# Spell

# to Write and Read

Overall Teacher's Manual for use with
*The Wise Guide for Spelling*

by Wanda Sanseri

Published by

Back Home Industries, Inc.
PO Box 22495
Milwaukie, OR 97269

Published in the United States of America
ISBN 13: 978-1880045-244
ISBN 10: 1880045-249

# DEDICATION

This book is dedicated to:


--My husband, **Gary,**

   without whom I would never have written this book,

--Our three home-schooled GRADUATES, **Samuel, Daniel,** and **Michael**,

   who taught and encouraged me as I taught them this system.

--**All my other students** including seminar alumni.

--My Lord and Savior, **Jesus Christ**,

   who in His sense of humor used me of all people

   to teach what was once my weakest subject.

# IN APPRECIATION

I want to acknowledge my indebtedness to teachers, colleagues, students, and editors who have been an inspiration and help to me. I value training from Dr. Diane Disney, my journalism teacher at RMSH in Rocky Mount, NC and from Dr. Emily Sullivan, my English professor at High Point University. Around 1975, Jeff Black, a Christian school teacher, patiently exposed me to *Writing Road to Reading (WRR)* by Romalda Spalding and introduced me to Lois Miller (fellow teacher at American Heritage Christian School in Hayward, California). Coupling my classroom experience teaching high school English and remedial reading with the new principles I learned from the above sources, I taught my oldest son to read. By first grade, he read at a sixth-grade level of comprehension. In 1981, I had the joy of meeting and training under Romalda Spalding for graduate level credit from the University of Hayward. Four years later, Jeannean Kintner encouraged me to join her in taking more college level teacher training in *WRR*. The instructor, Oma Riggs, had studied under Mrs. Spalding and successfully implemented her approach for years with amazing success. Mrs. Riggs invited me to team teach several teacher training seminars with WRR. When she retired, I focused on teaching my own children at home.

Meanwhile, educators kept asking me to show them how I had taught my sons. This grew into spontaneous classes. Friends told friends. By 1986, I created a fifteen-page outline, which by 1989 grew into an 87-page supplement to *WRR* called *Teaching Reading at Home*. To accommodate classroom teachers, I expanded the book and title to *Teaching Reading at Home and School (TRHS)*. I wanted to make sure that I accurately maintained the Spalding principles. I paid for a representative from the Spalding Foundation to observe and critique one of my seminars. She had minor corrections, but not regarding my understanding of the Spalding philosophy, my clarification of rules and phonograms, my research based modifications to the beginning word list, or my teaching style. Educators encouraged me to expand my spelling ideas to the whole program.

Mott Media's reprint of the book by Leonard Ayres showed that it was unnecessary to rigidly keep his spelling words in the WRR order. These words could be rearranged within each spelling difficulty level without losing any of the scientific support. I updated and expanded the Ayers List with current commonly used words and commonly misspelled words, and added tailored spelling enrichment activities. This turned an excellent spelling program into a more complete language arts curriculum. *Wise Guide for Spelling* was born. I appreciate the special parents and students who helped me field test this work at Tuesday School at our church. Two years later, *Spell to Write and Read (SWR)* with *Wise Guide* became a new stand alone program. SWR is both the name of this teacher's manual and the name used for the entire program. While I will always recommend *WRR* as a classic, it is no longer a necessary text.

Forty years have passed since I started teaching **spontaneous reading through systematic spelling**. Since that time, I have taught classes and tutored almost every age and ability level. I have been privileged to conduct teacher training seminars across the states, as well as in Canada and China. Along with my endorsed teacher trainers, we have conducted seminars in all but four states. Challenging questions and helpful observations made over the years by my many students of all ages have helped refine the work. Teaching others is an excellent way to learn.

I am especially grateful for the support and stimulating ideas I have gleaned from the dedicated team of Christians starting with Jean Evans, who I have trained and endorsed to teach seminars. I am indebted to Corina Treece and the members of the SWR loop she created as a support to educators using my program. I appreciate the faithful moderators headed by Liz FitzGerald. I am thankful to Grace Mahar, who allowed me to use a sample of her original work. I appreciate editing from Susan Eyk, Heidi Thomas, Rhonda Bedee, Dan Bosserman, Cindy Bowers, Sandra Nelson, Sam Sanseri, Lori Sekol, Elaine Selby, Jennifer Tarantello, Mary Tanksley, Sarah Moser, and Patsy Mugg. I also value help from Casey Gorsuch with the new cover design.

# Spell to Write and Read

## TABLE OF CONTENTS

\* For easy reference the Scope and Sequence Page is also duplicated on the inside front cover.

# GETTING STARTED

With a teacher-directed program, the first step is to prepare. All students regardless of age or ability will work with some or all of the 98 keys to the language (70 phonograms and 28 spelling rules) and will build each year a self-made textbook which we call a Learning Log. The teacher needs to understand our philosophy, collect and organize the supplies needed, start learning the phonograms, and begin building a teacher's edition of the Learning Log.

1. **Seek to understand our philosophy.** (For starters see the Introduction and Appendix A.) Most educators today teach reading first and expect that if a person reads a word often enough he will learn to spell it. Experience does not support that faulty theory. We start with spelling. Our students internalize the words they build from scratch and then easily recongize in print.

We use K-12 level spelling to teach how the English language works using little-known but reliable principles. Our student sounds out a word and writes it from guided dictation. He sees and reads the word he has written and analyzes it. The student uses the words to construct original sentences and practices reading the spelling words he has written and the sentences he has composed. Next he is ready to start reading books. Continue with spelling, teaching not only increasingly difficult words, but also using the words to learn other language arts principles. With our program reading is a more spontaneous process and a student is less likely to trip over spelling when he expresses thoughts in writing. Four verbs summarize the process.

With the right tools
all students can learn
to spell, write, and read!

| INTERNALIZE | (Spell) |
| RECOGNIZE | (Read) |
| COMPOSE and | (Write) |
| COMPREHEND | (Understand) |

2. **Collect and organize supplies.** (See Step 1* on page 13.)

3. **Start learning the phonograms.** (See Steps 5 and 6*.)

4. **Begin building a teacher's edition of the Learning Log.** (See Steps 8, 9, 10, *12). As a teacher new to the program you may want to begin a sample Log for beginners even if you will be teaching students in second grade or higher. You can place your students at a higher level in the program if they spell correctly the first ten words in the diagnostic test, but remember, words in Sections A-J of *Wise Guide* represent 60% of all we read and write. Only jump ahead if you are confident of a student's solid mastery of those vital words!

---

\* Some of the steps can wait until you start teaching students. These include pointers for teaching preschoolers (Step 2), the importance of reading aloud (Step 3), ways to evaluate the student's level (Step 4), how to write numbers (Step 7), and where to place students in Wise Guide (Step 11). When you actually teach a student you will move step-by-step.

---

# INTRODUCTION

One stormy evening last February, Bernadine Ruark, a 57-year-old stranger knocked on the door of a tutor using this program and pleaded, "Will you teach me to read? Doctors and teachers have told me that I have a brain problem. I've spent thousands of dollars on different tutors and courses but still can't read. I've heard you could help. Can you?"

Sandra Nelson assessed the situation in seconds. Bernie could see, talk, hear, think, express herself in clear, logical sentences, and she was highly motivated. "Yes, I can teach you how to read," Sandra replied with confidence. After three months of three 45-minute sessions each week, the once-illiterate woman could spell, write, and read independently. Today, the excited woman reads with understanding newspapers, magazines, and how-to books. She recently thanked her instructor, saying, "I was blind but now I see." Sandra is thrilled to have help transform a life this way but is not surprised. She proclaims, "I *knew* she could learn because I had a proven method of teaching her."

We rejoice that a program can work where so many others fail. When taught from the beginning, such a successful system can eliminate much unnecessary frustration and lost productivity. What makes this approach so victorious even over seemingly insurmountable odds?

## What We Teach

We present the language in a way that has few exceptions. One educator wrote on the internet, "I'm so happy to find a program that makes sense of our language rather than apologizing for it!" Typically phonics, if taught at all, is presented in incomplete or misleading ways filled with unnecessary rule-breakers.

We resurrect the historically successful idea of starting with phonics-based spelling. Most teachers today start with reading and cover spelling as an unrelated subject. When finally taught, spelling is often presented as a series of letter names divorced from the sounds they represent. Our students learn to read the "write" way by spelling their way into reading. The student hears a word and writes it (without copying) through a guided dictation technique. He reads the word after having written it accurately and analyzes it using a limited number of reliable rules. After a student can mentally think by sound to write a word correctly (spell), he can more naturally see a word and blend the sounds together (read).

Our spelling instruction is reinforced by simultaneously teaching other important topics. This integrated language arts approach includes phonics, penmanship, literature, logic, grammar, composition, vocabulary building, figurative language, dictionary skills, Greek and Latin roots, and comprehension. Such a well rounded presentation helps prevent or remediate spelling and reading failure.

## Whom We Teach

1. A SINGLE STUDENT OR A CLASSROOM GROUP. The system is presented the same way regardless of class size. This teacher's guide will rotate between referring to students as *he, she,* and *they* to demonstrate that the program is not restricted by gender or number of people taught together. We can teach male or female, one or many.

2. A VARIETY OF AGES. Preschoolers, school-age students, and adults can all profit. This program includes kindergarten to college-level words. Ideally this material should be mastered in the elemen-

```
+-------------------------------------------+
|              Suitable for All             |
|  ---------------------------------------  |
|                                           |
|                One or Many                |
|                                           |
|          Slow -- Average -- Gifted        |
|                                           |
|  Visual -- Auditory -- Vocal -- Tactile   |
|                  Learners                 |
|                                           |
|         Native Speakers or ESL            |
|                                           |
|               Young or Old                |
+-------------------------------------------+
```

tary grades, thereby freeing upper-level students to focus energy on higher-level reasoning skills, but everyone needs to learn the foundational aspects of the language. We provide a scientifically ordered plan for presenting these keys.

      a. <u>Beginning Non-readers</u>. We prepare a student to read before we expect him to read. Only after a student can smoothly identify individual words is he ready to comprehend sentences of thought.

      b. <u>Grade School Students</u>. This program will help fill in the missing pieces for students who can already read but struggle with comprehension or spelling.

      c. <u>Teens and Adults</u>. This program will remediate spelling or reading for any age.

3. A MIXTURE OF ABILITIES. Advanced, average, or delayed students can progress together. This system can challenge advanced students while stimulating stragglers.

One teacher had a first-grade class with a three-and-a-half grade range. Gary could not even spell his name while Karma could spell at a third-grade level. The class progressed as one unit, and by the end of the year all showed significant improvement. Gary jumped four grade levels. Although the class never reached words at Karma's beginning spelling level, she increased two grade levels in ability. She gained a more complete understanding of the language, even though the rules that govern English were illustrated with lower-level words. The same core principles that we teach with beginning spelling continue to apply with college-level work.

**Diagnostic Spelling Test**
First Grade

|  | Beginning of Year | End of Year |
|---|---|---|
| Gary | K | 4.2 |
| Janell | 1.5 | 3.7 |
| Karma | 3.5 | 5.7 |

4. PEOPLE WITH SPECIAL NEEDS. A variety of people benefit.

      a. <u>The Intellectually Gifted</u>. We encourage thinking and reasoning skills rather than random memory or inadequate splotches of phonics. The spelling principles taught work equally well with first grade or post-college-level words.

      b. <u>Those with English as a Second Language [ESL]</u>. With a logical, scientific presentation of our language, confusion subsides and learning progresses rapidly for the foreign student learning English.

      c. <u>Those with Learning Handicaps</u>. Many systems rely on visual learning alone. This program uses the techniques Dr. Samuel Orton developed to help correct dyslexia. Even children with severe language problems can learn to spell and read when vocal and kinesthetic senses (saying, writing) are simultaneously linked with hearing and seeing.

**How We Teach**

1. FOLLOW A LOGICAL PROGRESSION. We follow the sequence of instruction that has given the most reliable results. We teach from the known to the unknown, line upon line, precept upon precept. The same pattern works with non-readers or established readers. The speed may vary, but the sequence of instruction is the same.

      ✻ <u>Sounds of Speech</u>. We begin with the most elemental concept. Students learn to recognize and reproduce from memory the written symbols for the sounds of speech. We teach more than the single letters of the alphabet. The 26 letters alone are inadequate, because the English language has 45 sounds which we spell in 70 basic ways. Few people know these 70 basic phonograms. Many spelling problems would be solved if they did.

<table>
<tr><td>

* <u>Penmanship</u>. Students use legible handwriting as they say and write the phonograms. These are drilled in isolation, without picture clues. We avoid teaching anything, no matter how cute, that will interfere with the direct response between the symbol and the sound. We reserve songs and games for reinforcing other things.

* <u>Spelling</u>. We dictate spelling words, starting with the easiest to spell of the most frequently used words in English. Over four or so years we progress to post-college-level words. With only verbal assistance from the teacher, the student writes each new word, and then he reads what he has written.

* <u>Logic</u>. We stimulate logical thinking. The student learns to mark spelling concepts in words. We teach him to apply the basic rules of the language. He learns to think and not just guess.

* <u>Composition</u>. Students create original sentences using the spelling words. First, they compose them orally. After mastering 150 spelling words, they begin writing their own sentences.

* <u>Grammar</u>. Students learn correct grammar in application to their original sentences and as reinforcement activities with new spelling words.

</td>
<td>

**Teach from the Known to the Unknown**

---

sounds of speech
↓
penmanship
↓
spelling
↓
logic
↓
composition
↓
grammar
↓
SPONTANEOUS READING

</td>
</tr>
</table>

* <u>Spontaneous Reading</u>. We build spelling words from the part to the whole. In reading a word, we identify the whole. Reading is a spontaneous outworking of our type of spelling instruction. Some students connect spelling and reading instantly. Others need a longer time working with words before they recognize the magic of the code. The speed of understanding will vary, but with patient persistence all students can learn this way.

Rather than majoring on how fast a student will read, we concentrate on teaching the enduring principles that produce long-term success. None of our rules become outdated as the vocabulary expands. Our spelling list covers practically every pattern of English spelling and speaking. Teachers who faithfully teach this program consistently produce students who can spell and read well enough to be able to work independently for much of their subsequent education.

* <u>Comprehension</u>. Since the keys to the language are presented early, reading success is not dependent on material with a screened vocabulary. The student can read subjects that interest him. Many use the Bible as a first reader. After a student fluently recognizes words in print, *The McCall-Crabbs* books can help improve comprehension techniques.

2.    REINFORCE CONCEPTS IN MULTI-SENSORY WAYS.  Reading, primarily a visual skill, is taught best when involving all the key avenues to the mind (seeing, hearing, writing, saying). A third of the population, many with high intelligence, find reading nearly impossible to learn from a visual mode only. By linking speaking, spelling, and writing with reading, we connect four different pathways in the brain, thereby paving the way for virtually everyone to learn.

**Why We Teach This Way**

The best method is efficient, economical, and effective.

1. EFFICIENT. SWR is scientific, reasoned, and broad-based.

a. <u>Follows proven scientific data</u>. We follow up-to-date research on reading success as reported by Dr. Diane McGuinness. We hearken to the wisdom of the late Dr. Samuel T. Orton, a neurologist who specialized in the link between the brain and language. We draw from the findings of Dr. Jeanne S. Chall from Harvard University and a Stanford University study headed by Dr. Paul R. Hanna. We use the classic spelling list compiled by the late Leonard Ayres, the famous statistician who painstakingly sorted the most frequently used words in the language into levels of difficulty of spelling. (See bibliography.)

b. <u>Provides a precise, reliable rationale for spelling</u>. Streamlined rules harmonize with first-grade to adult-level spelling. Students internalize the keys that unlock the English language in amazingly consistent ways. One educator explains, "My fifth grader is now motivated! He's learning the rules that govern spelling. It is no longer just memory work and guessing."

c. <u>Integrates all language arts.</u> Basal readers with a limited vocabulary are unnecessary. Students can enjoy "living books." A home educator in Washington state wrote, "Six-year-old Katie is reading books like *Little House on the Prairie* and *Anne of Green Gables*, and she rarely misses any words on spelling quizzes." Another teacher shared the breakthrough she experienced with her eight-year-old daughter. "Before using this program she could not read past *Go, Dog, Go.* Now she reads *The Chronicles of Narnia!* Her writing skills are following suit. She rarely misspells words in applied writing."

2. ECONOMICAL. Our unified language instruction saves time and money. The SWR core kit covers multiple years and multiple skills. Adaptations each year are easier and less expensive than starting over with every grade change. Consumable workbooks are unnecessary. A classroom teacher from the East Coast writes, "Brand X gimmicky programs are costly. This program sticks to the essentials. By decluttering my language arts program, I can use my time to the best advantage."

3. EFFECTIVE. SWR lays an enduring language arts foundation. Usually good spellers become good readers. The reverse is often not true. "Researchers," according to Edna Furness, "note that in nine cases out of ten the most glaring handicap or deficiency of entering college freshmen is in spelling" (Furness, p. 57). Reading is a natural outgrowth of spelling mastery. Composition skills and grammar principles are taught as a way to reinforce spelling words.

> **Usually good spellers become good readers. The reverse is often not true.**

Key ideas are presented in a spiral fashion rather than concentrated and forgotten. An educator from California explains, "Rather than hold students back until they master each new idea thoroughly, we move ahead, keeping them excited while knowing that the concepts will be specifically addressed again for further mastery."

SWR helps teachers adapt the program to their students with simple, time-tested, evaluation tools. Diagnostic tests for spelling, writing, and reading measure growth, identify weaknesses, and determine placement for older students in the program.

This type of approach produces outstanding results. Starting in the 1920's Romalda Spalding served as a beacon to help preserve educational techniques no longer in vogue. Scattered teachers throughout the nation followed her lead in reviving tried and true methods from the past. Teachers who used these principles often endured ridicule and criticism for clinging to "outmoded" ideas but nonetheless maintained a high success rate. After a lifetime of using these methods, numerous class-room teachers report that they have NEVER failed to teach a child to read at grade level. The majority of their students tested far above their grade status. The speed may vary, but all willing students can learn with this foundation.

Teachers at American Heritage Christian School exposed me to this method in the early 1970's. Eight years later I joined their faculty for intensive, graduate level training under Mrs. Spalding. I homeschooled at the time. When my husband became terminally ill, I temporarily discontinued home education. Naturally, I enrolled my sons in the school that used the best appoach.

Robert Aukerman, in researching for his book, *Approaches to Beginning Reading*, came to observe my son's classroom. He gathered statistics. The entire first grade class averaged in the upper 90th percentile in reading on the Standard Achievement Test. My six-year-old son, himself, scored at the sixth grade level on the SAT. Others using the same program experienced similar success stories. Information, below reflects tests in the primary grades recorded in Aukerman's book (pp. 541-545). Outstanding results characterized all the schools he visited.

| School | Grade | Date | Test | No. Pupils Tested | Reading Median Score (in grade equivalent) |
|---|---|---|---|---|---|
| Francis Parker School Chicago, IL | 1 | 1979-1980 | SAT | 25 | 3.8 |
| St. Michael Dallas, TX | 1 | March 1981 | SRA | 51 | 2.9 |
| **American Heritage Hayward, CA** | 1 | March 1981 | SAT | 13 | 3.6 |
| Groveton Elementary Groveton, NH | 1 | March 1982 | SAT | 44 | 2.4 |
| Featherstone Elementary Woodbridge, VA | 2 | March 1982 | SRA | 8 | 4.5 |
| Our Savior Lutheran Aiea, HI | 1 | April 1982 | SAT | 28 | 4.2 |
| Taft Elementary Boise, ID | 2 | April. 1982 | SAT | 28 | 3.7 |
| Tri-City Christian Acad. Tempe, AZ | 1 | April 1982 | SAT | 22 | 2.9 |

Aukerman proclaimed, "When one finds reports of performance that are consistently and sig-nificantly above the national norms, one looks for causes. Can it be that the children are specially selected? Or that it is the teacher who is better? The results from 194 different classes taught by 194 different teachers in different and widely scattered small and large, public, private, and parochial schools led this writer to believe that it is the method that deserves the credit. . . . The results speak for themselves" (Aukerman, page 252). *Spell to Write and Read* clarifies and expands the program he reviewed several decades ago.

# SCOPE & SEQUENCE

*What* is taught in *SWR?* *(scope)* *When* is it first introduced? (sequence)

\* **P** = Primary Learning Log; **B** = Black Learning Log

\*\* **Spelling words (Step 12) form the backbone of the entire program.** The first 11 steps are preparatory to beginning spelling. Steps 13 to 40, listed in order of first appearance, cover a variety of language arts skills that will recur time and again in application to the spelling words from Section A to Section Z.

**Steps are keyed to** actual *Wise Guide* spelling words. Primary grades cover only the steps linked by the spelling level they reach. A student who finishes Section J will end the year at Step 28. Subsequent grades may begin Step 12 at a higher spelling level. *Wise Guide* will show you how to adjust the step sequence to fit later spelling sections.

**Understanding grows with intermittent repetition over time.** Total mastery of one step is unnecessary before moving to another. We return repeatedly to each step in application to increasingly difficult words. Although SWR will give an exhaustive coverage of each step, the teacher only needs to address what is appropriate for the level she is teaching.

## SCOPE AND SEQUENCE EXPANDED

This resource guide, together with *Wise Guide,* outlines the plan for teaching foundational language arts. The preceding page summarizes at a glance the concepts we teach (the scope) and the order (sequence) in which we first present them. The first step covers teacher preparation. Step 2 explains ways to prep the senses. Step 3 encourages reading aloud to students of all ages. Step 4 suggests ways to assess previously acquired skills of those who already read and write.

"What will my daily schedule be like with this program?" See several sample lesson plans in Appendix E. In general, start teaching how to say and write the phonograms and introduce several foundational principles (Steps 5 through 10). Place the student according to ability (Step 11) before the regular spelling routine is established. After Step 11, *Wise Guide* becomes the main source of daily lesson plans. Scope and Sequence Steps 12-40 list ideas in the order in which they are first presented for a student starting at the very beginning of the program. *Wise Guide* helps you adjust the step sequence to match the needs of students placing at a higher spelling level. Reference pages are best introduced when relevant to current work. *Wise Guide* tells you when to cover specific spelling rule pages and other concepts like composition and grammar. This manual adds detailed instructions on how to do so in a way tailored to the level of the student. *SWR* gives simple inital ways to first present each precept and then follow-up ways to dig more deeply as the student matures.

"How long will it take to teach each step?" An overall plan for K-5 is provided in Step 11, but this is only a sample. The same concepts are needed for all, but the speed of presentation may vary. Teachers use this book for elementary grades, older learners, and students learning English as a Second Language. A kindergarten teacher may need a month to introduce Steps 2- 6 (penmanship with the first 26 phonograms), while a sixth-grade teacher may need only minutes to review this material enough to start applying the information at the student level of demonstrated spelling mastery.. All students, regardless of age or ability, annually cover at least *SWR* Steps 1-11 before any dictation of spelling words in the front of the log.   (Some can omit Step 2 for preschoolers and Step 7 instruction for writing numbers.)

A kindergarten student or first grader will need four to six years to complete this program. If you are using the system to sharpen language skills for above average older students, you can move at a faster pace. Advanced high school students have been known to cover the material in four to six months. Older students needing remediation (students 9 years old or older who are below grade level) may take longer at first, but once students see the logic of this system and how it works, amazing gains can take place rapidly. Lost time can be made up, but it will take some extra patience at first. It is easier to learn the best way initially than to unlearn and replace automatic patterns.

 ## 1.  PLAN BEFORE TEACHING.

Objectives:
> To show the teacher what she needs to do to get ready.
> To summarize the resources needed.

Prepare to Teach:
> Gather required materials.
> Organize supplies.
> Start learning key foundational components to the program.

Those who try to teach without this preparation tend to flounder because they lack the big picture of the process. One user compared teaching this method to flying a jumbo jet. She said, "It takes a LOT of fuel to get it off the ground. BUT . . . soon you begin to be at a nice cruising altitude. The take-off of a plane uses TWICE the fuel burn per hour than will be needed in established level flight. Spelling for us is pretty much on autopilot now, but it required a lot of energy at first."

**Gather Required Teaching Materials**.

| TEACHER RESOURCES | | |
|---|---|---|
| **Essential** | **Highly Recommended** | **Optional** |
| *SWR Core Kit* (five items) <br> -- *Spell to Write and Read* <br> -- *Wise Guide to Spelling* <br> -- *Phonogram Cards* <br> -- *Phonogram CD* <br> -- *Spelling Rule Cards* <br> *A Learning Log* <br> Pencils (regular lead, red) <br> "Living" books <br> A good dictionary | *The Alpha List* <br> *SWR Seminars* <br> *McCall-Crabbs Test Lessons* <br> *Sanseri Suggested Book List* <br> *New England Primer of 1777* <br> *SWR Beginning Readers* <br> *Beginning Grammar Readers* <br> A blackboard or a whiteboard <br> Pencil sharpener <br> Press-on color tabs | *SWR Chart Pack* <br> *Companion CD for Review* <br> *Phonogram Game Cards* <br> *Ayres Research Findings* <br> *Cursive First* <br> *Writing Road to Reading* <br> *Supplemental grammar and composition for fourth grade +* |

1. ESSENTIAL TEACHER RESOURCES EXPLAINED. *Spell to Write and Read* is the basic manual for the whole system. The following teacher materials are required to go with this guide:

*The Wise Guide for Spelling* by Wanda Sanseri. The Wise List of 2000 words comes with two pages of lesson plans for every twenty words.

*70 Basic Phonogram Cards*. Hard stock flash cards were designed by Wanda Sanseri for teaching ease. Tutors or classroom teachers should have parents purchase these cards and the spelling rule cards, so that they can understand and support their children's work.

*70 Basic Phonogram CD* by Gary and Wanda Sanseri. Make sure you say the phonograms correctly by listening to this audio recording.

*Spelling Rule Cards*. Flash cards use symbols to represent each rule. While the students have the visual clues on the front of the card, the teacher can learn the exact dialogue from the back of the card. Good for fast-paced review before teaching new words.

A Learning Log. The teacher makes a sample of student self-made textbook. Select either *The Primary Learning Log* published by BHI for K-2 or ones new to the program, or *The Black Log*, a blank, 50-leaf sewn composition book, for students third grade and up.

Pencils. Use six-sided red and regular lead or mechanical pencils.

"Living" books. Collect interesting books of your choice to read aloud and books on the student's level for independent reading.

A good dictionary. The teacher can select any reputable book as a standard resource. If possible, find a dictionary published before 1957 at a used-book sale. The pronunciation key is more reliable in the older versions. Also, for stronger, more biblical definitions, try to locate a reprinted version of Noah Webster's 1828 *Dictionary of the American Language*.

2. HIGHLY RECOMMENDED TEACHER RESOURCES EXPLAINED. In addition to the essential items listed above, we strongly recommend some additional supplies.

*The Alpha List*. The Wise List (the spelling words in *Wise Guide)* is presented in alphabetical order and analyzed by phonograms and spelling rules. Derivatives and other information are included. Each word is cross-referenced to *Wise Guide* by the word number.

*SWR Teacher-Trainer Seminars*.  Seminars available throughout the country and in Canada are taught by either the author herself  or Christian women personally trained and endorsed by her.  For the most current dates and places see *www.BHIbooks.net*.  Two and three-day classes provide hands-on instruction.  Get to be the student under a trained instructor, observe the system at work, and ask questions.  Such exposure will enhance your effectiveness.  Unfortunately, not everyone can attend a workshop.  While the seminar greatly builds teacher confidence, many teach the program successfully without attending a class.

*McCall-Crabbs Test Lessons in Reading*, Books A-E.  This classic resource is useful for diagnostic testing in the beginning or for weekly reading activities.  See Step 31.

*The Sanseri Recommended Book List*.  A list of books the Sanseri family enjoyed, organized by grade level, and screened to be acceptable to most Christian families.

*The New England Primer of 1777*.   This textbook sold over three million copies and helped produce a high level of literate, self-taught citizens who valued righteousness and liberty.  BHI reprinted an expanded edition that includes nine simple stories using the beginning spelling words from *Wise Guide*.  This book with historic value can be used as a beginning reader.

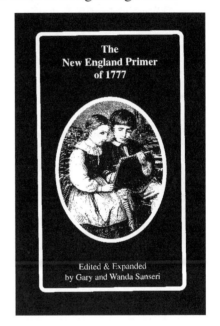

*SWR Beginning Readers*  Beginning readers use initial spelling words.  These include *Play by the Sea* and *Do You See What I See?*

Beginning Grammar Readers.  The student is the co-author, illustrator in these unique BHI publications such as: *I Can Run!* and *Up, Over, and Out*.

A blackboard or whiteboard provides a place for spelling dictation.  For blackboard work, you will need two colors of chalk (white and red).  For the whiteboard, you will need black and red dry-erase markers.

A pencil sharpener (preferably electric).

Press-on color tabs and highlight markers as aids in organizing teacher materials.

3.  OPTIONAL TEACHER RESOURCES EXPLAINED.

*Spell to Write and Read Chart Pack*.  The  reference pages without dotted lines are available on  8 1/2-by-11 heavy card stock paper.  Some bonus pages not available elsewhere are included.

*SWR Companion CD for Review and Mastery*.  A professional quality CD set includes a quiz on all spelling sections in WISE and the diagnostic spelling tests.  Six disks come in a convenient case.  An index guide makes accessing specific spelling sections easy!

*Phonogram Game Cards*.  A set of cards with the 70 phonograms in book face on white paper and a set of cards with the same phonograms in cursive on yellow paper.  Students can play the "Memory Game" or use the cards with any favorite game board.

Ayres Research Findings.  *A Measuring Scale for Ability in Spelling* documents the scientific research used for 1000 of the words in *Wise Guide* and our diagnostic spelling test in Appendix A.  Some express concern that the reordering of the words in Wise weakens the scientific norming established by Ayres.  Once we discovered that the words in each section are of equal value we realized that we could rearrange them to a great advantage.

*Cursive First*.  Elizabeth FitzGerald, one of our endorsed teacher trainers, has designed this guide for extra help teaching cursive to beginners.

*Writing Road to Reading* by Romalda Spalding.  The age-old principles preserved in this classic are foundational to this system. *Teaching Reading at Home & School*, the precursor to *SWR*, was a supplement to Mrs. Spalding's work.  We expanded the Ayres List, published in 1915, to reflect current research.  We reorganized the words within established ability-level groupings in order to teach derivatives and other supplemental skills.  We expanded the spelling rules to include plurals, contractions, and abbreviations.  We rewrote them in more lyrical and precise fashion for ease in group recitation. We redesigned reference pages for clarity of concepts. Though no longer necessary,  Mrs. Spalding's book still retains historic value.

Supplemental composition or grammar programs (4th or 5th grade and up). While *SWR* provides writing opportunities and introduces the key grammar concepts, it does not pretend to be exhaustive in these fields. Our spelling instruction reaches freshman-level in college, but the other aspects of language arts are not as extensive. Spelling is the backbone to this program, and ideally the technical mechanics of spelling are mastered in the elementary grades.  Grammar and composition skills need a longer time to perfect.  These disciplines are introduced from the beginning but are not covered in the same intensity. *Grammar Readers* we publish help make grammar come alive to the beginning reader. *Wise Guide* activities also pave the way for deeper grammar and composition understanding.  We recommend that the students spell their way into reading fluently before beginning any additional language arts programs.

**Gather Student Supplies**.

| STUDENT RESOURCES | |
|---|---|
| Required | Recommended |
| A Learning Log<br>A three-ring binder<br>Regular notebook paper<br>Red and lead six-sided pencils<br>A flat writing surface<br>Student reading materials | Press-on color tabs<br>A six-inch ruler<br>A plastic zipper pouch |

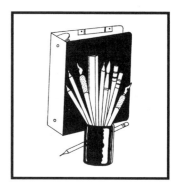

1.  REQUIRED STUDENT SUPPLIES.

A Learning Log.  The student needs a durable book that  he can transform into a personalized  spelling textbook by carefully following specific instructions.   See Appendix C for examples of reference pages in the two types of books.   Primary Learning Logs are designed for K-2 but may be used by older students new to the program. Black Learning Logs are for students third grade and above. We do not recommend a spiral notebook, since the pages tear out too easily and the spiral gets in the way, especially in the places where two facing pages need to be treated as one large page.

A three-ring binder with an inside pocket. Organize loose papers together with divider tabs for composition, homework, McCall tests, and quizzes.  Place the Log in the pocket.

Three-hole-punched regular-ruled notebook paper. Practice work, reinforcement activities in *Wise Guide,* spelling tests, and original compositions should be written on loose-leaf paper and organized into a binder.

Lined paper is essential for student work.  Dr. Hilde Mosse explains, "the best way to secure linear reading [learning to sweep the eye in the proper direction] is by having the child write on lined paper from the very start." (Mosse, p.187). Standard lined paper works fine. *The Primary Learning Log* has half lines to help the student do her best penmanship in the Log. We recommend standard regular lined paper for other work. It is best if the student does not become dependent on the half lines to mentally determine halfway.

　　　　Pencils. Each student needs both six-sided regular lead pencils (or mechanical pencils) and red pencils. Before dictation, students should have a back-up pencil sharpened (or loaded) to help avoid class disruptions.

　　　　A flat surface for writing. Students need either a desk or a table facing the teacher. If pupils are positioned across from each other at a shared desk, they will tend to look at each

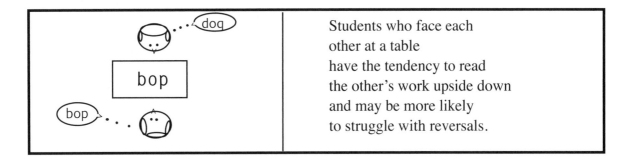

| | Students who face each other at a table have the tendency to read the other's work upside down and may be more likely to struggle with reversals. |

other's work upside down. Facing another student can confuse a child who does not have letter orientation firmly established. Students who face the teacher avoid distractions. They also see the teacher's lips clearly which is especially important for those with auditory processing problems or hearing difficulties. Some sounds taught are unvoiced and require that the student clearly watch the teacher's mouth. The kitchen table can be used in a home setting, but adjustments may be needed to boost the body to a more comfortable height (at elbows when seated) and to support the legs. Dangling legs promote fidgeting. A bar stool with rungs that can support the legs can be used.

　　　　Student reading materials. A basal reader is unnecessary, but a large supply of high-interest books will be needed. Easy readers of interest to children can be purchased or checked out of the library. Some students use the Bible as their first reader.

2. HIGHLY RECOMMENDED STUDENT SUPPLIES.

　　　　✐ Press-on color tabs. Tab the reference section of the Learning Log and sections of the three-ring binder for original sentences, phonogram drills, and other activities.

　　　　✐ A six-inch ruler for making neat brackets and underlines.

　　　　✐ A plastic zipper pouch to help keep pencils and ruler in the three-ring binder.

**Organize Teacher Supplies.**

　　　　1. PREPARE THE CARDS. Divide the sheets of perforated phonogram and spelling rules into individual cards. Before you laminate the spelling rule cards, read the backside of the title sheet. See optional suggestions to **add red pencil highlights to some** of the **spelling rule cards**.

　　　　2. ASSEMBLE THE MATERIALS IN ONE PLACE. Select a bag, box, binder, or attache-case where you can store all your SWR supplies in one portable but convenient place. Label the outside for easy recognition. Keep diagnostic test results, lesson plan ideas, and grading information in a folder or binder. Use a zipper pouch for smaller items like pencils, highlighters, and tabs.

3. HIGHLIGHT KEY WORDS. Use your own color scheme. I use an orange highlighter for links to the Primary Log and blue for links to the Black Log. I use a pink for the links to reference pages (example: SH Page) and green for grammar. With yellow I highlighted advanced phonogram references (example: gu = /g/). I use red pencil to underline other passages that I want to stand out.

4. CONSTRUCT LINES FOR THE BOARD. Mark off or permanently draw lines on a green chalkboard using a yardstick and a magic marker. Six to ten horizontal lines are ideal. A whiteboard can be marked off with graphic art tape. Train yourself to stand to the left of the written work. Students need to look from the teacher to the beginning of the written message.

A teacher should stand to the left of written work.

When teacher stands to the right, the student may glance from the teacher to the end of the word and read "was" for "saw."

**Preview the Program.**

Before teaching this program, spend a week or two working through Steps 1-12 in *SWR*. Don't just read about the process. Begin to learn the phonograms and start to build a sample Learning Log.

1. START LEARNING THE PHONOGRAMS (Steps 5 and 6). Listen to the phonogram CD in the core kit and practice saying each phonogram correctly, using the sound(s) rather than the letter name(s). Do not add a vowel sound to the consonants; for instance say /b/ for B instead of /buh/. Do not memorize the key words on the reverse of the card. This will slow down instant recall. Learn to respond immediately with the sound(s) each phonogram can make. Practice your penmanship. Take the test at the end of the CD to see how well you can reproduce each phonogram from hearing only. Your first goal is to get a general overview. A more solid mastery will come as you teach.

2. BEGIN CREATING A SAMPLE LEARNING LOG (Steps 8, 9, 10). This is essential. Take advice from one who tried to avoid this step. "Don't wiggle out of building a teacher's edition! If you just pick up *Wise Guide* and try to teach cold turkey as I did, you will lack the confidence and understanding that comes only by building your own Log first." Follow instructions carefully to construct your own edition of the student notebook. Your book should look like the textbook you expect your students to make from your dictation. We don't sell a ready-made textbook because we know people learn best by building this book for themselves. Our students will learn by doing. So will you.

Student built logs have two distinct sections. Reference pages are built in the back of the book like an appendix. Students use these pages to work through spelling rule concepts. New words are logged in the front. The student book is constructed entirely from teacher dictation. We teach several reference pages before we start the actual spelling lists.

Reference Pages. Steps 9 and 10 explain the some essential reference pages. We have two basic types of rule pages: fixed pages and collection pages. Most pages are collection pages. Fixed pages include the Consonant/Vowel Page (Step 9), the Silent Final E Page (Step 17), and the AEIOU Page (Step 19). The Multi-letter Phonogram Page is built over time with a young beginner but with older students can be taught as a whole. All other reference pages are "add as you go" pages. Build your master log in the same order you will use when you teach your class. Build the Consonant/Vowel Page and at least some of the Multi-letter Phonogram Page before you start with the spelling lists.

Spelling Words (Step 12).  Most teachers new to the program begin spelling instruction at Section A.  See dictation scripting on pp. 70-76.  You can, however, start with the word list that you will be teaching.  SWR is designed so students can begin their personalized log at the spelling section determined by the diagnostic test in Appendix A. Examples for many of the reference pages are drawn from the words being taught.  Tailor your teacher's log to the level of your class.

**Dictation is a crucial part of this program!** Carefully study the general outline for standard spelling dictation on p.76. Next study the dictation guide on the inside of the SWR back cover. This is your master guide.  Memorize the language used.  Practice this until the process becomes natural.

The spelling list will drive your lesson planning for the remainder of the year.  Teach new reference pages as directed on your current list in *Wise Guide*.   Look for instructions in one of three places: the Preliminaries, beside the words, or in the Spelling Enrichments.   Add words when you would have the students do so.  Do not just copy the sample pages in Appendix C!

> **A teacher MUST construct a personal master of the student Learning Log in order to learn this program!**

Let's see how this works. Turn to *Wise Guide* pp. 2-3.   In the Preliminaries to Section A you are reminded to teach Steps 1-11 before you begin.  You are told to add the beginning four phonograms to the Multi-letter Phonogram Page.  In the Spelling Enrichments on page 2 you are asked to add the words "six" and "ten" to the Number Page (Step 15).   Build your log in this manner, bit-by-bit as you progress through *Wise Guide*.   Later in Section G on p.19 beside the words a side note has you add "three"  to the Number Page.

While you are progressing through your prep, you can start some work with your students. With beginning non-readers you can try some of the non-threatening exercises of breaking words into individual sounds.  See if they hear them and verbally blend them together and say the word.   See Step 2 on Prep the Senses.  Give students who can already write and read the Diagnostic Test.  Start teaching the phonograms to any age.

Much of this material will be new to you.  Do not be alarmed.  Plan to learn as you go.

    a.  Complete understanding is not expected at first.  The first presentation exposes a concept and establishes a frame of reference. All the important concepts will recur over and over as you work through the program.  The first presentation plants a seed of thought and establishes a frame of reference.  Understanding grows for both the student and the teacher as key insights are repeated in application to a variety of words over a period of time.

    b.  What is hard for the teacher will not necessarily be hard for the student.  For most adults, the foundational stages of SWR will be more difficult than for the beginning non-reader. You will be amazed at what even kindergartners can grasp when taught this way.   Most teachers are glad for advance preparation time so that they can keep up with their students. Young minds are not cluttered with bizarre, useless spelling rules that they need to unlearn.

3. SEEK OUT OTHER USERS.  Find like-minded teachers either in person or on the Internet.   For a link to a support group loop for users of the program check the BHI web page at *BHIbooks.net*.  Share successes, problem-solve, or set goals.  Some people are more likely to complete an objective like finishing a master Learning Log when they have an accountability partner.

> **If possible build a support network with others who use the program.**

## 2. PREP THE SENSES.

Objectives:

To prepare a non-reader or a reluctant reader for success with future instruction.
To build phonemic awareness with oral games.
To develop the correct directional orientation for future penmanship exercises.

Prepare to Teach:

Start learning the 70 basic phonograms.
Make 3X5 cards with the numbers 1 through 12.

How can we prepare a student for this program? How should we reinforce concepts in informal times? We want to introduce language skills in ways that will not require unlearning later. Although writing is a key component of *Spell to Write and Read,* we don't have to wait for a child to have fine motor skills to start preparing her to write someday. Even babies can benefit from hearing the phonogram sounds. Some older students do not know how to segment a word into individual sounds.

**Inspire Phonemic Awareness**.

What is the subskill that best predicts future reading success? You may be surprised by the answer confirmed by recent research. It is not a sensitivity to rhyme. Noticing the lyrical quality of rhyming words may help one enjoy poetry but does not help a child learn to read. (Jose Morais tested illiterate poets. They could not read, but they had no trouble with rhyming.) Nor is it student IQ. Many have an excellent vocabulary and high intelligence and still have major reading problems. The most powerful predictor for reading success is the student's ability to hear and manipulate sounds in words. (McGuinness, chapter 6). This concept is the backbone of our program. What we will do constantly in written form can be first introduced and practiced in oral form. Practice orally breaking words apart and putting them back together is an extremely helpful prelude to SWR style spelling dictation. Even infants enjoy listening to the phonograms. They need these sounds for speech and appreciate hearing them in isolation.

When my preschool-age sons drew pictures, I would often ask them to identify what they had drawn (man, sun, rainbow, house, tree). Then I would repeat the word, sounding it out as distinctly isolated sounds. I remember the day my first-born had carefully sketched a tree with his crayons. Underneath, whispering one-by-one the sound of each phonogram, I wrote t-r-ee. I underlined the double E. My son shouted excitedly, "TREE!" His eyes sparkled and he hugged me with joy. He understood that a magic code could make words, and he eagerly begged to know more. The occasion reminded me of Helen Keller when she linked the liquid substance coming out of a pump to her teacher's finger-spelling for "water." At the age of six, my son could spell and comprehend at the sixth-grade level.

Without realizing it, I was building in my son phonemic awareness, the key ingredient for language success. Phonemes are the smallest units of sound. Phonemic awareness occurs when a student realizes that words are built by combining sounds together. For example, the word "hat" has three sounds blended together (/h/-/a/-/t/). Unless taught, few people automatically "sound out words" in this way. We can help someone develop phonemic awareness by teaching them to feel and describe the articulation of sounds.

*After I whispered /t-r-e-e/, my son shouted excitedly, "TREE!"*

**Build Reading Readiness with Oral Games.**

1. INVESTIGATE HOW SOUNDS ARE MADE. Casually study the lip shape when saying vowel sounds. Do your lips open normally, squeeze tight like a circle, or stretch out like a smile?

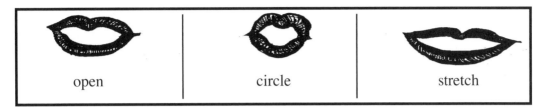

| open | circle | stretch |

Watch your mouth, and say: *bid, bad; tin, tan; pin, pan*. Can you see your jaw change and your tongue drop lower in words with /a/ than in words with /i/? Which is lower in these words: *bush, wash; put, what?* The tongue drops lower to make the /ah/ sound.

2. PLAY "SLOW WORD/FAST WORD." Say, "Words are made up of different sounds stuck together. See if you can name the word I'm saying by putting the sounds together fast." Slowly say distinctly separate sounds /h-a-t/. If the child says *at*, say, "Those sounds are in the word but that is not the word. Listen again." Say the word several times. First divide it into individual sounds and then, if need be, say it faster and faster until you blend it completely together.

Do some auditory activities each day. The goal is to show how sounds run together to make words. The word possibilities are endless. To get started, see samples below.

**Say and Do**: sit, stand, hop, run, jump, clap, bow, turn, tag, lean, fall, point, nod, wave, hug, sob, sleep, wake.

**Say and Find**: toy, cup, spoon, jar, mug, egg, rock, tree, car, ball, mat, game, tub, pet, bed, sink, rug, light, shoe.

**Say and Touch**: head, foot, chin, toe, lips, hip, cheek, eyes, knee, nose, hair, arm, side, ear, sock, hand, leg, mom.

> *The most powerful predictor for reading success is the student's ability to hear and manipulate sounds in words.*
>
> **—Dr. Diane McGuinnes**

**Say and See** (after the child says the word, pull the hidden object out of a bag): map, gum, cap, fan, jar, nut, pen, book, doll, leaf, bib, flag, sock, dish.

3. PLAY "UNGLUE THE WORD." Reverse the process by letting the student stretch out a word and have you blend the sounds together to guess their word. Throughout this program, we will constantly "glue" and "unglue" as we dictate new spelling words. The only difference is that we will add the written dynamic to what, in this step, is only verbal.

4. PLAY "COUNT THE SYLLABLES." A syllable is a rhythmic "chunk" of a word. A word has as many syllables as vowel sounds. English spelling rules are dependent on syllable divisions. We will be breaking spelling words into syllables throughout this program.

You can add kinesthetic reinforcement. The most reliable way is to have the student hum the word. Some call this "vowelizing the word." Close your mouth tightly and try to say, "apron." Hum-Hum. This is a two-syllable word. Say, "elephant." Hum-Hum-Hum. This is a three-syllable word.

You can add more action by humming the word and at the same time clapping once for each syllable or marching, stepping high for each syllable. Start with the left foot.

See *The New England Primer* for lists of words divided into one, two, three, four, and five syllables.

**Teach the Directional Orientation Needed for Writing.**

You can build early the patterns needed for proper orientation in writing. Precise handwriting instruction will be an important part of this program. We can train preschoolers orally in ways that will prepare them for the more formal pencil-and-paper instruction we will use later. (See Step 6 for a detailed description of teaching penmanship.) Use the expression "Go in the direction we read or write" to refer to movement from left to right. Train them to recognize the order of numbers around a clock. In this program we use a clock face to teach certain letters with circle parts. These letters need to be formed *counterclockwise*.

1. PLAY "RUN AROUND THE CLOCK." Arrange 3x5 cards with numbers 1-12 clock fashion in a big circle on the floor. Start the child at the 12 facing the 1. Have the child walk around the clock and stop at each card. You can say each number and have the child repeat it.

Later when the child is familiar with the numbers, have her stand at the 12 facing the 1 and follow your instructions. You might say, "Run around the clock until you get to 6." You might have the child connect the number with a time when key events happen at home. Run around the clock until you get to the time when we get up, have breakfast, eat lunch, take a nap, Daddy comes home, we go to bed, etc. When telling time we must move clockwise. We can't go back in time.

2. PLAY "CLOCK LETTER RELAY." After a child understands the numbers on the clock in clockwise order, we can play a different game. Explain, "When we tell time, we read the numbers going in number order. When we write, we will use the clock numbers, but we will do them in a funny order called "counterclockwise." Have the child stand by the 2 facing the direction of the 12. The child can skip around the clock saying, "All clock letters go from 2 this way."

To write a clock letter, we might go from 2 up and over to 10, continuing down around to 2. Vary instructions for them to follow. Say, "Go from 2 up over to 10, continuing around to 4." Or say, "Start at 2 and go until I say stop." Say, "Stop at 10. Stop at 8. Stop at 6. Stop at 4. Stop at 2."

**Surround Children with Books.**

Make books visible and available. C.S. Lewis describes growing up in a home filled with books. "In the seemingly endless rainy afternoons I took volume after volume from the shelves. I had always the same certainty of finding a book that was new to me as a man who walks into a field has of finding a new blade of grass." You know you have planted a good seed when your child gathers dolls or stuffed toys and pretends to read aloud to them.

Show that books are friends to respect and cherish. Isaac Watts said, "By the art of reading, we learn a thousand things which our eyes can never see, and which our own thoughts would never have reached. We are instructed by books in the wisdom of ancient ages. By reading we can sit at home and acquaint ourselves with what has been done in distant parts of the world. (Watts, p. 321).

You know you have planted a good seed when your child gathers dolls or stuffed toys and pretends to read aloud to them.

# 3.  READ ALOUD TO ALL AGES.

Objectives:
>       To expose students to excellent writing.
>       To demonstrate the joy and benefit of learning to read.

Prepare to Teach:
>       Search constantly for quality books.

Reading aloud is one of the most valuable things you can do as a parent or teacher. This verbal practice is more than a pleasurable activity that promotes closeness and nurturing. Students who listen to well-crafted books benefit in many ways.

**Demonstrate reading procedures**.

Reading aloud provides familiarity with the reading process. Don't be afraid to use your finger to point to the words as you read them. Show the child that English books are read from left to right, top to bottom. Words, not pictures, are read.

> You may have tangible wealth untold
> Caskets of jewels, and coffers of gold;
> Richer than I you can never be
> I had a mother who read to me.
>
> --Strickland Gillian

**Plant the desire for reading in students of any age.**

Model a love for books. Constantly hunt for a fresh supply of quality materials and share your delight in some of the worthwhile things you discover. Take frequent trips to bookstores and the library. As soon as a child can write his name, get him his own library card. Hunt for book bargains in garage sales and thrift shops. Let your students observe you read for practical reasons as well as for pleasure. Provide variety: chapter books, picture books, non-fiction, fiction, poetry, and biography.

**Inspire future reading success.**

After studying extensive research on literacy, the Commission on Reading reported, "The single most important activity for building the knowledge required for eventual success in reading is reading aloud to children. This is especially so during the preschool years." (Andersen, p. 23) Phonemic awareness provides the mechanics of reading. Reading aloud helps build the student's common knowledge and provides the motivation to learn.

> *Some of my fondest memories are of sitting with my mother's arm around me, listening to her read. Little did I know that she was doing much more than providing comfort and entertainment. She was paving the way for learning and for success.*
>
> --First Lady, Laura Bush

**Stimulate the intellect.**

Listening requires a higher level of imagination than watching a video or television. Rather than passively viewing an image on the screen, the listener has to picture the events in her own mind.

**Expose powerful ways to express ideas.**

The written word presents a higher degree of language excellence than normal conversational speech because a writer takes more time to organize thoughts. The grammar used is more correct and the word choice is richer and less repetitious than in a casual chat with a friend. Reading aloud exposes the student to well-structured sentences which display the textures and nuances of the English language. Students enlarge their vocabularies and gain ideas for developing their own writing styles.

**Expand horizons.**

Listening to a book enlarges the student's knowledge about persons, places, and things in the world. Even simple stories for young children provide an amazing array of background information on many varied subjects. Hearing stirring accounts of worthwhile endeavors and noble examples helps mold good character. Through books we gain the benefit of our ancestors' wise and judicious remarks without the fatigue of their long and painful experiments. By this means children may be led, in a great measure, into the wisdom of old age.

**Train minds to retell stories.**

Have the student repeat in his own words what you read. Such narration sharpens his listening and thinking skills. The ability to verbalize thoughts precedes the ability to write thoughts.

**Reading aloud is the best advertisement for learning to read and write.**

**Build valuable shared memories.**

Change your voice to match the characters in the book. Read with expression and feeling. Select books that you enjoy so you will be enthusiastic. Help the listener become actively involved. Ask questions to make sure they are following the story line. Pause to explain words that the listeners might not understand.

As First Lady of the United States, Laura Bush shared, "Some of my fondest memories are of sitting with my mother's arm around me, listening to her read. Little did I know that she was doing much more than providing comfort and entertainment. She was paving the way for learning and for success." (Felix, p. 35)

**Motivate the student.**

Reading aloud to students is one of the best advertisements for learning to read and write. An internally motivated child will learn more easily than one pushed. Don't restrict read-aloud selections to books marked at a certain grade level. Young children enjoy select, well-written passages from even adult-level books. When my boys were six, five, and one, I read highlights of the story, *Peace Child*. Several years later I saw a big grin on my active son's face as he spotted that inspirational book on the shelf and curled up to read it for himself.

You may want to read longer books a chapter at a time. If someone must wait in suspense for the next reading, she will long for the day when she can read for herself and not have to wait so long. Often, when Dad read to the children at night, our children would beg for one more chapter. Sometimes he would continue. Other times he would close the book. Sometimes he would continue reading silently, meanwhile smiling, laughing, or showing some appropriate emotion to the story unfolding. Then he would promise to read the rest tomorrow. Making them wait to experience what he enjoyed helped stir their desire to do this for themselves without being dependent on him. Half the job of teaching is planting the desire. The other half is showing how.

> **An internally motivated child will learn more easily than one pushed. Half the job of teaching is planting the desire. The other half is showing how.**

**4.**   # EVALUATE ACHIEVEMENT LEVEL.  (Delay for Non-Readers)

Objectives:
       To establish a benchmark for measuring future progress.
       To document degree of mastery of previously taught material.
       To measure application of spelling concepts to words not yet taught.

Prepare to Teach:
       Gather the Spelling Diagnostic Test, *McCall-Crabbs Test Lessons in Reading*, a recording
           device, and blank paper or photocopies of page 196.

## Understand Purpose of Tests.

     A non-reader does not need to take any of these diagnostic tests until after covering Section G of the spelling list in *Wise Guide*. A student who can already spell and read should be evaluated before beginnning a new year of instruction.

     A teacher needs easy, reliable tools for assessing literacy ability. Such tools evaluate more than just material studied that week. They reveal overall mastery of a subject and identify areas of weakness. Tests at the beginning of the year create a benchmark for comparing progress made during the year. Use the beginning of the year results to place students in *Wise Guide* and in *McCall*.

     Literacy areas to assess include: spelling, reading comprehension, oral reading ability, writing ability, and penmanship. I also like to evaluate any working knowledge of the phonograms. I hold up the cards one-by-one in a low pressure way. I ask if the student can tell me the sound(s) that each phonogram can make. All initial tests serve as a baseline for monitoring progress in subsequent months and years. Re-test every several months to identify problem areas, and note growth in ability. Date the work and keep it in a permanent place.

## Evaluate Prior Phonogram Knowledge.

     Give a cold turkey phonogram quiz for reading students new to the program. Flip through the cards and see how many the student can say correctly. In a subsequent year give a quiz on all 70 phonograms.

## Give Spelling Diagnostic Test.

     Give Diagnostic Test 1 in Appendix B to to establish a bench mark for the year. Use either the form on page 196 or a blank sheet of regular notebook paper. Continue to give a different one of the eight interchangeable tests once a month during the school year to monitor progress and pinpoint problem areas.

| +32 Grade level 6.0 mastery level R (1st missed #28) | Susie Best Test 1- Grade 4 9-6-02 |
|---|---|
| 1. go | 26. employ |
| 2. last | 27. connection |
| 3. will | X 28. entertane |
| 4. all | 29. publication |
| 5. over | X 30. treashure |

     A kindergarten or first-grade class may attempt only the first ten or fifteen words. More words can be given as students progress in ability. Follow the instructions given in Appendix B.

## Collect Oral Reading Sample.

     To document oral reading ability, record the student reading aloud. State the date, student's name and age, and the source of the selection being read. Later in the school year, have the student read the same selection again and compare the progress. Listen for smoothness, accuracy, speed, and enunciation. Does the student pause at commas and let his voice rise at question marks? Does his voice reflect the appropriate mood of sadness, suspense, or excitement? Does the student demonstrate the ability to sound out unfamiliar words?

**Administer Reading Comprehension Assessment**.

To check comprehension, assign five selections from the *McCall-Crabbs Test Lessons in Reading* and average the scores. Prior knowledge about a topic can increase comprehension for that lesson and give a false overall reading. These test lessons can be used as both an assessment aid and a tool for strengthening comprehension skills. See Step 31 for several samples from the McCall books.

**Request a Composition Sample**.

To check a student's ability to express thoughts on paper, give a simple writing assignment. Have the student write his name and the date in the upper right corner of the paper. The topic assigned could vary. Choose one of the following.

School
> I like (or don't like) school.
> I read a good book today.

Relationships
> I like many things about my best friend.
> My favorite family member is ____.
> I can help others in many ways.

How-to Instructions
> Making ___ is easy to do.
> Building ____ is fun for me.

Hobbies
> My favorite sport is ____.
> I enjoy playing ___ (musical instrument).

Miscellaneous
> Fall is my favorite time of year.
> I am thankful that _____.
> ___ is an important holiday.
> I remember a special vacation.

Evaluate the student's writing ability before you begin a new year.

Repeat the same assignment at the end of the year and compare the progress in penmanship, grammar, and the logical flow of ideas.

**Evaluate Penmanship**.

A separate test is not needed for penmanship assessment. Study the spelling test and the composition work. Is the penmanship neat and legible, or does the student need additional training? Do not alert the students that you will be grading their penmanship. Check their normal style.

Ask questions like:
> __ Do the letters rest on the base line?
> __ Are letters clearly short or tall?
> __ Are the T's crossed and the I's dotted?
> __ Is the T crossed with a tiny cross?
> __ Are words properly spaced?
> __ Are letter shapes consistent and legible?
> __ Can you clearly read each letter?

## **5.** **INTRODUCE PHONOGRAM SOUNDS**.

Objectives:
>    To consider the value and potential difficulty of isolating speech sounds
>    To understand the definition of "phonogram."
>    To see a way to stir student interest in wanting to learn the phonograms.
>    To grasp how a phonogram approach is better than a "look-alike" word approach.
>    To consider Chall's recommended progression of instruction from sound to reading.
>    To avoid common, but harmful, educational practices.

Prepare to Teach:
>    Laminate and cut apart the 70 phonogram cards.
>    Listen to the phonogram CD and make sure you say the phonograms correctly.
>    Practice saying sounds while you look in a mirror.
>    Optional: Read aloud the first chapter of *Michael Faraday: Father of Electronics* by Charles Ludwig. As a child, this famous scientist overcame the difficulty of pronouncing his R's. Once you start this well-written biography, you will probably want to continue.
>    Realize that phonograms should be introduced quickly but mastered over the course of the program.

**Consider the Value and Potential Difficulty of Isolating Individual Sounds in Speech.**

John Corcoran, author of *The Teacher Who Couldn't Read,* overcame a lifetime of hidden reading failure. Successful on the outside but hurting inside, he taught high school for seventeen years without being able to read the sign on a bathroom door. Finally, as a forty-year-old man, he turned to a tutor for help. She exposed him for the first time to phonics, and in a short time he learned to read, but he still faltered with many words. Later his conflict had a name: severe auditory conceptual dysfunction. The turning point that awakened his brain was what he called "mouth movement methodology."

Corcoran explains, "I had never consciously thought about how my tongue, lips, throat, nose, and the air affected the sounds that came out of my mouth. Feeling and watching myself in a mirror while my tongue and lips formed a sound were what made it click for me. Until then my hearing and vision processing had failed me with certain sounds; but now, using my kinesthetic sense, I was finally able to get it. It was like coming out of a coma" (Corcoran p. 212).

Have you ever considered how we use our throat, lips, teeth, palate, and tongue to produce the common sounds of English? Articulatory phonetics is a science worth studying someday, but, unless the student has major speech problems, at this point we need only make some observations.

Give each student a mirror so they can study their own mouths as they try to analyze what they do when they produce different sounds. When we get to the written language, we will learn that the same sound may be spelled in a variety of ways. For example, we spell the sound /f/ as F or PH. [Throughout this book slanted lines ( / / ) mean to think the letter sound, not the letter name.] First, we will just think about oral language.

Boy watching mouth in mirror

1. USE OUR MOTOR (Adding Vibration to the Vocal Cords). Say /b/. [Do not say /buh/!] Our lips make a line. Put your hand on your Adam's apple and say /b/ again. Did you feel a vibration in your throat? Yes. Now say /p/. How are these sounds alike? The lips are close together. How are they different? Our vocal cords vibrate when we say /b/, but not when we say /p/. We turn our motor on to say /b/, but it's off when we say /p/. To make motor-on sounds we use our vocal cords, but motor-off sounds are voiceless.

2. ADD FRICTION with the sound. Say /z/. Feel the friction as a stream of air passes through the narrow opening in the mouth. This is called a fricative (friction added).

3. USE THE NOSE. Next hold your nose and try to say /m/. Why couldn't you make the sound? (This voiced sound is made through the nose.) Hold your nose and say /n/. This one is nasal, too. How are they different? With /m/ the mouth is closed, but not with /n/.

4. USE THE LIPS AND TEETH. Say /p/ as in "pop." What did your lips do? The lips closed together and pushed the sound out in an explosive way. This is called a bilabial — bi- (two) + lips.

Say /th/ as in "the." Place your tongue between your upper and lower teeth as if you are slightly sticking out your tongue and biting. This is called an interdental (between the teeth).

Say /f/ and /v/. Describe the activity of your upper teeth on your lower lip.

5. USE THE THROAT. Some struggle saying /g/ or /k/. They may say "dame" for "game" or "tat" for "cat." The difference between /g/ and /d/ or /k/ and /t/ is the deepness of the source of sound. The /g/ and /k/ come from a deeper part of the throat. One nine-year old student had trouble saying either /k/ or /g/ until we did an activity to practice deep sounds. We would have her make a sound like a gargle. Then we would say /g/. When she slipped back into saying /d/ instead of /g/, I would just say, "gargle" and that reminded her to produce the sound from down in her throat. This one hint helped her say the sound correctly for the first time in her life.

Put your hand under your chin and say: /i/ as in "it," then /a/ as in "at." Both sounds are made closer to the front of the tongue. How are they different? The jaw drops lower for the /a/ sound. The /i/ is in the high front; the /a/ is in the low front.

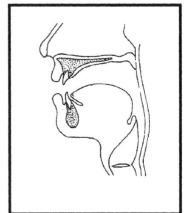

Now say: /a/ as in "at" then /ah/ as in "wasp." Can you tell how the sound for /ah/ comes from deeper back in the throat? When you say /ah/ I want to see your tonsils. While /a/ is in the low front, /ah/ is in the low back.

6. WATCH THE MOUTH. Say the long sound of A and the long sound of E. Watch the mouth. With which one does your mouth stretch out to form a big smile? (E).

7. USE THE TONGUE. Two tongue-lifter sounds give many people trouble. Many struggle with /r/. (Do not say /er/ or /w/.) To make the /r/ sound bring the teeth close together and turn the corners of the mouth down as when producing /E/. Make a sound like the growl of a little dog or a motor trying to turn over in winter. The tip of the tongue should turn up and back for this voiced sound.

Others struggle with /l/, particularly natives of the Pacific Northwest. Touch the tip of the tongue to the top center of the palate behind the upper teeth and, with your motor on, blow air out over the sides of the tongue.

**Define *Phonogram*.**

The teacher needs to understand and then define "phonogram" in an age-appropriate way. The Greek word *phono* means "sound" and *gramma* means "written symbol." A phonogram is a single letter or fixed combination of letters that symbolizes the sounds of speech. We have twenty-six letters in English, but forty-five sounds and seventy basic phonograms. The seventy phonograms cover the one thousand most frequently used words in the language. A limited number of advanced phonograms will be taught as needed with upper-level spelling (Step 38).

— A phonogram can have up to four letters. The word "eight" contains a four-letter phonogram (eigh) which makes the single sound /A/.

— A third of the phonograms represent more than one sound. For example, the letter C sounds like /k/ in most words (cat), but can sound like /s/ in others (cent). CH can make three sounds (/ch/, /k/, /sh/) as in *cheer, Christmas, chef.*

The basic seventy phonograms trace back to the research that Anna Gillingham did for Dr. Samuel Orton, a neurologist famous for his work with remedial reading. This profound breakdown of the language is still little-known by teachers because it is not commonly taught in schools of education. A university professor of linguistics who attended one of our seminars admitted that for the first time he understood his language. He told me, "You cannot imagine the stress you could have removed from my life if I could have taken your course twenty years ago." He admitted that our two-day workshop was more helpful to him than any other class he ever took. The majority of us, like the college instructor, have never learned a clear, consistent, reliable basis of the language, and it all starts with the phonograms!

### Stir Student Interest in Wanting to Learn the Phonograms

The teacher can say, "The forty-five sounds in English are written in seventy basic ways." Hold the stack of all seventy phonogram cards. "I have magic in my hands, and I'm going to teach you how to use it. With these cards (plus a few spelling rule cards that I will teach you later) I hold the secret for unlocking the written words in ALL the books in the library. You can use this information to write letters to friends or even to write books yourself. You will be able to spell words with a stronger level of correctness and understand the books you read with greater ease. Let's glance quickly through the 70 phonograms."

With non-readers, just show some or all of the seventy cards one at a time and say the sound or sounds each phonogram can make. The student can echo you if he likes.. This gives an overview of what they will learn and demonstrates that certain shapes represent certain sounds.

If students can already read, see how many of the phonograms they can identify by sound without help from you. If a phonogram can make two or more sounds, can they list them by frequency of use?

> **Just 98 cards hold the secret to unlock the English language.**

Most students who can read can say some phonograms correctly. Success is encouraging, but exposure to their need should stir curiosity to learn. Show pleasure at what they know and build excitement for what they will be studying.

What if you hold up the phonogram B and the student says, "BEE?" Ask students what sound a cat makes. "Meow." Cat is the **name** for the animal. Meow is the **sound** the animal makes. BEE is the **name** of a letter but it represents the **sound** /b/. When we build spelling words, we will focus on sound(s) and not letter names.

### Grasp How a Phonogram Approach is Better than a "Look-alike" Word Approach.

The phonogram cards are the code for either writing or reading messages.

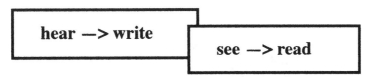

hear —> write

see —> read

The English language has vocabulary gathered from many different languages. We retain some of the flavor of the original when we Anglicize the word, or adjust it to fit our English spelling norms.

We use a limited number of symbols for the sounds of speech, which are phonograms, and a limited number of patterns called spelling rules. If we can learn this information, we will be able to logically understand words that others mistake as rule-breakers. Many people have trouble writing and reading because they do not know the phonograms and how to use them.

Many have been trained to look for the wrong things in words. Some try to watch for look-alike words. The problem is that numerous words LOOK ALIKE but DO NOT SOUND ALIKE. Other words SOUND ALIKE but DO NOT LOOK ALIKE. The following words appear irregular from a whole-language or rhyming perspective but are not irregular when taught as phonograms.

| Teach phonograms NOT appearance | |
|---|---|
| These words rhyme | These words do not rhyme |
| rapt<br>wrapped | food<br>good |
| rays<br>raze<br>raise | meat<br>threat<br>great |

**Consider the Best Sequence of Instruction Recommended by Dr. Jeanne Chall.**

Jeanne Chall, Reading Laboratory Director at Harvard University, describes five stages of reading development. (Chall as recorded by Spalding, pp. 15-16). Her scientific research matches the sequence of instruction in SWR. We begin by presenting the phonogram code clearly and quickly.

| Stages of Reading Development | Skills Involved in Each Stage |
|---|---|
| One | Link letters with the sounds. |
| Two | Master the alphabet sound code for a quick and automatic response. |
| Three | Develop comprehension skills, reading to discover the author's intent. |
| Four & five | Build higher-level analytical skills. |

Many programs bypass the reading readiness steps in order to get a student reading quickly, but an inadequate foundation in stages one and two (the primary focus of SWR) will always handicap the development of subsequent stages. Deficiencies with older students come in some measure from phonogram gaps in their initial foundation. Dr. Chall states, "Early stress on code learning . . . not only produces better word recognition and spelling, but also makes it easier for the child to eventually read with understanding." (Chall: *Learning to Read*, p. 83).

**Present Phonograms:**

Expose students to the phonograms in isolation, ahead of words, by sounds (not letter names), and with all the sounds from the beginning.

1.  IN ISOLATION.

a. <u>Without Picture Association</u>. We publish a set of cards that have only the letter(s) of a phonogram on the card. We avoid colorful additions like guide words or picture clues on the side of the card that we show the student. Our goal is to establish a fast trigger from sound to the symbol (spelling) or the symbol to the sound (reading). Pictures and word associations will block the instant response needed to read or write fluidly.

b. <u>With Speech, Not Music</u>. Some curriculum developers feel that it is too difficult for a child to remember phonograms in isolation, and so they develop songs, rhymes, or other props. "Cutesy" aids, though creative, can be counterproductive. They clutter the mind and defeat the long-term goal — instant recall.

Resist the temptation to teach through music facts that should be mastered to a second-nature level of automaticity. Our poetic, musical side can add joy and a special dimension to our lives. Singing, however, is not the most effective way to implant facts for rapid, instant recall. If we input facts through music, we need music to retrieve the information. Songs are stored in a different part of the brain from normal speech. Music and jingles can create a mental detour that unnecessarily slows down the thought process. Sing Bible verses or concepts that you can thoughtfully ponder. Memorize by speech the everyday keys to math or language.

c. <u>With a Focus on Spelling</u>. Some avoid teaching phonograms in isolation because sounds rarely exist in "pure" forms. The short A sounds different in "man" than it does in the unstressed syllable of "human." The distinct /a/ in "man" is muffled in "human." Children, even at a young age, can recognize that forest green, olive green, and chartreuse are all forms of green. The color may be slightly different, but it's still in the green family. While the sound of A may be slightly different in "man" and "human," they are both in the /a/ family.

For spelling, we think each phonogram sound precisely, even though we don't do so in normal speech. For example, we might misspell the second vowel if we write it as it sounds (hu-mun). To avoid that error, we mentally emphasize the unstressed syllable to match the way we spell it (hu-man). Some of our phonogram sounds appear controversial if you rigidly try to make them fit pronunciation. Focus instead on "what we must think-to-spell correctly." The way we say words can vary from one region of the English speaking world to another. Spelling, however, is amazingly consistent.

2. AHEAD OF WORDS. Rather than starting a student with the jumble of whole words written in sentences, we begin with individual phonograms, the symbols for speech. After the student is familiar with this code and has used it to spell and then read individual words, he will be more prepared to successfully write or read groups of words combined together into sentences.

The trend is to teach reading first and spelling as an afterthought. Supposedly, students will learn to spell correctly by seeing words in print. I do not see evidence of strong spelling success in our society as a result of this philosophy. Do you? The greatest deficiency of entering college freshmen is poor spelling skills. Historically, students do best when they spell themselves into reading.

3. BY SOUNDS, NOT LETTER NAMES. Dr. Hilde Mosse, in *You Can Prevent or Correct Learning Disorders,* explains: "Knowing the names of letters does not help a child with reading English, because the names of all consonants differ from their sounds and the names of all vowels indicate only one of their sounds. Learning the names of letters first, before learning their sounds, confuses

children. It is therefore better to teach their sounds first. . . The child can learn the letter names later" (Mosse, p.93). Recent research confirms Dr. Mosse's observations. McGuinness reports, "Knowledge of letter names did not promote good reading skills, whereas the knowledge of phoneme-to-letter correspondences did" (McGuinness, pp. 213-4).

We want the student to link the sounds of speech with the symbols used for spelling the words we use. If a child spells the word "cat" as "See, AY, Tee," say, " I'm glad you know the names of those letters. That will help you look up words in a dictionary someday, but we want to spell by sound. We will think to spell /k/-/a/-/t/ and read the word "cat."

The letters of the alphabet have a useful purpose for dictionary skills and spelling rules. Even though learning the ABC's is not the first order of business, people in our society commonly expect students to learn this information early. Can we teach this without harming young learners? It is possible if you use an ABC plan that uses capital letters like you can find in *The New England Primer of 1777*. Students see a capital letter G and say, "GEE, As runs the glass, our life does pass." Students can learn the alphabet in this way without confusing early attempts to read because our phonograms are all lower case letters.

G    As runs the Glass
     Our Life does pass.

H    My Book and Heart
     Must never part.

4. WITH ALL SOUNDS FROM THE BEGINNING. It is not difficult to learn the three sounds that O can make. Memory research has verified the efficiency of teaching all the sounds at once even with mentally challenged students. The brain can store the whole package together for easy retrieval. A student who knows only one sound for the vowel may be discouraged and confused that "open" does not begin with the same first sound as "odd." A student who knows the O makes more than one sound is prepared for this varied use of the same letter.

Recently we received a letter from a mom with adopted children. She confessed, "I had presupposed that knowing all sounds for all phonograms was too big a task for first graders (or at least first graders who were also just learning to speak English), so I was allowing my sons to just know the most common sounds." Then her family visited a school her sister and brother-in-law founded that uses our program. She admits, "I realized after watching them in a class of first graders, that they could easily memorize all sounds if I had been following your instructions. I have since gotten my act together a bit more, and they can do the phonogram drill as expected. As non-native speakers of English, they have come an amazing distance in 12 months. This curriculum has been key to their rapid progress."

MOVE QUICKLY FROM SAYING TO WRITING the phonograms! The Council for Basic Education insists, "Phonetics instruction should be FIRST and FAST." Instead of just building visual memory of the symbols with their sounds, add the tactile dimension to help implant these firmly in the brain.

Please do not drag out an introduction of the phonograms! The phonograms should be INTRODUCED within two months for a beginning school-age child. All 70 can be introduced the first week with most older students. With adult-level Spanish ESL classes, I present the single letter phonograms and some of the multi-letter phonograms in minutes. Total mastery of the phonograms is unnecessary before moving on to the spelling words. The typical learner needs to see how phonics works in order to retain early enthusiasm. **Throughout the four to five years you may use this program, you will review phonograms daily. They will be mastered in time. For now it is enough to start the process and move forward.**

**Phonetics instruction should be FIRST and FAST.**

## 6.  SAY AND WRITE NEATLY A-Z PHONOGRAMS.

<u>Objectives:</u>
>To teach the correct letter formation to those who cannot write,
>>who need help improving penmanship, or who have reversal problems.
>To "read" the phonograms: see them and say the sound(s) they represent.
>To "spell" the phonograms: to hear and write the symbols that spell the sounds.

<u>Prepare to Teach:</u>
>Practice penmanship using the instruction guidelines.
>Have a clock face or clock stamp available.
>Remember to go quickly to the next steps while continuing to review phonograms.

**Appreciate Multisensory Instruction.**

Penmanship does not need to be an isolated subject.  Have the student say softly the sounds of the phonograms as he learns to write them.  Students thereby link the **ear gate** (the way the phonogram sounds), and the **mouth gate** (the physical feel of saying the sounds), with the **hand gate** (the physical feel of writing the letters) and the **eye gate** (the way the phonogram looks).  Saying and writing the phonograms help build neuro-connectors that tie together four distinctly different areas of the brain and more strongly imprint the sound-symbol link for later recall.  Such multisensory instruction teaches to every child's strength and remediates every child's weaknesses.

**Use Methods that Help Reverse or Protect against Dyslexia.**

Students who do not write clearly and legibly are more likely to struggle with spelling, writing, and reading.  They often improve when good penmanship practice is combined with our type of spelling dictation.   Dr. Samuel Orton discovered that carefully taught, functional penmanship could help prevent or remediate tendencies to reverse or confuse letters.  He noted, "we find a very wide range of letter confusions—b's mixed with h's; m, n, and u are confused.  Such confusion is present in practically all children in the very beginning." (Orton, pp. 45-46).  Students benefit when they can produce accurately and see clearly the symbols that represent each sound in words.

1.  LIFT THE PENCIL FROM THE PAPER ONLY WHEN NECESSARY.  Teaching block letters, which require two strokes to make a lower case B or D, creates directional confusion in many children.  Letters, as much as possible, should be formed in a continuous motion.  Exceptions are when crossing the f, t, and x, dotting the i and j, and finishing the letter k.

2.  ESTABLISH CLEARLY THE DIRECTIONAL PATTERN FOR FORMING THE LETTERS.   Cross the f, t, and x in the direction we read or write and do not allow the students to retrace backward.  Establish a consistent connection between the visual image of a letter and the tactile feel of forming it.  While some penmanship is embellished with many swirls and fancy artwork,  we recommend starting with a more basic style.  Flair and slant can be added later.

**Save Energy for Learning.**

1.   ENCOURAGE GOOD POSTURE.  A slouched position puts unnecessary strain on the muscles in the back and neck.  Have the student sit up with hips, shoulders, and head in a line (stack his blocks straight), with his body not touching the desk, and his elbows just off the edge.

---

33

2. HOLD THE PENCIL CORRECTLY. Avoid undue strain on the arm, shoulder, and hand. Have the student place her pencil in an open palm. Ask, "Is it heavy?" She does not need to grip tightly to keep the pencil from falling over. If she holds her pencil correctly when writing, someone should be able to pull it out of her hand without any resistance.

Next, have the student hold the pencil between her thumb and her middle finger near where the paint ends. Point the index finger straight up, then drop it naturally on the pencil. Arch the side of the hand slightly above the paper, not lying on it. Curve all fingers gently.

Watch for signs of unnecessary tightening: student tiring quickly, heavy or uneven print, knuckles bent backward awkwardly, or twisted hand positions. Both left and right handers should keep their writing hand below the line on which they are writing (Mosse, p. 186).

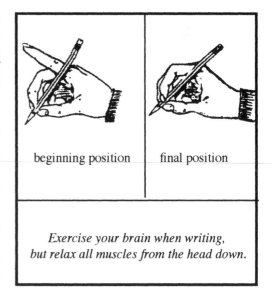

beginning position | final position

*Exercise your brain when writing, but relax all muscles from the head down.*

3. USE RECOMMENDED SUPPLIES. For phonogram drills we normally use regular six-sided #2 pencils and loose-leaf paper. Avoid a large pencil for small hands or hard-lead pencils which increase the pressure needed. To check whether the student is pressing down too hard, turn his paper over. The paper should feel smooth, not embossed. A mechanical pencil is a successful alternative even for kindergarten since the finer point requires less pressure, thereby facilitating neater handwriting.

Require students to have two pencils "ready to go" at the beginning of class. A back-up pencil helps avoid disruptions for sharpening the pencil or reloading the lead.

4. USE LINED PAPER. Dotted half-lines are optional and should not be used exclusively. Alternate practice with regular notebook paper and dotted-line work, such as will later be used in the Primary Learning Log. A student needs to learn early how to determine mentally what is halfway.

**Target Initial Instruction to Most Essential Things.**

1. BEGIN WITH LOWER-CASE LETTERS. Capital letters are used only in special places. When printers set font by hand a letter at a time, they placed the case holding the most frequent forms on a lower shelf for convenience. They called this box the "lower case." Capital letters were placed higher in a different box called the "upper case."

Recent research confirms, "Lower case is used far more often and should be taught first. Learning two sets of symbols with entirely different visual appearances adds an unnecessary memory load. Capital letters can be introduced later" (McGuinness, p. 214). Capital letters should be taught only as needed. The first capital used may be the first letter in a student's name. See later in this step for sample letter forms.

2. TEACH THE CLOCK LETTERS FIRST. We always learn most securely in our minds what we learn first. The clock letters are taught first because learning to form them correctly is of primary importance. Careful teaching here helps prevent or correct letter reversal like that in dyslexia. Younger children may need preliminary work in learning the points of a clock face. The eight clock-letter phonograms are A, C, D, F, G, O, QU, S. If you begin with cursive, omit F and S as clock letters.

Encourage a student to try to do his best work each day and to try to make it better than the day before. Especially watch for the way the letter is formed, not just the finished product. One of the ways to curb dyslexic tendencies is to carefully establish proper penmanship patterns: starting clock letters at 2, drawing lines from top to bottom and in the direction we read and write, and not retracing.

3. ADJUST INSTRUCTION TO VARIOUS AGES. Some older students have excellent penmanship and will not need to spend time learning how to write their letters. Other older students have developed poor habits that hinder their learning. The extra focus on trying to form letters correctly may force them to concentrate more intently, and thereby learn the phonograms more solidly.

What about preschoolers or students with delayed motor skills who are eager to learn? We recommend that the tactile aspect be incorporated even with a young or special-needs child. If the student's small-muscle coordination makes pencil-and-paper work premature, directional orientation and letter formation can be taught by using large muscles.

a. Use a game marker like a bingo chip. Give a beginner a large copy of the clock face, a sheet with two parallel lines about four inches apart, and a game marker from any board game. Have the student follow your instructions for letter formation by moving the marker around on the master.

b. Draw in the air. The child, while repeating the sounds, can also form the shape of each phonogram in the air, keeping his elbow straight to make it a gross motor activity.

c. Use nontraditional media. Possibilities include a pan of cornmeal, sand, a dab of shaving cream, a piece of velvet, the palm of his hand, a big paint brush on the sidewalk with water, a wet sponge on the blackboard, an individual sized chalkboard. A child can trace sandpaper letters, saying the sound(s) as they practice the form. Write a phonogram with chalk on the board and have the young child, starting at the beginning of the letter, trace the phonogram with his finger. A trail of his activity will be visible.

**Determine the Penmanship Style.**

1. BENEFITS OF MANUSCRIPT-FIRST INSTRUCTION. For eighty years, beginners have learned printing first. Manuscript has fewer strokes and appears easier. Some people assume students benefit when the first penmanship style learned looks closer to book-face type.

2. BENEFITS OF CURSIVE-FIRST INSTRUCTION. Although Mrs. Spalding, in *Writing Road to Reading*, recommends manuscript until the middle of second grade, we recommend teaching cursive first. Students who know only how to print have difficulty reading messages in cursive. Writers of cursive can read either. A remarkable decline is noticeable in penmanship today when compared to handwritten material a century or more ago. Teaching cursive first is more historically and scientifically sound.

a. Historically Sound. Before the 1920's, children across North America, Europe, and Asia learned cursive writing before manuscript printing. Consequently, most students developed lovely handwriting. Consider samples of penmanship preserved in early documents from the founders of our country or in museums. In those days printing was taught in high school so students could label maps, work with architectural drafting, prepare posters, or fill out job applications and other forms.

John Dewey, a leader of the misnamed "Progressive School Movement" inspired the switch to manuscript first instruction. The instituted changes proved to be more regressive than progressive. Overall academic achievement plummeted. The move to whole word instruction left many otherwise bright students illiterate. Many leaders today are restoring good practices lost at that time including cursive first instruction.
ABeka schools, for example, have been pleased to report that "kindergarten children learn cursive writing in a matter of months. . . .Both parents and teachers are pleased."

b. <u>Scientifically Sound</u>. Samuel Blumenfeld praises the practicality of teaching cursive first by explaining how the style developed. "The cursive alphabet is not an arbitrary set of forms devised to make life difficult for first graders. It is the ultimate refined product of hundreds of years of trial and error in which the need for legibility and speed required such compromises and refinements as to maximize both. It was devised to make life easier, not more difficult, to provide man with one of his most useful tools of self-expression and communication" (*How to Tutor* p.144).

(1) **Cursive is more natural for beginners.** Cursive uses more fluid motions. Watch how young children scribble, using flowing, swirly strokes. Cursive uses the most natural movements of the arm, wrist, hand, and fingers. We can write in cursive faster because connected writing involves less strain, requires fewer stops, and creates less fatigue. We have been amazed at the beautiful penmanship of beginners who learn cursive early. Though slightly more complicated to learn initially, once learned, connected penmanship is far less stressful.

(2) **Cursive is more permanent in usage**. Cursive is the ideal long-term form of penmanship. We learn best what we learn first and cling to what we learn initially. Many, especially men, who learned manuscript in the beginning years, will tend to print all their lives, even though printing is slower and more laborious. Others write with a mixed-up version of half printing, half cursive.

(3) **Cursive helps eliminate dyslexia**. Dr. Mosse, a reading specialist, reports, "Children with any form of directional confusion learn directions of letters and words better when taught cursive writing" (Mosse, p. 102).

Whether you teach cursive or manuscript first, you will eventually teach both. You can pick which to do first. In the past, students learned cursive first and then learned to print in high school.

## Prepare for Penmanship Instruction

1. SHOW THE STROKES NEEDED TO MAKE LETTERS.

a. Strokes Needed for Manuscript.

With just six strokes we can print all the letters of the alphabet. We start with the hardest to master. What we learn first we learn best. The clock letter stroke starts at 2 and goes counterclockwise. Other stokes include: a tall letter stroke, a short letter stroke, a letter with a tail part, a letter with a diagonal stroke, and a horizontal line. Line letters (letters that start with a line) start at the top. Horizontal lines (in letters e, f, z, t) move in the direction we read. Have students repeat, "Top to bottom, and the direction that we read or write." Avoid the terms "from left to right."

b. Initial Strokes Needed for Cursive.

clock  loop  uphill  hump

A cursive letter is like a printed letter with connectors added so strokes and letters can smoothly tie together or "hold hands." For cursive we use one of four beginning strokes depending on the type of letter: clock, loop, uphill, hump. (See p. 230 or the backside of the cover sheet to the phonogram cards printed since 2005 for added detail.) A child who struggles with the confusion of where to begin letters is helped if you start the clock letter at the baseline. Then all cursive letters will start at the same place. This is optional. Some teach cursive clock letters starting at 2 and line letters starting at the baseline. This book will illustrate cursive clock letters both ways.

## 2. TEACH PRINCIPLES OF PENMANSHIP.

✎ All letters sit on a "base line." All cursive letters start there.

✎ Tall letters DO NOT TOUCH THE TOP GUIDE LINE. Save room for underlining letters in words on the line above.

✎ Short letters are half as high as tall letters.

✎ Tails are parts that drop below the base line. If a letter hangs above the line or dangles below, it will get "tired." Tails can drape below the line, but other parts should not.

✎ Angled parts usually begin in the direction we read.

✎ Horizontal parts go only in the direction we read. You can teach young children the meaning of "horizontal" by calling nap time "horizontal hour."

✎ Clock letters involve a circular part that needs special attention. The clock face provides a stable reference point for round letters that have a stroke that goes from 2 up and over to 10.

✎ Underline all work in the direction we read. Work hard to build the subconscious patterns to move from left to right. Insist on the correct orientation for letter strokes. Failure to establish this pattern firmly may encourage letter reversals.

## Teach Letter Shapes and Sounds Together.

Say the sounds a single letter phonogram can make, and then teach the student how to shape the letter. Listen to the CD of the phonograms to double check your pronunciation. For example: The sound of L is not /el/ but only that of the last letter, the sound of B is not /buh/, and K is not /kuh/. We do not say /robuh/ but only /rob/. Don't say R as /er/. The mouth is more closed than when we say /er/. If the student has trouble have him say "red" then have him drop off the "ed." Practice with words like *rat, rake, rope*. Contrast the beginning and end sounds in rooster.

Teach proper penmanship from the beginning. Once formed, motor patterns are difficult to correct. When children write incorrectly, their mind registers the symbol incorrectly. Introduce as many phonograms as possible the first day, at least four or five for first grade students. See sample lesson plan in Appendix E.

## 1. TEACH FIRST CLOCK LETTER.

a. <u>Student learns phonogram sound(s)</u>.

| | |
|---|---|
| Instructor: | (Hold up card for A.) Say /a/-/A/-/ah/. (Speak in a quick but defined manner, keeping a spacing between each sound). |
| Student: | /a/-/A/-/ah/. |
| Instructor: | This phonogram can make three different sounds. The /a/ is used most often. Next is /A/. Sometimes the phonogram can also say /ah/. |

[In this program, if the letter(s) are surrounded by slashes (/a/), pronounce the sound indicated. If a single letter is capitalized (/A/), read it as the letter name. If a double letter is capitalized, read it as the long sound /OO/ as in "to" rather than /oo/ as in "put."]

b. <u>Student learns to write the phonogram for those sound(s)</u>. Carefully crafted penmanship instructions help students use reasoning ability as they write. They learn to follow directions.

Instructor: Our card shows how the phonogram looks in a book. This is a clock letter. [Hold up the clock face from the phonogram card pack.] Can you find 2? Do you see 10? We will use these points to describe how to write some of our letters with round parts.

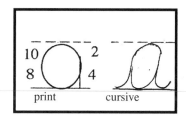

(1) **Manuscript a** -- short clock-letter.
*Start at 2 on the clock.* Go UP to 10, down and around to 2. Without lifting the pencil, pull a line sraight down to the base line.

(2) **Cursive a**.-- short clock-letter.
*Start at the base line with a clock connector stroke. At 2 stop.* Go UP to 10, down and around to 2. Without lifting the pencil, pull a line straight down towards the base line. *End with a slight uphill connector.*

Teacher: /a/ - /A/- /ah/. [Write the phonogram on the board.]
Student: /a/-/A/-/ah/. [Write the letter on looseleaf paper or other medium.]
Teacher: Does your phonogram look like mine?

## 2. TEACH OTHER CLOCK LETTERS.

**c** -- a short clock-letter. *Start at 2 on the clock.** Go UP to 10, down around to 4. **In cursive** end with a slight uphill connector.

**d** -- a short clock-letter with a tall part. *Start at 2 on the clock.** Go UP to 10, down around to 2. Continue a straight line up towards the top guideline. Without lifting the pencil retrace back to the base line. **In cursive** end with a connector.

**g** -- a short clock-letter with a tail. *Start at 2 on the clock.** Go UP to 10, down around to 2. Pull a tail down halfway past the base line. Curve from 4 to 8. **In cursive** continue up diagonally. Cross at the base line with a slight uphill connector.

**o** -- a short clock letter. *Start at 2 on the clock.** Go UP to 10, down and around to 2. **In cursive** end with a dip connector.

**qu** -- the first letter is a short clock-letter with a tail. *Start at 2 on the clock.** Go UP to 10, down and around to 2. Make a tail with a straight line going down from 2 past the base line. Add a flag in the direction we read and write. **In cursive** curve up from 6 to 12 to close at the base line. In cursive end with an uphill connector to the mid-point.

The second letter is a short line-letter. Pull a line straight down. Curve from 8 to 4. Continue straight up to the midpoint. Retrace down to the base line. **In cursiv**e end with a slight uphill connector.

**f** and **s** (manuscript only). In manuscript these are clock letters, but not in cursive. See the phonogram cards for manuscript instruction.

* For cursive substitute: *Start at the base line with a clock connector. At 2 stop.*

| Manuscript Clock Letters | Cursive Clock Letters |
|---|---|
| acdgo qu fs | a c d g o qu |

3. TEACH REMAINING LETTERS. Teach the rest of the letters either alphabetically or according to initial stroke. Cursive initial strokes -- loop letters, uphill letters, bump letters. See p. 230. Manuscript initial strokes -- tall letters, short letters, letters with tails.

**Show Connection between Book Face, Manuscript, and Cursive**.

Although we have three forms for writing letters (book face, manuscript, and cursive), all three are strongly related. Manuscript looks similar to bookface. In cursive we simply add strokes that connect letters together. Students who learn cursive first can easily read all three, but those who write only manuscript often have difficulty reading cursive.

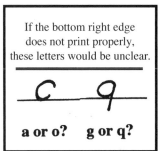

Why do the book face "a" and "g" look different from manuscript "**a**" and "**g**?" Early forms of printing type was a sophisticated form of rubber stamping. What happens with a rubber stamp if we don't push all sides down evenly? Part of the image is not clear. When the bottom corner of the "**a**" and "**g**" did not print evenly, the "**a**" could be mistaken for an "o" and the "**g**" could be confused with the letter "q." Swirls were added to "**a**" and "**g**" to solve this problem.

| bookface | manuscript | cursive | bookface | manuscript | cursive |
|---|---|---|---|---|---|
| l | l | l | t | t | t |
| h | h | h | u | u | u |
| i | i | i | v | v | v |
| j | j | j | w | w | w |
| m | m | m | x | x | x |
| n | n | n | y | y | y |
| p | p | p | | | |

Special attention needs to be given to make the cursive b, e, f, k, r, s, and z, but even in these letters the printed form of the letter is embedded in the cursive representation of the letter. The F can be more clearly seen if you make it longer and slide it down so that the horizontal line is at the point of the baseline. If we simply form the F by making an upswing in and out of the letter, it could be confused with an L that had an accidental line through it or with a T.

| b | b | b | k | k | k |
|---|---|---|---|---|---|
| e | e | e | r | r | r |
| f | f | f | s | s | s |
| | | | z | z | z |

1. PRACTICE USING THE CURSIVE STROKE TO CONNECT LETTERS. To demonstrate the link between bookface and cursive, give students a typed line of the letters. Have them connect them as in cursive.

a b c d e f g h i j k l m n o p  qu  r s t u v w x y z

a b c d e f g h i j k l m n o p  qu  r s t u v w x y z

2. FOLLOW PROCEDURES FOR PHONOGRAM INSTRUCTION.

   a. Introducing New Phonograms.

   | | |
   |---|---|
   | Teacher: | Holds up the card. Says the sound(s). |
   | Student: | Echoes the sound(s). |
   | Teacher: | Explains letter formation and demonstrates how to write the phonogram. |
   | Student: | Repeats the sound(s) and writes the phonogram on loose-leaf paper. |

   b. Reviewing Phonograms. The phonograms are a reversible code for spelling and reading. Give daily practice drills (quizzes) using them for either application. (Also see pp. 61-62.)

   1) "Spelling" the Phonograms (hear, say, write, and read).

   | | |
   |---|---|
   | Teacher: | Scrambles cards and calls out the phonogram without showing it. Include full spelling dialogue.   [CK: /k/, 2-letter /k/.] |
   | Student: | Repeats full spelling dialogue and writes each phonogram from hearing only. When finished with a list of phonograms, dictates them back to teacher. |
   | Student: | Reads each phonogram one-by-one. [CK: /k/, 2-letter /k/.] |
   | Teacher: | Writes the phonogram on the board from child's dictation. |
   | Student: | Proofreads and with red writes the correct answer to any missed. Counts total right. Writes at the top of the paper + and the number correct. |

   2) "Reading" the Phonograms (see and read).

   | | |
   |---|---|
   | Teacher: | Holds up cards. [Bring the cards from back to front so you can easily see the teacher's notes before showing the student the next one.] |
   | Student: | Sees phonograms and says the sound(s).  [CK: /k/.] Full spelling dialogue is not necessary. Students respond in unison. All seventy phonograms can be read eventually in about seventy seconds. |

**Additional Help with Cursive Instruction.**

   A separate handwriting program is unnecessary. Students practice penmanship as they learn the phonograms or write sentences. Elizabeth FitzGerald has organized consumable worksheets with detailed instructions and step-by-step practice sheets in *Cursive First* for those desiring extra help.

**Teach Capitals Only as Needed.**

   Have you seen children alternate between lower case and capitals in the middle of a word? This problem comes from teaching the lower case and capital letters at the same time. We first teach lower-case letters since those are the ones we mainly use. We teach capitals only as needed. The first capital letter the student will need will be the first letter of his name.

Clock letters always start at two-on-the clock. Cursive capital letters may have few or added swirls according to the preference of the teacher.   Letters are listed below grouped by starting point.

1. MANUSCRIPT CAPITALS
   a. Two on the clock: C, G, O, Qu, S, and maybe A
   b. Top to bottom: B, D, E, F, H, I, J,  K, L, M, N, P, R, T, U, V, W, X, Y, Z and maybe A

2. CURSIVE CAPITALS
   a. Two on the clock:  C, E, O, and maybe A and Qu
   b. Baseline forward:  G, S, and maybe A
   c. Baseline back: I, J, and maybe Qu
   d. Top to bottom:  B, D, E, F, H, K, L, M, N, P, R, T, U, V, W, X, Y, Z

**Manuscript alphabet with upper and lower case**

Aa  Bb  Cc  Dd  Ee  Ff  Gg  Hh  Ii  Jj
Kk  Ll  Mm  Nn  Oo  Pp  Qq  Rr  Ss  Tt
Uu  Vv  Ww  Xx  Yy  Zz

**Cursive alphabet with upper and lower case**

Aa  Bb  Cc  Dd  Ee  Ff  Gg  Hh
Ii  Jj  Kk  Ll  Mm  Nn  Oo  Pp
Qq  Rr  Ss  Tt  Uu  Vv  Ww  Xx
Yy  Zz

**Introduce the Phonograms and then Move Quickly to the Next Step**

If a student can't remember how to write the phonograms he hears, how can he spell a word from hearing only?  If he gets stuck you can help him out in a variety of subtle ways.  Write the phonogram on the board and quickly erase it.  Flash the phonogram card.  Give hints like "start at 2 on the clock" or "this was the same phonogram you used in the last word" and point to the phonogram on his paper.  Wean him from needing these clues, but please don't hold him back from spelling until he has mastered all the phonograms.  The biggest mistake that people make with the program is to spend too long on phonogram instruction alone. If you get stuck doing only phonograms day after day, your student will become unnecessarily bored.  Don't destroy the natural motivation a child has to learn in this way.

**Don't wait for total mastery of the phonograms before moving to spelling!**

**7.**   **TEACH NUMBERS FROM 0 to 9.**

Objectives:

To learn how to write the basic digits.

To show how a few digits can be used to write all the numbers in the world.

Preparation:

Write on the board: dif-fi-cult.

Under it write: 32,517,394,865.

**Introduce the Idea.**

The two most foundational school subjects (language and math) can be summarized by a few key things.

1. WORDS. All words, no matter how long, in all the books in the library, are made up of different combinations of **twenty-six letters**. If you can write these letters, you can write all the words in the dictionary. Learning to write our language doesn't sound as difficult when we think about it that way.

2. NUMBERS. All numbers, regardless of how large, are built from different combinations of **ten digits**. If you can write these ten numbers, you can write huge sums like 32,517,394,865 (32 billion, 517 million, 394 thousand, eight hundred sixty-five).

Later students will use numbers 1-6 for spelling markings. We might as well teach all the numbers now. In *Wise Guide*, spelling words are numbered, but students will not write the number of the words in their Learning Log. The words are numbered simply for teacher reference purposes.

We teach the single-digit numbers from 0 to 9 (instead of 1 - 10).

**Teach Penmanship Pointers for Writing Numbers.**

> The height of numbers is halfway between the height of a tall letter and a short letter.

> The clock face numbers are 0, 8, and 9. We elongate these letters slightly.

> Line numbers (starting at the top with a line) include 1, 4, 5, 6 and 7. Add the horizontal line to the 5 last, making sure the student forms it in the direction we read and write.

> Two numbers (2 and 3) violate the "2 to 10 on the clock" pattern we have so carefully learned. Unlike any other number or letter, these two go from 10 to 2. I helped my son remember this oddity by saying, "Two doesn't begin at 2 on the clock. Isn't that funny? Three doesn't either."

## 8.   <u>INTRODUCE THE LEARNING LOG</u>.

<u>Objectives:</u>

    To express special importance of the Log.
    To personalize log with name and date.
    To format a blank Black Log (if not using the preformatted one).

<u>Prepare to Teach:</u>

    Select one of three types of Learning Log for your student(s).
    Follow instructions for the type of log you will be using.
    Start creating a teacher's master guide. See Appendix C.

> **Students need to build a new log each year.**

Students create their own spelling textbook for more dynamic learning than the typical workbook. As the captain of a ship logs information about his travels, so students log new spelling words and illustrate the spelling rules. The log is tailored to ability level and built from teacher dictation. Each year the log repeats the essentials adding content and complexity. While it provides a springboard for language learning activities and a reference of spelling principles, it is not a place for practice work, quizzes, or homework assignments. These can be done on loose leaf paper and kept in a binder.

Tell students, "YOU will become the author of your own log! You will start by writing your name on the cover." **Treat these customized books with special respect as a place for a student to carefully do his best work.** Consider this as a potential "keeper," a valuable basis for comparison in future years. Use it as an encouraging record of improvement and growth. Many save one or more log to share with the next generation.

Each year, the student begins a new log. The contents will vary from year to year with some overlap. Similar reference pages will be constructed, but sample words will have growing complexity that matches the developing level of the student. Reconstructing these vital reference aids provides the review that helps cement concepts into long-term memory. A new book gives new beginnings. The child will feel a growing sense of accomplishment. The student and the teacher will combine the comfort of a familiar routine started earlier with a fresh start for a new year and its added challenges.

**Select One of Three Types of Log**.

Although the purpose of the log is the same for any student, the format and the contents will vary, depending on ability level. The Primary Learning Log works best for introductory level work for young beginners. Black log users have two options. A black log can be constructed from a blank, lined composition book. Better yet, Back Home Industries has now published a preformatted book for the students third grade to adult. The teacher makes a sample corresponding to the student's book.

**A log is a self-made textbook. Do not clutter with stickers (good job). Do not use for quizzes or practice work.**

1. PRIMARY LEARNING LOG (K-2, posssibly older students new to the program). The brown Primary Log has dotted-half lines to help the student write in their very best penmanship when building this important book. The front pages are pre-formatted for two columns of spelling words, with room at the bottom for the student's best original sentence for the week. A reference section in the back has preformatted pages for illustrating spelling rules. The rules themselves are written in tiny print on the page. These notes are not designed for young children, but for interested adults who never learned these principles. The small print can also serve as a note for the teacher, reminding her of the main point of the reference page.

2. NEW PREFORMATTED BLACK LOG (3rd grade and up). All the student needs to do to get started is to sign and date the book cover. This log is user friendly with bonus materials. It includes a built-in Table of Contents and an expanded set of reference pages. It provides a place for Greek and Latin numbers, roots and affixes, and a spot to collect examples for rules 17, 23, and 25. It covers spelling rules for subject/ verb agreement and gives a spot to collect heteronyms. A free download at www.bhibooks.net provides a teacher answer key for the sections not covered in Appendix C.

3. BLANK LEARNING LOG BUILT FROM SCRATCH. This type of log is a major project. See pages 46 and 47 for instructions. Most office supply stores sell blank black-and-white sewn composition books. We recommend ones with fifty-leaves. Blank pages in the thicker books tempt the teacher to keep using the notebook the next year, a practice that we do not recommend. An important dimension in developing long-term memory comes from the review involved in rebuilding a new book every year.

**Begin Instruction with the Log**.

Each type of log has two basic sections: one for new spelling words and the other reference pages for spelling rules. Follow the specific instructions below that correspond to the type of log your student will use.

1. INTRODUCE  THE PRIMARY LEARNING LOG (K-2 or older new students).

a. Sign the book cover and the signature page. Pass out the books. Have students study the log. Explain, "The book is not written in yet. You will be the author! Famous authors often autograph their books. We would like your autograph on this one. A famous man known for the way he signed his autograph was John Hancock. Can anyone tell us about him? We sometimes call the process of signing our name, 'giving our John Hancock.' Write your name on the top line of the inside front cover and date it." You can use numerals for the date.

b. Tab first reference page. Turn to the back of the book and find the Consonant and Vowel Page which is the first page of the reference section. We will need to be able to turn quickly to these spelling rule pages. Attach a Post-it ® tab to the edge of the page halfway down the right hand margin.

c. Add the table of contents to your master log, if you like. Photocopy the *Teacher's Table of Contents* on page 45. Glue it over the John Hancock chart in your Teacher's Edition of the Primary Learning Log. The students will not need this table of contents for themselves.

2. INTRODUCE FORMATTED BLACK LOG (3 grade+). The new Black Log includes all the concepts in the Primary and the built from scratch Black Log plus much more. Students with the preformatted log just add their name to the cover. All the other start-up work is done.

> **Each student will build from dictation his own personalized spelling textbook.**
>
> **He will log in words and illustrate spelling rules in this customized work.**
>
> **Stress neat, legible penmanship!**

(Attach the following table of contents to the teacher master log
over the John Hancock Signature Page on the inside the front cover.)

**The Primary Learning Log
Teacher's Table of Contents**

New Spelling Words

Appendix

3. INTRODUCE BLANK BLACK LOG BUILT FROM SCRATCH (grade 3+).

A student building his log from a blank composition book will do more in this step than just sign his name to the log. He needs to format the blank book.

a. <u>Write the name and date on the front cover</u>. Add a phone number and/ or address. In the unlikely event that you lose this book, you want people to know to return it to you.

b. <u>Number the reference pages in the back</u>. Go to the final page in the book. In the lower outer corner write 31. Continue to number each right and left page in decreasing order: 30, 29, 28, 27, 26. . . Be careful to turn each page and not accidentally miss any. Pages in the front of the book are reserved for new spelling words and will be identified by spelling section letter and division number. For example, the second set of words taught in Section R will be labeled R-2. Label these pages as you teach the corresponding section.

c. <u>Title the Reference Section</u>. On the unnumbered flip side of page one, around the ninth line down, center the label for this section of the book. Capitalize the first letter of all main words in titles. Write: *Notebook Reference Pages*.

d. <u>Format the Reference Pages</u>. We need to establish margins for columns of information. The easiest way to do this is to fold the pages with the creased fold serving as a margin. Each of the pages in the front of the book will be folded in half, but these should be done a page at a time as spelling words are taught. **The number of folds differs in the reference section,** and all of these should be formatted from the beginning.

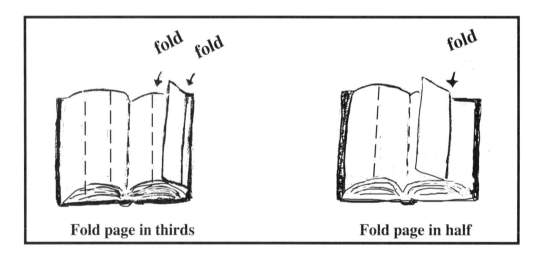

**Fold page in thirds**                          **Fold page in half**

Fold these reference pages in thirds:          Fold these reference pages in half:
         1-13, 20, 21, and 30.                           14-19, and 22-29.

Why do we need margin lines? We want these books to be neat and legible prized possessions. The folds give us guidelines so we can keep our list of words straight. We want each word to touch, or to come comfortably close to touching, the margin lines.

e. <u>Tab the first reference page</u>. We will need to turn quickly to the reference pages. Flag the title page for the reference section with a Post-it ® tab.

f. <u>Add the table of contents</u>. Photocopy "The Table of Contents for the Black Learning Log" on page 47, and glue it over the inside front cover. Make a copy of the table of contents for each student. This age level will need it.

**Paste the Table of Contents to the inside of the front cover of a built from scratch black log.**

(The new formatted Black Log already has a more extensive table of contents printed on the front page.
The new log student just writes his name and date on the cover to complete this step.)

---

### Black Learning Log Table of Contents

New Spelling Words

Reference Page Appendix:

---

**9.**   ## DICTATE CONSONANT AND VOWEL PAGE

| Rule # 1 |
| :---: |
| **q** |
| **qu** |
| *Q always needs a U* |

<u>Objectives:</u>
To build the Consonant and Vowel Reference Page in the Learning Log.
To define consonants, vowels, and syllables.
To apply and say rules 1, 2, 3, 4, 5, 6, 27. [Show rule cards after Step 20.]
To learn some spelling markings using the single underline and numbers.

<u>Prepare to Teach:</u>
Start by Building the Consonant Page in your teacher's Learning Log.

Note that Black Log students cover some additional, more advanced material.

Practice out loud the teaching dialogue as you create your log.

Compare your finished page with the sample for your type of log in Appendix C-- P1/ B1.

Add lines to a board as described in Step 1 or make an enlarged chart from SWR Chart Pack.

SWR Step 2 encourages orally blending sounds together to say words. In Steps 5 and 6, students start hearing, saying and writing phonograms using all their common sounds in the order of frequency. Step 9 is the first and most important reference page. This chart is taught at the beginning of every year, to every level of student. It divides the first 26 phonograms into consonants and vowels and teaches the difference. It moves from all the sounds a phonogram can possibly make to the particular sound it makes in a given word. It casually exposes students to one-fourth of the spelling rules. It introduces one-half of the SWR special spelling markings. **Note that a red pencil is reserved for reference pages to emphasize the focus highlighted by each particular chart**.

Kindergarten or younger students can just participate orally as the teacher builds this page on the board. Later, when their letter formation is no longer labored, come back and have them build the page in their log from your dictation. A first grade (primary) class is typically ready to build this page by the second week of school after an introduction of the first 26 phonograms. See sample lesson plan on p. 225. Older students may be ready to build this page on the first day or two of instruction.

**Introduce the Topic**.

"All people are either male or female. Each has strengths and weaknesses, and together we make up the human race. We would not last long without each other. Alphabet letters can be divided into two types." Hold up cards *a* and *c*. "What is the difference between these two phonograms?"

"Single-letter phonograms are either consonants or vowels. Consonants make short, quick sounds. Vowels make longer, louder sounds. Without a vowel no one could understand your call for help—/h-l-p/. They also would not know your need if you used only the vowel /e/. Combine them to get /h-e-l-p/. Try to say your name with only consonants or only vowels. We need both."

**Elicit Active Student Participation**.

Actively educate. Do not pass out a sheet of words or rules for students to copy. Do not introduce completed charts for students to study. Reference pages are built with direct student involvement. The instructor leads student discovery. Participation in the step-by-step construction of a reference page helps the student cement new concepts in his mind. He learns by doing.

This same reference material is covered again at the beginning of EVERY year that we teach this program. Think of the first presentation of this page as exposure. It provides the big picture and sets the stage for spelling dictation. Mastery of these concepts will come with review and application over time.

> **Reference Pages are built with step-by-step active involvement between teacher and student.**

All ages can benefit from this teaching. A preschooler can organize letters as consonants and vowels and see that a phonogram with three sounds will make only one of those sounds in a given word. He can hear how to blend sounds to make words. He can echo rules that apply. Challenge experienced students to dig more deeply, discussing some of the optional or advanced side notes. Cover the basic material and use the art of teaching to determine how much extra detail to give any particular class.

**Give Clear Instruction for Placement on the Page.**

In the Primary and formatted Black Logs, some information is preprinted. Build-from-scratch Black Log students add some of this information. When dictating, give precise horizontal and vertical directions for placement on the page. Use margin guides to create straight columns. Student work will be neater if the student starts at the corner where the vertical margin line and the base line meet.

Interaction with a teacher is vital. Follow the instructions to present this valuable material. Train your student to listen carefully and follow instructions accurately, engaging his mind to concentrate. Never let a student copy reference pages from this teacher manual or the teacher's master Log!

**Teach the Top Portion of the Consonant/Vowel Page.**

"Turn in your Learning Log to Reference Page One. This covers consonants and vowels."

1. DEFINE TERMS AS NEEDED. Before teaching the consonant portion, teach the meaning of consonants and vowels. Review the terms again in the vowel section. Then, when you start building actual words, explain the meaning of syllable. A word consists of one or more syllables.

**A consonant** is any letter that is not a vowel. The word *consonant* literally means "sounding with something." Consonant sounds are blocked by the organs of speech as the sound is pushed or exploded past throat, teeth, tongue, nose, or lips. (Point to each body part as you say the name for that part.) In forming a consonant, the voice is compressed or stopped. When voiced correctly, **we cannot shout a consonant sound.**

**A vowel** is any letter that is not a consonant. Our mouths are relatively open when we say a vowel; nothing blocks the sound. Vowels pass through the mouth and throat with little obstruction from teeth, tongue, or lips. Only vowels can say their letter names in words. **We can shout a vowel sound.**

**A syllable** is a rhythmic "chunk" of a word. A syllable is pronounced with one sound of your voice. **Every syllable must have a vowel.** We call syllables that end with a vowel "open syllables." Why? We end the syllable with our mouths open.

Different techniques help students grasp the meaning of *syllable*.

a. "Vowelize" the syllables. Tightly close your mouth, thereby stopping the production of any consonant sounds through the teeth, lips, tongue, or throat. Put your hand on your throat, and hum a word. This is the preferred and most reliable method.

| | |
|---|---|
| con-so-nant: | MM-mm-mmm (three syllables) |
| vow-el: | MM-mm (two syllables) |
| hip-po-pot-a-mus | mm-mm-MM-m-mm (five syllables) |

b. Clap or stamp. Count syllables by marching or clapping.

c. Use the hand under the chin. Put your hand under your chin and say the word. Feel the number of times your chin opens to say a vowel. Each syllable must have a vowel.

stamp syllables

2. DICTATE CONSONANTS. Read aloud the titles in the preformatted logs. Dictate them for build-from-scratch log students. For example, say: "Use the first line as a base line. Center the title, 'Consonants.' Capitalize the first letter of title words. Think to spell, Con-so-nants."

Teachers for all types of logs will say, "Under 'Consonants,' without skipping a line, write the consonants as I dictate them. Watch me say the phonogram sound or sounds and repeat it after me. Then look down and write it, saying it softly a second time as you write. Say it out loud with your mouth, not just in your head. Keep the letters close, side-by-side." The teacher refers to her log, but she writes point-by-point on the board so the student can proofread.

Dictate the consonants in alphabetical order. Leave an extra space the size of a round letter before and after QU, to show that this is a two-letter phonogram.

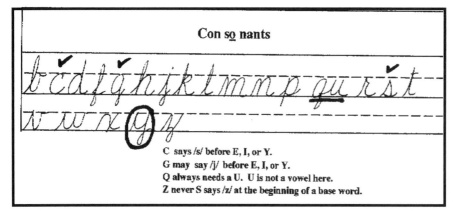

**Primary Learning Log**

Top portion of the
Consonant/ Vowel Page

See full page sample on p. 208.

Red markings in bold

3. ANALYZE THE CONSONANTS. The rules about the consonants are printed in small type in the Primary Learning Log. Do not expect young children to read these notes. When classroom teachers or tutors send the books home, parents will see ideas taught on the page. Instructors have the reminder of the key points as well. Black Log students will add sample words for the C and G rule. Compare the Primary Log and the build-from-scratch Black Log in Appendix C on pages 208 and 212.

a. Count the consonant sounds. "Let's read the consonants one by one. If a consonant has two possible sounds, say together: "Two sounds. Add a red check." When finished, ask: "How many can make more than one consonant sound?" (three).

Older students may know that QU and X can also make additional sounds. The second sounds will be taught later with the advanced-level phonograms in Step 38.

b. Notice the uniqueness of the phonograms QU and Y.

"QU is two letters. *Q always needs a U. U is not a vowel here* [R1]. With red, underline /qw/. In spelling words, we underline multi-letter phonograms. On a reference page, we mark **with red** ideas we emphasize on that page. An underline is a line UNDER (not on) the line."

"Y can be a consonant or a vowel. With red, **circle** the Y. **As a consonant, Y makes only one sound!** At the beginning of a base word it sounds like /y/ as in *yard, yes, yet, midyear, beyond (be+ yonder)*. The other two phonogram sounds for this letter are **vowels**. Y is the only single letter commonly used as either a consonant or a vowel." Y is a stand-in for I at the end of a word since *English words do not end in I* [R6].

c. Discuss the three consonants with two different sounds. "Rules sometimes help narrow down the sound in specific words."

— "*C usually says /k/, but C says /s/ before E, I, or Y.*" [R2]. We can tell which sound the C makes in a word by the letter next door. The C is very consistent.

— *"G usually says /g/, but G MAY say /j/ before E, I, or Y."* [R3]. G may also say /g/ before E, I, or Y. We say *get* not *jet*.

— *"Z, never S, says /z/ at the beginning of a base word."* [R27]. If S begins a word, it uses its first sound. In other positions it can make either sound, but most often will say /s/.

**Primary Log teachers should SKIP AHEAD now to SWR p. 53, point 6!**

**Black Learning Log**

Top portion of C/V Page

To dictate each word sample: say it, use it in a sentence and then help students sound it out sound-by-sound. Example: cap -- See the red cap. /k-a-p/.

**With red, bold the e, i, y in**

> *c*e*nt*, g*e*nt
> *c*i*ty*, g*i*n
> *c*y*st*, g*y*p

Older students new to the program wait until after completing the vowel portion to underline the O in Con-s*o*-nant.

.

d. <u>Illustrate the C and G rules.</u> (Dictate horizontally, leaving space between words.) "When will the C and G say their most frequent sound (their hard sound)?"

| First sound: | cap | → | gap | (before an A) |
|---|---|---|---|---|
| | cot | | got | (before an O) |
| | cuts | | guts | (before a U) |
| | clip | | grip | (before any consonant) |
| | arc | | bag | (before nothing) |

[The focus is where the single letter C can say /k/. Alternate phonograms spell /k/ in these locations: *kangaroo*, *chasm*, *koala*, *kumquat*, *khan*, *Christ*, ba*ck*, tre*k*, epo*ch*.]

"When will C and G say their second sound (their soft sound)?"

"C and G say their second sound only before E, I, or Y. The C consistently does. G usually does. With red, write the E, I and Y to highlight the reason for the change."

| Second sound: | cent | → | gent | |
|---|---|---|---|---|
| | city | | gin | |
| | cyst | | gyp | (or alternatives: *cym-bal, gym*) |

Teacher Note: In the next two steps, we will first demonstrate one of three ways we can spell the /k/ sound before E, I, or Y. Next, we will show how G can say /j/ only before E, I, or Y, but it does not have to say /j/. Words adopted into the language during the Old English time period have retained the hard /g/ before those letters. High frequency examples included in the *Wise Guide* spelling list: *get, give, girl, gift, begin, finger, together.*

"Other phonograms can spell /k/ before E, I, or Y. Beside *cent* write *Kent.*" On the same line with *city*, write *kitty*. On the same line with *cyst*, write *stinky*. No red is needed in the next two steps.

| e | cent | Kent | gent | |
| i | city | kit-ty | gin | |
| y | cym-bal | ink-y | gym | |

"Latin-based words, like *gent*, have G say /j/ before E, I, or Y. Beside *gent*, write *get* /g-e-t/. Add in parentheses *(not jet). Get* is an early English word. The G in Early English only said /g/. Today an English word MAY say /j/ before E, I, or Y. If it doesn't, we know why.

| e | cent | Kent | gent | get (not jet) |
| i | city | kit-ty | gin | be-gin |
| y | cym-bal | ink-y | gym | bog-gy |

4. REINFORCE **C/G** RULES. Ideas for digging more deeply with seasoned students:

a. Optional reinforcement of **C** [R2]: Write some or all of the following on the board. Ask students to identify each C sound and explain why.

| countenance | ice cream | circus | bicycle | succeed |
| accident | circumference | cynical | jaundice | efficacy |

The answer should be either C says:
—/k/ because it's NOT followed by (E, I, or Y).
—/s/ because it is followed by — (either E, I, or Y — whichever applies).

b. Optional reinforcement of **G** [R3]: Write some or all of the following on the board. Ask students to identify each G sound and explain why.

| geography | garbage | negligent | strategic |
| genius | gist | baggage | gigantic |

The answer should be either:
—/g/ because it's NOT followed by — (either E, I, or Y)
—probably /j/ because it's followed by — (either E, I, or Y )

5. APPRECIATE THE LONG-TERM VALUE OF THESE RULES. You will see the C/G rules concept show up again later in the program to explain other spelling rules and challenges.

—In **Step 17** we add a silent E to *notice* and *change* so C will say /s/ and G will say /j/.

—In **Step 29** we drop the E in *noticing* but not in notice*able.* In English words, a C before an I will say /s/ but not before an A. Likewise, we drop the E in *changing* but not in *changeable.*

—**With Latin derivatives that end with C**, we insert a K to keep the /k/ sound when adding an ending that starts with E, I, or Y. See Wise Guide p.126 *(picnic — picnick-ing).* Other examples: *mimicking, colicky, garlicky, panicky.* Without a K the C softens *(criticism, toxicity).*

—**In Step 38** we will learn advanced phonograms (*cu, gh, gu, ge, gi*), which are designed to accommodate the reliable C/G rules.

**Advanced:** Even tricky C and G can be easily explained.

"C usually says /k/, but C says /s/ before E, I, or Y." [R2]

(1)  Foreign words do not necessarily follow English spelling rules.

**Celtics** — /keltiks/ or /seltiks/?  The Gaelic form is /keltiks/.  When conformed to American spelling rules, we say /seltiks/, as in the sports team the Boston Celtics.

**Caesar** — AE is an advanced phonogram that says /E/. (See page 180.)  The C still precedes the sound of /E/ even though the next letter is not technically an E.

**façade** — The French use a cedilla to show the letter says /s/.  We adopted the foreign spelling but our typewriters may not have a key for ç.

(2)  Sometimes a C is retained for other spelling reasons.

**soc-cer** — The first says /k/ and closes the syllable.  The second C is silent.
**mus-cle** — The silent C in the root word is heard in the derivative *muscular*.
**cor-pus-cle** — The silent C in the root word is heard in *corpuscular*.

"G usually says /g/, but G may say /j/ before E, I, or Y." [R3]  French, Italian, and Spanish words create advance phonograms to clarify the G sound.  See SWR p. 180.

A *gh* or *gu* before E, I, or Y preserve the sound /g/ (spa**gh**etti, **gu**y).  A *ge* or *gi* before any letter other than E, I, or Y, indicates /j/ (pa**ge**ant, **Ge**orgia, re**gi**on).

---

6.  REVIEW THE MAIN POINTS ABOUT CONSONANTS  (all levels of students).

♥ Q never stands alone.  Q always needs a U.  [R1]

♥ The Y has only one consonant sound.  It also has two vowel sounds.

♥ Only three, single-letter consonants (c, g, s) make more than one consonant sound.

**Teach the Vowel Portion at the bottom of the Consonant/Vowel Page.**

1. DISCUSS THE NEXT SUBTITLE.  Build-from-scratch Black Log students skip a line and center "Vow-els." Capitalize the first letter. Underline /ow/; it's a two-letter phonogram. Put a 2 over the /z/; it makes the second sound. Review the definition of Consonant and Vowel. See page 49.

2. DICTATE SINGLE VOWEL PHONOGRAMS.  "On the first line in the first column under 'Vowels,' write the phonogram */a-A-ah/.*" Student says the phonogram sounds and writes *a.* The teacher writes it on the board. "Under */a-A-ah/,* write /e-E/." Student echoes and writes. Continue DOWN with *i, y, o, u.* **"With red**, circle the Y. At the beginning of a word, Y is a consonant. Elsewhere it substitutes for I. **Bracket I and Y**. These letters have a strong connection. **Y is** the **"stand-in" for I."**

3. SHOW VOWELS AS MORE COMPLEX.  "Most single consonants make only one sound. All single vowels make at least two; half of them make three. I will dictate a word for each vowel sound in the order of frequency. We'll discover one way a vowel regularly makes the second sound."

4. USE TEACHER DICTATION FOR WORDS. Give clear instructions where the student should write. For example, "On the same line with /a-A-ah/, in the next column, illustrate the sound /a/. Am. I <u>am</u> your teacher. — am." Next, "On the same line with *am* in the next column, write..."

Before a student writes, clarify which phonogram to use if more than one single letter can make that sound (See upcoming examples: *is, gym, cry.*) At first, he will need coaching. Ask a question and have him echo the reply. In time, the student will respond with fewer prompts.

---

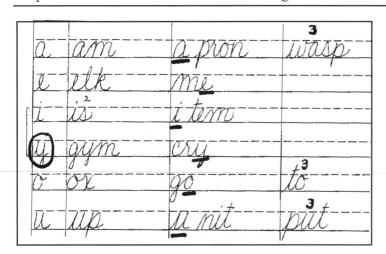

**Vowel Portion of CV Page**

—Same words used first year in either log. (Several advanced versions are provided on pp. 57-58 for older, returning students.)

—Red markings in bold.

—Fingergrams are extremely helpful. See SWR inside back cover for spelling dictation guide.

—Non-readers may watch and participate verbally as teacher writes on the board.

## Illustrate Vowel Sounds with Sample Words.

| **a** | /a/ | /A/ | /ah/ |
|---|---|---|---|
| | **am** | **apron** | **wasp** |
| | "I am your teacher." /a-m/ | "Wear an apron when cooking." Syllables? (*Two*) /A/- /p-r-o-n/ | "I see a wasp." /w-ah-s-p/ |
| | This is the most common sound for the phonogram. | Spelling words in the log are spaced between syllables and marked. | Teach Marking: *With red, put a 3 over /ah/.* [Student echoes and writes.] |
| | | Marking? *With red, underline /A/.* [Student echoes and writes.] | Why add a three? *It's the third sound of the phonogram.* [Student echoes.] |
| | Teacher Note: Single vowels can make the second sound, (taught next), in one of three ways. On this reference page, we orally introduce the most frequent reason in two parts: as it applies to A,E,O,U and as it applies to I and Y. Join the adventure to discover vital, but little known, secrets to the English language. | Why did it say /A/? *A said /A/ at the end of a syllable.* [Student echoes.] Does A usually say /A/ at the end of a syllable? *Yes! A-E-O-U usually say /A-E-O-U/ at the end of a syllable.* [Student echoes.] Why red? *It's what we're learning on this line.* [Student echoes.] . | Why red? *It's what we're learning on this line.* [Student echoes.] Note: We only use a 2 over a single letter phonogram when the reason for the second sound isn't governed by a rule. The underline in *a-pron* highlights one of four reasons that a vowel can make the second sound. Step 19 will later cover them all. |

| **e** | /e/ | /E/ | |
|---|---|---|---|
| | **elk** | **me** | [ **a** |
| | "An elk is a strong animal." /e-l-k/ | "Please, give it to me." /m-E/ | **e** **o** |
| | Marking? *No markings needed.* [Student echoes.] | Marking?: *With red, underline E.* Why /E/? *E said /E/ at the end of a syllable.* Usually? Yes, *A-E-O-U usually say /A-E-O-U/ at the end of a syllable.* Why red? *It's what we're learning on this line.* | **u** ] Add this sketch on the corner of the board and point to it when reciting the /A-E-O-U/ rule. |

| **i** | /i/ | /I/ |
|---|---|---|

|  | **is** | **item** |
|---|---|---|

| | "What is her name?"<br>/i-z/<br>Teacher clarifies: Use use /s-z/ | "What is the first item on the list?"<br>Syllables? (*Two*)<br>/I/-/t-e-m/ |

**item** column also contains the sketch box:

```
┌─ i ─┐
│  y  │
└─────┘
Add sketch on
board under
/A-E-O-U/ box.
```

| | **is** | **item** |
|---|---|---|
| | Markings? *With black put a two over the phonogram that says /z/.* [Student echoes.]<br><br>Why add a 2? *To show it is the second sound. No rule tells us to expect it.* [Student echoes.]<br><br>Why not use red? *The focus on this line is on a vowel. This is a consonant, not a vowel.* [Student echoes.] | Markings? *With red, underline /I/.*<br><br>Why did it say /I/? *I said /I/ at the end of a syllable.* Does I usually say /I/ at the end of a syllable? [Students often incorrectly say, "yes." If so, repeat together the A, E, O, U rule. An I is not on that list.]<br><br>Add above new rule sketch: *I and Y usually say /i/ at the end of a syllable, but **may** say /I/.* [Student echoes.]<br><br>If I says /I/ at the end of a syllable, we underline it. If it doesn't, we're not surprised.<br><br>Why underline with red?<br>*It's what we're learning on this line.* |

| **y** | /i/ | /I/ |
|---|---|---|

| | **gym** | **cry** |
|---|---|---|
| | "Play basketball in the gym." — *gym*<br>Teacher: Use /g-j/; use stand-in for /i/<br>/j-i-m/ | "If you don't like me, I will cry."<br>Clarify: Use /k-s/; use stand-in for /I/<br>/k-r-I/ |
| | Why does G say /j/? *G may say /j/ before E, I, or Y.* [Student echoes.]<br><br>Markings? *No markings needed.* [Student echoes.] G makes the second sound, but the reason is visible in the word.<br><br>The vowel Y stands-in for I. This is the first of its two vowel sounds. [Student echoes.]<br><br>———<br>Teacher Note: See SWR page 220 for a summary of all spelling markings. | Markings? *With red, underline the stand-in for I.*<br><br>Why did Y say /I/? *Y said /I/ at the end of a syllable.*<br><br>Usually? *No! Y usually says /i/ at the end of a syllable, but **may** say /I/.* [Student echoes.]<br><br>If the letter Y says /I/ at the end of a syllable, we underline it. If it doesn't, we're not surprised.<br><br>Why underline with red?<br>*It's what we're learning on this line.* |

Teacher Note: Unstressed vowels can be hard to distinguish by sound alone. The classic approach is to exaggerate these muddled sounds to match them to the written word. This builds a strong mental link to actual spelling without making us talk funny. We think-to-spell the unstressed O in *a'-pron* as /o/, the unstressed vowel Y at the end of words like *bod'-y* as /i/, and the unstressed E in *i'-tem* as /e/.

The way we treat these types of unstressed vowels is discussed in detail on SWR Step 12.

— Pages 78-79 address an unstressed vowel at the end of a syllable like *a-bout'* or *ex'-tra*.
— Pages 82-85 address the importance of keeping the Y/I connection and the E/I distinction.
— Page 87 covers an unstressed vowel within a syllable like *hu'-man*.

| **O** | /o/ | /O/ | /OO/ |
|---|---|---|---|
| | **ox**<br>"The <u>ox</u> pulled the wagon."<br>/o-x/<br><br>Marking? *No markings needed.* | **go**<br>"May I <u>go</u> to the store?"<br>/g-O/<br><br>Marking? *With red, underline O.*<br><br>Why underline? *To show the reason that O said /O/.* [Student echoes.]<br><br>Why did O say O?<br>*O said /O/ at the end of a syllable.*<br><br>Does O usually say /O/ at the end of a syllable? *Yes.*<br><br>Prove it! *A-E-O-U usually say /A-E-O-U/ at the end of a syllable.*<br><br>Why underline with red? *It's what we're learning on this line.* | **to**<br>"I want <u>to</u> go <u>to</u> the store."<br>/t-OO/<br><br>Marking? *With red, put a 3 over /OO/.*<br><br>Why a three? *It's the third sound of the phonogram.*<br><br>Why with red? *It's what we're learning on this line.*<br><br>⌐ **a**<br>  **e**<br>  **o**<br>└ **u** |
| **u** | /u/ | /U/ | /oo/ |
| | **up**<br>"Go <u>up</u> the stairs."<br>/u-p/<br><br>Marking? *No markings needed.* | **unit**<br>"We will finish this <u>unit</u> soon."<br>Syllables? (*Two*)<br>/U/-/n-i-t/<br><br>Marking? *With red, underline U.*<br><br>Why underline? *To show the reason that U said /U/.* [Student echoes.]<br><br>Why did U say /U/?<br>*U said /U/ at the end of a syllable.*<br><br>Does U usually say /U/ at the end of a syllable? *Yes.*<br><br>Prove it! *A-E-O-U usually say /A-E-O-U/ at the end of a syllable.*<br><br>Why underline with red? *It's what we're learning on this line.* | **put**<br>"Put your feet on the floor."<br>/p-oo-t/<br><br>Marking? *With red, put a 3 over /oo/.*<br><br>Why a three? *It's the third sound of the phonogram.*<br><br>Why with red? *It's what we're learning on this line.* |

During the year, reinforce these key concepts by referring back to this reference page. For example, when discussing the marking of a new word, you can ask, "Like what word on the Consonant/ Vowel Page?" The segment, <u>Reviewing Consonant and Vowel Rules</u> on volume one of the <u>Hidden Secrets</u> DVD, available at BHI, demonstrates how to review this entire page.

Please don't expect either yourself or your students to understand all the ins and outs of this material at first. This program starts with a rapid exposure of the key puzzle pieces to the language. We introduce the essential principles and continue to use them. Some people need more repetition to see the big picture. Keep moving. All concepts will be reiterated as you go. Understanding will grow day by day. In time these concepts will be retained.

## Alternative Words for the Consonant Vowel Reference Page

Students repeating the program multiple years might enjoy a variation from the basic sample words in the vowel section. The different sounds for single vowels can be illustrated using names of books in the Bible, words from the chemistry periodic table, or states in the United States. Reserve these alternate pages for students well experienced in the program. Several of the sounds are not covered by the categories. Substitutes are provided with a related link described below the list.

**Use names of books in the Bible.**  (Red markings are in bold.)

| | | | |
|---|---|---|---|
| a | Acts | A̲ mos | Ez ra [3] |
| e | Ex o̲ dus | Pe̲ ter | |
| i | Le̲ vit i cus | Ti̲ tus | |
| y | Tim o̲ thy | cry̲ | |
| o | Prov e̲rbs [2] | Jo̲ el | to [3] |
| u | Num be̲rs [2] | Sam u̲ el | bush [3] |

cry   —   Jeremiah would *cry* so much he is known as "the crying prophet."
to    —   The full title for the book of Romans is "The Epistle *to* the Romans."
bush —   A *bush* is what Moses saw burning.

An alternative to Peter would be E̲-ze̲-ki-el. An alternative to Samuel would be Josh̲-u̲-a. [3]

**Use chemicals from the Periodic Tables.**   (Red markings are in bold.)

| | | | |
|---|---|---|---|
| a | cal ci um | ti̲ ta̲ ni um | co̲ balt [3] |
| e | nep tu̲ ni um | ne̲ on | |
| i | sil i con | ni̲ tro̲ gen | |
| y | ox y gen | hy̲ dro̲ gen | |
| o | cop pe̲r | bo̲ ron | to da̲y [3] |
| u | gal li um | ru̲ bid i um | full [3] |

today — "*Today* we know many elements in chemistry, but you may discover another."
full    — "Do you have a *full* understanding of periodic tables?"

Red markings should be used only for the vowel emphasized at that point. For example, in the word *nitrogen* both the I and O are underlined, but only the I should be underlined with red because we are teaching the vowel sounds for the I at this point. Likewise, *Alabama* below illustrates all three sounds for the letter A. We mark with red only the 3 over the final A because that is the sound we are illustrating with that word.

**Use the states in the United States.** (Red markings are in bold.)

| | | | |
|---|---|---|---|
| a | Kan sas [2] | A las ka [3] | Al a bam a [3] |
| e | Tex as | Or e gon * | |
| i | Con nec ti cut | I o wa [3] | |
| y | Ma ry land | Wy o ming | |
| o | Wis con sin | O hi o | tomb [3] |
| u | Ken tuck y | U tah ** | bush el [3] |

tomb — "Where is the *tomb* of George Washington?" (Virginia -- at Mount Vernon)
bushel — "Name a state known for growing corn by the *bushel*." (Iowa)

---

* An alternative to Oregon would be Min-ne-so-ta. [3]

** *ah* (in Utah) is an advanced two-letter phonogram. See Step 38.

**Joke related to a state name:**

I asked my friend, "Where was your mom born?" He replied, "Alaska." I said, "Never mind. I'll ask her myself."

**Fun Bonus Question:**

Why do *Arkansas* and *Kansas* look alike but sound different?

Both words trace to Native Americans.

*Arkansas* follows a French influence. The last A says /ah/ and the final S is silent. In French "bas" means "low" and rhymes with "pa."

*Kansas* more closely matches the English pronunciation where the A in a closed syllable usually says /a/ and a final S is rarely, if ever, silent.

> **The Consonant/Vowel Page does more than meets the eye at first. Expose students to these ideas, but don't worry about full understanding in the beginning. Keep moving in the program. After repetition over time, the patterns taught will be internalized.**

# 10. START MULTI-LETTER PHONOGRAM PAGE.

ea

th

sh

Objectives:
    To introduce the multi-letter phonograms in thirteen weeks or less.
    To show how some letters combined may represent new sounds.
    To provide a reference page of these phonograms in the Learning Log.
    To realize the importance of moving to the next step before mastery of the phonograms.

Prepare to Teach:
    Listen to the CD for correct pronunciation.  CD follows order on p. 221.
    Organize cards by presentation order according to the preliminaries in *Wise Guide*.
    Practice the connecting strokes for cursive using the multi-letter phonograms.
    Consider different ways to drill and quiz phonograms.
    View completed Consonant Page in Appendix C -- P2 or B3.

    Multi-letter phonograms need to be introduced more quickly than most educators realize.  Once students can blend phonograms together into words, they will soon be frustrated unless they know certain letters may behave differently when they get together.  For example, if we know the sounds of E, I, G, and H, we would never guess that together these four letters can say /A/.  To master English, we need to learn not only the sounds of single letters, but also the sounds of certain phonogram sets.

    Don't get stuck for long doing ONLY phonogram work or students will become bored in what may seem to be exercises in futility.  Writing and saying phonograms is not a dead-end activity.  Children who realize the value of these tools will be motivated to work harder to acquire them.  Romalda Spalding, in the appendix of the 1962 edition of *The Writing Road to Reading*, wrote, "It has proved best to move forward rapidly with the drill in the phonogram sounds and handwriting --two of the basic tools -- not expecting these to be learned fully by every child before he starts the writing of words and reading of them."

    By week thirteen, a student will typically get 80% of phonograms correct on a quiz.  Ultimately, they need to say phonograms as fast as the teacher can show them in order to have them in long-term memory.  They should be able to write them without pause or contemplation in order to use them at the speed of thought in spelling.  Such complete mastery will come only with repetition over time.  From the beginning to the end of this program, you should include some phonogram work daily, even if only for a minute a day.

**Teach at Least Some Phonograms before Starting Spelling**.

    Your daily lesson plan will include the phonogram work (new and review), spelling words (from *Wise Guide*), and reinforcement of words using varying aspects of language arts.

    Starting at the beginning of the program teach new phonograms as listed in *Wise Guide* preliminaries.  Before Section A teach: *sh, th, oo, ee, er*.  (Delay adding *er* to the reference page until later to join it with the other basic spellings of /er/.)  With each spelling section introduce more phonograms until all are taught.  The Reference Page on p.62 shows the order.  Note: We moved *ew* from Section C to Section I-1.

    For students who place higher in Wise List (as explained in the next step), review all the basic multi-letter phonograms quickly and add them to the reference page BEFORE you begin spelling.

**Avoid getting stuck
doing ONLY phonograms!
Students become bored
if they don't see the
magic of these tools in action.**

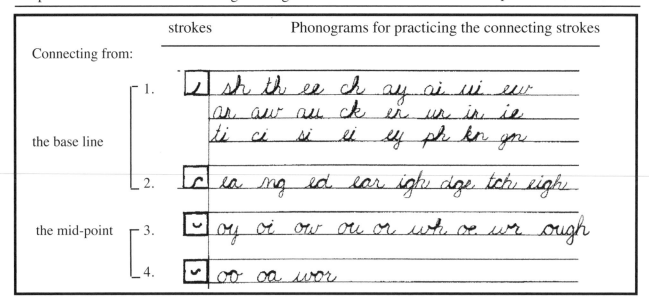

| | strokes | Phonograms for practicing the connecting strokes |
|---|---|---|
| Connecting from: | | |

**Apply Cursive Instruction to Multi-letter Phonograms**.

Practice connecting letters while learning multi-letter phonograms. See chart above.

1. <u>Simple upswing</u>. Smoothly connect from where one letter ends to where another begins: sh, th, ee, ch, ay, ai, ui, ew, ar, aw, au, ck, er, ur, ir, ie, ti, ci, si, ei, ey, ph, kn, gn.

2. <u>Upswing with a curve to 2</u>: ea, ng, ed, ear, igh, dge, tch, eigh.

3. <u>Midway dip</u>. Four letters (b, o, v, w) end at half line: oy, oi, ow, ou, or, wh, oe, wr, ough. (No multi-letter phonograms use b or v. Practice with words like *bat, blue, vat, vow.*)

4. <u>Dip with a curve</u>. If a dip letter joins a clock letter, it needs to curve up to 2: oo, oa, wor.

**Drill Phonograms Regularly**.

Reinforce phonograms daily in a variety of ways. (Focus some days just on those most needing extra drill as well as the ones listed in the Preliminaries to *Wise Guide* words.) Other times review all of them. Some days students can say and write the phonograms. Other days have them simply see and say the phonogram sounds. Rotate between spelling dialogue ("oy—the /oy/ that we may use at the end of English words") and reading dialogue (/oy/). Routinely scramble together the phonograms taught so far and test on all of the cards.

1. GIVE WRITTEN QUIZZES. Use written quizzes to help achieve mastery of the phonograms. Students do not need to number the paper for a phonogram quiz. Follow clear procedures.

a. Prevent midstream retracing. In written quizzes, if a student underlines in the direction we read and write or forms letters using the right orientation but then retraces going the opposite way, she may confuse the mental patterns we are carefully trying to establish.

b. Create a record of phonograms needing more work. If the student can't remember a phonogram on a quiz, have him underline the space where the answer would have gone. This will save room so he can fill in the correct answer in red later.

c. Let student proofread his quiz using a red pencil. On non-graded practice quizzes let the student correct his own work. Have students dictate the quiz back for the teacher to write the answer on the board. If the student misses any, she should write the correct phonogram in red. The red marking will help to emphasize the areas needing extra study.

    d. Mark non-graded quizzes with the number correct. When a student is still learning the phonograms, focus on how many phonograms she wrote correctly rather than the number she missed. Put a plus sign and then the number at the top of the paper (+11).

    2. KEEP A LIST OF PROBLEM PHONOGRAMS. The teacher should keep a dated record of the phonograms students miss and review them often.

    3. ROTATE BETWEEN READING AND SPELLING PHONOGRAMS. The same code is used for both reading and spelling. In reading we need to simply see the phonogram and say the sound. For spelling we may need to distinguish between more than one phonogram with the same sound. Students who have excelled with this program drill selected phonograms every day. Once the phonograms are mastered, it only takes a minute and fifteen seconds to read all seventy.

    4. ANSWER QUESTIONS THAT STUDENTS RAISE. We have certain phonogram pairs because English words do not end with I (ay, ai; oy, oi; ey, ei) or U (aw, au; ow, ou; ew, eu). If English words do not end in I or U what about words like *ski* and *menu?*

**If English words
do not end with U,**

**why does *you*
end with a U?**

    Some imported words are never adjusted to English spelling conventions. Nonconforming spelling commonly happens with words used heavily in advertising. In a restaurant it may sound more exotic to call the list of foods available a *menu* and to identify food items by their foreign names. Some of these become so popular that we continue to use the foreign spelling: *tofu, tiramisu, sushi, chili, calamari, spaghetti, macaroni, zucchini. Ski* is a Norwegian word that has retained its spelling probably because of the advertisements for Ski (not *sky*) Resorts.

    Rare exceptions to this principle are the Anglo-based words, *you* and *I.* Stir curiosity by asking students why these words end with U and I. Give them time to think about it before revealing my secret answer. "YOU and I are special!" (A more technical answer is that the Old English spelling for "you" was "eow" but was changed by the French after the Norman Invasion of England (1066-1350). French words can end in U. The word "I" is a shortened form of the German word "ich.")

    5. VARY ROUTINE TO HELP KEEP INTEREST HIGH.

    a. Organize the phonograms in some pattern. Alphabetize the first 26 letters or divide them into consonants and vowels. Group them by the type of connecting strokes.

    b. Add an occasional special perk for mastery. Stand across the room and hold up phonograms, one at a time. The student hops forward when she reads a phonogram correctly and jumps backward when she misses. The goal is to reach the teacher and collect a hug.

    c. Change the manner of checking knowledge. Spread out phonogram cards on the table. Call out the sounds for the student to find the corresponding card. Clap if correct. Honk if wrong. Trade places for the student to call out the sounds to you. Watch for other ideas in *Wise Guide.*

    6. LET STUDENTS TEACH OTHERS. Advanced students can give the phonogram drill. Coach students to drill each other with the phonograms. Since teaching is more challenging than simply learning, they can mutually strengthen skills this way. Stay nearby to monitor information correctness and intervene if the "pupil" becomes silly or the "teacher" too strict.

**Build a Reference Page in the Learning Log of the Multi-Letter Phonograms**.

The students build a page of the multi-letter phonograms in their Learning Log. Start adding to this page before starting Section A in the *WISE Guide* and finish it some weeks later after you have introduced all the phonograms that year. Except for ER the phonograms are added in the order they are first introduced in WISE Guide. Several advanced ones (eu, our, yr) may be added later. All students, regardless of their level in the program, will build this page. Note the limited variation between the Primary Learning Log and the Black Learning Log.

1. BRACKET RELATED PHONOGRAMS. After dictating all the phonograms, go back and bracket any related to each other. In most cases they make the same sounds. OW and OU make the same first two sounds but OU makes two additional sounds. EIGH shares the first sound with EI and EY. Linking these together helps the student remember that the most frequent sound for EI is /A/.

2. INDICATE WITH RED THE NUMBER OF SOUNDS. After you have finished dictating, go back and read each phonogram, looking for any that has more than one sound. "**With red**, come out two spaces after the phonogram and write the number of sounds it can make."

| Primary Learning Log | |
| --- | --- |
| **Multi-letter Phonogram Page** | |
| | |
| **See P2, Appendix C** | |
| **for placement on page.** | |
| (P2 means Primary Log page 2.) | |
| | |
| **Red markings are in bold.** | |
| Optional: Write W in *wor* in red. | |
| | |
| Advanced phonograms (eu,gu, etc.) | |
| are added with red | |
| later when they occur in spelling. | |
| | |
| For the **Black Learning Log** | |
| | |
| See B3-4, Appendix C | |
| (B3 means Black Learning Log page 3.) | |

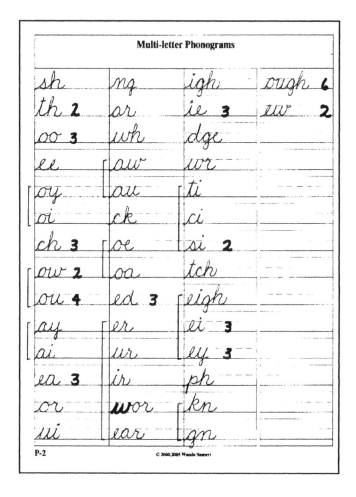

3. TEACH ADVANCED PHONOGRAMS ONLY AS NEEDED. The Multi-letter Phonogram Page in the Learning Log is designed as a reference of the phonograms learned. Our basic seventy cover the phonograms needed to spell the one thousand most frequently used words. Additional phonograms will occur with more advanced words starting with Spelling Section N-2 or can be taught as needed. Additional spellings for /er/ (OUR, YR) are introduced in Section Q-5 of the Wise List and EU is introduced in U-2. See Step 38 for further information on advanced phonograms.

## 11. DETERMINE PLACEMENT IN *WISE GUIDE*.

Objective:

    To determine where to start in the spelling list.

Prepare to Teach:

    Study the results of the diagnostic test in Step 4.
    Determine mastery level in the spelling test in Appendix B.
    Read information on McCall Crabbs books in Step 31.

In the introductory year with K-1 or with a non-reader of any age, start at Step 1 in *SWR* and Section A in *Wise Guide*. The Wise List words form the backbone of this entire program and are organized by ability level into sections with letter names. Section A includes the simplest words. Section Z is freshman level in college. The two thousand words compose the base to over 80 percent of what a student will ever read or write. Ideally we cover the full scope of these spelling levels in the elementary years. Think of spelling as the base for all other aspects of language arts. Exposure to the big picture of how English spelling works helps prepare the student for a lifetime of new vocabulary development.

Many students did not receive a solid foundation. It is never too late to fill in the missing gaps. Older remedial students can be placed by ability and taught at a speed appropriate for them. *Wise Guide* is designed so you can pick it up at different points according to your situation and need.

**Complete Steps 1-11 Every Year with All Students**.

All teachers need to work through the first eleven steps before beginning spelling in *Wise Guide*. Plan before teaching (Step 1). Build Readiness (Step 2). Select age-appropriate read-aloud material (Step 3). Evaluate the achievement level of any student who can read (Step 4). Introduce or review phonograms. Continue phonogram work daily each year at every level (Steps 5, 6, 10). Check the ability to write numbers (Step 7). Start a new Learning Log for the year (Step 8). Dictate the Consonant/Vowel Page (Step 9). The time needed to jump start this introductory material will vary. The beginning first grade student needs about two weeks. A returning student may need only several sessions.

**Place Students at the Appropriate Place in the Wise List**.

Placement varies according to previous exposure to the program and mastery of spelling.

1. START YOUNG CHILDREN. Young beginners follow the regular sequence. Kindergarten and first grade students start spelling in Section A at least two different years and then move consecutively through the list as far as they can get that particular year. See the sample chart on the next page.

2. TEACH STUDENTS EIGHT YEARS OLD OR ABOVE. **Use the diagnostic test to place older students new to the program. Think of the test as a placement aid their initial year and a monthly monitoring of long term mastery after that.** Some teachers who transition older students to this program like to start with Section A words as a way of introducing the SWR rules and marking system. Everyone, however, does not need to start the year back at the beginning of the Wise List. Use the diagnostic test, the proposed outline on the next page, and your own judgment to determine the beginning spelling section for the year. The interest level is higher if the student is stimulated by at least some unknown spelling words as he masters concepts he may have missed. See point 3 on p. 65.

**Reteaching last year's new words will help ensure long-term retention.** Our goal should be for the student to spell words correctly in the natural process of life, not just on a test. Solid mastery happens only by repetition. The Wise List words have many stimulating reinforcement activities. Save some spelling enrichments for subsequent years and plan to repeat favorite ones.

# TEACHING THE WISE LIST IN DIFFERENT GRADES

Student backgrounds and aptitudes vary, but general guidelines can help determine how much to cover each year. Use the diagnostic spelling test in Appendix B to monitor individual progress and to determine placement for students entering the program for the first time after second grade. The words in *Wise Guide* and their derivatives represent 80% of the words we read and write and encompass the principles of the language as a whole.

Spelling instruction using active student interaction should be the heart of all foundational language arts instruction. If you skimp here, your students will suffer for years to come. When spelling is internalized phonetically, the student's mind is freed up for higher level comprehension and composition. The longer you delay, the greater will be the difficulty to correct the problems in this area. Students more naturally learn spelling in the early elementary years. Don't miss this limited window of opportunity!

| Grade | Words a Week | Possible Wise List Sections Covered in a Year | | | | | | | |
|---|---|---|---|---|---|---|---|---|---|
| K | 10 | A--> I | | | | | | | |
| 1st | 20 | Repeat A--> I | New J--> L | | | | | | |
| 2nd | 40 | | | Repeat J--> L | New M*--> O | | | | |
| 3rd | 40 | | | | | Repeat M*--> O | New P --> S | | |
| 4th | 40 | | | | | | | Repeat P --> S | New T --> Z |
| 5th | 20 | | | | | | | | Repeat T --> Z |

With this schedule, all words are taught by dictation into the spelling textbook (the Learning Log) in two different years: the year they are first introduced and again the following year. This overlap of instruction promotes long-term mastery of the key words to the language. Vary the reinforcement activities from year to year. *Wise Guide* often has more than enough enrichment ideas for any given year. By fifth grade, the students should have mastered the conventions of English spelling and can focus on developing vocabulary, strengthening reading comprehension, and polishing composition skills. Remedial work can be done at any age but will be more difficult than teaching this foundation solidly from the beginning.

---

* Each lesson in M and N suggests 15 to 20 review words from A through I. Students write these as a spelling test on loose-leaf paper. Only misspelled words require full dictation. A triple exposure helps cement the words which compose 60% of all we read and write.

The chart on the facing page follows a typical student who starts in kindergarten and continues through to fifth grade with the program. The teacher uses an overlapping pattern where all words are taught two separate years.

**Kindergarten** -- Teach 260 words (A-I) ranging up to second grade, fourth month level (2.4).

**First grade** -- Reteach last year's words at a stepped up pace of 20 words a week. Introduce 380 new words covering up to the third grade, third month (3.3) level.

**Second grade** -- Reteach the 380 words from the year before (J-L) and introduce 420 new words (M-O) reaching 4.3 grade level. Sections M and N have a built-in review of A-I, giving extra coverage to the words, which make up 60% of all we read and write.

**Third grade** -- Reteach M-O and introduce 500 new words (P-S) reaching 6.0 grade level.

**Fourth grade** -- Reteach P-S and introduce 440 new words (T-Z) reaching 13.0 grade level.

**Fifth grade** -- A student who has been in the program for years can now reduce time spent on spelling. Drop to 10 or 20 words a week and reteach T-Z. While the number of words has decreased, the spelling difficulty ranges from sixth grade, second month to freshman level in college.

Many teachers move at a livelier pace with great success. A first grade teacher using this program for the first time in a classical school sent me the following update in late March.

*We will be heading into Section L. The children are doing beautifully. They are reading and thinking about their spelling beyond what I thought they could do. On the diagnostic test given a month ago, all scored 2.5 and above. We are now tackling 30 words a week. My year has been enjoyable. In some ways I have felt like I have been just one step ahead of the students in regard to the curriculum, but it has been a wonderful challenge. I'm eagerly looking forward to next year.*

3. TEACH IN ALTERNATIVE SITUATIONS. How do you place a student second grade or above who has never done this program, a remedial student in junior high or above, an illiterate adult, a special needs student, or a person who is learning English as a second language? Think in terms of acquired knowledge rather than age or grade level. Refer to the diagnostic spelling test given in Step 4 using Appendix B. Count the number of words the student spells correctly. The total correct shows the overall spelling ability of the student but does not indicate placement in the program. Placement depends on tension of learning level. What is the first word missed on the test? Look on the evaluation table in Appendix B to find the corresponding level in the Wise List.

| Place new student by SWR Diagnostic Test | |
| --- | --- |
| 1st missed | Section |
| 1-10 | A |
| 11-12 | J |
| 13-14 | K |
| 15-16 | L |
| 17-18 | M |
| 19-20 | N |
| 21-23 | O |
| 24-25 | P |
| 26-27 | Q |
| 28-30 | R |
| 31-32 | S |
| 33-50 | T |

Can a student new to the program who places in Section P start there without missing vital information in the sections skipped? If the student has truly mastered the earlier words, you can pick up this program at any point before Section T without missing any key component in the program. If you want to assure that beginning words are covered, start older students between J and M. All of the A-I words are incorporated as a review activity in Sections M and N.

All older students can benefit from SWR instruction. It can fill in gaps for the student with average to strong language skills as well as one who struggles with reading and spelling. The speed of presentation may vary.

a. <u>Older students with strong language skills</u>. Many educators realize the value of giving a systematic presentation of the language to students who have average or above-average spelling ability. These students usually progress rapidly.

b. <u>Older students who struggle with reading and spelling</u>. Those performing below grade level usually need careful systematic instruction to reverse ingrained negative patterns. Remediation for people nine years old or older generally takes longer than teaching the right foundation from the beginning. The National Institute of Child Health and Human Development reports, "What could be addressed in 30 minutes a day in kindergarten now can take two hours a day by the 4th grade. The 8th grade teacher will have it even tougher with more ground to cover to even catch up—not to mention the failure that the student has already experienced and the toll that takes on self-esteem." (Rubin, p. 1). In my experience with this program, the prospect is not as bleak. Once they comprehend how to use these precise language tools, they often make up for lost time quickly.

4. TEACH MULTIPLE LEVELS IN THE SAME CLASS. We use the same foundational principles of the language in teaching words from first grade level to freshman level in college. Concepts taught have multiple levels of understanding. The same rule that helps a beginner spell the word *me* can be used to explain why we have only one S in the word *occasion*. A student who has good spelling skills can benefit alongside a student who knows little. Likewise, a student who has limited knowledge can profit by working alongside a student who understands much more. While some individual time may be needed, much work can be done together with mixed ability levels. In general, evaluate all the diagnostic tests and then teach from the average ability level in the group.

5. TEACH RELUCTANT OR DELAYED LEARNERS. Some students are easier to teach than others. Some have a natural knack with language in the same way that some people can play piano by ear. Others may never learn to read without carefully guided help. What does a teacher of the reluctant or developmentally challenged **school-age** student do? Should she stop and wait a while, go more slowly, or change programs?

a. <u>Stop and wait a while</u>? Some late bloomers respond well to a break. We want to motivate, not frustrate. However, a lengthy delay may be harmful. You have information that a student needs for long-term success. A student who lacks the natural ability to play the piano by ear does not improve piano playing skills by waiting and doing nothing. Likewise, the epidemic number of intelligent but illiterate high school graduates demonstrates that time alone will not solve a problem with language. A person's mind does not hibernate when you stop. Words surround him in everyday life. Odds are that the student in limbo will start to devise his own scheme to attack English. Someone already struggling is unqualified to appraise a complex language successfully. The longer you wait, the larger the mountain of misconceptions will grow for you to surmount. The older the student becomes, the less likely will he delight in learning to spell. The best window of opportunity for teaching spelling skills is in the lower elementary grades.

b. <u>Go more slowly</u>? Sue wisely focused on spelling and delayed having her daughter read books aloud to her. However, her daughter was "struggling to learn 10-20 words a week." An experienced veteran advised her to SPEED UP to teaching 30 words a week or more. Sue confessed, "At first, my daughter hated it, but soon, she was THINKING TO SPELL and I'm thrilled with her progress." Within several months this educator developed a new, more desirable problem. Her once-reluctant reader started sneaking books to read. Sue reports, "Yesterday, I found her hiding out when she was supposed to be doing math (which she's pretty good at), and discovered she was halfway through a

> **"My daughter has been a reluctant reader, so finding her sneaking books to read when she's supposed to be doing other things is really a great thing. (Just don't tell her!)"**

chapter book! This child that a few months ago hated to read anything, actually chose to read on her own. Now I have to figure out appropriate discipline. I don't dare punish her for reading, but I want her to read when she's not supposed to be doing something else!"

c. <u>Change programs</u>? If you are tempted to switch programs, read the Senate Hearing Speech in the Appendix A. Does the new program display any of the weaknesses described? A home educator tried switching. Her child still struggled. Since the mother kept inserting information she had learned from our material, she eventually decided to switch back. The mom told the relieved daughter, "We're going to drop reading for a while and just work on spelling." Struggling teachers can take advice from this parent. "Those who wonder if this program really works, I have to say YES, just stick with it. Don't stop for long, go too slowly, or switch."

6. APPLY THE ART OF TEACHING. Certain situations may require a brief departure from the step-by-step presentation of the program. I once taught a remedial high school group. All the students had high IQ's but poor spelling and weak reading comprehension skills. On the first day of class they nervously lingered outside my room until no one was looking and then, when the coast was clear, quickly dashed inside. These bright students were ashamed to be seen in my room. When I perceived the situation, I changed my lesson plan for the day. I wrote on the board four words that most students in the school did not know. I said, "It looks like you didn't want your friends to see you in my class." Heads nodded around the room. I asked, "How would you like to play a trick on them?" They sat up tall and grinned. I had their attention.

We spent the next hour learning to pronounce, spell, and use the words on the board.

lo-qua-cious — given to continual talking
*I dread sitting by a <u>loquacious</u> person.*

mag-nan-i-mous — loftiness of spirit
*The <u>magnanimous</u> man quickly forgave me.*

fas-tid-i-ous — delicate to a fault
*She was a <u>fastidious</u> dresser.*

pro-cras-ti-na-tor — one who delays or puts off
*The <u>procrastinator</u> finally answered my letter.*

I photocopied the following note: "For homework define and use in a sentence the following: fastidious, loquacious, magnanimous, procrastinator." I told them the real assignment was for them to ask their friends to help them with their homework. Word got out that my class was for the talented and gifted. The next day my students held their heads high when they came in the room. Now they could trust me to take them back to the foundations of the language and help them fill in the missing holes of their Swiss-cheese education.

**Avoid Common Mistakes that Perpetuate Uncooperative Learners**.

1. DON'T GET STUCK IN ONE PLACE. Avoid spending too much time on details that make sense only when the bigger picture is provided. Some people press for total mastery of phonograms before continuing. They teach phonograms, play phonogram games, drill phonograms, and quiz phonograms. Day after day their ONLY activity is phonograms. It's like eating tuna every meal for a year. Tuna may be good, but we long for variety. With school-age students the season exclusively for phonograms should be short, so they will not become bored and resist instruction.

Intersperse phonogram review in a fast-paced way with spelling instruction. When I dictate spelling words and a student freezes, I may give him a sneak peek at the phonogram needed. I could show the card itself or simply write the phonogram on the board long enough for the student to see it and then erase it quickly. I might start giving the language we used for forming that letter: "Start at 2 on the clock." I could point to the phonogram in another word she has already written. A student can still learn phonograms as we weave them into spelling words. Knock down obstacles and keep going. Give occasional hints but wean them to become increasingly independent.

If a student freezes during spelling dictation, I may give a sneak peek at the phonogram needed.

2. RESIST MAKING UNREALISTIC DEMANDS. Avoid expecting the student to perform a task that you have not adequately taught. Some highly intelligent students have dyslexic tendencies. Teaching such a student reading before spelling can add internal frustration. Some teachers become impatient and force daily "torture reading." Pressuring a child to decipher a page full of words when he still struggles with individual words is counterproductive. Resist fleeing to workbooks as a means of overcoming a roadblock. Workbooks rarely forge a major breakthrough for the struggling scholar.

**Learn How to Reverse a Negative Situation**.

1. PROVIDE POSITIVE MOTIVATION. An eager child is easy to teach. Stir the student's curiosity and be ready to challenge the blooming desire. If the student can taste success and realize the advantage of learning, he will start working with you instead of against you.

2. PERSIST PATIENTLY. Faithful work will yield fruit if you continue straight and steady. The magic of blending phonograms into words happens easily for some, but for others it takes multiple spelling words and extra time. Don't give up. Most students learn a new word, forget it, learn it again, and forget it again. Keep reviewing. Eventually they will retain the word. Continue plodding with spelling dictation. I have often seen students transform overnight from non-readers to fluid readers.

3. ELIMINATE VISUAL HANDICAPS. Some need glasses; others need "vision therapy." A small minority of people cannot keep both eyes consistently in focus as their eyes scan across a page of print. Signs of a visual-motor problem include: turning sideways to read, moving the head instead of the eyes from left to right, squinting at the book, covering one eye when trying to read, or repeatedly rubbing eyes when reading. With therapy from a trained professional, this disorder is highly correctable.

> **Pressuring a child to read sentences when he still struggles with individual words is counterproductive.**

4. PRACTICE FROM A STUDENT'S STRENGTHS. If a child lacks writing readiness, go back to oral teaching with preschoolers in Step 2. Continue to read aloud to the student from dynamic books. Watch for signs of interest in the written word as a clue that the student is ready to resume writing.

A teacher of a delayed learner wrote and asked what to do with his daughter. He had been teaching the program for three years but had only covered Sections A-J. On her diagnostic test she started missing words back at Section I. After all this time with a small number of words, she still did not retain some of the words taught. The teacher asked if he should start her back at A (gulp!) or pick up at Section K and move forward. A student of this age needs to experience higher level spelling. She has been through A-J two to three times. Move ahead. Showing the bigger picture is possible only by plowing on in the list. To fill in the gap indicated by the Section J word missed on the diagnostic test, review five or ten words from Section J each week. Call out these words as a quiz on separate paper and teach through full dictation any words misspelled on the quiz.

**12.** 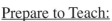 ## BEGIN DAILY SPELLING IN THE WISE LIST.

<u>Objectives</u>:

    To learn to write new words from the teacher's guided dictation.
    To sound out spelling words, analyze them, and mark spelling rules.
    To construct a personalized student Learning Log.
    To learn to spell and read words quickly and accurately.

<u>Prepare to Teach</u>:

    Learn standard spelling dictation which will be continued throughout the program.
    Make a teacher's edition of a student's Learning Log.
    Practice sounding out the words for dictation. (See Dictation Guide on inside back cover.)
    Select age-appropriate sentences for your students or compose alternatives.
    Check your understanding of the spelling markings and the rules that apply.
    Realize Step 12 will be continued in parallel with subsequent steps.

**Understand SWR Spelling Dictation**.

    Our spelling instruction differs from most programs. Teacher investment in learning this new approach pays large dividends. Why? Most programs teach spelling as a mindless memory approach. The student may be given a list of words to copy or trace. Even when phonics is included, it is usually incomplete and misleading. Phony, pokey, and fickle phonics are all discussed on pages 191-193. We have found a way to teach all learning styles, satisfy the logical thinker, and train the student for a lifetime of language learning. This not only aids spelling mastery but also aids better reading comprehension and composition skills.

    New spelling words are best put into the brain in the same manner they will be retrieved: drawing words from our brain to the paper. Most programs teach new spelling the opposite way: from paper (or tiles, magnets, etc.) to our brain. In our program, however, the teacher guides the student in sounding out and shaping a new word correctly BEFORE the student sees it written on the board. With sounds that can be spelled more than one way, the instructor uses phonogram language (not letter names) to alert the student which to use. She tells him when to add a silent letter. Thus, a student is mentally engaged when a new word is first presented, and he is able to write the unseen word accurately without any guessing. **Repetition will be needed for long-term mastery,** but he should strive from the beginning to take ownership of each new word. We want him to think, not just memorize.

    1. EMPLOY ALL THE AVENUES TO THE MIND SIMULTANEOUSLY. We link auditory, vocal, kinesthetic, and visual stimuli with logic. Multisensory instruction is the most powerful way to fix information firmly in the mind! Our students, with guidance from a teacher, write a word before seeing it. Next they analyze the word and mark the spelling rules.

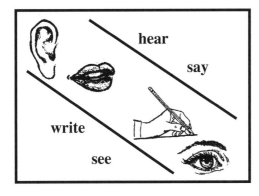

STUDENTS:

★ HEAR the word,

★ SAY the word,

★ WRITE the word,

★ SEE the word as they read it, and

★ THINK, using logic to MARK the rules.

    2. DICTATE WORDS FOR STUDENTS TO WRITE. Beginners can practice on the board or on any medium, including loose-leaf paper. Eventually, students will write all new words directly

into the log. We never have a student copy a new word. He must first say the word, repeat it in his own voice, write it with his own hand, and then read the word -- all BEFORE he sees you write it.

3. ENCOURAGE ANALYTICAL THINKING. The spelling list is purposely NOT grouped by rules. This helps prevent the student from guessing any letters in a way he might do if all the words rhyme or illustrate a particular spelling concept. He must consider each word as a separate unit.

**Illustrate Spelling Dictation with Section A Words.**

Section A words, the first words in the program, are scripted below. A generic description of spelling dictation for any level is given on page 76 and the inside back cover to SWR. Rehearse giving dictation as you might practice a play. Keep it crisp and lively. Dragging it out too slowly will cause student attention span to wane. Train your student(s) for a lifetime of language learning. Enjoy!

1. START SPELLING AT THE FRONT OF THE LOG. Dictate words for the student to write neatly, beginning with the first page of his student-built textbook. Additional work, quizzes, and re-inforcement activities should go on loose-leaf paper and be kept in a three-ring binder. Each spelling section has two facing pages in *Wise Guide*. Section A words can be found on pages 2-3.

2. NOTE TEACHER DIRECTIONS. Say the sound, not the letter name, for letters within slash marks. Students do not number words. Numbers are for teacher cross reference. For the spelling lists use regular pencils. **Save the red pencil for spelling rule reference pages in the back of the log.**

3. DICTATE SECTION TITLE. Give clear instruction for placement. For example,"In the first column, on the first line, center a capital A. I will show you how." See student sample on p. 75.

Since Section A is only one-syllable words, the syllable-count question is omitted below. Placement directions are given in enough words to show the pattern. Give vertical and horizontal instructions as to where the student should write each word.

### *Section A Spelling Words*

*top* (1)  **Teacher**: <u>Pencils down.  Eyes on me</u>.
**Placement**: On the next line, under A, starting at the margin line, we will write ***top***.
**Sentence**: "Can you climb to the *top? Top."* <u>Say the word with me</u>.
**Together**: top
**Teacher**: Think-to-spell /t-o-p/. <u>Help me sound it out</u>.
**Together**: /t-o-p/. (As student says each sound, teacher shows matching fingergram.)

---

OPTIONAL: Use "fingergrams" as an added visual prompt for phonograms.

/t/ -     /o/ -     /p/

Teacher faces student with a closed fist. As student says each sound, the teacher, using right-hand pinkie first, lifts a finger(s) for each phonogram said. (See p. 82 for multi-letter phonograms.) Student should see the fingers move in the direction he reads and writes.

---

**Teacher**: (Points to student log.) <u>Say it as you write it</u>.
**Student**: Top. (Picks up pencil, whispers, and writes /t-o-p/.)
**Teacher**: <u>Say the word and dictate it back</u>.  (Teacher puts chalk in ready position.)
**Student**: *top*. /t-o-p/. (As student says each sound, teacher writes it on the board.)
**Teacher**: <u>Does your word look like mine</u>? If not, fix it.
**Marking?** No marking. All first sounds. (I may omit this question if no markings.)
**Reviews**: (Teacher and student in unison.) <u>Think</u> /t-o-p/. <u>Say</u>, "top."

---

*but* (2)     **Teacher**: <u>Pencils down. Eyes on me.</u>
             **Placement**: Under *top*, we will write ***but.***
             **Sentence**: "You can do that, *but* be careful. *But.*" (Student echoes, "but.")
             **Teacher**: Think-to-spell /b-u-t/. <u>Help me sound it out.</u>
             **Together**: /b-u-t/. (Student says each sound. Teacher shows matching fingergram.)
             **Teacher**: (Points to student log.) <u>Say it as you write it.</u>
             **Student**: But. (Picks up pencil, whispers, and writes /b-u-t/.)
             **Teacher:** <u>Say the word and dictate it back.</u> (Teacher puts chalk in ready position.)
             **Student**: *but.* /b-u-t/ (Teacher writes on board.)
             **Teacher**: (Points to the word.) <u>Does your word look like mine</u>? If not, fix it.
             **Reviews:**. *(Teacher points to each sound one-by-one.)* <u>Think</u> /b-u-t/.
                    (Teacher then runs her finger under the word quickly.) <u>Say</u>, "but."

*and* (3)     **Teacher**: <u>Pencils down. Eyes on me.</u>
             **Placement**: Under *but,* we will write ***and.***
             **Sentence**: "You *and* I are friends. *And.*" (Student echoes, "and.")
             **Teacher**: Think-to-spell /a-n-d/. <u>Help me sound it out.</u>
             **Together**: /a-n-d/.
             **Teacher**: (Points to student log.) <u>Say it as you write it.</u>
             **Student**: And. (Picks up pencil, whispers, and writes /a-n-d/.)
             **Student reads word and dictates back**: *and.* /a-n-d/. (Teacher writes on board.)
             **Teacher**: (Points to word.) <u>Does your word look like mine</u>? If not, fix it.
                    We bracket words to show some kind of relationship.
                    *But* and *and* can both be used to connect ideas. We call them *conjunctions.*
             **Reviews**: <u>Think</u> /a-n-d/.    <u>Say</u>, "and."

*cat* (4)     **Teacher**: <u>Pencils down. Eyes on me.</u> (Continue to give placement for each word.)
             **Sentence**: "A *cat* can eat a rat. *Cat.*" (Student echoes, "cat.")
             **Teacher**: Think-to-spell /c-a-t/. <u>Help me sound it out.</u>
             **Together**: /k-a-t/. (Teacher points back to the first letter and says, "Use /k-s/."
             **Teacher**: (Points to student log.) <u>Say it as you write it.</u>
             **Student**: Cat. (Picks up pencil, whispers, and writes /k-a-t/.)
             **Student reads word and dictates back**: *cat.* /k-a-t/.
             **Teacher**: (Writes *cat* on the board.) <u>Does it look like mine</u>? (Student proofreads.)
             **Reviews**: <u>Think</u> /k-a-t/.   <u>Say</u>, "cat."

*red* (5)     **Teacher**: <u>Pencils down. Eyes on me.</u>
             **Sentence**: "The sky is *red* -- *Red.*" (Student echoes, "red.")
             **Teacher**: Think-to-spell /r-e-d/. <u>Help me sound it out.</u>
             **Together**: (Student) /r-e-d/. (Teacher shows fingergram.)
             **Teacher**: (Points to log.) <u>Say it as you write it.</u>
             **Student**: Red. (Picks up pencil. Whispers and writes /r-e-d/.)
             **Student reads word and dictates back**: *red.* /r-e-d/.
             **Teacher**: (Writes on board.) <u>Does your word look like mine</u>?
             **Reviews**: <u>Think</u> /r-e-d/. <u>Say</u>, "red."

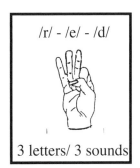

/r/ - /e/ - /d/

3 letters/ 3 sounds

*six* (6)     **Teacher**: <u>Pencils down. Eyes on me.</u>
             **Sentence**: "The child is *six*. *Six.*" (Student echoes, "six.")
             **Teacher**: Think-to-spell /s-i-ks/. <u>Help me sound it out.</u>
             **Together**: /s-i-ks/. (A single finger shows /ks/ is one letter.)
             **Teacher**: (Points to log.) <u>Say it as you write it.</u>
             **Student**: Six. (Picks up pencil, whispers, and writes /s-i-ks/.)
             **Student reads word and dictates back**: *six.* /s-i-ks/.
             **Teacher**: (Writes on board.) <u>Does your word look like mine</u>?
             **Markings?** No marking. All first sounds.
             **Reviews**: <u>Think</u> /s-i-ks/. <u>Say</u>, "six."

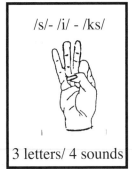

/s/- /i/ - /ks/

3 letters/ 4 sounds

**³all** (7) **Teacher**: <u>Pencils down. Eyes on me</u>.
   **Sentence**: "I like *all* of you. *All*." (Student echoes, "all.")
   **Teacher**: Think-to-spell /ah-l-l/. <u>Help me sound it out</u>.
   **Together**: /ah-l-l/. (Student says sounds. Teacher shows fingergrams.
      Go back and point to first finger. Say, "Use /a-A-ah/."
      Point to 3rd finger. Wiggle it. Whisper, "Add a silent /l/.")
   **Teacher**: (Points to log.) <u>Say it as you write it</u>.
   **Student**: All. (Picks up pencil. Says and writes /ah-l-l/.)
   **Teacher**: At this point the teacher has been saying, "<u>Dictate it back</u>." In time the
      teacher can just put her chalk on the board to silently signal the next step.
   **Student reads**: *all* and **dictates**: /ah/-/l/. Add a silent /l/.
   **Markings?** Put a 3 over /ah/. Why? It's the third sound of the
      phonogram. Like what word on the Vowel Chart? (wasp)
   **Teacher**: Let me teach you a new rule. We often double L after a single vowel at the end of
      a base word [R17]. Repeat after me. (Student echoes the rule.)
   **Reviews**: <u>Think</u> /a-l-l/. <u>Say</u>,"all."

/a/ -/l/ - /l/

3 letters/ 2 sounds

**m<u>y</u>** (8) **Teacher**: <u>Pencils down. Eyes on me</u>.
   **Sentence**: "*My* teacher teaches me good things. *My*." (Student echoes, "my.")
   **Teacher**: Think-to-spell /m-I/. <u>Help me sound it out</u>.
   **Together**: /m-I/. (Teacher holds up one finger per letter as student says sound. Say the phonogram sound /I/
      and not the letter name for Y.)
   **Teacher**: We need the stand-in for I. Can you explain the reason?
   **Student**: English words do not end with I. (Teacher may say the answer. Student can echo.)
   **Teacher**: (Points to log.) <u>Say it as you write it</u>.
   **Student**: My. (Picks up pencil. Says and writes /m/-/I/.)
   **Student reads** and **dictates**: *my*. /m-I/. (Teacher writes *my* on the board. Student proofreads log.)
   **Markings?** (In time he will answer independently. At first he probably needs coaching.)
      Student: Underline the phonogram that says /I/.
      Teacher: Like what word on the Consonant/Vowel Page? (cry)
      Teacher: Explain the reason we underline the phonogram that says /I/.
      Student: Y said /I/ at the end of a syllable.
      Teacher: Does Y usually say /I/ at the end of a syllable?
      Student: No, Y usually says /i/ at the end of a syllable, but may say /I/. [R5]
   **Reviews**: <u>Think</u> /m-I/. <u>Say</u>,"my."

**not** (9) **Teacher**: <u>Pencils down. Eyes on me</u>.
   **Sentence**: "Do *not* withhold good. *Not*." (Student echoes, "not.")
   **Teacher**: Think-to-spell /n-o-t/. <u>Help me sound it out</u>.
   **Together**: /n-o-t/. (Teacher shows fingergrams. Points to log.) <u>Say it as you write it</u>.
   **Student**: Not. (Picks up pencil. Says and writes /n-o-t/.)
   **Student reads** and **dictates**: *not*. /n-o-t/. (Teacher writes on the board.)
   **Teacher**: <u>Does your word look like mine</u>? If not, fix it.
   **Markings?** No marking. All first sounds.
   **Reviews**: <u>Think</u> /n-o-t/. <u>Say</u>,"not."

**ten** (10) **Teacher**: <u>Pencils down. Eyes on me</u>.
   **Sentence**: "A dime is worth *ten* cents. *Ten*." (Student echoes, "ten.")
   **Teacher**: Think-to-spell /t-e-n/. (Not /t-i-n/!) <u>Help me sound it out</u>.
   **Together**: /t-e-n/. (Teacher shows fingergrams. Points to log.) <u>Say it as you write it</u>.
   **Student**: Ten. (Picks up pencil. Says and writes /t-e-n/.)
   **Student reads** and **dictates**: *ten*. /t-e-n/. (Teacher writes on the board.)
   **Teacher**: <u>Does your word look like mine</u>? If not fix it.
   **Markings?** No markings.,
   **Reviews**: <u>Think</u> /t-e-n/. <u>Say</u>,"ten."

**Teacher**: Let's start at the top. Count the words. (The top word is *top*, the sixth word is *six*, and the tenth word is *ten*. Fun things like this are seeded throughout *Wise Guide*. Enjoy!)

*hat* (11)

> **Teacher**: <u>Pencils down. Eyes on me</u>.
> **Placement**: On the same line with *top*, in the second column, write ***hat.***
> **Sentence**: "Lincoln had a top *hat. Hat*."
> **Teacher**: Think-to-spell /h-a-t/.
> **Together**: /h-a-t/. (fingergrams)
> **Student**: Hat. (Says as he writes /h-a-t/.)
> **Student reads** and **dictates**: *hat*. /h-a-t/.
> **Teacher**: <u>Does yours look like mine</u>?
> **Markings**? No marking. All first sounds.
> **Reviews**: <u>Think</u> /h-a-t/. <u>Say</u>, "hat."

<u>*be*</u> (12)

> **Teacher**: <u>Pencils down. Eyes on me</u>.
> **Placement**: On the same line with *but*, under *hat*, we will write ***be.***
> **Sentence**: "If you walk with wise men, you will *be* wise. *Be*."
> **Teacher**: Think-to-spell /b-E/.
> **Together**: /b-E/. (fingergrams)
> **Student**: Be. (Says as he writes /b-E/.)
> **Student reads** and **dictates**: *be*. /b-E/.
> **Teacher**: <u>Does yours look like mine</u>?
> **Markings?** Underline /E/.
> **Teacher**: Why do we underline /E/?
>> E said /E/ at the end of a syllable.
>> Teacher: Like what word on the Consonant/Vowel Page?
>> Student: *me*
> Teacher: Does E usually say /E/ at the end of a syllable?
> Student: Yes, A-E-O-U usually say /A-E-O-U/ at the end of a syllable." [R4]
> **Reviews**: <u>Think</u> /b-E/. <u>Say</u>, "be."

| List A Spelling Words in *Wise Guide* | | |
|---|---|---|
| **Words for Section A** | | |
| 1 | top | Start from the *top* and count the words. |
| 2 | but | You can do that *but* be careful. |
| 3 | and | Christ is all, *and* in all. -- Colossians 3:11 |
| 4 | cat | A *cat* can eat a rat. --Webster's *Bluebacked Speller* |
| 5 | red | The sky is *red*. |
| 6 | six | Lincoln read the Bible through *six* times during his youth. |
| 7 | all | God is with me at *all* times. --*McGuffey Primer* |
| 8 | my | *My* mother teaches me good things. |
| 9 | not | Do *not* withhold good. --Proverbs 3:27 |
| 10 | ten | A dime is worth *ten* cents. A shilling is worth *ten* pence. |
| 11 | hat | Abraham Lincoln removed his top *hat* to pray. |
| 12 | be | If you walk with wise men you will *be* wise. |
| 13 | am | He is ten and I *am* six. |
| 14 | is | The cat *is* purring. |
| 15 | bed | My *bed* is a little boat. --Robert Louis Stevenson |
| 16 | run | All rivers *run* into the sea, and yet the sea is not full. |
| 17 | ran | All six boys *ran* up a hill. |
| 18 | go | You can *go* play after lunch. |
| 19 | do | I cannot what I will not *do*. -- Shakespeare |
| 20 | did | Today, I do; yesterday, I *did*. |

The dividing line after every ten words in *Wise* means to begin a new column. See the line on the sample page.

*am* (13)  **Teacher**: <u>Pencils down. Eyes on me</u>.
> **Sentence**: "He is ten and I *am* six. *Am*." (Student echoes, "am.")
> **Teacher**: Think-to-spell /a-m/. <u>Help me sound it out.</u>
> **Together**: /a-m/. (fingergrams.) <u>Say it as you write it.</u>
> **Student**: Am. (Picks up pencil, whispers, and writes /a-m/.)
> **Student reads** and **dictates**: *am*. /a-m/.
> **Teacher**: <u>Does yours look like mine</u>? If not, fix it.
> **Reviews**: <u>Think</u> /a-m/. <u>Say</u>, "am."

*is*² (14) **Teacher**: <u>Pencils down. Eyes on me</u>.
> **Sentence**: "The cat <u>*is*</u> purring. *Is*." (Student echoes, "is.")
> **Teacher**: Think-to-spell /i-z/. <u>Help me sound it out.</u>
> **Together**: /i-z/. (Two single letters can spell /z/ in this location. When teaching a new word do not pressure the student to guess which one.) Teacher uses fingergrams and clarifies: Use /s/ -/z/.
> **Student:** Is. (Picks up pencil, whispers, and writes /i-z/.)
> **Student reads** and **dictates**: *is*. /i-z/. (Teacher writes *is* on the board.)
>> Before she writes /z/ the teacher may ask: Which /z/? (This is reviewing, not guessing.)
>> Student: /s/-/z/. (Answer with phonogram sounds, not the letter name.)
> **Teacher**: <u>Does your word look like mine</u>? If not, fix it.

**Markings?**  (Teacher helps as needed.)
       Student:  Put a 2 over the /z/.  Teacher may ask, "Why?"
       Student:  It's the second sound of the phonogram.
**Reviews**:  *Think* /i-z/.  <u>Say</u>, "is."

**Teacher**:  Bracket *be, am,* and *is.*
A bracket shows some kind of relationship.
These are all verbs that describe a state of being.

> ⌈ be  *He will **be** there.*
> ⎢ am  *I **am** his sister.*
> ⌊ is  *She **is** happy.*

***bed*** (15)  /b-e-d/.  Use standard dictation, all first sounds.

***run*** (16)  /r-u-n/.  Use standard dictation, all first sounds.

***ran*** (17)  /r-a-n/.  Use standard dictation, all first sounds.

**Teacher**:  Bracket *run* and *ran.*   What is the relationship between these words?
       *I run today; yesterday I ___ (ran).*
       The only difference is the timing.  We call these present and past tense verbs.

**g<u>o</u>** (18)  **Teacher**:  <u>Pencils down.  Eyes on me.</u>
     **Placement**:  Under *ran,* on the same line with *all,* we will write ***go.***
     **Sentence**:  "You can *go* play after lunch.  *Go.*"  (Student echoes "go.")
     **Teacher**:  Think-to-spell /g-O/.  <u>Help me sound it out.</u>
     **Together**: /g-O/.  (Student says sounds.  Teacher shows fingergrams.)  <u>Say it as you write it.</u>
     **Student**:  Go.  (Picks up pencil, whispers, and writes /g-O/).
     **Student reads** and **dictates**: *go.*  /g-O/.  (Teacher writes on the board.  Student proofreads.)
     **Teacher**:  <u>Does you word look like mine?</u>  If not, fix it.
     **Markings?**  (Teacher helps as needed.)
        Student:  Underline /O/.
        Teacher:  Why?
        Student:  O said /O/ at the end of a syllable.
     **Reviews**:  *Think* /g-O/.  <u>Say</u>, "go."

**d<u>o</u>**³ (19)  **Teacher**:  <u>Pencils down.  Eyes on me.</u>
     **Placement**:  Under *go,* we will write ***do.***
     **Sentence**:  "I cannot what I will not *do.*  *Do.*"
        Make a stubborn, pouty look when you quote Shakespeare. The statement means that
        if we're not willing to try, we cannot do something, even if we had the ability to do it.
     **Teacher**:  Think-to-spell /d-OO/.  <u>Help me sound it out.</u>
     **Together**: /d-OO/.  (Teacher shows fingergrams.  Clarifies last phonogram.) Use /o/-/O/-/OO/.
     **Student**:  Do.  (Picks up pencil.  Whispers and **writes** /d-OO/.)
     **Student reads** and **dictates**:  *do.*  /d-OO/.  (Teacher writes on the board.)
     **Teacher**:  <u>Does you word look like mine?</u>  If not, fix it.
     **Markings?**  (Teacher helps as needed.)
        Student:  Put a 3 over the /OO/.
        Teacher:  Shouldn't O say /O/ at the end of a syllable?
        Student:  It usually does, but not always.
        Teacher:  Like what word on the Consonant Vowel Page?  (Turn to P1 in the log.)
        Student:  *to*
     **Reviews**:  *Think* /d-OO/.  <u>Say</u>, "do."

> **Dictation is a learning tool to teach a word, not a spelling test!**

***did*** (20)  Use standard dictation.
     **Teacher**:  Bracket *do* and *did.*  Why bracket these words?
     "These are present and past tense verbs.  The words show the timing when it happened."
     *Today I do; yesterday I ___ (did).*

# Spelling Section A

## Primary Learning Log

## Front page

Vary your dictation order to help keep attention. Call out words in a column going down the page. With other sections switch and dictate a word in column number one and then the facing word in column number two. Such movement across the page helps students build their left-to-right eye movement.

Beginning non-readers
will not write original sentences
until step 21.

| A | | Some prefer a capital A that is a tall version of the lower case A. |
|---|---|---|
| top | hat | |
| but | be | |
| and | am | |
| cat | is | |
| red | bed | |
| six | run | |
| all | ran | |
| my | go | |
| not | do | |
| ten | did | |

*Best original sentence for this lesson rewritten neatly.*

Six cats ran and ran.
Ten did not go.

---

## Avoid The Following Spelling Dictation Faux Pas

1. Asking the student to copy new spelling words or build new words by arranging tiles. (Save visual for last, since it builds a stronger mental imprint.)

2. Mumbling the word or omitting the "think-to-spell" memory aid. (Speak clearly as we think **and** as we say.)

3. Calling out words using letter names. (Think /k-a-t/ and read "cat.")

4. Mixing letter names and phonogram sounds in dictation. (Don't say, "Use H to write /h/.")

5. Saying a word as a series of phonograms. (Do not spell "has" as /h/ - /a-A-ah/ - /s-z/.)

6. Failing to clarify which phonogram to use when more than one can work.

7. Dragging out the dictation. (Keep it crisp.)

8. Ignoring left-to-right pattern with fingergrams, penmanship, and spelling markings. (Do not re-trace underlines. Start left to cross the T or draw the bridge for silent E. Mark the spelling word in sequential order.)

9. Allowing the student to write new words without saying each sound softly as he writes.

10. Letting the student mark his word before student proofreads from the teacher's work.

11. Doing all the mental thinking for the student. (Engage him fully: have him identify syllable breaks, drive the teacher's fingergrams and chalk, proofread the word, and analyze it.

12. Assuming the student properly corrected the words. (Double-check the student log.)

13. Allowing the student to correct a portion of a misspelled word. (He should erase the entire word to sound it out and rebuild.)

# STANDARD SPELLING DICTATION OUTLINED
Goal:  Train students to independently spell, analyze, and read words.

## TEACHER (while students have pencil down on desk):

**Shows placement**. Give reference points on the page: "Beside __ , under__ , we will write _."
**Says word** as in normal conversation.
**Uses it in a sentence**. Read sentences in *Wise Guide* or make up your own.
**Repeats word.**    Student echoes the word.
**Syllables?**  Student listens carefully and identifies the number of syllables ("three syllables").
   If needed he can clap, hold his hand under his chin, or close his mouth and hum the word.
**Think-to-spell**. Segment the word into individual sounds exaggerated to match spelling.  Some words sound funny this way!  The focus is on spelling over proper pronunciation in the flow of speech.

   Shows Fingergrams. Student sounds the word out (with help as needed). As he says each sound, the teacher lifts corresponding finger(s).  One finger represents one letter.  Two fingers stuck together represent a two-letter phonogram.  A finger that wiggles represents a silent letter.   Teacher, facing the student, starts with her right hand so that the student sees her movements going in the direction the child will read and write.  (I prefer pinkie first, but permit other ways as long as the directionality movement appears left to right for the student.)  Change hands for each syllable.  See p.80.

   Clarifies the Phonogram if need be.  If the letter A says /a/ we do not need to say anything.  That is the most expected spelling.  If /A/ is spelled some other way, the teacher should alert the student.  For example with *eight* we say, "Use the four-letter /A/."   Give helpful information so that the student can successfully, and without undue stress, write the unseen word accurately the very first time.  Our goal here is to teach a new word, not to test the student.  See Appendix D for phonograms.

## STUDENTS (in unison):

**Say and Write**. The teacher points towards the student log. Command, "Say it as you write it." In time she can drop the verbiage and just point to the log as the signal for the student to pick up his pencil and whisper as he writes. It is important that he says the word from his mouth and not just in his head. After the dictation pattern is established, strive to maintain a lively pace of one minute per word.

**Read** the word. Beginners need extra help reading the word they just spelled. Although all students can learn how the language code works, some learn to blend sounds together more slowly than others.

**Dictate** back syllable-by-syllable, sound-by-sound. Develop a signal for the class to dictate back to you in unison. The teacher should spell the word correctly from their direction. If students are silent, look at them blankly and say, "You are driving my chalk."  Translation: "Tell me what to write."

**Proofread** work against the board and correct if need be.  (Teacher should double-check later.)

**Analyze** the word.  Students explain how to mark the word, moving in the direction we read.  The teacher may clarify markings or check understanding by asking, "Why?"  Recite rules, not rule numbers.  Markings and rules are explained in Appendix D.

## TEACHER & STUDENTS TOGETHER:

**Review**. Unglue the words and blend them back together.
   *We think* /t/-/o/-/p/. [Point to each phonogram and say the sound it makes in that word.  Go bit-by-bit like a recording on slow speed.]
   *We read, "top."* [Slide a pointer or finger quickly under the word. Say it normally.]

**Reinforce**. After teaching a list of words, have students collectively or one-by-one read the words from the Log going across the page.  Have each student compose original sentences, read aloud his own sentences,  take practice quizzes, and complete suggested reinforcement activities in *Wise Guide*.  Also use generic activities in SWR Step 13.

Spell to Write and Read

Begin Daily Spelling in the Wise List — Step 12

**Understand Spelling Markings used in Learning Logs.**

The marking system graphs the way our language works. Markings are only used when dictating words in the log or for extra help with troublesome words. Markings are not used on spelling tests or original sentences. Words should not be marked in readers.

1. UNDERLINES. Underlines should be"under the line" or clearly distinct from the base line. Single underline letters to emphasize particular spelling rules (4, 5, 7) or multi-letter phonograms. Underline twice silent letters that need special recognition (unusual silent letters or examples of rules 7, 14, 15). Silent letters for rules 17 and 29 do not need to be marked.

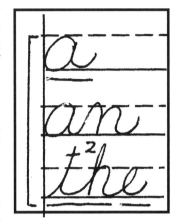

2. NUMBERS AND X'S. The number used to distinguish a phonogram sound and the X used to indicate an exception should be written above the middle of a multi-letter phonogram. They should be kept separate from the phonogram so that the word can be easily read.

3. BRACKETS. Brackets are placed one space before words. They should be clearly separate. The bracket starts at the mid-point of the top word and stops just under the base line of the bottom word. Use a ruler or straight edge to make neat brackets.

Some spelling words may have more than one possible way to mark them. Invite discussion. Any focus on the word helps reinforce proper spelling. **As a novice, don't try to rebuild the system!** Do not test the students on markings. The goal is to establish an internal second sense of how the language works as well as to learn to spell correctly. For a fuller explanation of the special spelling markings and rules see Appendix D.

**Determine the Number of Words to Study Each Week.**

Teach from ten to forty new words a week depending on the level. In general, kindergarten students do ten, first grade students twenty, and second grade and above forty. On the weeks you build an extensive reference page in the Learning Log, dictate few, if any, new words. Some students seem to write a word once and —*voila*— remember it forever. More typically, students need regular activity with words before claiming ownership.

Small blocks of time can produce big results. Plan practice quizzes on phonograms and spelling, and sprinkle exposure to the words throughout the day. One day a week, test all new words plus ten unannounced review words or phonograms. Make students accountable all year for any spelling words in their Logs. Build long-term memory by training them for more than the weekly test. See Step 13 for ideas in reinforcing troublesome words.

**Continue through the SWR Steps as You Teach Spelling.**

Spelling words in *Wise Guide* form the backbone of this program. Steps are intertwined in a user-friendly fashion. Compare the SWR steps to dance steps or juggling. The first step is introducing phonograms. Resist the temptation to teach only phonograms until they are totally mastered and then put them aside to start teaching spelling words. Continue phonogram review in your lesson plans throughout the program.

In this system we continue to use the spelling concepts we introduce while adding new concepts.

Dance steps adjust to the music. SWR steps adjust to the spelling list for the week. In spiral learning, all the concepts will be covered repeatedly along the way. SWR gives the full scope of each step. Apply it to where you are in the Wise List.

© 2015, Wanda Sanseri

77

Step 12 addresses spelling dictation from the beginning words all the way to the final spelling lesson. Along the way, we weave in a variety of other steps.

Step 13          Reinforce new spelling words in generic ways.
Step 14          Sprinkle touches of literature in teacher dictation and read aloud selections.
Step 15          Collect spelled numbers for the Number Page in the Learning Log.
Step 16          Present grammar principles using spelling words as early as Section C.
Step 17          Teach five reasons for silent final E's.
Step 18          Collect /sh/ words in the spelling list to add to the SH Reference Page.
Step 19          Analyze the various ways that vowels can say AEIOU.
Step 20          Use spelling rule cards to reinforce rules first taught orally.
Step 21          Train students to compose original sentences using spelling words.

*Spell to Write and Read* gives the global picture of each step. *Wise Guide* shows when they apply to specific spelling words along the way. Older students starting higher in the list will not follow the beginning step order. Adjust the steps to match the spelling words at their level in *Wise Guide*.

**Teach Students to *Think-to-Spell.***

Many words have sounds that are hard to precisely pinpoint from speech alone. "Think-to-spell" means to verbalize the spelling code as a memory aid to correct spelling. We think /Wed-nez-day/, but say /Wens-day/. We can do the same thing with vowels in unstressed syllables. Treating all unstressed vowels as a vague sound, the schwa (ə), unnecessarily complicates spelling. (See page 234 for a definition of schwa.) Was it *-ant* or *-ent?* Was it *-ance* or *-ence?*

| ə | cli-*ent* | cur-*rant* | cur-*rent* | de-fi-*ant* | ca-d*ence* | in-st*ance* |
|---|-----------|------------|------------|-------------|------------|-------------|
|   | hu-m*an*  | sud-d*en*  | cous-*in*  | gal-l*on*   | Brook-l*yn* | moun-t***ai****n* |

Exaggerate each vowel to match the actual phonogram used, then, say the word with a slight whisp of the sound linked to spelling. This mentally harmonizes the code for spelling and reading. Our speech becomes more precise and our spelling is more accurate. The language makes more sense.

This "think-to-spell" approach works anywhere in the world to teach English spelling and reading because **the primary emphasis is not on pronunciation**. English speaking people around the globe vary the way they pronounce words. In *Albion's Seed,* David Fischer says Yankee speech drops some R's (*Harvard* is said as /Haa-v'd/) and adds others (*follow* becomes /foller/). Virginians add syllables where New Englanders subtract them (p. 258). We don't need to speed up what Fischer calls the "soft, slow, melodious drawl" in Southern speech or to slow down the rapid tongue of a New England native.

The Thorndike High School Dictionary explains the unpredictable nature of pronunciation.

"No two speakers pronounce a sound in exactly the same way.... Even the simple question, 'How do you pronounce the word THE?' never has a single answer. One's pronunciation of this word and of other words depends on neighboring sounds, accent, speed of utterance, and in many cases, on the style of discourse, formal or informal.... Linguistic scientists have never agreed on all matters of pronunciation.... Educated people do not pronounce English in exactly the same way in Chicago, New York, Boston, and Atlanta" (Thorndike, p. xiv, xv).

In Noah Webster's classic 1828 dictionary, words are not respelled for pronunciation. Instead some letters are marked on the correctly spelled word. He adds the stress mark to the stressed syllable. That vowel sound will be more distinct. The other vowels will be more muffled in the flow of speech. His classic approach highlights what English speakers share in common. (See Step 36). *Spell to Write and Read* phonograms and spelling markings follow that same tradition.

In *Wise Guide* some words may cause you to ponder. This section will help explain "extra attention think-to-spell words." The points below are organized by the order of first occurrence in the spelling list. Each category lists each example word by its word section in the *Wise Guide*.

| "Extra Attention" Think-to-Spell Words | 1st example | Section/ word # | |
|---|---|---|---|
| 1. Exaggerate an unstressed vowel in an open syllable. | the | B | 28 |
| 2. Divide words into syllables. | in-to | C | 45 |
| 3. Deal with exception words. | of | C | 50 |
| 4. Exaggerate an O with a French overtone. | moth-er | D | 68 |
| 5. Maintain the E/Y distinction and the Y/I connection. | ba-by | E | 100 |
| 6. Sound out silent letters. | lit-tle | F | 102 |
| 7. Exaggerate an unstressed vowel within a syllable. | ba-con | G | 131 |
| 8. Mark a single vowel before an R. | ver-y | I-4 | 244 |
| 9. Handle a one-syllable word that may sound like two. | fire | J-6 | 379 |
| 10. Add a syllable for thinking to spell. | bu-y | L-2 | 548 |
| 11. Exaggerate OR, AR, AI in a muffled syllable. | col-or | M-1 | 641 |
| 12. Teach advanced phonograms. | guide | N-2 | 803 |

1. EXAGGERATE AN UNSTRESSED VOWEL IN AN OPEN SYLLABLE . When a vowel at the end of a syllable is muffled, we think-to-spell the sound we expect in that location.

---

***the*** — Section B (28)

**Think-to-spell**: In speech the vowel sound for *the* varies depending on the next word after it. Either way, we will apply R4 and *think-to-spell*: /th-E/.

**Markings**:

| | | |
|---|---|---|
| Student: | Underline /th/ with a 2 over it. | Teacher: Why? |
| Student: | It's a two-letter phonogram— 2nd sound. | |
| Student: | Underline E. | Teacher: Why? |
| Student: | E said /E/ at the end of a syllable. | Teacher: Prove it. |
| Student: | AEOU usually say /A-E-O-U/ at the end of a syllable. | |

---

Other examples of the many R4 words to exaggerate as a long vowel at the end of a syllable:

| | | | | | | | |
|---|---|---|---|---|---|---|---|
| a-bout' | H-1 | a-rith'-me-tic | M-2 | re-fuse' | O-1 | cel- e-bra' tion | T-5 |
| a-like' | I-2 | pro-vide' | M-3 | o-blige' | P-2 | col' o-ny | U-1 |
| e-lev'-en | J-4 | re-gret' | M-5 | a-mount' | P-4 | ca' reer | V-1 |
| a-long' | J-5 | e-vent' | M-6 | va'-ca-tion | P-7 | sep' a-rate | W-2 |
| sum'-ma-ry | K-1 | a-mong' | N-1 | bound'-a-ry | Q-4 | math'-e-mat-ics | X-1 |
| a-cross' | K-7 | wo-man' | N-2 | sal'-a-ry | R-2 | cem' e ter-y | Y-2 |
| a-bove' | L-2 | his'-to-ry | N-5 | nat'-u-ral | S-1 | flam' ma-ble | Z-1 |
| be-fore' | L-6 | de-pen'-dent | N-6 | cen'-tu-ry | S-2 | sym' pho-ny | Z-2 |

Examples of R18 where we exaggerate A as /ah/. "When a word ends with A it says /ah/."

| | | | | | | | |
|---|---|---|---|---|---|---|---|
| ex'-tra | M-6 | i-de'-a | R-2 | di-lem'-ma | T-2 | or'-ches-tra | X-1 |
| um-brel'-la | Q-6 | a-re'-a | R-5 | ba-nan'-a | T-5 | pneu-mo'-ni a | Z-2 |

2. DIVIDE WORDS INTO SYLLABLES. Some rules relate to a letter's placement within a syllable. To understand English spelling, we must divide words into syllables. The words are divided for you already in *Wise Guide*. Unless indicated otherwise, we follow classical dictionary syllable breaks.

> **ę lev en —** Section J: (324)
>
>> **Teacher dictates:** Say the word normally and use it in a sentence. Student learns to hear the word and count the syllables. With multi-syllable words, we need to exaggerate the unstressed vowel sounds to match actual spelling.
>> **Think-to-spell:** [Teacher says. Student echoes.] /E-lev-en/.
>> **Student repeats:** [Teacher shows fingergrams.] E - lev (l-e-v) - en (e-n).
>>
>> [Teacher uses a new hand for each syllable and fingergrams for each sound.]

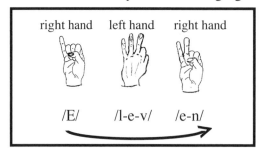

right hand    left hand    right hand

/E/     /l-e-v/     /e-n/

student's view

>> **Student says:** "Eleven," picks up pencil and sounds it out as he writes /e-lev-en/.
>> **Student reads:** "Eleven."
>> **Student dictates for teacher to write on the board:** E - lev (l-e-v) - en (e-n).
>> **Teacher writes, student proofreads and, if need be, corrects:** *e-lev-en.*
>> **Analyze together:** Underline the first E. "Why?" E said /E/ at the end of a syllable.
>> **Review together:** <u>Think</u> /e-lev-en/. <u>Say,</u> "eleven."

3. DEAL WITH EXCEPTION WORDS. Rule-breakers are rare for us. We put an X over a phonogram when it makes a different sound from that taught with the phonograms and we are unable to *think-to-spell* the sound. We have only twenty-five words out of the 2000 in the Wise List that we need to teach as an eXception. In all but five, the problem is with only one phonogram.

> **oḟ̽ —** Section C: (50)
>
>> **Teacher dictates:** "The next word "of" has a rare exception. — of."
>> **Think-to-spell:** [Teacher says. Student echoes.] We say /o-v/. We *think* /o-f/.
>> **Student repeats:** [Teacher shows fingergrams.] /o-f/.
>> **Student writes and dictates back to teacher:** of. /o-f/.
>> **Teacher writes, student proofreads and, if need be, corrects:** *of*
>> **Teacher explains new marking:** Put an X over the /f/. It is a rare eXception.
>> **Review together:** <u>Think</u> /o-f/. <u>Say,</u> /o-v/.

"Why do we use the /f/ to make the /v/ sound?"
     1. English words do not end with V [Rule 6]. Spelling changed to match rule.
     2. The letters look unrelated but do have a connection. Help student discover how. Have him watch you carefully as you say /f/ and /v/. The mouth is shaped the same. What is different? Have him put his hand on his throat and say /v/ and /f/. We turn on our motor (vibrate our vocal cords) to say /v/, but we turn off our motor to say /f/. The /v/ is voiced; the /f/ is unvoiced. The word "of" is probably the only time that F says /v/ in English.

Bonus sidenote: Words like *wife* and *wives* show a connection between F and V, but the spelling changes to match the sound change. (See page 142 for a list of common words where the F changes to V when making the word plural.)

The Rest of the of Rule-Breaker Words in this Program (See Wise List for markings):

*said* (342); *says* (738) — Use AI and AY to say /e/. In Scotland many still say /A/.

*should* (422); *would* (423); *could* (424)  — See *Wise Guide* p.59.

*any* (441); *many* (442) — Americans now tend to say the A more like /e/.

*who* (649); *whole* (973); *whose* (1221); *whom* (1252) —Use WH to say /h/.

*sew* (650) — Use EW to say /O/. It gives distinction between *so, sow,* and *sew.*

*broad* (708) — Use OA to say /ah/.  Usually it says /O/.

*does* (737) — Think "do" and add -es. We end up with the OE phonogram saying /u/.

*pretty* (779) — Think "pret" but we tend to say /prit/.

*been* (861) — Some say /b-E-n/. Most Americans say /b-i-n/.

*blood* (903) — Use OO to say /uh/. In Scotland many still say /oo/.

*friend* (950) — IE says /e/ from the Dutch word *vriend*.  Some think as two syllables, fri-end.

*bus y* (1366) — Use U to say /i/. Think to spell /buz/ and then say /biz/.

*ser geant* (1522) — Use ER to say /ar/. Looks like the French derivative (ser-); sounds like the Spanish (sar-). The GE = /j/. In this advanced phonogram, the silent E is added to make the G say /j/ [See Rule 3].

*bus i ness* (1601) — Sometimes in the development of English, British people adopted spelling from one part of the island and pronunciation from another. Though we say busy ("bi-zzy") and business ("bizness") we use the western England spelling  (Bryson, p.124.)

*col o nel* (1677) — Initially spelled in English with an R like the Old French word *coronelle* meaning "a military column," this word was adapted from the Italian *colonello*.  For a hundred years some people spelled it with an R.  For another hundred years some people used L and others used R.  In an illogical compromise, the word became standardized with the Italian spelling and the French pronunciation (Bryson, p.122).

*aisle* (1719) — The only word in 20,000 words where AI says /I/. The silent S was gained by well-meaning meddlers in the seventeenth century who tried to make English conform to Latin ideals in this word and in *island*.

*height* (1695) — Use EIGH to say /I/. In the 1828 dictionary, Webster noted that some spelled it "height" and others spelled it "hight."  He preferred "hight" to go with the root word "high."  Unfortunately, his wisdom did not prevail.

*heif er* (1825) —  Use EI to say /e/.

Exception words not marked with an X:

*one* (153)  — The root word to *lone* and *alone*.  We used to pronounce it /O-n/ as in *lone*.  Now we say the word to match the sound of /won/. This one defies our normal markings.  Simply bracket *one* together with *lone* and *alone*.

*once* (551) — *One* and *once* use old East Midland dialect but South England pronunciation. We say /wun/ and /wunce/ but spell like "own" and "ownce" (Bryson, p.124). Words *lone* (151), *alone* (152), and *only* (443) match East Midland spelling and pronunciation.

*eye* — Section K-5 (478)

The two E's are silent. Romalda Spalding suggested an artistic marking. Students write the word a second time and turn it into a happy face with a big smiling mouth. The E's become the eyes. The tail of the Y looks like a nose. For fun I like to underline each of the E's twice. They are silent in the word. These are "bags" under the eyes. Put a 2 over the Y. It has the second vowel sound in an unexpected place. The 2 is like "wrinkles" on the brow.

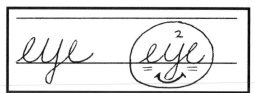

4. EXAGGERATE THE FRENCH OVERTONE. English words like *come* were once spelled with a U, but the French conquered the island. The French language reigned over four hundred years. The way Frenchmen tried to say /u/ in some stressed syllables sounded more like /o/. While the French controlled education on the island, the spelling changed to O, but native Englishmen continued to say /u/. Today, we retain the original English pronunciation but use the French modified spelling.

*moth er* — Section D: (68)

**Teacher dictates:** The word *mother* uses the French overtone. "We say this word in a silly way to remember how to spell it. Your *mother* is not a *moth*, but we will think-to-spell /moTH/- /er/."

| student view | | | |
|---|---|---|---|
| teacher<br>pinkie first<br>right hand<br>palm out | /m-o-TH/ | /er/ | teacher<br>pinkie first<br>left hand<br>palm in |

**Fingergrams:** As student says the first syllable /m-o-TH/, the teacher shows the related fingergrams with her right hand. For /er/ she uses her left hand.
**Student says:** *Mother* and writes /m-o-TH/ - /er/.
**Student reads:** *Mother*  (Saying it as we talk normally.)
**Student dictates for teacher to write on board:** moth (m-o-TH) —er.
**Student proofreads his word against teacher's** then gives markings.

| | |
|---|---|
| Student: | Underline /TH/ and put a 2 over it. |
| Teacher: | Why underline it? |
| Student: | It's a two-letter phonogram. |
| Teacher: | Why 2? |
| Student: | Second sound. Underline /er/. It's a two-letter phonogram. |

Examples in the Wise List using the French Overtone:

| love | E | won | J-5 | be come' | L-6 | com' pa ny | O-6 |
|---|---|---|---|---|---|---|---|
| come | G | broth' er | K-6 | col'or | M-1 | won' der ful | Q-2 |
| some | H-1 | done | L-1 | month | M-5 | on' i on | S-4 |
| oth'er | H-2 | a bove' | L-2 | in come' | M-7 | | |
| son | J-1 | hon' ey | L-2 | some' thing | N-1 | | |
| cov'er | J-2 | a noth' er | L-5 | com'fort | O-4 | | |

5. MAINTAIN THE E/Y DISTINCTION AND THE Y/ I CONNECTION. For spelling purposes, we eliminate much confusion by keeping the I and Y distinct from E. Classic dictionaries code *eternity* as (e-ter-ni-ti). Modern dictionaries give the conflicting code (i-tur-nE-tE). Linking the unstressed sound of E to /E/ and I and Y to /i/ is more reasonable **practically, linguistically**, and **historically.**

**Practically**, keeping the distinction between E, I and Y narrows spelling choices. If we teach three single letters that all spell /E/, students will have a greater tendency to mix them up. <u>At the end of a syllable</u> we think-E as /E/ *(a-rith-m**e**-tic)* and I as /i/ *(ra-d**i**-o)*. <u>At the end of a word, we think E</u> either as a silent E *(bab**e**)* or /E/ *(tama'l**e**)*. <u>At the end of a word, think an unstressed Y</u> as /i/ *(ba'b**y**)*. After the Great Vowel Shift, the spelling of *"babi"* changed to *"baby."* (See *Wise Guide* p.174.)

<table>
<tr><td colspan="8" align="center">**The E and Y Distinction**</td></tr>
<tr><td colspan="8" align="center">Keeping Y in the I family and E in the E family reinforces proper spelling.</td></tr>
<tr>
<td>en'emy</td><td>ses'am**e**</td><td>po'ny</td><td>ac'n**e**</td><td>final'ly</td><td>final'**e**</td><td>econ'omy</td><td>epit'om**e**</td>
</tr>
<tr>
<td>To'by</td><td>ado'b**e**</td><td>sil'ly</td><td>sim'il**e**</td><td>tro'phy</td><td>stro'ph**e**</td><td>zip'py</td><td>rec'ip**e**</td>
</tr>
<tr>
<td>ea'sy</td><td>Boi's**e**</td><td>pot'ty</td><td>kara't**e**</td><td>hank'y</td><td>psy'ch**e**</td><td>bo'ny</td><td>abalo'n**e**</td>
</tr>
</table>

The classical approach connects sounds to the rules that govern English. Y stands in for I at the end of a word *(baby)*. English words do not end with I. Y changes back to the I (not E) when we add ANY ending *(babies)* except one that begins with an I *(babyish)*. I and Y are linked with two-letter phonograms *(ay/ ai; oy/ oi; ey/ ei)*. Greek-based words use Y for /i/ *(fist/ cyst)*. Latin-based words link I to the consonant Y *(million)*. Retaining the I/Y connection simplifies spelling mastery.

| The I and Y Connection | | | |
|---|---|---|---|
| Function in Word | | I | Y |
| At the end of a word | y = /i/ <br> y = /I/ | babied <br> mine | baby <br> my |
| At the end of a syllable | | ti-ny <br> li-cense | ty-rant <br> ly-ing |
| 2-letter phonograms | ai —> ay <br> oi —> oy <br> ei —> ey | daily <br> rejoice <br> their | day <br> joy <br> they |
| With a silent final E | i _ e / y_ e | size <br> time <br> bite | par-a-lyze <br> thyme <br> byte |
| Within a syllable | i or y | Jim <br> mist | gym <br> mys-ter-y |
| Spellings for /er/ | ir or yr | mirth <br> stir | myr-tle <br> mar-tyr |
| Latin spelling. <br> In speech the vowel sound /i/ sometimes degenerates into /y/ thus eliminating a syllable. | i = /y/ | William <br> convenient <br> onion <br> familiar | yam <br> yen <br> yon <br> yard |
| IE phonogram  2nd/3rd sounds <br> English words do not end with I. <br> Just add E or change I to Y. | ie or y | tie <br> cal-o-rie | ty-ing <br> glo-ry |

An emphasis on the Y and I relationship helps build the auditory memory for spelling. We can exaggerate the sound of Y to harmonize with I for spelling and still say the word normally. Many adults struggle with thinking Y as /i/ in *baby*. Children rarely have this problem. Margaret Bishop explains, "The difference in sound between unstressed long E and unstressed short I is nearly undetectable to the layman, and the student reader is most certainly a layman" (Bishop, p.151).

> **Focus on the closest sound to how *we* <u>spell</u>, rather than the closest sound to whatever *you* <u>say</u>.**

**<u>Linguistically</u>**, /E/ is a tense sound in contrast to the lax /i/. The tongue stretches more tightly to say /E/ but is more rounded to say /i/. Liz FitzGerald's pathology/audiology class in college set out to pinpoint the sound of Y. Using a spectrograph, a scientific gauge for measuring sound, they found that people who insisted that they said /E/ in a word like "baby" did not actually do so **in the flow of speech**. A word (like *baby*), when spoken in isolation, gains stress to the final letter. However, when *baby* is spoken normally in context, the Y is more clearly lax. (*H<u>e</u> s<u>ees</u> the baby on my kn<u>ee</u>.*)

Treating Y as /i/ in these types of words may be challenging for you as a teacher, because your ear has been taught to hear a sound inconsistent with English spelling. You don't have to pass on this same confusion to your students. Even if the Y does sound more like /E/ to you, teaching Y as /E/ creates long term spelling problems for them. Use *think-to-spell*, and all will be well.

**<u>Historically</u>**, in the first edition of his 1783 speller (*A Grammatical Institute of the English Language, Part 1*), Noah Webster wrote on page 23, "Some instructors have absurdly taught their pupil to pronounce *y* at the end of words like long *e*." For two centuries his perspective was standard. *Wise Guide* has 414 words with an unstressed *e, i,* or *y* (classically treated as normal) that current dictionaries often move unpredictably to a conflicting vowel family. Over a third of the words treat E as /i/ (be-gin'.) Other altered-code cases either mark an unstressed single I and Y as /E/, or /ə/. Classic dictionaries code *illicit* as /il-lic'-it/ and *elicit* as /ē-lic'-it/. Current dictionaries code them both identically as /i-lis'it/. Which is easier to remember for correct spelling? Classical dictionaries and SWR markings apply technical linguistic accuracy based on etymology, science, and history.

a. <u>Y saying /i/ at the end of a word in an unstressed syllable.</u>

*b<u>a</u> by* — Section E: (100)

**Think-to-Spell**: /bA/ -/bi/. Use the stand-in vowel. English words do not end with I.
**Student says and writes**: /b-A/ /b-i/.
**Student reads the word as we say it normally**: baby.
**Teacher asks**: Why do we use the stand-in for I here?
**Student**: English words do not end with I.

**<u>Other examples of Y = /i/ at the end of an unstressed syllable by spelling section</u>:**

| | | | | | |
|---|---|---|---|---|---|
| stormy | I-2 | glory | L-5 | nobody | O-1 |
| very | I-4 | early | L-6 | weary | O-2 |
| happy | J-1 | ready | M-4 | navy | O-3 |
| funny | J-4 | daily | M-5 | worthy | O-4 |
| twenty | K-1 | pretty | M-7 | truly | O-5 |
| story | K-2 | study | N-1 | company | O-6 |
| clearly | K-3 | womanly | N-2 | nearly | P-4 |
| many | K-4 | energy | N-3 | heavy | P-5 |
| party | K-5 | fancy | N-4 | family | P-7 |
| country | L-1 | history | N-5 | primary | Q-2 |
| bury | L-2 | actually | N-6 | boundary | Q-4 |
| body | L-4 | dairy | N-7 | magnify | Q-5 |

| | | | | | |
|---|---|---|---|---|---|
| eternity | R-2 | accompany | T-1 | missionary | V-1 |
| angry | R-3 | discovery | T-3 | testimony | V-2 |
| injury | R-4 | ninety | T-4 | library | W-1 |
| poverty | R-6 | stationary | T-5 | accuracy | X-1 |
| temporary | S-1 | ceremony | U-1 | preliminary | X-2 |
| century | S-2 | necessary | U-2 | bibliography | Y-1 |
| sympathy | S-3 | majority | U-3 | extraordinary | Y-2 |
| dictionary | S-4 | necessity | U-4 | penitentiary | Z-1 |
| society | S-5 | probably | U-5 | proficiency | Z-2 |

b. <u>**Y** and **I** connection with two-letter phonograms</u>. Consider phonogram pairs.

| | | | |
|---|---|---|---|
| day/ daily | F/ M-5 | joy/ rejoice | J-5/— |
| lay / laid | H-1/— | they/ their | K-7/ Q-6 |
| pay/ paid | J-3/ — | pray/ praise | N-2/ M-3 |

c. <u>**I** functions as the consonant sound of **Y**</u>. The Y can be a consonant /y/ or a vowel to represent a sound of I. In limited cases, the vowel I can also assume the consonant sound of /y/.

### *fash i on* — Section L-5: (620)

**Think-to-Spell**: Think 3 syllables for spelling (fash-i-on). The I in the past may have been pronounced as a short vowel. In the *New England Primer of 1777, -tion* was considered two syllables. If you think to spell the I as the vowel sound /i/ and then blend the word quickly, you will see how we get /fash-yon/.

Note: In *Wise Guide* the word on the left-hand page will be divided as in the dictionary (fash-ion), but on the right-hand page, the way we think-to-spell it (fash-i-on).

Other examples where we add a syllable to help think /i/ when we actually say /y/.

| | | | | | |
|---|---|---|---|---|---|
| pe-cu-li-ar | S-1 | o-pin-i-on | S-4 | con-ven-i-ent | X-2 |
| bril-li-ant | S-1 | on-i-on | S-4 | pneu-mo-ni-a | Z-2 |
| un-i-on | S-2 | com-pan-i-on | S-5 | Cal-i-for-ni-a | — |
| be-hav-i-or | S-2 | fa-mil-i-ar | T-1 | cham-pi-on | — |
| mil-li-on | S-3 | re-bel-li-ous | U-2 | Sav-i-or | — |

6. SOUND OUT SILENT LETTERS. We add silent letters for a number of reasons. Some are ghosts of forgotten sounds. Many are covered by Rules 7, 14, 15, 17, 29 (See p. 222 in Appendix D) and our phonograms (kn, gn, igh, ough, eigh, dge, tch, ck, wr). Some silent letters help clarify word meaning. [In *plumb* the silent B sets off meaning from *plum*.] Other silent letters show the origin of the words. The silent M and P at the beginning of words such as *mnemonics* and *psyche* show Greek origin. Still other silent letters are retained to link them to the root words or some of the derivatives.

### *lit tle*₋₄ — Section F: (102)

**Syllables?** Two.
**Think-to-Spell**: lit-tl. Add a silent E. [Note: Both the second T and the E are silent.]
       Optional: Quote the rule:"Double consonants in multisyllable words should both be
       sounded for spelling but not in normal speech." — R 29
       <u>Help me sound it out</u>.
**Student says**: /l-i-t/ - /t-l/. Add an E. (Teacher shows fingergrams. Wiggles finger for silent E.)
**Student reads word** and **dictates it back**: lit /l-i-t/. tl /t-l/. Whispers, "Add a silent E."
**Markings**? Underline E twice and put a 4 by it. Every syllable must have a vowel.
**Review**: <u>Think</u> /lit-tl/. Whisper, "Add a silent E." <u>Say</u>, /lit-l/.

$\overset{3}{t\underline{\underline{w}}o}$ — Section K-1: (387)

**Think-to-Spell**: /t-w-OO/. We say /to/.
**Student**: Underline W twice.
**Teacher**: Why?
**Student**: It's a silent letter needing special attention.
Put a 3 over the /OO/. It's the third sound.
**Teacher**: Bracket the related words. Explain how they
all link with the meaning *two.* Maybe in the base
word, the W is the ghost of a forgotten sound.

Silent Letters in the root word may be still heard in derivatives.

| | | |
|---|---|---|
| thum**b** | P-3 | thimble |
| crum**b** | — | crumble, crumbly |
| de**b**t | Q-6 | debit |
| hym**n** | T-3 | hymnal |
| **h**eir, **h**eirloom | U-3/ Y-1 | inherit, inheritance |
| solem**n** | V-2 | solemnity |
| colum**n** | V-2 | columnist, columnar |
| mor**t**gage | Y-1 | mortal, mortician, mortuary   [< mort (death)] |
| bom**b** | — | bombard, bombardier |
| condem**n** | — | condemnation, condemnable |
| mus**c**le | — | muscular |
| **h**erb | — | herbivorous, herbaceous |

Letters may be sounded in the root word but silent in the derivative.

| | | | |
|---|---|---|---|
| soft/ soften | H-1/ — | fast/ fasten | —/ M-7 |
| nest / nestle | — | Christ/ Christmas | — |

Other examples on the Wise List with ghosts of forgotten sounds:

| | | | | | | | |
|---|---|---|---|---|---|---|---|
| **h**our | K-2 | half | L-1 | calm | Q-2 | wrestle | T-4 |
| should | K-3 | climb | M-4 | calf | Q-2 | folks | T-4 |
| would | K-3 | exhaust | N-5 | honor | R-1 | whistle | T-4 |
| could | K-3 | honest | N-6 | sword | R-1 | adjourn | U-1 |
| talk | L-1 | exhort | P-6 | listen | S-5 | yacht | V-1 |
| walk | L-1 | answer | P-6 | often | S-6 | isthmus | W-1 |

Most letters can occasionally be silent as illustrated by these words not on the Wise List:

| | | | | | |
|---|---|---|---|---|---|
| B | comb | dumb | lamb | limb | numb |
| | plumber | subtle | tomb | womb | succumb |
| S/H/D | debris | shepherd | John | handsome | handkerchief |
| L | balm | chalk | embalm | fault | Holmes |
| | palm | Psalm | qualm | salmon | yolk |
| N/P | autumn | Psalm | corps | raspberry | cupboard |
| T | apostle | bristle | bustle | castle | chestnut |
| | debut | depot | epistle | glisten | hasten |
| | hustle | jostle | mistletoe | tsunami | tzar |

Misled scholars centuries ago incorrectly added silent letters supposedly to link words more
closely to Latin. The words, however, were not Latin-based. Words caught in this misfortune include:

| | | | | | | | |
|---|---|---|---|---|---|---|---|
| B | doubt (S-3) | S | island (S-4) | | aisle (U-3) | P | receipt (X-2) |

Our phonograms cover some ghost letters. For example, in Chaucer's day, the K and G were pronounced in ***know*** and ***gnat.*** (Bryson, p. 128). The GH in phonograms IGH, EIGH, AIGH, and some AUGH and OUGH words represents an Old English sound now lost (Bishop, p. 134.)

7. EXAGGERATE AN UNSTRESSED VOWEL WITHIN A SYLLABLE. Any vowel can sound like the indistinct mumbled schwa sound /ə/ in an unstressed syllable. Some programs group words (like those in the first column below) and tell you, "These all say /əl/. Make sure you remember the right spelling to use." Such programs expect visual memory alone to support this confusing muddle. Rather than emphasizing the similarity of sounds in these words, SWR exaggerates the precise vowel needed. This auditory reinforcement helps students overcome a troublesome part to accurate spelling.

| | |
|---|---|
| to-**tal** | Think-to-spell /al/ |
| reb-**el** | Think-to-spell /el/ |
| coun-**cil** | Think-to-spell /il/ |
| cap-i-t**ol** | Think-to-spell /ol/ |
| con-s**ul** | Think-to-spell /ul/ |

***ba̲ con*** — Section G (131)

> **Think-to-spell**: In speech the vowel in the second, unstressed syllable is indistinct. Think /bA/ - /con/. (Say the O as /o/ rather than /ə/).
> **Student says**: Bacon. Dictates back to teacher: bA (b-A) - con (c-o-n).
> **Markings**: Underline A. Why? A said /A/ at the end of a syllable.

A few of many examples where we think the actual vowel sound within an unstressed syllable:

| | | | | | |
|---|---|---|---|---|---|
| sea' s**on** | I-2 | de pend' **ent** | N-6 | con' stant | S-1 |
| sev' **en** | J-4 | sec'**ond** | O-2 | sys'tem | S-3 |
| cot' t**on** | K-5 | per' fect | O-4 | au'di ence | S-5 |
| free'd**om** | K-6 | dis' tant | O-5 | stom' ach | T-3 |
| li'**on** | K-7 | trav' **el** | P-3 | sum' mon | T-5 |
| les's**on** | L-2 | sev'er **al** | P-4 | ig' no rance | U-4 |
| pock' **et** | L-3 | bot' t**om** | P-5 | prin' ci p**al** | V-1 |
| pen' c**il** | M-1 | im por' tance | Q-1 | ac'cu-rate | W-2 |
| thou'sand | M-2 | pres'i dent | Q-2 | in tel' li gent | X-1 |
| bal'ance | N-1 | com' m**on** | R-1 | par' **al** lel | Y-1 |
| cus' t**om** | N-3 | gen' er **al** | R-3 | per sis' tence | Y-1 |
| mar'ket | N-4 | dif' fer **ent** | R-4 | priv'i lege | Z-1 |

8. MARK A SINGLE VOWEL BEFORE AN R. Some two-letter phonograms are a combination of a single vowel and R (ar, er, ir, or, ur). However, a vowel may sit next to R without sounding like one of these two-letter phonograms. In these cases, we put a one (1) over the vowel to indicate that we need to think of the two letters as separate phonograms.

> ¹
> ***ver y*** — Section I-4: (244)
> **Syllables?** Two.
> **Think-to-Spell**: /vĕr/ -/i/. Help me sound it out.
> **Together**: /v-e-r/. [Teacher shows three stand alone fingers.] /i/
> **Student reads word and dictates back**: *very. ver (v-e-r). /i/.*
> **Teacher**: We need a special marking for this word. We will put a one over the /e/. We do not read E-R as the phonogram /er/. The one (1) shows that we are thinking the first sound of the vowel. It says /e/. This is not /er/. Why use the stand-in vowel? English words do not end with I.
> **Review**: Think /vĕr/-/i/. Say, "Whatever you say."

Other examples of R influenced words in the Wise List:

| | | | | | | | |
|---|---|---|---|---|---|---|---|
| where | K-4 | terrible | Q-2 | arrive | S-5 | paramedic | Y-1 |
| orange* | M-1 | arrest | Q-4 | carriage | S-6 | parallel | Y-1 |
| forest* | M-1 | experiment | R-1 | error | T-4 | cemetery | Y-2 |
| there | N-1 | tomorrow | R-3 | foreign* | U-2 | embarrassment | Z-1 |
| carry | N-4 | marry | S-2 | anniversary | W-1 | kerosene | Z-1 |
| sorry | N-5 | marriage | S-2 | character | W-2 | souvenir | Z-2 |
| arrow | N-7 | paragraph | S-4 | parable | Y-1 | | |

*Some pronounce OR as a two-letter phonogram. If so, you can underline it. Others think of the sounds individually. If so, put a one over the /o/ to indicate to think the first sound of the phonogram.

9. HANDLE A ONE-SYLLABLE WORD THAT MAY SOUND LIKE TWO. R and L often trip us up because of the way they are made in the mouth. They want to be vowels, but they're NOT! We may tend to pronounce words like this with two syllables. However, if we think two syllables, students continually mix up the R+ silent E (correct spelling) with the ER phonogram (incorrect spelling).

*fire* — Section J-6: (379)

**Think-to-spell** with the first type of silent final E. Draw a bridge from the I over the consonant to the E. Underline the E twice. In speech we say this quickly like "far" but with the definite sound of /I/ in the middle.

Other examples:    while (M-4)    wire (M-6)    rule (N-1)    tire (N-7)    weird (T-2)
Not in Wise List:   tile            lyre           mule        mire       style

10. ADD A SYLLABLE TO *THINK-TO-SPELL*. Establish a clear sound picture for spelling. Add an extra syllable to include a phantom sound. [In normal speech we do not say the O in *people*]. Add an extra syllable to clarify a surprise pronunciation. [In *soldier* and *cordial*, say the d+i fast. Hear how the sounds /d/ and /i/ blend together to sound like /j/.]

*bu̅ y* — Section L-2: (548)

**Think-to-Spell**: *Buy* is a one-syllable word. To help remember the ghost of a forgotten sound, we will give it a sound just for spelling. This forces a second syllable.

**Student Marks**: Put a one over the U to show that we think the first sound.

*ques-ti-on* — Section N-2: (814)

**Think-to-Spell**: *Question* is a two-syllable word that we think as three. After the student has written it, discuss why. Our eyes see the Latin suffix -tion, but our tongue cannot blend two hissing sounds together (/s/ + /sh/). Think /t/ and /i/ as single letters. Say /t-i/ -/o-n/ fast to see how TI here ends up sounding more like /ch/.

Additional words where we add a syllable for spelling:

| | | | | | | | |
|---|---|---|---|---|---|---|---|
| pe-o-ple | L-6 | vi-ew | P-5 | car-ri-age | S-6 | le-o-pard | X-2 |
| bu-ild | M-3 | bea-u-ty | P-7 | bus-i-ness | T-3 | par-li-a-ment | X-2 |
| he-art | M-6 | bea-u-ti-ful | P-7 | cho-ir | T-3 | ex-tra-or-di-nar-y | Y-2 |
| bu-ilt | N-8 | sol-di-er | R-5 | cor-di-al | W-2 | li-eu-ten-ant | Z-2 |
| o-ce-an | O-4 | mar-ri-age | S-2 | flu-o-res-cent | W-3 | Wed-nes-day | (Num. Pg.) |

Also see page 81 for an option for exception word *fri-end*. See page 85 point 5c for the few words like *fash-i-on* where an I sounds like /y/. We add a syllable to think its vowel sound for spelling.

11. **EXAGGERATE A PHONOGRAM IN A MUFFLED SYLLABLE.** We think the sounds the way they are spelled to create a "sound" picture in the mind. This is especially true with the phonograms OR, AR, AI.

**col <u>or</u>** — Section M-1: (641)

> **Think-to-Spell**: <u>Think</u> /col/- /or/. <u>Say</u> a slight whisp of /or/, or whatever you say.

**[ or ]**    Examples where **OR** may not be a distinct /or/ in speech:

| | | | | | | | |
|---|---|---|---|---|---|---|---|
| doctor | N-2 | tailor | P-6 | behavior | S-2 | senator | U-4 |
| author | O-1 | correct | P-6 | bachelor | S-5 | calculator | W-1 |
| sailor | O-1 | honor | R-1 | scissors | T-3 | thorough | X-1 |
| comfort | O-4 | neighbor | R-6 | emperor | U-3 | endeavor | Y-2 |
| favor | P-1 | visitor | R-6 | attorney | U-3 | humorous | Z-1 |
| mayor | P-6 | janitor | R-6 | majority | U-3 | demeanor | — |

Also: actor, anchor, creator, educator, flavor, harbor, horror, inventor, mirror, odor

**[ ar ]**    Examples where **AR** may not be a distinct /ar/ in speech:

| | | | | | | | |
|---|---|---|---|---|---|---|---|
| war | L-3 | sugar | N-8 | popular | R-4 | burglar | T-3 |
| warm | L-3 | caterpillar | P-4 | familiar | T-1 | calendar | W-1 |
| collar | M-6 | similar | Q-1 | circular | T-1 | leopard | X-2 |
| dollar | N-3 | grammar | Q-3 | | | | |

Also: altar, cellar, liar, lunar, quart

**[ ai ]**    Examples where **AI** may not be a distinct /A/ in speech:

| | | | | | | | |
|---|---|---|---|---|---|---|---|
| mountains | M-4 | curtain | O-6 | certain | S-1 | Britain | — |
| again | M-5 | bargain | R-3 | porcelain | Y-2 | chaplain | — |
| captain | O-1 | against | R-6 | villain | Z-1 | fountain | — |

Margaret Bishop refutes the concern that AI can make numerous sounds. In 98% of English words the AI says a clear /A/ as in *rain*. Muffled sounds can be exaggerated as /A/ with our *think-to-spell* technique. Some have historic roots. Scotsmen still use the long A when saying *said* and *plaid* (Bishop, pp. 7-8). The word *aisle* is explained as an exception word on page 81.

12. **TEACH ADVANCED PHONOGRAMS** as they occur in spelling words or in other subjects: *ae, ah, aigh, augh, cu, eau, et, eu, ge, gh, gi, gu, our, pn, ps, pt, rh, sc, yr.* See Step 38.

**gui͡d̲e̲** — Section N-2: (803) History is a better *guide* than good intentions — *guide*.

> **Think-to-Spell**: /g-I-d/. Use GU as a phonogram to spell /g/. G before I usually says /j/, but adding the silent U separates the G from the I and thus eliminates any confusion about reading the G as the hard sound. The I says /I/ because of a silent E.

In some advanced words we find an additional sound for the basic seventy: *ai, au, ay, qu, x.*

**con qu̲er̲** — Section N-4: (851) We can *conquer* the English language — *conquer*.

> **Think-to-Spell**: /con/ - /ker/. Use QU to say /k/ in this word. This spelling for /k/ is used in French and Spanish-based words. Can you think of a Spanish word meaning "one who conquers"? (conquistador)

# 13. REINFORCE SPELLING WORDS IN A VARIETY OF WAYS.

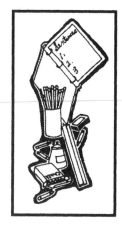

Objectives:

    To assure long-term mastery of the words taught.

    To strengthen other valuable skills while learning spelling.

Prepare to teach:

    Follow a weekly routine for studying the week's words. See Appendix E.

    Choose spelling enrichment activities from *Wise Guide.*

    Pick additional reinforcements from *SWR* p. 91 or *Wise Guide* p.16.

Dictating words to the Learning Log is only the beginning. Strive for mastery of the words introduced. Use blocks of time for study as well as tidbits of practice trickled throughout the day.

**Follow a Weekly Routine for Studying the Week's Words.**

1. READ WORDS. Student reads words from his Learning Log moving across the page. A class can read in unison. Periodically record the length of time it takes a student to read a page. Later he can race against his previous time until he can read the page smoothly and naturally.

2. COMPOSE ORIGINAL SENTENCES DAILY. In Sections A through F, beginners compose original sentences orally as a non-threatening preparation for writing original sentences starting with Section G. Assign one to five sentences daily, depending on the skill level. Students should underline the spelling words. Teacher's option: For every day they submit perfect sentences (grammar correct, spelling correct, and penmanship neat), they can have a day off from sentence writing.

3. ENLARGE SHORT-TERM MEMORY. Time permitting, immediately after dictating the week's list, have the student close the log and take a quiz on the new words. Hesitation on any word reveals areas needing extra attention. With beginners you can do this after each new word.

4. GIVE PRACTICE QUIZZES AND TESTS ON WORDS. Give a daily quiz on some of the words. You can give prompts on a quiz. At the end of the week give a graded test where you do not give any hints. Do not require markings on a quiz or a test! Grade only actual spelling.

5. DICTATE SENTENCES MADE UP OF SPELLING WORDS. With Section A you could dictate: *My bed is red. Six ran. All ten did not run.* Some sentences for dictation are suggested as spelling enrichment activities. Make up additional ones as well. A student can more easily spell words in isolation on a test than by dictation in the flow of a sentence. Test both ways.

6. PUT A CHECK IN THE LOG BESIDE WORDS MISSED. Hold students accountable for words studied. Put two red checks in the student log beside any word missed on the end-of-the week test. The student sees the word correctly spelled and is alerted that this word needs extra attention. The following week checked words may be included on the week-end test. If the student spells a review word correctly, erase one red check. Erase the second check the second time a review word is spelled correctly. Since red pencil never erases completely, each student's log maintains a personalized record of his challenge words. If the backlog of unmastered review words becomes too large, take a break to focus just on mastering those words.

**Choose Spelling Enrichment Activities from *Wise Guide.***

Select one or more of the specific ideas given with each list of new words. Suggested spelling enrichment activities for Section A words include making contractions, trying to identify opposites, writing numbers on the Number Page, and composing original oral sentences. The ideas change from list to list to help keep interest high. These activities help a student practice new spelling words as well as learn something else at the same time. Dynamic reinforcement is better than mindlessly copying a spelling word five times. Select age-appropriate activities for your class.

**Pick Additional Reinforcement Activities as Needed**.

How can students mentally correct their challenge words? Although it is best to learn words correctly from the beginning, many methods can help overturn words learned incorrectly.

1. SIGNAL MISTAKES IMMEDIATELY. On practice quizzes give immediate hints if the student starts to write a word incorrectly. I make a buzzer type warning sound, "Honk!" This haults an error before it is implanted. My students laugh and usually correct the mistake without further help.

2. USE AN AUDIO RECORDING FOR INDEPENDENT SPELLING PRACTICE. Use the Companion CD for Review and Mastery (see page 15) or have him record his troublesome words onto a cassette tape. If he makes his own recording, have him begin with the date. He should say each word, use it in a sentence, and repeat the word. The student can listen to one word at a time on the CD or tape, push the pause button, and write it. He can use his log to correct his own work when finished.

3. CREATE 3 x 5 CARDS. One mom wrote, "We make word cards with the *Wise Guide* word number on one side and the word on the other. I color code them by Section for ease of keeping them organized. Each day my daughter practices reading her new words from the flashcards. Whenever she misses a word on a spelling test, we place its card with other such word cards in her index file. At the end of each section, we review all the flashcards from that section to continue building fluency and speed."

Some make cards only of troublesome words, mark each word, and highlight with a yellow highlight marker the portion the student tends to miss. If the student misspelled the word "do" as "doo," highlight the O.

4. VARY THE MEDIUM. Quizzes may be done different ways.

 a. <u>Chalk</u>. Most students enjoy writing on the board.
   (1). Line up several students. Have all write the word at the same time.
   (2). Arrange students into pairs. One calls out words for the other to write.
   (3). Give students individual chalkboards. Call out a word. When each student holds up his slate, the teacher can quickly check the spelling.

 b. <u>Magnetic letters</u>. Use magnetic letters on a magnetic white board or the refrigerator at home. Call out a word and have students form it correctly. See page 24 in *Wise Guide* for a master for making your own magnetic letters.

 c. <u>Crayons</u>. Student writes especially troublesome words in crayon, saying the sounds, then traces over it twice with two different colors.

 d. <u>Other</u>: Finger paints, Post-it ® notes, letter tiles, sidewalk chalk.

5. WALK AND REWRITE. Place the student Learning Log (or a list of challenge words) on a table. Student looks at a word with red checks in the Log (or a word on the list of challenge words), says the word, sounds it, and then walks across the room to write it on another paper.

6. ANALYZE TROUBLESOME WORDS. Sometimes it helps to give a student a list of his troublesome words properly spelled and have him take the words apart. Beside the correctly spelled word he is to divide the word into syllables and add spelling markings. After he has finished all the words, have him check his work against his Learning Log.

7. ADD KINESTHETIC LINKS. Teach the computer keyboard (see page 34 of *Wise Guide)* or deaf finger spelling of the alphabet (see page 82 of *Wise Guide)* or Morse Code. Practice spelling words with this new skill. See other suggestions in *Wise Guide* pages 8, 16, 52, 146.

**14.** **EXPOSE TO CLASSICAL LITERATURE**. (After *Wise Guide* Section A)

Objective:
>    To develop a love of language.
>    To train the student to appreciate noteworthy expressions of thought.

Prepare to Teach:
>    Before you dictate a new set of spelling words, read through the sample sentences in the *Wise Guide*. Pick at least one sentence to discuss.
>    Realize that this step is completed little by little over time.

Edgar Work defines *literature* as "the kind of writing that frames noble and useful thought in forms that excel" (Work, p. 16). Noah Webster, in his first edition of *The American Dictionary of the English Language* in 1828, calls literature "learning; acquaintance with letters or books. *Literature* comprehends a knowledge of the ancient languages, denominated classical, history, grammar, rhetoric, logic, geography as well as the sciences. A knowledge of the world and good breeding give luster to *literature.*" The 1998 edition of *Webster's American Family Dictionary* defines *literature* as "writing regarded as having permanent worth through its intrinsic excellence."

**Use Quality Sentences When Dictating Spelling Words**.

In the spelling dictation routine, we use each word in a sentence. It takes no longer to say a meaningful sentence than an empty one; the challenge is finding a meaningful sentence. *Wise Guide* provides sample sentences to stimulate the mind and model excellent writing. Many selections are quotes from famous people, well-known proverbs, and excerpts from world literature. Several authors --Shakespeare, R.L. Stevenson, John Bunyan, and Benjamin Franklin -- deserve special attention.

1. SHARE WISDOM FROM WORLD LEADERS.

    a. Presidents of the United States:

| | |
|---|---|
| John Adams | Ulysses S. Grant |
| James A. Garfield | Andrew Jackson |
| Abraham Lincoln | James Madison |
| Ronald Reagan | Theodore Roosevelt |
| Franklin Roosevelt | Zachary Taylor |
| George Washington | Woodrow Wilson |

    b. Statesmen:

| | |
|---|---|
| Samuel Adams | Otto von Bismarck |
| Edmund Burke | Winston Churchill |
| Alexis DeTocqueville | Benjamin Franklin |
| Patrick Henry | Aleksandr Solzhenitsyn |
| Margaret Thatcher | Queen Victoria |
| Daniel Webster | William Wilberforce |

    c. Scientists and Musicians:

| | |
|---|---|
| Johann Sebastian Bach | Thomas Edison |
| Henry Ford | Johannes Kepler |
| Robert Fulton | Sir Isaac Newton |
| Booker T. Washington | |

George Washington
Winston Churchill
Martin Luther
Henry Ford
Booker T. Washington
Thomas Alva Edison

d. <u>Religious leaders</u>:

Augustine of Hippo        Jim Elliott
Thomas Carlyle            Francis of Assisi
Bill Gothard              Martin Luther
D. L. Moody               Francis Schaeffer
Hudson Taylor             Tertullian

f. <u>Famous educators</u>:

William McGuffey          Noah Webster

2. REVIEW PROVERBS FROM MANY LANDS. Words of wisdom are included from different tongues and nations: English (J-5), Russian (H-2), Hebrew (I-1), Chinese (I-4), German (L-1), Spanish (N-2) and African (Q-2).

3. TASTE QUOTES FROM RESPECTED AUTHORS OF WORLD LITERATURE. One sentence from a classical masterpiece can only be called a tiny taste, but we can begin to whet the appetite for excellence of thought and expression even with young scholars. The authors quoted come from a variety of nations and the span of world history from classical Greece and Rome to contemporary times.

Molière (Jean-Baptiste Poquelin)

Charles Dickens

Johann Wolfgang von Goethe

Miguel de Cervantes

(George Gordon, Lord Byron)

a. <u>Classical Greece and Rome</u>:

| | | | |
|---|---|---|---|
| **Cicero** | 106-74 BC | Roman statesman, orator, writer | (J-4) |
| **Euripides** | 485-406 BC | Athens' poet and dramatist, author of *Medea* | (U-4) |
| **Hesiod** | 700 BC | Poet from ancient Greece | (Y-1) |
| **Homer** | 8th century BC | Greek author of *The Iliad* and *The Odyssey* | (R-5) |
| **Plutarch** | 1st century | Greek writer; resource for Shakespeare's Roman plays | (R-6) |
| **Virgil** | 1st century | Roman author of *The Aeneid*, the epic of Western civilization | (K-4) |

b. <u>Euro-Asia</u>:

| | | |
|---|---|---|
| **Cervantes**, Miguel | Spanish 17th-century author of *Don Quixote* | (S-5, S-6) |
| **Dostoevski**, Fyodor | Russian 19th-century author | (V-3) |
| **Goethe**, Johann | German poet, playwright, novelist | (E, K-5, P-7, V-2, W-2) |
| **Moliere** (stage name) | French 17th-century playwright | (Q-3) |
| **Tolstoy**, Leo | Russian author of *Anna Karenina, War and Peace* | (J-3) |
| **Zola**, Emile | French 19th-century master of realistic novel | (L-3) |

c. <u>The British Isles</u>:

| | | |
|---|---|---|
| **Addison**, Joseph | 17th-century English essayist | (O-2, S-1, T-4) |
| **Blake**, William | 18-19th-century English poet | (K-2) |
| **Browning**, Robert | 19th-century English poet | (M-5) |
| **Bunyan**, John | 17th-century author of *Pilgrim's Progress* | See p. 97 |
| **Byron**, Lord | 19th-century English poet | (K-1, N-8, O-4) |
| **Carroll**, Lewis | 19th-century author of children's literature | (O-1) |
| **Chaucer**, Geoffrey | 14th-century author of *The Canterbury Tales* | (J-5) |
| **Christie**, Agatha | 20th-century mystery writer | (P-4) |
| **Coleridge**, Samuel T. | 19th-century English poet | (J-2, K-5) |
| **Dickens**, Charles | 19th-century English novelist | (P-6, T-3) |

| | | |
|---|---|---|
| **Donne**, John | 16-17th-century metaphysical English poet | (N-8, T-5) |
| **Dryden**, John | 17th-century Poet Laureate and dramatist | (K-6, Q-5) |
| **Johnson**, Samuel | 18th-century lexicographer, poet | (K-5, O-1, P-3, U-3) |
| **Keats**, John | 19th-century English poet | (O-6, R-3) |
| **Kipling**, Rudyard | English author born in Bombay, India | (I-2, J-5, R-1, S-2) |
| **Lamb**, Charles | 19th-century author of *Tales from Shakespeare* | (N-8) |
| **Lewis**, C.S. | 20th-century Christian apologetics and author | (O-3) |
| **MacDonald**, George | 19th-century Scottish children's author and novelist | (N-4) |
| **Milton**, John | 17th-century author of epic poem *Paradise Lost* | (M-5, P-6) |
| **Orwell**, George | 20th-century novelist born in Bengal, educated in England | (Q-4) |
| **Pope**, Alexander | 17th-century poet learned to write by paraphrasing classics, Chaucer and Psalms | (J-5, K-4, Q-2) |
| **Rossetti**, Christina | 19th-century English poet, author of *Caterpillar* | (P-4) |
| **Saki** | Pseudonym for 19-century author, H. H. Munro | (J-6, S-1) |
| **Shakespeare**, William | Quoted frequently in *Wise Guide* | See below. |
| **Spenser**, Edmund | 16th-century author of *The Faerie Queene* | (Q-1) |
| **Stevenson**, Robert L. | Quoted extensively in *Wise Guide* | See below. |
| **Swift**, Jonathan | 18th-century satirist, author of *Gulliver's Travels* | (T-2) |
| **Tennyson**, Alfred Lord | 19th-century poet | (M-4, N-7, W-2) |
| | Author of *Charge of the Light Brigade* and | (P-6) |
| | *Idylls of the King* with the story of King Arthur | (K-5) |
| **Thackeray**, William | 19th-century novelist born in Calcutta to Anglo-Indian parents | (M-6) |
| **Wilde**, Oscar | 19th-century Irish playwright, novelist, poet | (N-7) |
| **Wordsworth**, William | The celebrated English Romantic poet | (K-4, N-8, Q-3) |

d. America:

| | | |
|---|---|---|
| **Beecher**, Henry Ward | Writer during the War Between the States | (L-5, M-1, P-7, S-1) |
| **Brink**, Carol Ryrie | Author of Newbery Prize winner *Caddie Woodlawn* | (J-4) |
| **Dickinson**, Emily | 19th-century American poet | (J-6, M-2, R-3, V-1, W-2) |
| **Emerson**, Ralph Waldo | 19th-century American essayist and poet | (Y-1) |
| **Fitzgerald**, F. Scott | 20th-century American novelist and short-story writer | (T-3) |
| **Franklin**, Benjamin | 18th-century statesman, scientist and author | See below. |
| **Frost**, Robert | 20th-century American poet, Pulitzer Prize winner | (L-2) |
| **Hawthorne**, Nathaniel | 19th-century American author | (M-4) |
| **Irving**, Washington | Early American writer with international reputation | (J-2) |
| **Keller**, Helen | Blind and deaf 19th-century American author | (R-1) |
| **Lindsay**, Vachel | 20th-century American poet | (L-2) |
| **Longfellow**, Henry W. | 19th-century American poet | (N-7, T-4, Y-2) |
| **Nash**, Ogden | 20th-century American poet | (U-4, V-3) |
| **Nesbit**, Edith | Children's author of *The Railway Children* | (P-7) |
| **O. Henry** | Pen name for short-story writer William Sydney Porter | (W-2) |
| **Rogers**, Will | 20th-century American humorist | (J-4, K-6, L-3) |
| **Steinbeck**, John | 20th-century American novelist | (R-2) |
| **Twain**, Mark | Pen name for Samuel Clemens | (I-3, L-3, M-7, T-5, Y-2) |
| **Wallace**, Lew | Author of *Ben Hur* | (U-2) |
| **Whittier**, John Greenleaf | 19th-century American poet | (N-5) |

**Select a Key Sentence from Each Spelling Section.**

With each spelling section, pick one or more sentences for special reflection and discussion. For example, in Section A consider the quote from William Shakespeare, "I cannot what I will not do." If the student doesn't know what that means, you might ask, "Remember the other day when you feigned great fatigue and begged to be excused from schoolwork? Why just five minutes later did you zoom down the driveway on your rollerblades faster than the speed of sound? You had the energy to rollerblade because that is what you wanted to do. Desire to do something greatly influences whether you ever do it."

**Train the Students to Value the Rich Heritage of English Literature.**

Geoffrey Chaucer

John Wycliffe supervised the translation of the Bible from Latin into the vernacular of the people, and a follower of his, Geoffrey Chaucer, used his gift of storytelling to expose massive corruption of church leadership. The two men not only paved the way for the Reformation but also helped give birth to middle English. Historian Charles Coffin reports, "When Doctor [Wycliffe] selected the Midland dialect for his translation of the Bible, and when Geoffrey Chaucer used it in writing his Canterbury stories, they little knew that they were laying the foundations, as it were, of the strongest and most vigorous language ever used by human beings for the expression of their thoughts... the one aggressive language of the world — the language of Liberty" (Coffin, p. 53-54). Edgar Work explains, "Let men live generation after generation in the atmosphere of this Book [the Bible], reading its language and absorbing its thought, and their speech will grow more expressive, and more weighty, as if some mysterious mastery had possessed their lips, and exacted tribute of their tongues" (Work p. 25). By the following century, England produced some of the greatest authors of all time, including William Shakespeare.

Several of the British writers are quoted frequently in *Wise Guide:* Robert L. Stevenson, John Bunyan, and William Shakespeare.

1. ROBERT L. STEVENSON. In 1885 Stevenson released the book now known as probably the most famous children's poetry book, *A Child's Garden of Verses.* This volume is readily available at most libraries and referenced often in *Wise Guide.* In addition to just reading the sentence, later in the week you may want to study the entire poem. Read it aloud and discuss the meaning. Stevenson captures the imaginative powers of a child in memorable ways. For ease in linking the poems to the spelling words, see the poem title followed by the section in *Wise Guide* that quotes a sentence from it:

| | |
|---|---|
| My Bed is a Boat | (A) |
| Where Go the Boats? | (I-2) |
| Armies in the Fire | (I-3) |
| The Swing | (J-5) |
| Where Go the Boats? | (J-6) |
| To Any Reader | (K-4, M-5) |
| System | (K-5) |
| Travel | (K-7) |
| Marching Song | (L-3) |
| Bed in Summer | (M-3) |
| The Land of Story-Books | (N-8) |
| Foreign Lands | (O-3) |
| Block City | (O-6) |
| My Shadow | (P-3) |
| The Wind | (Q-3) |
| Rain | (Q-6) |
| The Land of Counterpane | (R-5) |

*How do you like to go up in a swing*
*Up in the air so blue?*

A key quote in Section A comes from "My bed is like a little boat." What does the poet mean? Is his bed floating in the river? No. Listen to the poem.

*My Bed is a Boat*

*My bed is like a little boat;*
*Nurse helps me in when I embark:*
*She girds me in my sailor's coat*
*And starts me in the dark.*

*At night, I go on board and say*
*Good-night to all my friends on shore;*
*I shut my eyes and sail away*
*And see and hear no more.*

*All night across the dark we steer;*
*But when the day returns at last,*
*Safe in my room, beside the pier,*
*I find my vessel fast.*

*I shut my eyes and sail away*
*And see and hear no more.*

When he goes to bed at night, he considers it to be like a trip. He sails off to dream land. His nurse helps him into his pajamas and says, "Good-night." In the morning when he awakes, the bed is back safely in his room.

"Marching Song" is not quoted in L-3 but it could be used with the spelling word *march*.

*Marching Song*

*Bring the comb and play upon it!*
*Marching, here we come!*
*Willie cocks his highland bonnet,*
*Jonnie beats the drum.*

"The Land of Counterpane" quoted in R-5 can be used to help train a student to interpret poetry. The title word, "counterpane," is a British word for bed cover.

*When I was sick and lay a-bed,*
*I had two pillows at my head,*
*And all my toys beside me lay*
*To keep me happy all the day.*

Read the poem aloud. Discuss the poem verse by verse. Ask questions like: What is the setting? (A child's sick bed.) What did the boy do to keep himself entertained? (Played with toys while he was propped up by two pillows.)

The last stanza says:            *I was the giant great and still*
*That sits upon the pillow-hill,*
*And sees before him, dale and plain,*
*The pleasant land of counterpane.*

Ask: Who is the giant? (The boy presiding over the toy world he created. He looks like a giant in contrast to his toy soldiers. He peers down into another, smaller world and observes the play figures move over the bumps in the covers that create imaginary hills and valleys.)

2. JOHN BUNYAN. This seventeenth-century tinker spent years locked away in prison because he preached a message different from the state church. While incarcerated, he wrote *Pilgrim's Progress,* one of the most influential books of all time. He also composed a series of poems that BHI has reprinted in an attractive hardback edition and renamed *Lessons from Nature.* Quotes in the *Wise Guide* reveal some of the lessons he learned in bondage behind bars.

> *In some countries trees bear no fruit because there is no winter there.* (K-2).
> *The best prayers have often more groans than words.* (L-2).
> *The egg is no chick by falling from a hen, nor man a Christian till he's born again.* (M-6).
> *Prayer is a shield to the soul, a sacrifice to God, and a scourge for Satan.* (P-2)
> *One leak will sink a ship, and one sin will destroy a sinner.* (P-5)

3. WILLIAM SHAKESPEARE. Unequalled in brilliance as an author and as an observer of the ways of men, William Shakespeare is considered as possibly the best writer of all times. No one can be considered truly literate without some familiarity with his works. To a large measure his success stems from the wisdom he gleaned from Holy Writ.

"The England into which Shakespeare was born was an England that had welcomed the Bible in the vernacular, and that was becoming saturated in every pore with Biblical speech and thought. It is scarcely possible to exaggerate the extent to which the new English versions [of the Bible: Wycliffe, Tyndale, Coverdale, Geneva] had permeated the life of the country. Shakespeare's knowledge [of God's Word] is not casual and accidental, like that of one who has touched it lightly, and with indifference. . . The thoughts of Scripture appear to be running through his mind, and the very language of the Book comes readily to his pen. When he refers to the Bible, it is done naturally and without effort—he does not strain his point. He does not drag his references in by force." (Edgar Work, pp. 156-160)

More than twelve hundred references to the Bible appear in Shakespeare's works. He includes the creation, the temptation, the fall, the story of Cain and Abel, the flood, Job, the patriarchal histories, Pharaoh, Samson, David, Nebuchadnezzar, and many other Bible characters and events. He scarcely omits an important character from Adam to Jesus and his disciples. In five different plays he refers to the parable of the Prodigal Son. The overall themes of his dramas carry a biblical theme or ideal like the age-old conflict between good and evil. He demonstrates the consequences of sins like greed, deceit, and violence, as well as the need of repentance and faith.

William Shakespeare

Some desire to censor his plays because he employs witches and ghosts. So does Scripture. The characters do not entice the audience to follow them into the occult, rather they expose evil and guilt. Shakespeare's tragedies showcase the doctrines of sin, retribution, and atonement. He believes in Providence and shows the folly of unjust gain. "There is a divinity that shapes our ends, rough-hew them how we will." Henry VI asks, "Can we outrun the heavens?" He studies the human soul. In Henry VIII, he charges, "Fling away ambition; By that sin fell the angels; how can man, then, the image of his Maker, hope to win by't?" (Edgar Work, pp. 166-172)

Can small children enjoy Shakespeare? My sons attended their first Shakespearean performance when they were in the primary grades. Before we went to the play, I read them a summary of the story from *Tales from Shakespeare,* by Charles and Mary Lamb. Although I'm sure they missed many of the intricacies of the language (I do myself), they watched the production with delight. I'll never forget the day, not long after that, when I found eight-year old Daniel sitting in his Dad's chair with a big grin on his face as he read the actual play for himself.

Many of the Shakespeare quotes in *Wise Guide* demonstrate in a small way the influence of God's Word on his plays. In addition to reading the quote, you could look for a biblical parallel. Have students analyze some of his well-phrased ideas. Memorization activities strengthen mental capacity. Budding authors do well to learn well-phrased sentences from the master craftsman of words.

Spelling Section                    Quotes from Shakespeare

| | |
|---|---|
| A | *I cannot what I will not do.* |
| F | *Woe to the land that is governed by a child!* |
| G | *Heat not a furnace for your foe so hot that it does singe yourself.* |
| I-1 | *It's one thing to be tempted, another thing to fall.* |
| J-3 | *There is a divinity that will shape our ends.* |
| K-3 | *Repentance is the heart's sorrow, and a clear life ensuing.* |
| L-1 | *I clothe my naked villainy with Holy Writ and seem a saint when most I play the devil.* |
| L-6 | *When I was a little tiny boy, a foolish thing was but a toy.* |
| N-2 | *Confess yourself to heaven; repent what's past; avoid what is to come.* |
| N-6 | *There is no small choice in rotten apples.* |
| N-8 | *With devotion's visage and pious action we do sugar over the devil himself.* *A greater power than we can contradict hath thwarted our intent.* |
| O-1 | *A thief doth fear each bush an officer.* |
| O-2 | *A good deed will shine in a naughty world.* |
| P-2 | *Desire of having is the sin of covetousness.* |
| P-4 | *To several subjects heaven hath my empty words.* |
| P-5 | *There is no vice so simple but assumes some mark of virtue on his outward parts.* |
| Q-1 | *Like doth quit like and measure still for measure.* *Suit the action to the word, the word to the action.* |
| Q-2 | *To thine own self be true, and thou canst not then be false to any man.* |
| R-3 | *No beast is so fierce but knows some touch of piety.* |
| R-6 | *Though this be madness, yet there is method in it.* |
| S-4 | *To rain a shower of commanded tears, an onion will do.* |
| S-6 | *God made him; therefore, let him pass for a man.* *Some people sell their peace in eternity to get a toy.* |
| T-2 | *The world is still deceived with ornament... a gracious voice obscures the show of evil.* |
| T-4 | *To show unfelt sorrow is an office which the false man does easily.* |
| U-2 | *I'm not in the giving vein today.* |
| U-3 | *You will hang like an icicle on a Dutchman's beard.* |
| U-5 | *Assured through only the merits of Jesus Christ, I partake life everlasting.* |
| V-3 | *Deny us for our good; so find we profit by losing of our prayers.* |
| W-1 | *The fool multitude choose by show.* |
| W-2 | *Extreme fear can neither fight nor fly.* |
| X-1 | *Good name in man or woman is the immediate jewel of his soul.* |
| X-2 | *Suspicion always haunts the guilty mind.* |
| Y-2 | *Tomorrow creeps in this petty pace from day to day to the last syllable of recorded time.* |
| Z-2 | *Parents "to their children ... are heaven's lieutenants."* |

## Consider Classical Ancient Literature.

Morals taken from *Aesop's Fables* occur frequently in *Wise Guide*. Many versions of these fables are in print. Some editions do not have the morals at all, others have them worded different ways. Although the morals can stand alone as a sentence worth considering, if you can find the accompanying story, you may enjoy reading it out loud and discussing how it relates to the moral. Student can also rewrite the story in their own words. The morals in the *Wise Guide* come from the following stories.

Spelling Section          *Aesop's Fable* which illustrates the moral

I-1      The Vain Crow
J-1      The Lion and the Mouse
J-5      The Wolf and the Lion
K-1      Frog and the Well
L-1      The Fox and the Crow
L-5      The Monkey and the Dolphin
M-3      The Shepherd Boy and the Wolf
O-2      The Travelers and the Bear
P-1      The Milkmaid and Her Pail
P-4      The Bundle of Sticks
P-5      The Hare and the Tortoise
R-3      The Goose that Laid the Golden Egg
R-4      Belling the Cat (also called The Mice in Council)
U-2      The Miller, His Son, and Their Donkey
V-3      The Mountain in Labor
W-3      Eagle and Arrow
Z-1      The Wild Boar and the Fox

*"What is evil won is evil lost."*

*--The Wolf and the Lion*

## Present American Literature.

Though American history is short in contrast with ancient history or the British Isles, we have valuable contributions to the world of letters. American statesman Benjamin Franklin wrote a book full of wise sayings called *Poor Richard's Almanack*. *Almanac* is not misspelled. The reprint of Franklin's book which I bought in Philadelphia uses the spelling used at the time. Even the Webster's 1828 dictionary retains the K at the end of *almanac*. The following quotes appear in the *Wise Guide*.

Spelling Section          Quotes from *Poor Richard's Almanack*

D        *You may delay, but time will not.*
J-4      *Lost time is never found again.*
J-5      *A soft tongue may strike hard.*
J-6      *Eat to live; live not to eat.*
K-3      *No price can recompense the pangs of vice.*
K-4      *Think of whence you came, where you are going,*
             *and to whom you must give account.*
K-5      *Danger is sauce for prayers.*
L-3      *Wish not to live long, as to live well.*
L-5      *Sin is not hurtful because it's forbidden;*
             *it is forbidden because it's hurtful.*
M-6      *Clean your finger before you point at my spots.*
N-5      *Hear reason, or she'll make you feel her.*
O-4      *A quiet conscience sleeps in thunder.*
O-5      *Getting into debt is getting into a tanglesome net.*
P-1      *He that waits upon fortune is never sure of a dinner.*
P-5      *Three things are extremely hard: steel, a diamond, and to know one's self.*
P-6      *An undutiful daughter will prove to be an unmanageable wife.*
Q-2      *He that cannot obey, cannot command.*
Q-4      *Remember that time is money.*
R-2      *There is no little enemy.*
R-3      *The fool does say, "Tomorrow, I'll reform."*
S-6      *Changing countries or beds cures neither a bad manager nor a fever.*
V-3      *Experience keeps a costly school. The fool will learn in no other.*

BENJAMIN FRANKLIN
Benjamin Franklin

**15.** **START NUMBERS PAGE.** (After *Wise Guide* Section A)

Objective:
>To log numbers taught in spelling to a reference page.
>To link the cardinal *(one)* and ordinal *(first)* numbers.
>To connect numbers to other related words *(dozen, decade)*.

Prepare to Teach:
>Notice that this reference page needs no red markings.
>Realize that this page is built little by little over time.
>Combine this assignment with a calendar activity or a math lesson.
>View a page in progress in Appendix C (P12/ B15).

The Learning Logs collect numbers that we learn to spell. Space is provided for the days of the week and the months of the year. These proper names are not on the spelling list. Teach them when appropriate. See page 200 of *Wise Guide* for a sample completed page.

Add appropriate words to the Number Page after they are taught. The numbers occur in *Wise Guide* by difficulty in spelling. The number in parentheses is the assigned spelling order.

| | | | | | |
|---|---|---|---|---|---|
| *six(th)*, *sixteen(th)** | A | *first* | K-4 | *fourth* | O-3 |
| *ten(th)* | A | *zero* | K-7 | *fourteen(th)** | O-3 |
| *three* | G | *four* | L-2 | *forty,* *fortieth** | O-3 |
| *one* | H-1 | *third* | L-6 | *ninth* | P-4 |
| *five* | H-1 | *thousand(th)** | M-2 | *hundred(th)** | P-4 |
| *nine,* *nineteen(th)** | I-4 | *dozen* | N-5 | *thirteen(th)** | Q-4 |
| *seven(th)* | J-4 | *fifth* | N-5 | *thirty, thirtieth** | |
| *seventeen(th)** | | *fifthteen** | | *decade* | R-6 |
| *eleven(th)*** | J-4 | *fifty, fiftieth** | | *century* | S-2 |
| *twenty** | K-1 | *second* | O-2 | *midcentury** | S-2 |
| *twelve*** | K-1 | *eight(h)* | O-2 | *million(th)** | S-3 |
| *twelfth* | K-1 | eighteen | | *millennium* | X-2 |
| *two* | K-1 | | | | |

If you are beginning the year higher in the spelling list, watch for notes in Wise Guide that say, "Add to Number Page." First, add ALL the bold number words taught prior to where you are teaching. Continue to collect more new number words each time you see the "Add to the Number Page" instruction.

**Number Page -** *Primary Log*
**Student at Section L-2**

No red is used on this page.

Some numbers (13-20, 30, 40, 50) will only be in the Formatted Black Log.

---

*non-bold items only in new black log

** *Eleven* and *twelve* come from German meaning "one" and "two" left over. *Thirteen - nineteen* mean "ten more than." The reason for the shift is lost in antiquity.

| Numbers | | | | | Months of the Year |
|---|---|---|---|---|---|
| • *zero* | | | | | |
| 1 *one* | 1st *first* | | | | |
| 2 *two* | 2nd | | | | |
| 3 *three* | 3rd | | | | |
| 4 *four* | 4th | | | | |
| 5 *five* | 5th | | | | |
| 6 *six* | 6th *sixth* | | | | |
| 7 *seven* | 7th *seventh* | | | | |
| 8 | 8th | | | | |
| 9 *nine* | 9th | | | | *September* |
| 10 *ten* | 10th *tenth* | | | | |
| 11 *eleven* | 11th *eleventh* | | | | |
| 12 *twelve* | 12th *twelfth* | | | | |

**INTRODUCE GRAMMAR PRINCIPLES.** (After *Wise Guide* Section C)

<u>Objectives</u>:

    To teach students to write in complete, grammatically correct sentences.

    To expose students to grammar terms and concepts.

    To provide a way to practice new spelling words in a worthwhile and engaging way.

<u>Prepare to Teach</u>:

    Read the instructions for grammar Spelling Enrichments in *Wise Guide*.

    Purchase for each student a set of *SWR Grammar Readers*. (optional)

    Read aloud the appropriate Ruth Heller's *World of Language* book. (optional)

    Preview the Grammar Pages for Black Learning Log students. See Appendix C (B27-31).

In an early exercise students divide spelling words into lists of nouns that can name a person, place, thing, or idea. Activities sprinkled throughout the Wise List expose a student to grammar concepts using spelling review words. Much can be done with the student's original sentences. Capitalize the first word in a sentence. Use appropriate end punctuation. Correct improper word usage.

**Make Grammar Terms Come Alive.**

While we make no attempt to cover grammar extensively, we do introduce many aspects of grammar in a hands-on way.

1. ACT OUT PREPOSITIONS. Introduce grammar terms with a hands-on activity. For "preposition," use a stuffed dog and a shoe box (a pretend dog kennel) as you review the spelling sentences. (See the paragraph on prepositions in Section C of *Wise Guide*.) The word **preposition** comes from the prefix **pre-** meaning "before" and the word **position**. A preposition comes before a word and shows the position of one word in relation to another. *Up, Over, and Out* is a *Grammar Reader* on prepositions.

2. IDENTIFY THE SUBJECT AND VERB. Use Grammar Reader: *I Can Run!* The student reads and illustrates sentences made with spelling words. He demonstrates his comprehension by illustrating the passage. He learns to identify and diagram the simple subject/verb.

3. DEMONSTRATE THINGS THAT CONNECT. For conjunctions, play with Legos®, tinker toys, or some building game where you have a connector piece that joins two other items. The word **conjunction** comes from the prefix **con-** meaning "together" and the Latin word **jungere** meaning "to join." A conjunction connects thoughts together.

The dog is on the kennel.

4. READ ALOUD THE BOOKS ON GRAMMAR BY RUTH HELLER. Even young children can enjoy learning grammar ideas with these books with full-color artwork on every page and a poetic cadence. In *Merry-Go-Round: A Book About Nouns*, she starts with a lady and a dragon and the script, "Nouns name a person, place, or thing." On the next page we see a king, a castle, and medieval flags with the words: **a king**. These NOUNS are all COMMON, and they're very nice, but PROPER NOUNS are more precise. **King Arthur** is a person." I have read Heller's books even to preschoolers. They are not only good tools for children, but also an excellent form of adult remediation.

5. DRAW TO ILLUSTRATE ADJECTIVES.

An artwork project can help capture the purpose of adjectives. The word **adjective** comes from the prefix **ad-** meaning "to" and the Latin word **jacere** meaning "throw." An adjective modifies, or restricts, the meaning of a noun. The word *man* is a general description of an adult male. If we add the adjective *old,* we "throw to" or "clarify" the more general word.    Draw pictures that reflect the different adjectives for man: old man, strong man, short man, tall man, thin man, fat man.

**Teach Grammar with Spelling Words**.

### Adjectives

old man    strong man

tall man    short man

1. INTRODUCE ALL EIGHT PARTS OF SPEECH.  The following Sections in *Wise Guide* address parts of speech.

| | |
|---|---|
| Prepositions: | C, J-2, N-1 (See SWR page104). |
| Nouns: | D, G, H-2, K-2, Q-1, R-2, R-6, S-2, S-3, U-3, V-1, W-2 |
| Pronouns:* | C, I-3, M-6, Q-3 |
| Verbs: | D, E, H-2, I-1, I-3, J-3, K-3, L-l, L-4, M-3, N-5, P-6, Q-4, S-3, S-5, T-2, W-2 |
| Adjectives: | F, J-4, J-6, K-2, K-5, M-6, N-3, N-6, Q-2, S-2, W-2. |
| Adverbs: | J-5, M-5, N-6, O-5, Q-2, R-3, R-6, S-1 |
| Conjunctions: | A, M-1, N-8, T-4 |
| Interjections: | H-2 (Well!), J-6 (Help! Fire!); P-3 (Good grief!); Z-2 (Hallelujah!) |

2. PRESENT MECHANICAL AND STRUCTURAL GRAMMAR SKILLS. The main practice with mechanics will come with the ongoing weekly original sentences. The following places in *Wise Guide* also address the following aspects specifically:

Capitalization:

| | |
|---|---|
| Proper names: | Student's name, Sections I-3, O-1, P-3, Y-1, Z-1 Months, Days of Week on Number Reference Page |
| First word in a sentence: | B |
| Titles: | Spelling Section Titles A-Z and Reference Pages |
| First word in a line of poetry: | M-4, O-1, P-3, Q-6, S-6, T-4, Y-1 |

Punctuation:

| | |
|---|---|
| Period: End of a sentence: | B, C, F, N-8 |
|     With abbreviations: | See Step 25. |
| Exclamation point: | C, N-8 |
| Question mark: | B, C, F, I-2, L-2, N-4, N-8 |
| Direct Quotes: | J-6, N-2 |
| Colon: | I-2 |
| Commas: | |
|     Clauses: | G, Q-6 |
|     Compound sentence: | H-2 (dictation) |
|     Salutations, closings: | I-1 (thank you note), J-1 (personal letter),  N-5, Z-2 |
|     Appositives: | W-1 |
|     Series: | I-2, W-2 |
| Apostrophe: | |
|     contraction: | See Step 28, I-1 |
|     possession: | I-1, U-3, V-1, W-1 |

Correct Word Usage:

| | |
|---|---|
| Subject/ Object Pronouns: | C, I-3, M-6, Q-3 |
| Misplaced Modifiers: | N-7, R-4, S-1 |
| Subject/ Verb Agreement:* | O-1, P-6, S-5 |

| | |
|---|---|
| Kinds of Sentences: | L-2, N-8 |
| Complete Sentences: | D, L-4, M-3 |

---

* See helpful new reference pages in the formatted Black Log for Personal Pronouns (B31) and Subject/Verb Agreement (B32). For answer key go to www.bhibooks.net > Free Downloads.

---

3. TEACH SENTENCE DIAGRAMMING. When specific parts of speech are presented, the diagram symbol can be introduced. If the students are studying adjectives, just diagram the noun / adjective. If they are studying prepositions, you can diagram the prepositional phrase.

Adjectives: F-1. *I ate old bread.*

bread
old

Prepositions: J-2. *He came from the ship.*

from  ship  the

Subject/ verb: L-4. *Mother held the baby.*

mother | held

4. ADD TO THE BLACK LEARNING LOG. Space is provided in the final pages of the Black Learning Log for some grammar reference material.

a. Parts of Speech. Build a reference page with the eight basic parts of speech. First construct the overall outline of pages B27, B28. See the sample B27 on page 219 to determine the number of lines to skip between terms. With red, underline each part of speech.

|  | **Define** | **Illustrate** |
|---|---|---|
| noun | | |
| pronoun | | |
| verb | | |
| adjective | | |
| adverb | | |
| preposition | | |
| conjunction | | |
| interjection | | |

As each different part of speech is covered in the reinforcement activities, add the definition of that part of speech. On the facing page add some examples.

b. Sentence diagramming. The skeleton outlines of sentence diagramming with examples can be added to page 29. If you would like an additional resource for diagramming, we recommend the guide by Louise Ebner, *Learning English with the Bible: English Grammar Diagrams Based on the Book of Joshua.*

c. Pronouns. A common grammatical error is using the wrong pronoun. Pronouns must match the function in the sentence. An optional reference chart for page 31 of subjective, objective, and possessive pronouns will help clarify which pronoun to use when. See *Wise Guide* M-6 for a table of personal pronouns. This is not duplicated in Appendix C.

d. Prepositions. On page B30 collect the fifty words that might be used as preposi-tions. You may build this list following the order of presentation in *Wise Guide*. The words are identified by spelling number in the Wise List. The starred prepositions are derivatives of spelling words. With fourth grade or above you may prefer using an alphabetical order.

## English Prepositions

| | | | | | | |
|---|---|---|---|---|---|---|
| in | 41 | (C) | upon | 503 | |
| by | 42 | | across | 518 | |
| out | 43 | | behind | 519 | |
| to | 44 | | within | 543 | (L) |
| into | 45 | | above | 544 | |
| up | 46 | | before | 630 | |
| on | 47 | | off | 680 | (M) |
| onto | * | | below | 712 | |
| over | 48 | | beside | 717 | |
| at | 49 | | past | 745 | |
| of | 50 | | beyond | 785 | (N) |
| like | 94 | (E) | among | 786 | |
| for | 126 | (G) | except | 918 | |
| about | 143 | (H) | through | 975 | (O) |
| after | 198 | (I) | throughout | * | |
| down | 257 | | aboard | 976* | |
| with | 266 | (J) | until | 994 | |
| under | 279 | | during | 1032 | |
| outside | 282 | | regarding | 1066* | (P) |
| inside | 283 | | since | 1126 | |
| from | 286 | | beneath | 1187 | |
| along | 343 | | underneath | * | |
| near | 378 | | toward | 1427 | (R) |
| between | 382 | (K) | against | 1439 | |
| without | 390 | | concerning | 1626* | (T) |
| around | 394 | | | | |

\* A derivative of spelling words

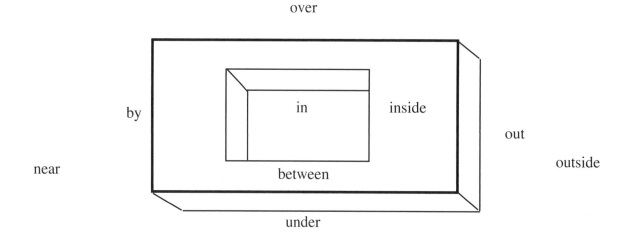

## 17. **TEACH SILENT FINAL E PAGE.** (Before *Wise Guide* Section D)

Objectives:

  Introduce Silent Final E's. (Mastery will come in application to words in *Wise Guide*.)
  Build the Silent Final E Page in the Learning Log annually, regardless of level.
  Teach five reasons for silent final E's in English words.

Prepare to Teach:

  View the sample completed page in Appendix C: P6/B9.
  Practice the dialogue for teaching Silent E's as you build your Silent Final E Page.

**Review Rules Learned**.

  In Sections A-C we had some words that end with E. Find them in your Learning Log-- *be* (12); *the* (28); *me* (52); *he* (54); *she* (56); *we* (59). Dictate them to me, so I can write them on the board. What sound did the last letter make? (/E/) Why? (E said /E/ at the end of a syllable.) [Advanced words also follow rule 4: *abalone, acne, adobe, apostrophe, calliope, canape, coyote, catastrophe, epitome, facsimile, finale, Gethsemane, hyperbole, kamikaze, karate, provolone, psyche, recipe, sesame, simile, tamale, ect.*]

  In English most final E's are silent for one of five reasons. Do you know what they are? Few people have ever learned this valuable information. As a result they think many words are irregular when they are not. They are more likely to make spelling errors like adding a silent E when one is not needed or forgetting one that is. Are you ready to learn the five reasons? This will be fun. Then we can watch for silent E's as we learn new words.

> What sound does the E make in these words?
> An E at the end of an English word is usually silent.
> Can you explain five reasons for a silent final E?

  Teacher's Note: In *Wise Guide* almost 25% of the words have a silent final E. Numerous other words on the list are derivatives of silent final E words. Throughout the program we will locate and analyze silent E's until the student can see and identify at a glance the reasons for the added E. It will help students overcome the tendency to indiscriminately add E's after almost every word. These valuable, but little-known, concepts clarify why we can or cannot drop the E in certain words (notice, noticing, noticeable). Our students can logically explain what seems puzzling and strange to many scholars.

**Follow Dialogue for Dictating Silent Final E Reference Page.**

  1. **SILENT FINAL E -- TYPE ONE**

| | | |
|---|---|---|
| Teacher: | I will use the word "dime" to demonstrate the main reason for a silent final E. *I traded two nickels for a <u>dime</u>.* Write the sounds you hear in "dime." | **dim** |
| Student: | /d/-/I/-/m/ | |
| Teacher: | Read what you have written. | |
| Student: | dim | |
| Teacher: | Add an E to make the word "dime." Repeat after me; "/I/ said /I/ because of the E". This type of E can work with any single vowel + consonant (s) + a silent E. In general we say, "**The vowel sound changes because of the E.**" | |

Markings:   With red (using a red pencil), draw a bridge from the vowel over the consonant(s) to the E. Underline the E twice. A double underline indicates a silent letter.

This type of E can also work with 2 consonants between the vowels: *paste, clothe, change.*

## 2. SILENT FINAL E -- TYPE TWO

Teacher:    Our second type of E is illustrated by the word "have." *I have a love for reading.* Under "dime" write the sounds you hear in "have." Don't add the E yet.

Student:    /h/-/a/-/v/

Teacher:    Read what you have written. The word sounds fine. Why do we add an E? Without the E, the V would fall over. (Use magnetic letters to demonstrate. Try to have the V stand up alone. Then put an E after it to prop it up.)  Seriously, we need an E because **English words do not end with V.**

Markings:   With red, underline V once to show that's why we needed an E. Underline E twice because the letter is silent. Put a little 2 beside the double underline to show it is the second type of silent final E.

Teacher:    On the line with "have" in the second column we will illustrate another type two E with the word "true." *Think on those things that are true.* Write the sounds you hear in "true."

Student:    / t/-/r/-/U/

Teacher:    Add an E. From what we have learned can you say why?

Student:    **English words do not end with U.** [If not tell them.]

Markings:   With red, underline U to show that's why we need an E. Underline E twice to show it's silent. Put a little 2 beside the double underline to show it's the second type of silent final E.

V and U take 2

## 3. SILENT FINAL E -- TYPE THREE

Teacher:    Our third type of E is illustrated with the word "dance." *She was so happy she did a little dance.* Under "have" write "dance." Use the / k/-/s/. Don't add an E yet.

Student:    d-a-n-c

Teacher:    Read what you have written.

Student:    /dank/. C says /s/ only before E, I or Y.

Teacher:    Add an E. **The C says /s/ because of the E.**

Markings:   With red, underline C once, because that's why we needed an E. Underline E twice because it's a silent letter. Put a small 3 beside the double underline to show it's the third type of silent final E.

Teacher:    On the line with "dance," under "true," we will illustrate another type three E with the word "large." *Large families are special.* Use the /g/ - /j/. Don't add an E yet.

Student:    l-ar-g

Teacher:    Read what you have written.

Student :   /larg/. G says /j/ only before E, I, or Y.

Teacher:    Add an E. **The G says /j/ because of the E.**

Markings:   Underline /ar/. With red, underline G once, because that's why we needed an E. Underline E twice because it's a silent letter. Put a small 3 beside the double underlines to show it's the third type of silent final E.

C and G take 3

A helpful ditty to help remember the number is **"V and U take 2,  and C and G take 3."**

### 4.  SILENT FINAL E  -- TYPE FOUR

Teacher:        Our fourth type of E is illustrated with the word "Bible." *Capitalize the word "Bible" because it is the title of a book.* — *Bible*. (Some use the alternative word, "apple" to teach the type four E.)
Student:        Two syllables.
Teacher:        Sound it out as you write it but don't add the E yet.
Student:        "Bi" (/b/-/I/)  "bl" (/b/-/l/)
Teacher:        Why do we need an E?  Is it to make the I say /I/?
Student:        No, the I says /I/ at the end of a syllable.  Underline I.
Teacher:        Then why do we need the E? **Every syllable must have a vowel.** Add an E.
Markings:       With red, underline E twice with a small 4.

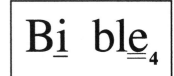

L and R are "vowel wanna-be's."  Say /l/ and /r/. While the tongue does obstruct the sound some, there is less obstruction than with other consonants.  The sound is close enough to help make a syllable without any vowel sound, but in order to ensure having a vowel in every syllable, we add the silent E. The fourth type of E applies to words ending with syllables *ble, cle, dle, fle, gle, kle, ple, sle, tle, zle,* or words like *a-cre* and in British spellings like *cen-tre.*

We usually underline book titles, but the Bible is so well known the underline is unnecessary.

### 5.  SILENT FINAL E  -- TYPE FIVE

Teacher:        Our fifth type of E is illustrated by the word "were." *Were you happy when I gave you money?*  Under "Bible" write "were."  Don't add the E yet.
Student:        /w-er/
Teacher:        Read what you have written.
Student:        /wer/
Teacher:        Does it need the E for any of the reasons above?

         1st    — Does the vowel sound change?
         2nd    — Would the word end with V or U?
         3rd    — Would the word end with C or G?
         4th    — Does the syllable need a vowel?

If we answer all the questions "no," this is a type five E, also known as *the odd job E.*

What is the fifth reason for an E? [Pause so they can think.]

Teacher:         Sometimes we can tell why we have a type five E; sometimes we are not sure. **An "Odd Job E" is one needed for any reason not covered by the first four.**
Markings:       Underline /er/.  With red, underline E twice with a small 5.
Teacher:        Why do we underline the E twice?
Student:        It's a silent letter.
Teacher:        Why do we write a 5?
Student:        It's a type five silent final E.

What does the word "odd" mean?   One meaning is "unusual." *I did a number of odd jobs today.*  What are *odd* jobs that a mother might do?  She might repair a broken toy, replace a light bulb, re-pot a plant, remove a splinter from a child's hand,  answer Aunt Sue's letter, patch a hole in her son's jeans, and hang a new picture, all in one day.

What are some odd jobs that a type five E might do?

1.  The E can keep a word from looking like it ends with the suffix -S.

| | | | | | | | | |
|---|---|---|---|---|---|---|---|---|
| *goose* | not | goos | *please* | not | pleas | *moose* | not | moos |
| *tease* | not | teas | *false* | not | falls | *tense* | not | tens |
| *dense* | not | dens | *purse* | not | purrs | corpse | not | corps |

2.  The E can add length to a short main-idea word.
    Examples: *awe, ewe, rye, owe.*

3.  The E can give a distinction in meaning.

| | | | | | | | | |
|---|---|---|---|---|---|---|---|---|
| *cleanse* | not | cleans | *belle* | not | bell | *breathe* | not | breath |
| *hearse* | not | hears | *aide* | not | aid | *caste* | not | cast |

4.  The E can be left over from Middle English or a foreign language where the final E was once pronounced: *are, come, gone, some, were, ease, done, treatise, giraffe.*

    A fun way to illustrate this one is to pretend to talk using 14th century speech. Sound the silent E's in the following sentences. *Come-e to my house-e. Where-e else-e can you eat some-e goose-e?*

**Refer to Reference Page When Teaching New Words.**

When you come to a word on the spelling list, such as *home*, ask, "How do we mark the E?" Students should learn to respond: "Draw a bridge from the O [or whatever vowel was used in the word] over the consonant to the E. Underline the E twice." MEMORIZE THIS WORDING and repeat it each time you mark type one silent final E words.

After the students say how to mark a silent final E word, you may ask, "Like what word on the Silent E Page?" Often students can recite the sample word without looking.

**Sample of Silent Final E Page**

**Primary Learning Log**

(Note use of *apple* as an alternative word to *Bible* for a type four E.)

All markings are red except AR in *large,* ER in *were,* and the I in *Bible.*

**Mark  Double Duty Words.**

What do we do when a silent E has more than one job?  How will we mark the word?  We will follow the Law of First Order.  That means we will mark the first kind of E that works.

1. TYPE ONE PLUS TYPE TWO E'S.

| | |
|---|---|
| cav͜e | The A says /A/ because of the E.  (Type One E) |
| | English words do not end with V.  (Type Two E) |

*One* comes before *two*.  *A* comes in the word before *V*.  Although we mark only the type one E, our smart head tells us the E does double duty in this word. Other examples in the Wise List:

| | | | | | | | |
|---|---|---|---|---|---|---|---|
| wave | (90) | live | (132) | five | (155) | gave | (187) |
| brave | (248) | drive | (412) | grave | (457) | save | (561) |
| behave | (1478) | arrive | (1536) | vague | (1886) | opaque | (1899) |

2. TYPE ONE PLUS TYPE THREE E'S.

| | |
|---|---|
| ac͜e | The A says /A/ because of the E.  (Type One E) |
| | The C says /s/ because of the E.  (Type Three E) |

*One* comes before *three*.  *A* comes in the word before *C*.  We will mark the type one E, but our smart head tells us the E does double duty in this word.

Examples of type one plus type 3 where the C is softened by the E:

| | | | | | | | |
|---|---|---|---|---|---|---|---|
| ice | (106) | lace | (230) | nice | (233) | face | (249) |
| race | (302) | place | (309) | twice | (384) | price | (436) |
| surface | (987) | palace | (1047) | produce | (1090) | trace | (1091) |
| mice | (1265) | brace | (1288) | advice | (1429) | sacrifice | (1794) |

Examples of type one plus type 3 where the G is softened by the E:

| | | | | | | | |
|---|---|---|---|---|---|---|---|
| page | (197) | age | (298) | change | (655) | village | (809) |
| strange | (927) | range | (932) | oblige | (1097) | language | (1114) |
| cabbage | (1189) | voyage | (1195) | engage | (1290) | courage | (1295) |
| stage | (1324) | marriage | (1467) | carriage | (1558) | mortgage | (1939) |

**Learn a Back-up Way to Illustrate Silent Final E's.**

Initially teach the E's with word examples only.  This plants the most direct neurological image of the concept.  Later you can reinforce the idea with the cartoon E characters on the spelling rule cards.

1. The Strongman E silently stands behind a consonant or two. Although he says  nothing, when a timid vowel peeps around the consonant(s) and sees him, she  may become  brave and say her name. In "mane," A said /A/ because of the E.
2. The Supporter E holds up a V or U so they will not fall over.
3. The Softening E helps soften the sound of the C or G.
4. The Sidekick E tags along to help give the last syllable a vowel.
5. The Odd Job E is used for some reason not named above.

## 18. START SH /TI REFERENCE PAGE. (*Wise Guide* Section E)

Objectives:

    To collect /sh/ words on a reference page (after Section E).

    To teach the four most common ways to spell /sh/ (after H-1).

Prepare to Teach (after Section M):

    Prepare teacher's master tailored to where you are in the program.

    Realize that this page is built little by little over time.

    View completed SH/ TI Page in Appendix C. (P3/B7)

    Pull out phonograms *sh, ti, ci, si,* and spelling rule cards 10 and 11.

How do you spell /sh/?

### Start Building the /sh/ Collection Page in the Learning Log.

We have four basic ways to spell /sh/. A reference page helps organize these spellings by the rules that govern English. Students collect spelling words along the way that use one of these phonograms. We have some words that use the most common spelling very early in the program before we have even taught the other ones. Start this page with the concept of rule 10 and several SH spelling words. See the sample of Primary Learning Log below. See the teacher instructions in *Wise Guide* Section E. Look both in the Preliminaries and also beside the word *wash*. Additional words, one or two at a time, will be added to the SH Page in this manner as you teach through the list.

**On this Reference Page with red underline SH. Use regular pencil for all other markings.**

| SH Spells /sh/ | |
|---|---|
| . . . at the beginning of a word | . . . at the end of a syllable |
| *she* | *fish* |
| *short* | *wash* |

SH is the most common way to spell /sh/. By Section H-1 all four basic phonograms that spell /sh/ will be introduced.

### Illustrate Both /sh/ Rules (after H-1 or higher on the list).

    1. GRAB STUDENT ATTENTION. Show cards. Ask:

       ❏ What do these have in common? (They can say /sh/.)

       ❏ Which spells /sh/ at the beginning of a word? (sh)

       ❏ At the end of a word? (sh)

       ❏ At the beginning of any syllable after the first one? (ti, ci, si)

       ❏ With the suffix -ship? (sh)

       ❏ Which one commonly has 2 sounds? (si)

*sh*

*ti*

*ci*

*si*

    The next two points are notes which apply mainly to students at Section M or above.

    2. DEMONSTRATE THE NEED. Many people use the wrong phongram to spell /sh/. We will collect words to help reinforce the correct one. Here are some helpful observations.

       ❏ Short, common words most often use SH.

       ❏ Latin endings use TI 90% of the time.

       ❏ Often the base word influences the ending.

| | | |
|---|---|---|
| elect | **+ ti** | — elec**ti**on |
| face | **+ ci** | — fa**ci**al |
| manse | **+ si** | — man**si**on |

    3. UNDERSTAND PHONOGRAM SELECTION OF TI. Some educators ask why we don't teach TION as a phonogram. Learning TI, CI, SI as a set helps connect the three for ease in learning.

TI should not be restricted to TION when TI says /sh/ with at least six other suffixes and in *ratio*.

| TI- + | -al | *confidential, differential, essential, impartial, influential, potential, preferential, presidential, providential, residential, substantial* |
|---|---|---|
| | -an | *dietitian* |
| | -ary | *penitentiary* |
| | -ate | *differentiate, propitiate* |
| | -ent | *patient, sentient, quotient* |
| | -ous | *ambitious, cautious, fictitious, infectious, nutritious* |

TI, CI, SI are used only at the beginning of any syllable after the first one.  TI is the most common.

**Build the SH/TI Page Fresh Every Year.**

In subsequent years students start building this reference page whenever a link "add to the SH Page" occurs in *Wise Guide*.  The teacher starts off the page reviewing rules 10 and 11 and dictating some /sh/ words from preceding spelling sections.  As new /sh/ words come up during the year, students determine the appropriate column and add them.  The page will "grow as you go."  Each /sh/ word is listed below under the proper category and cross references to its spelling section in *Wise Guide*.

1. ALL SH WORDS IN *WISE GUIDE* BY ORDER OF APPEARANCE.

**SH spells /sh/ . . . at the beginning of a base word**

| she | C | shape* | J-3 | shoe | L-3 | shield | P-2 |
|---|---|---|---|---|---|---|---|
| short | E | shore* | K-2 | shop | M-3 | shallow | P-3 |
| shot* | F | shall | K-3 | shine | O-2 | share | P-6 |
| show | I-1 | should | K-3 | shed | O-4 | shelf | R-2 |
| ship | J-2 | shut | K-4 | shrink* | O-4 | sheep | R-2 |

[*Affixes do not interfere with the rule:  up**sh**ot, re**sh**ape, a**sh**ore, pre**sh**rink]

**. . . at the end of a syllable**

| fish | B | dash | L-1 | fashion | L-5 | reddish | P-3 |
|---|---|---|---|---|---|---|---|
| wash | E | push | L-2 | furnish | M-7 | publish | Q-5 |
| finish | K-3 | wish | L-3 | fresh | N-6 | distinguish | U-4 |
| | | | | | | accomplishment | W-3 |

**. . . BUT not at the beginning of any syllable after the first one** (See TI, CI, SI),

**. . . EXCEPT for the ending -ship.**

The rule applies to base words.  *Battleship* combines two base words.  -SHIP may also be a suffix which does not mean boat:  *office, status or rank* (governorship); *quality, state, or condition* (kinship); *acts, power, or skill of* (horsemanship); *relation between* (comradeship).

Derivatives of spelling words formed by adding -SHIP.  (son -> sonship; lead -> leadership)

| son*ship* | J-1 | head*ship* | K-2 | court*ship* | N-7 | mayor*ship* | P-6 |
|---|---|---|---|---|---|---|---|
| lord*ship* | J-1 | king*ship* | K-5 | friend*ship* | O-1 | assistan*ship* | S-3 |
| hard*ship* | J-2 | leader*ship* | L-5 | judge*ship* | O-4 | worship | T-1 |
| | | | | | | [<OE worth + ship] | |

2. ALL LATIN SPELLINGS OF /SH/ IN *WISE GUIDE* BY ORDER OF APPEARANCE. Select words for the reference page for each phonogram (TI, CI, SI). Use spelling words, derivatives (words in italics below), or words from outside study. Tailor the page to your student's level of spelling. As students progress in *Wise Guide*, Latin spellings for /sh/ will become more prominent.

| Phonogram | Section | Words | | |
|---|---|---|---|---|
| **TI** | M | solution (671) | *contraction* (696) | *collection* (735) |
| | N | definition (824)<br>*inspection* (866) | *subjection* (843)<br>*expectation* (868) | *exhaustion* (865)<br>*intention* (929) |
| | O | station (978)<br>*projection* (1023) | *location* (1006)<br>*rejection* (1024) | population (1020)<br>resurrection (1051) |
| | P | *visitation* (1086)<br>*subtraction* (1122) | *obligation* (1097)<br>*correction* (1175) | election (1120)<br>vacation (1191) |
| | Q | position (1204)<br>connection (1216)<br>*conviction* (1273)<br>addition (1297) | action (1211)<br>direction (1218)<br>*declaration* (1276) | section (1214)<br>*selection* (1227)<br>information (1292) |
| | R | *resignation* (1325)<br>convention (1336)<br>*combination* (1375)<br>patience (1395)<br>*preparation* (1409) | *congratulation* (1329)<br>*temptation* (1337)<br>*distribution* (1386)<br>education (1400)<br>objection (1413) | patient (1332)<br>attention (1339)<br>publication (1391)<br>*illustration* (1408)<br>creation (1418) |
| | S | impartial (1441)<br>motion (1482)<br>ambition (1505)<br>*investigation* (1539) | examination (1465)<br>mention (1488)<br>dictionary (1513) | condition (1468)<br>emotion (1492)<br>affliction (1524) |
| | T | nation (1591)<br>*competition* (1622)<br>celebration (1658) | national (1592)<br>exception (1634)<br>invitation (1659) | conversation (1611)<br>fraction (1657)<br>stationary (1660) |
| | U | *conservation* (1661)<br>*calculation* (1745) | *suggestion* (1692)<br>application (1746) | confidential (1729)<br>consideration (1756) |
| | V | association (1766)<br>confectionery (1829)<br>destruction (1862)<br>conjunction (1926)<br>stationery (1993) | superstition (1780)<br>*appreciation* (1841)<br>concentration (1876)<br>procrastination (1972) | organization (1806)<br>*separation* (1844)<br>alliteration (1906)<br>penitentiary (1980) |

| **CI** | | | | | | |
|---|---|---|---|---|---|---|
| *facial* | I-1 | electrician | T-3 | atrocious | X-1 |
| facial | R-1 | official | T-4 | pediatrician | X-2 |
| spacious | N-8 | ancient | U-4 | especially | X-2 |
| special | Q-6 | delicious | U-4 | suspicious | X-2 |
| precious | R-1 | social | U-5 | mortician | Y-1 |
| gracious | R-3 | artificial | W-2 | physician | Y-2 |
| musician | S-5 | beneficial | W-3 | sufficient | Y-2 |
| crucial | T-1 | *financial* | X-1 | proficiency | Z-2 |
| racial | T-1 | | | | |

CI words not in Wise List:

| | | |
|---|---|---|
| commercial | delicious | glacier |
| judicial | official | optician |
| politician | superficial | vicious |

**SI**

| | | | | | |
|---|---|---|---|---|---|
| *expression* | L-2 | profession | R-1 | discussion | V-3 |
| *confession* | N-2 | missionary | V-1 | session | V-3 |
| *progression* | Q-6 | mansion | V-1 | *ascension* | W-3 |
| tension | R-1 | compression | V-3 | dissension | Z-2 |

SI words not in Wise List:

| | | | |
|---|---|---|---|
| (com)passion | concession | congressional | depression |
| digression | expansion | expulsion | fission |
| pension | recession | Russia | suppression |

**SI [2]**

| | | | | | |
|---|---|---|---|---|---|
| *confusion* | O-5 | television | T-2 | occasion | V-2 |
| *inclusion* | Q-6 | conversion | U-4 | decision | X-1 |
| provision | R-1 | vision | U-5 | explosion | Z-1 |
| division | T-2 | | | | |

SI-2 words not in Wise List:

| | | | |
|---|---|---|---|
| abrasion | adhesion | allusion | ambrosia |
| collision | delusion | erosion | excursion |
| explosion | fusion | illusion | incision |
| intrusion | invasion | leison | version |

Note: In the Primary Learning Log the titles are ordered as TI, SI, CI. The sequence is changed in the Black Log to allow more room for the word examples under CI.

3. ALL CH WORDS IN *WISE GUIDE* THAT SPELL /SH/. Delay connecting CH with the other /sh/ spelling rules until later in the program unless a student asks. CH can spell /sh/ in French-based words. No words using the CH to spell /sh/ occur until well over halfway through the program. Only three words using CH to say /sh/ are in the Wise List at all.

**CH**          **machine**     R-5      **chandelier**     Y-1         **chauffeur**     Z-1

Other French-based CH words not in *Wise Guide:*

| | | | | |
|---|---|---|---|---|
| cache | chagrin | chaperon | champagne | chaperone |
| chateau | chauvinism | chef | chenille | Chevrolet |
| chic | Chicago | chiffon | chute | cliche |
| crochet | echelon | gauche | Michigan | mustache |
| nonchalance | parachute | pistachio | | |

4. RARE EXCEPTION FOR SH RULE. In at least one common word outside of the words in *Wise Guide,* SH spells /sh/ at the beginning of a syllable after the first one. The word, **mar-shal**, is a foreign spelling coming from an old German compound word (horse + servant).

Rather than conform to English spelling, proper names often reflect word origin. **Me-shach** is the Persian name given to one of the friends of Daniel, and Daniel was renamed **Bel-te-shaz-zar**.

**19.** **DICTATE A-E-I-O-U PAGE.** (Before F in *Wise Guide*)

Objective:

    To discover the three reasons for a single vowel to say its letter name.
    To build a reference page contrasting the short and long vowel sounds.

Prepare to Teach:

    Build a teacher's sample page.  See Appendix C. (P8/ B2)
    Pull out the single-vowel phonograms.
    Pull out spelling rule cards 4, 5, 7, 19.
    Realize that this step should be repeated once per year.

|  |
|:--:|
| **fin** |
| **fi-nal** |
| **fine** |
| **find** |
| What can make a single vowel say its name? |

**Illustrate the Concept You Want to Teach.**

    Have the student quickly "read" the single vowel phonograms.  Now read ONLY the most frequent sounds of these letters: /a, e, i, o, u/.  Next read them with ONLY the second sound.  When do they say /A-E-I-O-U/ in words?  We have three categories that cover the key reasons.  This page should be built each year for all levels.  The word examples used are the same for all ages.

**Locate the Reference Page.**

    1. TURN TO PAGE 8 IN THE PRIMARY LEARNING LOG.  The page is already formatted.  The teacher simply dictates the sample words and explains where the student should place the words.

    2 FORMAT PAGE 2 IN THE BLACK LEARNING LOG.  The page has already been divided into thirds (Step 8).  Dictate the main titles using horizontal and vertical reference points.  Teach students to carefully follow instructions as to placement on the page.

    Center on the first line (omit a top guideline): **A-E-I-O-U.**

Skip a line. Two spaces before the red guideline,
    write the number **1**.
After the red line write, ***at the end of a syllable***.
Under *at*, after the red line, write a lower case **A**.
Under A write a lower case **E**.
Under E write a lower case **O**.
Under O write a lower case **U**.  Bracket the four vowels.
Under U write a lower case **I**.
Under I write a lower case **Y**.    Bracket the two vowels.

Skip a line.  Under 1, write **2**.
After the red line write ***before a silent final E***.
Under "before," after the red line, write a lower case**A**.
Under A write a lower case **E**.
Under E write a lower case **I**.
Under I write a lower case **O**.
Under O write a lower case **U**.
Under U write a lower case **Y**. Bracket the six vowels.

Skip a line.  Under 2, write **3**.
After the red line write ***before 2 consonants***.
Under "before," after the red line, write a lower case **I**.
Under I write a lower case **O**.  Bracket the two vowels.
Skip a line.  Under 3, write **4**.
After the red line write ***unknown reason***.

|  |  |
|:--:|:--|
|  | *A-E-I-O-U* |
|  |  |
| *1.* | *at the end of a syllable* |
| ⌐ | *a* |
|  | *e* |
|  | *o* |
| ⌐ | *u* |
| ⌐ | *i* |
| ⌐ | *y* |
|  |  |
| *2.* | *before a silent final E* |
| ⌐ | *a* |
|  | *e* |
|  | *i* |
|  | *o* |
|  | *u* |
| ⌐ | *y* |
|  |  |
| *3.* | *before 2 consonants* |
| ⌐ | *i* |
| ⌐ | *o* |
|  |  |
| *4.* | *unknown reason* |
|  |  |

**Demonstrate the Primary Reasons for Vowels Saying Their Names**.

To guide the discovery process, the teacher should stimulate student interest, give precise instructions, elicit a student's response, and review using a preset dialogue.

1. STIMULATE INTEREST. A-E-I-O-U are the only phonograms that can say the sounds of their letter names in words. In the first column of words, we will illustrate the more common use of the vowels. In the next column we will demonstrate ways to make that vowel change to the long sound.

2. DICTATE PRECISE INSTRUCTIONS. Give clear enough instructions for a student to write words accurately without seeing them. After a student is finished or almost finished, the instructor writes the words on the board, so the student can proofread his work.

| | |
|---|---|
| Teacher: | Under "1. at the end of a syllable," after the first fold, beside /a-A-ah/, write **cat**. *The cat is purring.— cat* |
| Students: | One syllable. cat. /k/-/a/-/t/ |
| Teacher: | On the same line with *cat*, in the last column write **cater.** *The deli will cater our dinner. — ca-ter* |
| Students: | Two syllables. First syllable: /kA/ /k/-/A/. Second syllable -ter /t/-/er/. With red, underline A. |
| Teacher: | Why does A say /A/? |
| Students: | A said /A/ at the end of a syllable. [A-E-O-U **usually** say /A-E-O-U/ at the end of a syllable.] |

When marking the long vowel sounds, teach the class to say "with red, underline the __ (whichever vowel is used)." The reverse, "underline with red" may lead someone to underline with black pencil before they focus on the word red.

| | | | | |
|---|---|---|---|---|
| Continue as above: | e | met | me ter | E said /E/ at the end of a syllable. |
| | o | rob | ro bot | O said /O/ at the end of a syllable. |
| | u | cub | cu bic | U said /U/ at the end of a syllable. |

3. ELICIT A STUDENT'S RESPONSE. Engage student thinking with questions.
   ❏ Why do we mark with red? (It's what we're emphasizing on this page.)
   ❏ Why don't we underline ER in red? (We're not teaching ER on this page.)
   ❏ Why only A,E,O,U? (We have a different rule for I and Y. I and Y usually say /i/ at the end of a syllable but **may say** /I/.)

| | |
|---|---|
| Teacher: | Under *cub*, beside I, write **dilemma**. *We will solve the dilemma -- dilemma.* |
| Students: | Three syllables. di-lem-ma. *Think to spell* /i/ (See pages 83-85) and /ah/. Put a 3 over /ah/. If a word ends with A it says /ah/. [R18] |
| Teacher: | Next, we will illustrate the first syllable (di) with a changed vowel sound. On the same line with *dilemma*, in the second column write **diet.** *Go on a diet.* |
| Students: | Two syllables. /dI-et/. With red, underline I. I said /I/ at the end of a syllable. |
| Teacher: | Does I usually say /I/ at the end of a syllable? |
| Students: | No, I and Y usually say /i/ at the end of a syllable but may say /I/. |
| | |
| Teacher: | Under *dilemma*, beside Y, write **hobby**. *A hobby is fun.* Think /hob-bi/. The Y stands in for I because English words do not end with I. [R6] We use the same syllable but change the vowel sound. In the next column write **by.** *Sit by me -- by.* |
| Students: | One syllable. /bI/. With red, underline the phonogram that said /I/. |

4. REVIEW WITH PRESET DIALOGUE. What rules cover vowels at the end of a syllable?
   *a. A-E-O-U usually say /A-E-O-U/ at the end of a syllable.* [R4]
   *b. I and Y usually say /i/ at the end of a syllable but may say /I/.* [R5]

**Illustrate the Second Reason a Vowel Can Say its Name.**

Under **2**, beside **A**, using the first fold as the guideline, write **can.** *(I can do it.)* Under *can* write **pet**. *(I have a pet cat.)* Under *pet* write **pin**. *(I need a straight pin.)* Under *pin* write **rod**. *(Have you seen my fishing rod?)* Under *rod* write **cut**. *(Did you cut your finger?)* In the adjoining column write the word again but add an E: **cane, Pete, pine, rode, cute.**

**Can** becomes **cane** because of the E.
With red, draw a bridge from the vowel, over the consonant to the E. Underline E twice.

**Pet** becomes **Pete** because of the E.
With red, draw a bridge from the vowel, over the consonant to the E. Underline E twice.

**Pin** becomes **pine** because of the E.
With red, draw a bridge from the vowel, over the consonant to the E. Underline E twice.

**Rod** becomes **rode** because of the E.
With red, draw a bridge from the vowel, over the consonant to the E. Underline E twice.

**Cut** becomes **cute** because of the E.
With red, draw a bridge from the vowel, over the consonant to the E. Underline E twice.

Under **cut**, write **gyp.** Under **cute**, beside **gyp**, write **type.** In Greek-based words, the Y is used as a substitue for I within a word. Fewer words fit this category.
YP as in *gyp* changes from **/ip/** to **/Ip/** in *type* because of the E.
With red, draw a bridge from /I/ over the consonant to the E. Underline E twice.

**Illustrate the Third Way a Vowel Can Say its Name.**

Under 3, on the same line with **I**, under **gyp** write **mint**. In the next column write **mind**. On the same line with **O**, under **mint**, write **pond**. In the next column write **poll**. *I and O MAY say /I/ and /O/ before two consonants.* [Rule 19]. No markings are necessary. The reason can be seen in the word.

Questions to help clarify why we use no markings for words like *mind* and *poll*.

Q. Why don't we put a two over a vowel when it says its name at the end of a syllable?
A. A two isn't needed over a second sound, IF the reason is seen in the word.

Q. Why did we underline these vowels?
A. All six vowels can change their sounds at the end of a syllable, and frequently do so. We added a special marking just for this rule because we needed to draw extra attention to it.

Q. Why don't we put a two over the vowels with a strongman E?
A. A two isn't needed over a second sound, IF the reason is seen in the word.

Q. Why did we use a special marking?
A. To distinguish five different types of silent E's.

Q. What would we be saying if we put a two over the vowel in words like *mind* and *poll?*
A. We would be saying that the vowels say their name without a visible reason.

Q. Does this final rule need a special new marking for special emphasis?
A. No. It involves only two of the six vowels and even then only half the time. The two consonants provide marking enough. These words don't need any additional marking.

**Illustrate When to Put a 2 over a Vowel that Says its Name (Black Log only).**

On the same line as **4**, under **poll**, write **control**.  Why does the second O in **control** say /O/?

    * Is it at the end of a syllable?        [R. 4, 5]       (No)

    * Does it have a silent final E?       [R. 7]         (No)

    * Is it followed by two consonants?  [R. 19]       (No)

With red, put a 2 over the second /O/ in **control**.  We put a 2 over vowels that say their second sound for any reason not covered by the Rules 4, 5, 7, or 19.  Only four other words in the Wise List will need a 2 over the vowel: *danger* (474), *angel* (810), *union* (1477), *ancient* (1727).  Examples outside the Wise List: *creosol* (a colorless, oily liquid), *extol, patrol, sheol, sol*.  A 2 over a single vowel will be extremely rare!  *Control* no longer needs the 2 with the derivative *controlled* where the O says /O/ before two consonants [R19].  The English language is much more regular than most people realize!

| A-E-I-O-U | | | |
|---|---|---|---|
| 1. | at the end of a syllable | | |
| | a | cat | ca ter |
| | e | met | me ter |
| | o | rob | ro bot |
| | u | cub | cu bic |  Rule 4 |
| | i | di lem ma | di et |
| | y | hob by | by |  Rule 5 |
| 2. | before a silent final E | | |
| | a | can | cane |
| | e | pet | Pete |
| | i | pin | pine |
| | o | rod | rode |
| | u | cut | cute |
| | y | gyp | type |  Rule 7 |
| 3. | before 2 consonants | | |
| | i | mint | mind |
| | o | pond | poll |  Rule 19 |
| 4. | unknown reason | | con trol |

Also known as: *Ways a Single Vowel Says its Name*

Primary Log p.8/ Black Log p. 2

Note:  Point 4 -- Black Log only

**Summarize the Vowel Rules with Bonus Examples.**

At a later time you can check the understanding of the **A-E-I-O-U** concept by writing on the board one of the five sets of words below such as: *fin, final, fine, find*.  Ask, "Can you use these words to illustrate the 3 ways the single **I** or **O** can change from saying /i/ and /o/ to saying /I/ and /O/?"

| /i/ | **fin** | **pin** | **bin** | /o/ | **rod** | **cod** |
|---|---|---|---|---|---|---|
| /I/ -- R. 5 | **fi**-nal | **pi**-ne-tum | **bi**-nary | /O/ -- R. 4 | **ro**-dent | **Co**-dy |
| /I/ -- R. 7 | **fine** | **pine** | com-**bine** | /O/ -- R. 7 | **rode** | **code** |
| /I/ -- R. 19 | **find** | **pi**nt | **bin**d | /O/ -- R.19 | **ro**ll | **co**ld |

## 20. DRILL RULE CARDS REGULARLY. (After Section F)

Objectives:
> Learn the spelling rules on cards (also in Appendix D).
> Understand how to use the rule cards for review.

Prepare to Teach:
> See the "Instructions for Prompt Cards" in the card set.
> Highlight with red the areas suggested.
> Laminate the cards for ease in handling and durability.
> Cut them out.
> Pull out the rules taught in Sections A-F:
> > Rules 1-8, 10-13, 17-19, 25.

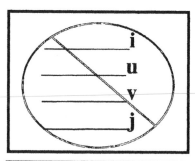

English words do not end with I, U, V, or J. [R. 6]

Hold up Spelling Rule Card #1. Say, "Silently study the card and see if you can identify the rule that it represents. Don't say anything, but raise your hand if you know. Give others a chance to think a little." When everyone is ready, repeat the rule in the box on the back of the card and have the students repeat it after you. Continue in a similar fashion with the rules listed above. From now on, the cards can become a handy way to review spelling rules. In the preliminaries before each lesson, you will often find a listing of rules that will come up with that lesson. You can flip through the cards quickly and repeat in unison the rules before dictating the new spelling words for the day. The rule itself is surrounded by a box on the back side of the card.

The cards help the students and the teacher learn the rules faster. You get to see the wording of the rule on the back side while the students look at the front side. Those who learn best visually are especially helped by this valuable tool. Say the rules exactly as stated. The wording has been fine tuned for clarity. Memorize it by constant review.

In general it is best not to introduce any of the rule cards until the concept is needed with spelling. For example, in Section G, after teaching the word **box**, you can show the card for Rule 20. Ask the students what we would do if we wanted this word to refer to more than one **box**. If we have more than one **day** we just add an -s. Can we just add an -s to **box** to make it plural? No. *X is never directly before S.* We add -ES.

**Identify Rule-Breakers.**

If he had known our phonograms and spelling rules, George Bernard Shaw would never have claimed that "ghoti" could logically spell "fish." GH does say /f/ as a part of the OUGH phonogram team but never alone or at the beginning of an English word. The O does say /i/ but only in one word in the dictionary, "women." TI is used to say /sh/ but only at the beginning of a syllable, never at the end of a word. English is much more reliable than most people comprehend.

Someone recently asked, "What gives **permission** for the A to say /A/ in an-gel?" She's thinking of the rule: A-E-O-U usually say /A-Ē-O-U/ at the end of a syllable [R. 4]. In angel the A says /A/ without being at the end of a syllable. Does the rule say that the A **must** say /A/ at the end of a syllable? No, only that it *usually* does. When a vowel makes the second sound of the phonogram in an uncommon place not covered by a rule, we mark the vowel with a 2 over it. The rareness of such words demonstrates the amazing predictability of Rule 4.

Language is not like math. Spelling rules provide principles for spelling, but they cannot accommodate all the languages on earth or words that float our way from various sources. Proper names and advertising terms often defy English spelling rules. Our rules should not be viewed as absolutes, but rather as aids in understanding. You'll be pleasantly surprised how well they work.

## 21. COMPOSE ORIGINAL SENTENCES DAILY. (After Section G)

Objectives:

    To define "sentence" and to show the standard form.
    To demonstrate the link between talking/ writing and listening/ reading.
    To encourage students to compose sentences using spelling words.

Prepare to Teach:

    At least one sentence should be written daily using new spelling words.
    Purchase the *SWR Grammar Readers* as optional aids.
    Realize that once started, writing sentences is an ongoing process throughout the program.
    Keep the process fresh with a variety to the assignment. Refer to *Wise Guide* or use ideas at
        the end of this step for additional ways to inspire students to write.

    After presenting words through Section G, the student can begin to write original sentences on separate sheets of loose-leaf paper. Keep these papers together in the student three-ring binder with the most recent papers to the front. Primary students neatly and correctly write in their Learning Log the teacher-approved best sentence for the week.

**Teach the Meaning of "Sentence."**

    1. EXPLAIN THAT A SENTENCE EXPRESSES A COMPLETE THOUGHT. A sentence needs a naming part (the subject) and a telling part (the verb or predicate). Example: *People sing.*

        a. Ask: Is this a complete thought?
            *A huge, yellow lion.*   (No)       *The lion roared.*    (Yes)
            *Then he.*           (No)       *Then he saw her.*  (Yes)
            *Come!*                  (Yes. *You* is the understood subject.)

        b. Introduce the SWR Simple Subject/Verb Grammar Reader: *I Can Run!*

    2. SHOW STANDARD FORM FOR WRITING A SENTENCE.
        a. Begin the first letter of a sentence with a capital. (Step 6 covers capital letters.)
        b. Conclude a sentence with end punctuation. (. ? or !)

**Assign Original Sentence Composition.**

    Throughout this program, students write original sentences using spelling words. We not only reinforce the correct spelling this way, but we also teach foundational grammar using their own work, rather than with boring, ineffective workbook pages. If the student needs help to spell new words in his original sentences, assist only with the part of the word he cannot do alone. Use the dialogue we learned with the phonograms.

    Occasionally "prime the pump" for student-composed sentences by dictating sentences you have created from the words he has learned. Consider the following examples.

*I love my mother and she loves me.*    *Come stand by the heat.*    *I like my pet fish.*
*Will you trade a book for a toy?*      *The dog must have a shot.*   *I can pet my cat.*
*Read the book by the cold, green sea.*   *The boy has a cat and a dog.*   *My hat is red.*

**Have Students Read Sentences Aloud.**

    The first assigned reading in this program is from the student's own writing. He can read with understanding his own thoughts expressed on paper. In this way we teach in a multi-sensory manner from the known to the unknown.

Dr. Harvey Wiener, in his book, *Any Child Can Write*, says,

"There is a close relationship between [writing and reading] especially in the initial learning stages. . . Part of the ability to recognize a word develops from the ability to write the word and to read it back; for many people, including adults, the tactile aspect of writing is an indispensable feature of the learning process. When I teach reading, I try, wherever possible, to use the student's writings to help me teach the skills. When the context is part of their own lives, students' paragraphs are fertile grounds for building knowledge in reading. . . Practice in writing is a vital part of practice in reading. . .

Certainly, the youngster needs to read at some time what others write, but in the early stages of language awareness the writing activity is an integral part of reading. I'd like to see someone experiment with a systematic approach to reading through writing. Could not an entire program in reading skills development revolve around directed writing for children?"

We agree with Dr. Wiener. In fact we have done what he suggests and it works fantastically. One user of our program shared the benefits in following this plan.

"Last year I had John read from his writing journal every day. He loved this!!! The results were incredible. I cannot emphasize enough having a beginner student write and write and then read and read what they have written. Their writing journal (or whatever) becomes the reader long before published books. It also emphasizes to the student the need for legible handwriting.

**Inspire Students to Write**.

At first we should be excited if a student can read a spelling word or two and compose a correct sentence that properly uses the word. As time passes, variety in sentence writing assignments will help keep interest high. Composing sentences is very threatening to many. Help get the student's creative juices flowing by discussing ways we could use the words. Do some preliminary work on the board. Then let her try to work on her own. Some of the following ideas can be used to inspire writers. Some suggestions are more advanced than others. Help students grow into them.

1. COMBINE ADJOINING WORDS. Read words from the student log across the page. Combine two adjoining words in a sentence. See example using the words from Section G:

| | | |
|---|---|---|
| *ask* | *bacon* | — **Ask** mother for the **bacon**. |
| *let* | *live* | — **Let** the **live** fish go. |
| *then* | *live* | — **Then** he can **live**. |
| *gas* | *heat* | — Do you have **gas heat**? |
| *read* | *box* | — Did you **read** the **box**? |
| *for* | *three* | — I can eat **for three**. |
| *yes* | *if* | — **Yes**, you may go **if** you ask. |
| *door* | *stand* | — **Stand** by the **door**. |
| *now* | *come* | — Will you **come now**? |
| *lot* | *wing* | — I ate a **lot** of the **wings**. |

2. CONSOLIDATE SENTENCES. Tell the students they will need to use every spelling word in a complete sentence. They can write twenty sentences, or if they can do so correctly, they can write only one, but each sentence must make logical sense. Teachers humorously report that some students actually spend twice the time composing one sentence with many of the words thinking they will reduce their work. The following sentence uses all twenty words from Section G.

*Yes, **now** we can heal the **live** pet with **three wings if** you **ask for gas** for **heat** and a **lot** of **bacon**, **then come stand** by the **door** where you **live** and **let** me **read** the **box**.* (The words in bold are spelling words.)

3. INCLUDE ONE SELECTED WORD. Each sentence must contain both new spelling words and the selected word. With Section G you might choose **box**. Underline other spelling words.

*Ask if he will* **box** *the bacon for you.*
*Let the live bug out of the* **box**.
*Can you read the* **box**?
*I will ask for three* **boxes**.
*The wall fell and then we had to live in a* **box**.
*Do not put the* **box** *near the gas heat.*
*Yes, you can have the* **box** *if you want.*
*Now come in the door and stand by the* **box**.
*I have a lot of chicken wings in the* **box**.

4. TIE ALL SENTENCES TO A SPECIFIC THEME. Have all sentences relate to one subject. For example, all the words in Section I-2, p. 28 of *Wise Guide* can be tied to seasons. Have students name the seasons as you write them on the board. Beside each season write a spelling word that could somehow link with it: Fall — corn; winter — storm. Brainstorm this way together. Feel free to also include spelling words from previous sections.

*What season is the best? Each spring the wind blows; then trees put out buds. In summer we can have dinner by the river. Each fall we thank God for corn. In winter we may have an ice storm. The seasons are not alike, yet I do not like one more than the other. What season is the best? I like them all.*

5. CREATE A STORY. Write the following words across the top of the board.

who?          when?          where?          what?          how?

A story must have characters (who), a setting (where, when), a problem (what), and a resolution (how). Together look for spelling words that fit each category. With J-1 words, who could be the characters? (girl, daddy, son, lord) Where is the location? (Daddy reading the Word) What could be the conflict? (proud, forget) How is it resolved? Next start working on the beginning of a story together.

*Every night was the same. Our Daddy read the Word and would talk about the Lord. Life was fine until I became proud.*

Then ask, "How could we finish the story?" After we've used our imaginations this way, then I ask them to write their version. They can work from the story we started, or make any changes they like. The only requirement is that they write in complete sentences and include all the spelling words -spelled correctly- of course.

6. INCLUDE A GRAMMAR PRINCIPLE. See the activity for J-2, p. 40 in *Wise Guide* as an example. Study prepositions. The first ten words in Section C are prepositions. By this time the students have also covered other prepositions for spelling: *after, down, for, from.* Students should write original sentences that include both spelling words and at least one prepositional phrase using one of the prepositions. Be sure to give examples, so the students understand the assignment.

**After** *lunch come* **inside** *the house and hang the oil painting* **of** *the ship* **on** *the wall.*

prepositional phrases: ⌐ after lunch
                       | inside the house
                       | of the ship
                       ∟ on the wall

Prepositions can be taught using SWR Beginning Grammar Reader: *Up, Over, and Out.*

**22.** **EXPLAIN ED RULE.** (After Section H-2)

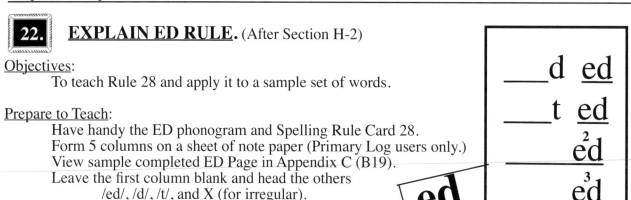

Objectives:

To teach Rule 28 and apply it to a sample set of words.

Prepare to Teach:

Have handy the ED phonogram and Spelling Rule Card 28.

Form 5 columns on a sheet of note paper (Primary Log users only.)

View sample completed ED Page in Appendix C (B19).

Leave the first column blank and head the others
/ed/, /d/, /t/, and X (for irregular).

**Introduce the Idea.**

Hold up ED. Recite together: "/ed/ -/d/ -/t/, past tense ending."

Explain: When ED is added to a verb to make it past tense, it will say one of three sounds.

Dictate for students to write in the first column: *land, heat, play, jump, run, do, hit, give, let.*
Say, "Help me make these words past tense."

| | | | |
|---|---|---|---|
| We **land** the plane today. | Yesterday we __ (landed). | Add to which column? | (/ed/) |
| We **heat** today. | Yesterday we __ (heated). | Add to which column? | (/ed/) |
| We **play** today. | Yesterday we __ (played). | Add to which column? | (/d/) |
| We **jump** today. | Yesterday we __ (jumped). | Add to which column? | (/t/) |

Q. Why does *play* not say /play-ed/ or *jump* /jump-ed/?

A. Hold up rule card 28. Recite together, *E-D forms another syllable if the base word ends with /d/ or /t/. If not, the E-D sounds like /d/ or /t/.*

Verbs usually become past tense by adding ED. Put an **irregular verb** in the X column as an eXception. Irregular verbs come from primitive German (singen, sang, gesungen - sing, sang, sung). Core beginning words come from that side, therefore, most irregular words appear early in the program.

**Build the Reference Page and Assign Independent Study.**

Introduce the concept using review words like sample below with A-G words. Later collect more examples from current spelling words adding them to either loose-leaf paper or the black log.

| | ed | ²ed | ³ed | X |
|---|---|---|---|---|
| land | land ed | | | |
| heat | heat ed | | | |
| play | | played | | |
| jump | | | jumped | |
| run | | | | ran |
| do | | | | did |
| hit | | | | hit |
| have | | | | had |
| let | | | | let |

Optional Q. Is there a way that we can tell which word will say /d/ and which will say /t/?

✧ If the final letter is voiced, use the voiced /d/. Voiced sounds include all the vowels and the consonant sounds: /b, g, j, l, m, n, ng, r, TH, v, z, zh/. Some can be spelled in several ways.

✧ If the final letter is unvoiced, use the unvoiced /t/. Unvoiced sounds include: /ch, f, h, k, p, s, sh, th, x/. Some can be spelled in several ways (/f/ --staffed, graphed).

For H-2 homework, change the first ten words (plus "box") into past tense using the same format.

| | **ed** | $^2$**ed** | $^3$**ed** | **X** |
|---|---|---|---|---|
| call | | called | | |
| row | | rowed | | |
| salt | salt ed | | | |
| belong | | be longed | | |
| bring | | | | brought |
| bite | | | | bit |
| get | | | | got |
| send | | | | sent |
| coat | coat ed | | | |
| tell | | | | told |
| box | | | boxed | |

Check understanding. > Why do we say "salt-ed"?   The base word ended with T.
                   > Why not say "call-ed"?   The base word didn't end with D or T.
                   > Why not say "bring-ed"?   This verb is irregular.

At any time in the program, you can analyze verbs this way, perhaps using current spelling words plus review words. Note the following examples.

**Section I-3**

| | ed | $^2$ed | $^3$ed | X |
|---|---|---|---|---|
| sing | | | | sang |
| miss | | | missed | |
| add | add ed | | | |
| lace | | | laced | |
| plant | plant ed | | | |
| come | | | | came |
| go | | | | went |
| give | | | | gave |
| robe | | robed | | |
| storm | | stormed | | |
| shoot | | | | shot |
| bag | | bagged | | |
| wave | | waved | | |
| back | | | backed | |
| spring | | | | sprang |
| thank | | | thanked | |
| blow | | | | blew |
| foot | foot ed | | | |
| put | | | | put |
| lift | lift ed | | | |
| wash | | | washed | |

**Section J-5**

| | ed | $^2$ed | $^3$ed | X |
|---|---|---|---|---|
| say | | | | said |
| strike | | | | struck |
| make | | | | made |
| still | | stilled | | |
| want | want ed | | | |
| forgive | | | | forgave |
| win | | | | won |
| rest | rest ed | | | |
| room | | roomed | | |
| air | | aired | | |
| fudge | | fudged | | |

| | | ed | $\overset{2}{ed}$ | $\overset{3}{ed}$ | X |
|---|---|---|---|---|---|
| Section K-7 | draw | | | | drew |
| | feel | | | | felt |
| | owe | | owed | | |
| | herd | herd ed | | | |
| | keep | | | | kept |
| | join | | joined | | |
| | water | | wat ered | | |
| | grow | | | | grew |
| | cost | | | | cost |
| | stamp | | | stamped | |

In the remainder of *Wise List* there will be few irregular verbs. Just as the carpet is more likely to be worn in the high traffic areas, so verbs are more likely irregular in the more common words.

| | | ed | $\overset{2}{ed}$ | $\overset{3}{ed}$ | X |
|---|---|---|---|---|---|
| Section N-2 | demand | de mand ed | | | |
| | excuse | | ex cused | | |
| | offer | | of fered | | |
| | question | | ques ti oned | | |
| | pray | | prayed | | |
| | confess | | | con fessed | |
| | mumble | | mum bled | | |
| | repent | repent ed | | | |
| | criticize | | cri ti cized | | |
| | reason | | rea soned | | |
| Section N-7 | mark | | | marked | |
| | front | front ed | | | |
| | wonder | | won dered | | |
| | note | not ed | | | |
| | cause | | caused | | |
| | bridge | | bridged | | |
| | court | court ed | | | |
| | smoke | | | smoked | |
| | tire | | tired | | |
| | mean | | | | meant |
| | check | | | checked | |
| | except | ex cept ed | | | |
| Section P-1 | button | | but toned | | |
| | match | | | matched | |
| | regard | re gard ed | | | |
| | value | | valu ed | | |
| | count | count ed | | | |
| | repair | | re paired | | |
| | catch | | | | caught |
| | teach | | | | taught |
| | support | sup port ed | | | |
| | favor | | fa vored | | |
| | double | | dou bled | | |
| Section X-1 | finance | | | fi nanced | |
| | seize | | seized | | |
| | counterfeit | coun ter feit ed | | | |
| | perceive | | per ceived | | |
| | digest | di gest ed | | | |
| | accommodate | ac com mo dat ed | | | |
| | possess | | | pos sessed | |

## Other Irregular Verbs in the Wise List

For additional optional reinforcement of irregular verbs, you can draw from the following examples in the Wise Guide or their italicized derivatives.  These irregular verbs are listed alphabetically.

| Present | Past | Wise Section | |
|---------|------|------|------|
| am/is | was | A | D |
| are | were | D | L-4 |
| bear | bore | K-5 | — |
| begin | began | L-5 | L-5 |
| break | broke | M-2 | — |
| build | built | M-3 | N-8 |
| buy | bought | L-2 | M-7 |
| cast | cast | J-2 | J-2 |
| choose | chose | R-5 | R-5 |
| drink | drank | K-2 | — |
| drive | drove | K-2 | — |
| eat | ate | J-6 | O-2 |
| fall | fell | I-2 | L-4 |
| feed | fed | L-1 | — |
| fight | fought | L-3 | — |
| find | found | I-3 | J-4 |
| fly | flew | K-2 | L-4 |
| forget | forgot | J-1 | J-4 |
| freeze | froze | M-7 | — |
| grind | ground | — | L-4 |
| hang | hung | J-2 | — |
| hear | heard | N-1 | M-2 |
| hold | held | M-2 | — |
| hurt | hurt | K-3 | K-3 |
| know | knew | L-4 | O-3 |
| lay | laid | H-1 | M-7 |
| leave | left | L-2 | J-3 |
| lie (down) | lay | O-6 | H-1 |

| Present | Past | Wise Section | |
|---------|------|------|------|
| lose | lost | R-3 | J-4 |
| meet | met | L-3 | — |
| pay | paid | J-4 | — |
| read | read | J-1 | J-1 |
| ride | rode | L-2 | L-4 |
| rise (arise) | rose (arose) | L-3 | L-4 |
| see | saw | E | J-3 |
| sell | sold | — | I-4 |
| set | set | K-6 | K-6 |
| shed | shed | O-4 | O-4 |
| shrink | shrank | O-4 | — |
| shut | shut | K-4 | K-4 |
| sleep | slept | J-6 | — |
| speak | spoke | M-3 | — |
| spend | spent | P-5 | I-4 |
| spread | spread | P-5 | P-5 |
| stand | stood | G | M-2 |
| steal | stole | N-6 | — |
| *sweep* | swept | O-5 | |
| swim | swam | M-3 | — |
| take (mistake) | took (mistook) | I-2 | M-7 |
| tell | told | H-2 | I-4 |
| think | thought | J-1 | N-1 |
| throw | threw | O-2 | O-2 |
| understand | *under*stood | M-7 | M-2 |
| wear | wore | R-3 | — |
| wind | wound | J-3 | — |
| write | wrote | N-1 | — |

| Irregular Verbs not in the Wise List | | | | | | | |
|---|---|---|---|---|---|---|---|
| No change | | Similar change | | | | Others | |
| beat | beat | creep | crept | bend | bent | bite | bit |
| bet | bet | weep | wept | lend | lent | sat | sit |
| bid | bid | kneel | knelt | bleed | bled | hide | hid |
| fit | fit | dwell | dwelt | flee | fled | dig | dug |
| rid | rid | sink | sank | tear | tore | drag | drug |
| split | split | stink | stank | swear | swore | seek | sought |

| British spelling sometimes varies from American spelling in forming past tense verbs. | | | | | |
|---|---|---|---|---|---|
| American: | dreamed | leaped | learned | spelled | strove | lit |
| British: | dreamt | leapt | learnt | spelt | strived | lighted |

**23.** **ASSIGN READING IN BOOKS.** (After Section I-1)

Objectives:

    To make the transition from reading original sentences to reading books.

    To build reading confidence and establish a lifetime love of books.

Prepare to Teach:

    Constantly search for books of high interest and lasting value.

Teaching someone to read is one of the greatest joys in life. A child's success will largely depend on mastery of this vital skill. Reading is the foundation to all academic subjects. The late Richard Wurmbrand once showed his son a poem by one of the best poets of their fatherland and asked his son what he saw. The boy replied, "Black letters on white paper." We teach the code that brings life to written symbols. Someone who knows the keys to the language never needs to be forced to read.

A formal reading curriculum is not required. Focus on the mechanics of spelling until students can read their spelling words fluently. We don't have to teach a student to spell every word before he can read it. We teach the "formation" of words not just the "information" needed to learn a few specific words. Some will learn to blend words faster than others. Once they grasp that foundational skill, they quickly start to read material way above their level.

My greatest challenge was finding enough books to satisfy my son's cravings. We made regular trips to the library. A bookstore near me would let customers return used books bought from them and trade them two for one. We went every week for the exchange. I kept our favorites and then recycled the others. I found used copies of Bob Jones and A Beka readers. We rarely did the activities in these books and we ignored all phonics questions. I bought six volumes of Pathway Readers secondhand. My sons finished them all in several weeks.

**Avoid "Torture Reading."**

If a student cannot read at a glance most of the words in a reader, he is not ready for the book. Keep teaching the spelling process. The reading skill will come as a spontaneous side effect. If you try to force reading prematurely, you will never have the same results. My adult friends who learned through "torture reading" still resist reading today. With whole word instruction, a student must see a word repeatedly before eventually memorizing it. Whole language instructors endure the laborious process of having a child read aloud before he is ready and then patiently (or not so patiently) correcting him as he slowly guesses at each word. The books used have a limited, screened vocabulary and lots of pictures. Often the stories are composed of an unnatural combination of words using only short vowel sounds *(Pat sat on a hat. Ben can send men.)* or memorized "sight words" which need to be repeated over and over in these painfully boring books.

**Seek Long-Term Reading Success over Speed in Starting to Read.**

The standard for evaluating a reading program in many circles is how quickly a student starts "reading." Many gimmicks are designed to produce the appearance of early success. Teachers, parents, and students often get a false sense of progress. Rather than making our thrust how fast a student will read, we concentrate on giving a solid foundation for long-term reading success.

One friend, a teacher herself, considered her son to be an excellent reader until he missed school for sickness one day in second grade. She decided to have him read aloud at home the lesson he missed. He looked blankly at the page and shook his head. "I can't read that yet," he said with pleading in his eyes. Then he added, "I can read last week's assignment with my eyes closed." The teacher soon discovered with horror that not only her son, but many of her other students had been memorizing the stories. They could not read at all. She switched to this system with amazing results. Her teaching colleagues started complaining to the principal for giving all the better students in the school to this teacher.  The principal wisely suggested that they should ask her what she had been doing.  Others copied her and soon had similar success.

Teaching reading before spelling is like putting up the walls to the front of a home and painting them before the foundation is finished.  With this program, the time frame when reading activities are assigned may be slower, but our students quickly surpass the reading ability of their peers using controlled vocabulary texts.  We move from teaching phonograms, to studying spelling, to assigning original sentences, and then to reading books.  A student who no longer struggles with the structural analysis of words can read sentences and paragraphs more fluidly.  Students who lack this information are handicapped.  Anyone who must exhaust unnecessary attention capacity to just identify the words in the text will be hindered in grasping the author's intent.  A reader can move to higher levels of understanding only when his mind is free to concentrate on the message itself.

After Step 23, we will strengthen both spelling and reading. The student who masters the spelling words in this program from teacher-directed dictation and learns to apply the 28 spelling rules has the tools to readily decipher almost any new English word.  This foundation is well worth the discipline and work required of both the teacher and the pupil.  A student who can read and spell well can work independently for much of his subsequent education.

**Learn to Select "Living" Books**.

What we read is as important as learning to read.  If we read things based on wrong philosophy or debased themes, we become educated fools.  A student of this program can read interesting materials from the beginning.  My sons' first reader was the Bible. *The Suggested Book List from the Sanseri Homeschool* provides a good listing of favorites that we enjoyed.  The BHI catalog lists our latest discoveries.

**Rather than push a student to read quickly, we concentrate on building a solid foundation for long-term reading success.**

BHI has reprinted in a heritage hard-cover edition *The New England Primer of 1777*.   Many of our founding fathers learned to read using this historically significant book.  Nine simple stories based on ninety-nine of the first spelling words in the Wise List have been added.  Each story has a moral theme and a Bible verse to illustrate the theme.  Wanda Sanseri wrote another good beginning reader called *Play by the Sea*. This story of family closeness uses all 120 of the first spelling words in *Wise Guide*.

Romalda Spalding recommends books in the appendix to *The Writing Road to Reading*.  Our favorite beginning books include *Are You My Mother?, The Little Red Hen,* and *Little Bear*.  Judy Blume wrote a cute book titled *Freckle Juice*, which Mrs. Spalding recommends for grade three.  Although this particular book is funny and enjoyable, I cannot recommend Judy Blume's later books.

*Books Children Love* by Elizabeth Wilson serves as a comprehensive guide to the best in children's literature.  This grandmother of four looked for works that would catch and hold children's attention, were finely written, and reflected basic Judeo-Christian values.  She includes catchy descriptions of books and indicates appropriate grade level and subject category.  I used this guide extensively.

**Encourage Students to Select Books that Motivate Them**.

While teachers should be constantly looking for gems to savor, students also profit from selecting books for themselves.  The first book Ben Carson read all the way through was *Chip the Dam Builder*.  He discovered it after his mother forced this failing fifth grader to visit a library and write a report on a book he read. He had an interest in animals and the book caught his eye. He describes the experience. "For the first time in my life I was lost in another world.  No television program had ever taken me so far away from my surroundings as did this verbal visit to a cold stream in a forest and these animals building a home."  That led to books about plants and, after exhausting that subject, to books on rocks. Today Ben Carson is a pediatric neurosurgeon at Johns Hopkins Children's Center.

**24.**   **DEVELOP VOCABULARY.** (After Section I-2 in *The Wise Guide*).

Long Term Objectives:

To grasp the importance of derivatives.
To explain compound words, prefixes, suffixes.*
To recognize synonyms and antonyms.
To practice spelling in engaging ways.
To introduce homophones, heteronyms, and homographs.*
To introduce Greek and Latin roots.*

| over | time | |
|---|---|---|
| | time | ly |
| un | time | ly |
| bed | time | |
| | time | li ness |
| | time | less |
| spring | time | |
| winter | time | |
| | time | s |

Prepare to Teach I-2 Prefix/Suffix Activity:

Write on separate, blank cards: **in, out, over, time**.
Photocopy for you and each student onto cardstock paper
the suffixes, p. 98 of *Wise Guide* and prefixes on p. 116.

To master a complex subject start with the basic components that can give us double duty, the things that we use over and over again. The phonogram is the smallest unit that we use recurringly. Root words and derivatives are the next smallest. Show students how one word is the key to knowing many others. The majority of words in the dictionary are built from a pool of foundational words. New words are developed by combining two root words together or by adding a prefix and/or a suffix to a root word. The Wise List is made up of 2000 words, but these basic words are the core of a multitude of additional words. If we can spell and understand the base word, and we learn key prefixes and suffixes, then we can easily learn to spell and understand most words derived from the base.

**Define Terms.**

1. A ROOT (OR BASE) WORD is the smallest form of a word. Some base words have one syllable (boy), but others are polysyllabic (apple).

2. A COMPOUND WORD is the combination of two or more root words to form a new word. (door + way = doorway)

3. A PREFIX is a letter or syllable that can be added to the beginning of a word to help form a new word. Mid- is a prefix that can mean "the middle of." (mid + day = middle of the day)

4. A SUFFIX is a letter or syllable that can be added to the end of a word to help form a new word. The suffix -Y can mean "characterized by." (salt + y  = characterized by salt)

5. A WORD FAMILY is a group of words built from the same root or base. Unrelated look-alike or rhyming words are not true word families (fall, tall, small, hall; corn, horn, morn, born; moon, spoon, noon). What relationship does "fall" have to "hall" or "tall"? How are "born" and "horn" associated? Is a "moon" a kind of "spoon"?

— The **"fall"** family includes: *falling, unfallen, waterfall, downfall, fallout, pitfall.*
— The **"moon"** family includes: *moonlight, moonless, moonbeam, moonlit, moony.*
— The **"corn"** family includes: *corncob, cornstalk, cornstarch, popcorn, corny.*

**Explore Vocabulary Building with Lessons after I-2**.

Vocabulary means "the sum of words that a particular person can use or understand." Educators should help students efficiently enlarge their stock of words. Instead of just expanding their word banks one word at a time, we teach tools that can be used over and over to help understand many words.

*The formatted Black Log adds pages for Prefixes (B36), Suffixes (B37), Homphones (B38), Heteronyms (B39), and Greek and Latin Roots (B33-35). For an answer key see www.bhibooks.net > Free Downloads.

1. EXPLAIN COMPOUND WORDS. Hold up "in" and move it down the spelling list on the board to discover one or more words that can be combined to make new compound words (input, intake). What about "out?" Move the card in front and then in back of the words (output, blowout). What about "over" (overtake)? What about "time?" Move the card down the front. See if any student will suggest that you try moving it down the back (springtime, wintertime).

2. ILLUSTRATE WORDS WITH PREFIXES OR SUFFIXES. Compound words are introduced as early as Section B, but Section I-2 is the first time we introduce prefixes and suffixes.

    a. Prefix. Hold up the card for the prefix MID-. Ask if this would be a word by itself. No, it can't stand alone. What does it mean? (in the middle) Let's see if we can add *mid-* to any of our words. Should I try the beginning or the end? (the beginning— *pre-* means before. A prefix is something that is fixed before.)

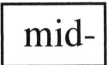

What new words can we make from this prefix?

| | | |
|---|---|---|
| midsummer | — | in the middle of the summer |
| midwinter | — | in the middle of the winter |
| midseason | — | in the middle of the season |

    b. Suffix. Hold up the card for the suffix -Y. Would this be a word by itself? No, it can't stand alone. The dash in the front shows it is a suffix, a word part that will be added to the end of a word. This suffix can mean "full of, having, small, resembling."

What new words can we make using this suffix?

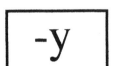

| | | |
|---|---|---|
| corny | — | full of corn, slang for trite |
| moony | — | like the moon |
| springy | — | full of springs, resembling springs |
| summery | — | like the summer |
| wintry | — | like the winter |
| stormy | — | having storms |

**Strengthen Word Understanding.**

Ownership of words comes from use. Many reinforcement activities in *Wise Guide* enlarge a student's vocabulary. Students will write original sentences using the words, select synonyms and antonyms, answer analogies, learn multiple meanings, and build derivatives.

1. WRITE ORIGINAL SENTENCES. You need to understand the meaning of a word in order to use it intelligently in a sentence. This activity is ongoing throughout the program. Avoid sentences such as: My spelling word is ___. My teacher used the word ____ today.

2. SELECT SYNONYMS AND ANTONYMS. The SAT for college entrance requires the students to work with synonyms and antonyms. Rarely is time spent in school developing this skill.

    a. Define terms.
      (1) **Synonym** comes from the Greek **syn-** meaning "together" and **onyme** meaning "name." A synonym is another way to say the same thing *(small, tiny)*.
      (2) **Antonym** comes from the Greek **anti-** meaning "opposite, against" and **onyme** meaning "name" *(good, evil)*.

    b. Note frequency of occurrence on the Wise List. Work with synonyms and antonyms appears in the following spelling Sections: A, B, E, F, K-1, L-4, L-5, L-6, N-6, N-7, O-3, P-1, Q-5, R-5, S-1, S-6, T-2, T-3, U-2, U-4, V-2, W-3, X-1, Y-2, Z-2.

3. HOMONYMS. Homophones and homographs are addressed in Step 30.

4. ANSWER ANALOGIES OR LINKING ASSOCIATED WORDS. The student will follow a train of thought and provide a corresponding answer. For example: Night is to dark as day is to ___ (light). Exercises of this type are provided in Sections:  H-1, I-1, L-2, L-5, M-4, O-4, P-6, Q-6, R-1.

5. LEARN MULTIPLE MEANINGS OF HOMOGRAPHS. Some common words have a variety of unrelated meanings. For example: **Ball** can mean "a round object" or "a party." Specific work with multiple meaning words occurs in Sections: H-2, I-4, J-3, P-1, R-5.

6. BUILD DERIVATIVES.   A derivative word can be traced back to a base word. **Derivative** comes from the Greek *de-* meaning "down from, away from" and *rivus* meaning "brook, stream." The secondary word derives its meaning from the original word like a stream that branches out away from a river. We use the meaning of the root word to understand other words that use that root.

Derivative work occurs in practically every spelling lesson, but it may be labeled in different ways in *Wise Guide:* verbs (p. 31), prefixes (p. 33), compound words (p. 37), vocabulary enrichment (p. 43), plurals (p. 44), derivatives (p. 47), suffixes (p. 58), past tense verbs (p. 71), 1-1-1 review (p. 74), degrees of comparison (p. 81), Dismiss L Rule (p. 92),  change in spelling (p. 123),  adding endings (p. 143), -LY adverbs (p. 150), subject / verb agreement (p. 185), Greek roots (p. 193),"one who" derivatives (p. 194),  Latin roots (p. 219), and change the endings to change the part of speech (p. 228).

7. WRITE DEGREES OF COMPARISON.  Instead of a mindless activity copying a word five times, we build new words using the spelling word.  Students can complete degrees of comparison.

| **thick** | **old** | **cold** | **long** | **wild** |
|---|---|---|---|---|
| thicker | older | colder | longer | wilder |
| thickest | oldest | coldest | longest | wildest |

Degrees of comparison activities occur in Sections I-4, J-5, L-6, N-6, P-5, and R-3. The usual pattern for showing a gradual change in meaning is to simply add  *-er* and *-est*.  One exception is *good, better, best*.  Also the word *far* needs some special attention (*far, farther, farthest*).   In longer words, instead of changing the base word itself, we just add the adverbs *more, most, less, least.  More* and *most* show improvement (*more comfortable, most comfortable*). *Less* and *least* show decreasing value (*less comfortable, least comfortable*).

**Learn the Foundation for Building Many Words**.

Ninety percent of the lessons in the Wise List have some type of derivative activity.  The Wise List has 2000 spelling words. Words built from reinforcement activities more than double the base list to make 4500 words directly taught in *The Wise Guide*.  When we apply the principles taught in this program we can multiply many times over the value of the original list. For example, the word **"act"** taught in Section N-1 is foundational to at least eighty-five other words.

> *Good, better, best*
> *We will never rest*
> *'Til our good is better*
> *And our better best.*
>
> — author unknown

1. BUILD MANY WORDS FROM ONE.  A simple word like **act,** meaning "anything done, being done, or to be done," can be enlarged to many words with the help of eighteen suffixes (-able, -ant, -ary, -ate, -ed, -ess, -ing, -ion, -ism, -ist, -ity, -ive, -ly, -ment, -ness, -or, -s) and/or six prefixes (counter-, in-, en-, inter-, re-, trans-). A three-letter word plus twenty-four common word parts can be combined to produce at least eighty-five other words.  Amazing!

a. Add prefixes to ACT: *counteract, enact, interact, overact, react, transact.*

b. Add suffixes to ACT: *acted, acting, action, activate, activated, activating, activation, activator, active, actively, activeness, activism, activities, activist, activity, actor, acts.*  The word *actress* is made with the addition of an R (*act+ r + ess*).

c. Add prefixes and suffixes to ACT:

| | | |
|---|---|---|
| *counter-* | + *act* + | *-ed, -ing, -ion, -ive, -ively, -s* |
| *en-* | + *act* + | *-able, -ed, -ing, -ive, -ment, -or, -ory, -s* |
| *in-* | + *act* + | *-ion, -ivate, -ivated, -ivating, -ivation, -ive, -ively, -ivity* |
| *inter-* | + *act* + | *-ant,-ed, -ing, -ion, -ional, -ive, -ively, -s* |
| *over-* | + *act* + | *-ed, -ing, -ive, -iveness, -ivity, -s* |
| *re-* | + *act* + | *-ance, -ant, -ed, -ing, -ion, ionaries, -ionary, -ionist, -ivate, -ivated, -ivating, -ive, -ively, -iveness, -ivity, -or, -s* |
| *trans-* | + *act* + | *-ed, -ing, -ion, -ional, -or, -s* |

> ## *act*
> **+ affixes**
>
> **= 82 words**

Knowing the meaning of the prefixes helps determine the  meaning of the derivative.

| prefix | meaning | derivative build with prefix + act | |
|---|---|---|---|
| counter- | against, opposite | counter**act** | to **act** against |
| en- | to cause to be | en**act** | causing to be an **act** |
| in- | lacking, not | in**act**ion | lacking **act**ion |
| inter- | between, among | inter**act** | to **act** on each other |
| over- | to excess | over**act** | to **act** to excess |
| re- | back, again | re**act** | to **act** back in opposition |
| trans- | across | trans**act** | to **act** across |

Suffixes help determine the meaning or the function of a word in the sentence.  For example: *nation* (noun), *national* (adjective), *nationally* (adverb) and *nationalize* (verb).

| suffix | meaning or function | derivative built with act + suffix | |
|---|---|---|---|
| **-able** | able to (adjective) | en**act**able | able to be enacted |
| **-ant** | a person or thing that | inter**act**ant | that which acts upon |
| **-ary** | related to (adj. or noun) | re**act**ionary | one who reacts |
| **-ate** | cause, makes (verb) | **act**ivate | make active -<u>Activate</u> the bomb. |
| **-ed** | past tense (verb) | **act**ed | *She <u>acted</u> yesterday.* |
| -ess | feminine(noun) | **act**ress | *The <u>actress</u> forgot her line.* |
| **-ing** | present participle (verb) | **act**ing | *<u>Acting</u> is a challenging job.* |
| **-ion** | process or outcome of (noun) | **act**ion | process of acting, deed |
| **-ism** | practice or result of (noun) | **act**ivism | practice of vigorous action |
| **-ist** | one who does (noun) | **act**ivist | one involved in activism |
| **-ity** | the state of (noun) | **act**ivity | *Swimming is a favorite <u>activity.</u>* |
| **-ive** | (adjective) | **act**ive | *The <u>active</u> boy fell.* |
| **-ly** | (adverb) | **act**ively | active like —*He <u>actively</u> played.* |
| **-ment** | means, action, state (noun) | reen**act**ment | *I saw the civil war <u>reenactment</u>.* |
| **-ness** | state of (noun) | **act**iveness | *His <u>activeness</u> annoyed me.* |
| **-or** | one who (noun) | **act**or | one who acts in plays |
| **-s** | plural form of noun, present singular verb | **act**s | *The play had two <u>acts</u>.* (n.) <br> *The boy <u>acts</u> strange.* (v.) |

2. LEARN  GREEK AND LATIN ROOTS.  Many foreign root words form the base to English words. Individual words using Greek and Latin roots occur in almost all sections after N-4 and as reinforcement activities in Sections P-4, S-2, T-2, V-3, W-1, W-2, W-3, X-2, Y-1, and Z-2.

Teachers can increase student exposure to foreign roots. Jeannean Kintner, one of our endorsed trainers, teaches in a Christian school that introduces ten Greek and Latin roots in kindergarten. Every year they add ten more and review all roots introduced previously.  By fourth grade they have exposed their students to fifty foreign roots.

<u>Illustrate Greek and Latin Roots</u>. "Ject" in English words is derived from the Latin word "jactum" which means "to throw." Combine various prefixes + *ject* to determine word meanings. Introduce the idea with words not in *Wise Guide* like: *deject, eject, inject,* and *interject*. Collect additional *-ject* words as well as *-fer* (bring, carry) and *-mit* (send) words on preformatted Black Log B34. Print a new formatted Black Log Answer Key as a free download at www.bhibooks.net.

| | | | | |
|---|---|---|---|---|
| **de-** | (down) | **deject** | (throw down) | |
| **e-, ex-** | (out) | **eject** | (throw out) | |
| **in-** | (in, into) | **inject** | (throw into) | |
| **inter-** | (between) | **interject** | (throw between) | |
| **sub-** | (under) | **subject** | (throw under) | N-4 |
| **ob-** | (against) | **object, objection** | (throw against) | O-1, R-5 |
| **pro-** | (before) | **project** | (throw before, throw forward) | O-5 |
| **re-** | (back) | **reject** | (throw back) | O-5 |

<u>Illustrate Greek and Latin Numbers</u>. Number words are taught in *Wise Guide* (see section in parentheses). Explore these **advanced** ideas more deeply in the formatted Black Log: B16, B33.

| | | |
|---|---|---|
| **ONE** | *mono-*<br><br>*uni-* | *mono*tone (K-2), monotonous (W-3), *mono*syllable (Y-2), monolith, monopoly, monologue, monarch<br>union (S-2), universal (T-1), unanimous, unicorn, unicycle, uniform, unilateral, unique, unison, unite, universe, university |
| **TWO** | *di-*<br>*bi-* | division (T-2), dilemma, dichotomy, dichromatic<br>*bi*monthly (M-5), *bi*centennial (S-2), bicycle (W-3), biceps, bicuspid, bilateral, biped, bipartisan, bisect, billion, binoculars, biplane, bifocal |
| **THREE** | *tri-* | *tri*monthly (M-5) *tri*centennial (S-2), triangle (W-3), triad, triple, trio, trillion, tricycle, trifocal, trinity, trilogy, triplet, tripod, triceps, triune |
| **FOUR** | *tetra-*<br>*quart-* | tetrameter, tetragon<br>quart (N-8), quarter (O-3), quarterly, quartet, quatrain, quadrant |
| **FIVE** | *penta-*<br>*quint-* | pentagon, pentangular, Pentateuch (first 5 books of Bible)<br>quintuplet, quintet |
| **SIX** | *hexa-*<br>*sext-* | hexagon, hexameter<br>sextet, sextuplet |
| **SEVEN** | *hepta-*<br>*sept-* | heptagon<br>September (seventh month of the Roman calendar), septuagenarian |
| **EIGHT** | *octa-*<br>*octo-* | octagon, octagenarian, octave<br>October (eighth month of the Roman calendar), octopus |
| **NINE** | *nona-*<br>*novem-* | nonagon<br>November (ninth month of the Roman calendar), novena |
| **TEN** | *deca-*<br>*dec-* | Decalogue (Ten Commandments), decade, decathlon, decasyllable<br>decimal (P-4), December (10th month of Roman calendar) |
| **HUNDRED** | *hecto-*<br>*cent-* | hectogram<br>cent (K-2), century (S-2), centennial (S-2), centimeter, centigrade (S-2) |
| **THOUSAND** | *kilo-*<br>*milli-* | kilometer (Y-1), kilogram, kilowatt, kiloliter<br>million (S-3), millionaire, millennium (X-2), millipede, milligram |

## 25. COLLECT ABBREVIATIONS. (Before I-3)

"Teacher, what does one'st st mean?"

Objective:

To teach and illustrate abbreviations.
To collect abbreviations of spelling words.

Prepare to Teach:

Have ready to use Spelling Rule Card 12.
Preview Appendix C (B25).

Write the initials of your name (eg. W.K.S.) and/or abbreviations of words taught recently. Ask students to read the abbreviations you have written. For some this may be the first introduction to the idea of abbreviations. Hold up the spelling rule card and teach the rule, having the students repeat after you. **Abbreviations use a few letters to represent a larger word.** An oddity of English is that the term meaning "a short representation of a word" is a five-syllable, twelve-letter word. A big word is representing a small thing.

From here on out, at any given year you may want to teach abbreviations for spelling words up to the place where you are currently teaching. Add more as you go. We use many other abbreviations in English including the days of the week, the months of the year, the states, the books of the Bible, and the basic parts of speech.

| Abbreviations | | | | | | | | |
|---|---|---|---|---|---|---|---|---|
| (49) | @ | = | at | | (797) | no. | = | number |
| (67) | St. | = | Street, Saint | | (859) | mkt. | = | market |
| (157) | yr. | = | year | | (874) | doz. | = | dozen |
| (172) | yd. | = | yard | | (911) | Ct. | = | Court |
| (194/226) | ft. | = | foot, feet | | (934) | qt. | = | quart |
| (219) | ea. | = | each | | (944) | capt. | = | captain |
| (231) | Mr. | = | Mister | | (969) | sec. | = | second |
| (238) | W | = | west | | (981) | N | = | north |
| (266) | w/ | = | with | | (982) | S | = | south |
| (326) | gal. | = | gallon | | (1048) | co. | = | company |
| (335) | in. | = | inch | | (1111) | Mrs. | = | Mistress |
| (344) | E | = | east | | (1135) | amt. | = | amount |
| (373) | lg. | = | large | | (1261) | pres. | = | president |
| (390) | w/o | = | without | | (1368) | sq. | = | square |
| (404) | hr. | = | hour | | (1437) | Ave. | = | Avenue |
| (412/804) | Dr. | = | Drive, Doctor | | (1463) | cm | = | centimeter |
| (453) | 1st | = | first | | (1469) | gov't | = | government |
| (482) | lb. | = | pound* | | (1504) | Is. | = | Island |
| (489) | bro. | = | brother | | (1522) | sgt. | = | sergeant |
| (496) | wk. | = | week | | (1593) | min. | = | minute |
| (513) | mi. | = | mile | | (1597) | TV | = | television |
| | mph | = | miles per hour | | (1616) | vol. | = | volume |
| (532) | Rd. | = | Road | | (1695) | ht. | = | height |
| (663) | pd. | = | paid | | (1705) | atty. | = | attorney |
| (672) | acct. | = | account | | (1766) | assoc. | = | association |
| (714) | mts. | = | mountains | | (1801) | wt. | = | weight |
| (726) | mo. | = | month | | (1973) | misc. | = | miscellaneous |

* [< L. libra pondo (pound by weight)]

## 26.  __START ER PAGE__. (Before J-1)

<u>Objectives</u>:

     To illustrate the five spellings of ER.

     To collect ER words for our reference page in the Learning Log.

<u>Prepare to Teach</u>:

     Separate out the five /er/ phonogram cards.

     Start building the ER page in your teacher's edition of the Log.

     Plan to spend an entire lesson introducing this concept initially. You will review and add to the reference page as you continue in the program.

     Preview a completed page at the end of a sample year in Appendix C (P4/ B5).

**Explain Why We Need a Reference Page for ER Words.**

| er | ur | ir | wor | ear |
|----|----|----|-----|-----|

|  | In a core list of 20,000 words |
|--|--------------------------------|
| er | 2063 times |
| ur | 247 times |
| ir | 114 times |
| wor | 51 times |
| ear | 31 times |

Hold up the five /er/ phonogram cards. We use the ER phonogram the most. In *The ABC's and All Their Tricks* Margaret Bishop analyzed 20,000 words. Not counting words that use ER as a suffix meaning "one who" (farm + er), the ER spelling occurs over five times as often as all the others put together. Each remaining ER's occurs about twice as often as the one after it.

How do we spell /s-er/? Write possible spellings on the board: ser, sir, sur, sear. How do we know which phonogram to use in the following sentence? *Serve sirloin* as a *surprise* to the *worried search* party. We cannot tell which /er/ to use by hearing alone. More words will use ER because that is the most common, but no rule governs when to use what. We must memorize the standard form acceptable for each word.

Why do we have so many ways to write the same sound? The spelling often traces back to the origin of the word, but not always.

| ser- | *serve* |
|------|---------|
| sir- | *sirloin* |
| sur- | *surprise* |
| wor- | *worried* |
| sear- | *search* |

| | | |
|---|---|---|
| **serve** | Middle English | *servus* (slave) |
| **surprise** | Old French | *sur* (over) + *prendre* (take) |

**Log ER Words onto the ER Page.**

Students past Spelling Section J-1 can start building the ER Reference Page when spelling words in the Wise List include one of the ER'S *(ur, ir, wor, ear)*. These words will be flagged in *Wise Guide* with a note, "Add to the ER Page." Provided there is still room in that column, add the word.

A guide sentence at the top of the reference page will help us remember the different spellings of ER. We recommend the sentence: ***Her church first worships early***. Some teach in a setting that censors any reference, however vague, to Christianity. Those teachers can substitute the sentence: ***Winter hurts birds' worm search***.

Word examples for the ER Page are taken from the Wise List. A first grade student and a fourth grade student will both construct an ER Page but the word examples may vary according to where the student is in the *Wise Guide*. Add ER words to the Reference Page as they occur in regular spelling work. Some teachers make a standard teacher's master Primary Learning Log and Black Learning Log but use Post-it ® notes to track words as they are added to the student's books that year.

    1. ADD BEGINNER WORDS TO A PRIMARY LEARNING LOG. After teaching Wise List J-1, dictate into the first column of the ER Page all the ER words learned to date. With red, underline the ER's and with regular pencil add all other spelling markings. See the sample on the facing page.

| Her o v**er** 2 moth **er** 2 oth **er** pa p**er** af t**er** sum m**er** win t**er** riv **er** din n**er** let t**er** | church | f**ir**st | w**or** ships | **ear** ly. |
|---|---|---|---|---|
| | | Introducing the ER Page for students at J-1 | | |

So far we have used only one /er/ in the Wise List. These are the most common. Now we'll start collecting examples of the others. After each new spelling lesson, we will try to add words to our ER Page. Sometimes we will find ER words in our other work as well. After J-1 add: *every, word, girl, never, under.* Since the "ER of HER" words are so common, after we fill up the first column we won't worry about adding any more of them. We're mainly looking for the more rare ERs.

| Five Spellings of /er/ | | | | |
|---|---|---|---|---|
| er | ur | ir | wor | ear |
| Her | church | first | wor ships | ear ly. |
| o ver | spur | girl | word | earth |
| moth er | hurt | third | work | earn. |
| oth er | burn | thirst | worms | world |
| pa per | turn | sir | | |
| af ter | purse | third | | |
| sum mer. | curl | birth day | | |
| win ter | | | | |
| riv er | | | | |
| din ner | | | | |
| let ter | | | | |
| every | | | | |
| nev er | | | | |
| un der | | | | |
| word | | | | |

**Sample Primary Learning Log Reference Page after teaching through all of Section L**

Note: *purse* and *curl* are not in the Wise List. These illustrate words added from outside work.

2. ADJUST THE **ER PAGE** FOR BLACK LOG USERS. The example words on this page will reflect the spelling level of the students. Select some review words from an easier level and then load additional examples from the list as they occur. It is not necessary to begin the ER Page in the black log until a new /er/ word other than *the /er/ of her* shows up in the Wise List. Watch for a reminder in *Wise Guide* as to when to begin or add words to this reference page. A suggestion in the preliminaries may say, "If you have not done so already this year, teach the ER Page." A sidenote to new words with an /er/ may say, "Add to the ER page." It is generally less confusing if you wait until all new words have been dictated for the day before plugging new examples onto reference pages.

If you begin the year at Section N, the first /er/ reference (nor counting the /er/ of her words) is *pearl*. After teaching N-3 words, dictate the ER guide sentence and then dictate selected ER, UR, and IR review words. See page 138-140 of this book for all the ER words in the Wise List organized by section and word number. Next dictate all of the WOR and EAR words taught previously in the program along with some of their derivatives. Personalize the page. Add words that a student misspells in other student work or other personally relevant words. Perhaps a friend is named *Bert* or *Katura*. Maybe you live in *New Jersey*, *Vermont*, or *Virginia* or plan to cook *turkey* for Thanksgiving.

Continue adding ER words as they come up during the year. When you run out of space for the /er/ of her words, discontinue adding to that column. These words are "a dime a dozen." On our reference pages we mainly collect the more scarce spellings, the ones that need special attention. In the first column, ignore the red guideline. With red underline each /er/.

| Her | church | first | wor | ships | ear | ly |
|-----|--------|-------|-----|-------|-----|-----|
| re cov er | pur ple | girl | word | | earth | |
| thun der | re turn | bird | work | | earn | |
| fin ger | fur nish | thirst | team | work | heard | |
| mem ber | hur dle | sir | han di | work | learn | |
| num ber | bur i al | third | worm | | pearl | |
| per son | curb | birth day | world | | | |
| teach er | hur ry | swirl | | | | |
| of fer | tur key | dirt | | | | |
| mat ter | | | | | | |
| en er gy | | | | | | |
| leath er | | | | | | |
| oys ter | | | | | | |
| con quer | | | | | | |
| cen ter | | | | | | |
| suf fer | | | | | | |
| yes ter day | | | | | | |
| won der | | | | | | |

**Sample Black Learning Log Reference Page (after teaching Section N)**

3. INTRODUCE OUR and YR as advanced phonograms. See Section Q in *Wise Guide* p. 157 as well as Section Y on p. 233. Add *adjourns* to the final column of the ER Page making the guide sentence say, *Her church first worships early and adjourns.* If you used the alternate sentence add *journey* making the sentence read: *Winter hurts birds' worm search journey.*

**Provide Additional ER Exercises.**

1. QUIZ. On loose-leaf paper or on the board label 5 columns: *er, ur, ir, wor, ear.* Call out an ER word, and have student add it to the correct column.

2. RACE FOR THE ER CARD. Spread the ER cards on a table. If you have a magnetic surface, mount them with a magnetic backing. Divide the class into two competing lines. Call out a word with an ER and have the front student in each line race to collect the correct ER card.

3. RECONSTRUCT PAGE FROM MEMORY. Have the student write as many examples of words for each /ER/ column as he can think of in a given time.

4. ANNOUNCE A SENTENCE CONTEST. Ask students to write sentences using as many /ER/ words as possible. Give 1 point for each /er/, 2 for /ur/, 3 for /ir/, 4 for /wor/, and 5 for /ear/. Grant five bonus points for including all /ers/ in one logical sentence and ten for listing them in frequency order.

5. DICTATE ER WORD SENTENCES. The teacher can dictate one or more of the following sentences any time after the Section listed below.

Section        Sentences Using the Basic ER Words

L        Winter hurts the birds' worm yearnings.
         Supper spurs a girl's work on earth.
         Never burn with a thirst for the world's earnings.

N        Father curbs dirty words earnestly.
         Order the purple swirl with handiwork pearls.

O        Sister burped thirsty worried earthling.
         Every turn, sir, you worry about what you learn.
         Offer burial for short skirts unworthy of yearnings.
         Conquering hurdles, sir, is worth learning.
         The river hurdles confirmed worthless earthworks.
         A perfect undisturbed birthday is worth pearls.

P        The clerk furnishes the girl's worthless hearse.
         After she returns, swirl around the worse hearse.

*Winter hurts birds' worm search journey.*

Q        Sister's surprise birth worried Earl.
         Nervous disturbing squirming worsens learning.
         Yesterday hurt firm's network earnings.
         Tenderly turn the skirt with handworked pearls.
         Passenger curbs dirty words earnestly and courageously.
         The teacher surprisingly confirms, "All the words are learned."

R        Better purposes stir worthwhile yearnings and journaling.
         Laughter blurs thirsty, overworked researchers.
         Paul's letter on the resurrection stirred a worthy search.
         Soldier returned from third world and heard encouragement.

T        Never burglarize confirmed workers' earnings.
         Government burned dirty worthless earthenware.
         Lawyer urges virtue worth learning.
         Teacher returns circled handiwork from earlier journals.

U        Writer reimburses girl's work earnings.
         Herds survive first worldwide earthquake.
         Daughter nurtures virtue worth rehearsing courteously.
         Emperor hurries third work rehearsal.

Y        Superintendent's church affirmed worship and heard martyr's journal.
         After surviving, the girl works yearningly for the courage of martyrs.

Z        A customer purchased a virtual world of pearly nourishing myrrh.

**Refer to the ER Word Index**

The /ER/ words taught in the Wise List are indexed by type, spelling section, and word order. Some derivatives from the spelling enrichment activities have been added.

| /er/ | Section | Base Words and Derivatives Identified by Word Number | | | |
|------|---------|-----|-----|-----|-----|

**ER**

| | J | never (275) | under (279) | cover (299) | |
| | | perch (303) | sisters (331) | supper (336) | |
| | K | better (405) | danger (474) | afternoon (486) | |
| | | brother (489) | herd (506) | water (511) | |
| | L | power (531) | were (584) | butcher (587) | flower (598) |
| | | another (607) | feather (610) | herself (614) | order (622) |
| | | ever (624) | however (625) | silver (632) | father (637) |
| | M | recover (685) | thunder (719) | finger (751) | member (760) |
| | N | number (797) | person (801) | teacher (805) | offer (813) |
| | | matter (826) | energy (836) | leather (838) | oyster (840) |
| | | conquer (851) | center (854) | suffer (857) | |
| | | yesterday (880) | wonder (905) | | |
| | O | weather (968) | farther (991) | quarter (993) | perfect (1010) |
| | | personal (1012) | liberty (1045) | rather (1053) | |
| | | everything (1059) | | | |
| | P | pattern (1095) | laughter (1100) | verb (1115) | several (1124) |
| | | caterpillar (1138) | newspaper (1139) | passenger (1162) | |
| | | daughter (1166) | clerk (1170) | answer (1173) | whisper (1180) |
| | Q | term, midterm (1219) | wonderful (1226) | murder (1234) | |
| | | property (1240) | tender (1243) | tenderhearted | tenderly |
| | | exercise (1254) | either (1267) | remember (1274) | |
| | | serve (1287) | nerve (1298) | perhaps (1320) | |
| | R | lawyer (1349) | prisoner (1350) | eternity (1357) | general (1367) |
| | | different (1388) | together (1394) | consider (1396) | |
| | | entertain (1402) | prefer (1406) | soldier (1410) | service (1415) |
| | | poverty (1425) | disaster (1435) | | |
| | S | certain (1449) | fertile (1456) | centimeter (1463) | |
| | | government (1469) | theater (1472) | concert (1494) | |
| | | temperature (1506) | difference (1508) | grocery (1516) | |
| | | celery (1519) | handkerchief (1547) | neither (1550) | |
| | T | universal (1575) | conversation (1611) | discovery (1619) | |
| | | whether (1621) | concern (1626) | altogether (1632) | |
| | | confer (1644) | refer (1646) | conference (1654) | |
| | U | conserve (1661) | kernels (1678) | emperor (1703) | |
| | | customer (1706) | interfere (1739) | interference (1740) | |
| | | reverence (1743) | consideration (1756) | | |

| V-Z | artillery | (1775) | berth | (1777) | superstition | (1780) |
|---|---|---|---|---|---|---|
| | reference | (1798) | heifer | (1825) | anniversary | (1831) |
| | emergency | (1833) | treachery | (1834) | controversy | (1840) |
| | character | (1852) | persevere | (1857) | sovereign | (1871) |
| | transmitter | (1879) | counterfeit | (1884) | perceive | (1887) |
| | superintendent | (1902) | alliteration | (1906) | persistence | (1934) |
| | kilometer | (1935) | kindergarten | (1940) | discern | (1961) |
| | rhinoceros | (1982) | maneuver | (1985) | | |

**UR**

| | | | | | | |
|---|---|---|---|---|---|---|
| J | spur | (339) | furniture | | | |
| K | hurt | (430) | burn | (439) | | |
| L | **church** | (534) | churchyard | | | |
| | turn | (571) | turnout | | turnover | |
| M | purple | (644) | return | (686) | furnish | (762) |
| | hurdle | (771) | | | | |
| N | burial | (834) | curb | (841) | hurry | (850) |
| O | surface | (987) | curtain | (1049) | resurrection | (1051) |
| P | blur | (1104) | nurse | (1163) | | |
| Q | murder | (1234) | surprise | (1302) | | |
| R | purpose | (1387) | | | | |
| S | purchase | (1533) | further | (1551) | furthermore | |
| T | burglar | (1612) | | | | |
| U | survive | (1662) | survival | | surviving | |
| V-Z | surgeon | (1770) | occurrence | (1963) | surveillance | (1991) |

UR words not in the Wise List:

| | | | | |
|---|---|---|---|---|
| blurt | burden | burp | churn | concurred |
| current | curl | curdle | curse | disturb |
| extracurricula | flurry | fur | imperturable | lurk |
| precursor | purge | purse | Saturday | Saturn |
| slurp | scurrious | spurn | suburb | surplus |
| Thursday | turkey | turtle | urchin | urge |

**IR**

| | | | | | | |
|---|---|---|---|---|---|---|
| J | girl | (274) | bird | (333) | | |
| K | **first** | (453) | thirst | (477) | sir | (514) |
| L | third | (621) | birth | | birthday | (631) |
| M | swirl | (681) | | | | |
| N | dirt | (849) | dirty | | | |
| O | confirm | (989) | skirt | (1025) | stir | (1058) |
| Q | firm | (1247) | firmest | | affirm | |
| | thirteen | (1264) | circus | (1266) | | |
| R | virtue | (1392) | virtuous | | virtual | |
| T | circular | (1577) | circle | (1589) | circulate | |
| U | circumference | (1663) | circumstance | (1664) | | |

IR words not in the Wise List:

| | | | | |
|---|---|---|---|---|
| birch | chirp | circuit | circumloction | circumspect |
| circumvent | dirge | fir | firmament | flirt |
| girdle | infirmity | mirth | shirt | skirmish |
| smirk | squirrel | squirm | squirt | thirteen |
| thirsty | thirty | twirl | virgin | whirl |

### WOR

| | | | | |
|---|---|---|---|---|
| J | word | (272) | work | (372) |
| L | worms | (619) | world | (638) |
| O | worry | (999) | worth | (1001) |
| T | **worship** | (1580) | worshipful | |

WOR word derivatives not in the Wise List:

| | | |
|---|---|---|
| bookworm | crossword | fireworks |
| handiwork | network | overwork |
| silkworm | teamwork | workable |
| workshop | underworld | unworthy |
| worse | worsen | worshiping |
| worst | worthless | worthwhile |

Note:  At least four words use WOR without being ER words: sword, wore, worn, sworn.  We do not call these words rule-breakers.  Our rule prepares us for this.  "OR usually says /er/ when W comes before O-R" [R. 8].

### EAR

| | | | | |
|---|---|---|---|---|
| K | earth | (462) | | |
| L | earn | (606) | **early** | (629) |
| M | heard | (668) | learn | (740) |
| N | pearl | (827) | | |
| P | hearse | (1140) | | |
| R | search | (1393) | | |
| U | earliest | (1665) | rehearse (1666) | rehearsal |

EAR words not in the Wise List:

| | | |
|---|---|---|
| dearth | earl | earlier |
| earldom | earnings | earthenware |
| earthworm | earnest | earnestly |
| earnestness | earthquake | overheard |
| research | searchlight | unearthly |
| unlearned | yearn | yearning |

## ADVANCED PHONOGRAMS FOR /ER/

### OUR

| | | | | |
|---|---|---|---|---|
| Q | journal (1291) | courage (1295) | courageous | |
| U | **adjourn** (1667) | journey (1711) | courtesy (1751) | |

OUR words not in the Wise List:

| | | | |
|---|---|---|---|
| discourtesy | discourage | encourage | flourish |
| glamour | journalist | journalism | nourish |
| nourishing | nourishment | | |

### YR

| | | |
|---|---|---|
| V-Z | martyr (1949) | martyrdom |

YR words not in the Wise List:

| | | | |
|---|---|---|---|
| myrrh | myrtle | zephyr | satyr |

## 27. <u>DICTATE PLURALS PAGE</u>. (Before Section J-4)

one child

two children

<u>Objectives</u>:

To review the meaning of noun.
To show ways that words can be made plural.
To build a plural reference page. See Appendix C (P11/ B14).

<u>Prepare to Teach</u>:

Have available spelling rule card #22.
Plan to spend an entire lesson introducing this concept.
Build your teacher's edition of the log.
Do not use regular spelling markings on this page.
With red write the letters that cause the change to -es.

**Teach the Plural Rule Page**.

Teach the rule: *To make a noun plural, just add an -S, UNLESS the word hisses, changes, or may end with O. In these cases add -ES. Occasional words have no change, an internal change, or a foreign spelling.* Select review words that illustrate each part of the rule as you initiate the Plural Page. Add additional sample words later as space permits.

**Explain the Words and Phrases in the Plural Rule.**

1. TO MAKE A NOUN PLURAL. What is a noun? A noun names a person, place, thing, or idea. Illustrate with review words. For example, in J-1, have students find two or more words that could be used to name a person: *son, daddy, girl, lord.*

In J-2 any two or more words that could name a place: *arm, ship, sun.*

In J-3 identify any two or more words that could name a thing or an idea: *race, perch, bill.*

Do not become overly concerned if one thinks that *arm* is a place and someone else calls it a thing. Both can be right. (He broke his arm — thing; A wasp is on her arm — place.) The important thing is recognizing nouns as naming words.

Some words can be different parts of speech depending on the use in a sentence. If you *saw* me, "saw" is a verb. It shows action. If you cut wood with a *saw,* "saw" is a noun. It names a thing. Two hints help us identify a noun.

a. **Number.** Most nouns can be singular or plural (foot/feet). Collective nouns never change.
b. **Noun indicators**. The articles *a, an, the* indicate a noun will follow (a boy, an ostrich).

2. JUST ADD AN -S. The most common way to make a noun plural is by just adding an -S. Many words can fit into this category: sons, banks, girls, arms. If you want some challenge words try: boys (not a single vowel Y), gulfs (the F sound doesn't change), stomachs (the CH says /k/ and doesn't hiss), horses (the S hisses but is already closed by an E. We just add -s.)

3 UNLESS THE WORD ENDING HISSES. Words that end with *s, sh, x, z, and sometimes ch,* may hiss. Sample words for each are listed below by Section. With red write the letter(s) that hiss.

| | | | |
|---|---|---|---|
| CH -- | rich (I-4) | perch (J-3) | inch (J-4) | church (L-1) |
| | watch (L-3) | march (L-3) | pitch (M-3) | match (P-1) |
| | branch (Q-2) | speech (T-1) | approach (U-3) | wrench |
| S -- | class (K-6) | glass (K-6) | cross (N-1) | press (N-2) |
| | address (O-1) | toss (Q-3) | recess (S-4) | canvas (S-4) |
| | witness (S-6) | business (T-3) | process (T-3) | chorus (T-3) |
| | guess (T-5) | apparatus (U-3) | | |

SH -- fi**sh** (B)        wa**sh** (E)        fini**sh** (K-3)    da**sh** (L-1)    pu**sh** (L-2)    wi**sh** (L-3)
X --  si**x** (A)         bo**x** (G)         fi**x** (M-3)       ta**x** (N-1)     prefi**x** (R-2)  wa**x**
Z --  qui**z** (R-5)      bu**zz**            walt**z**

4. CHANGES:  This includes nouns where a Y changes to an I or an F changes to a V.

   a. Y to I — English words do not end with I; we substitute a Y.  When other letters are added to the end, the stand-in Y is no longer needed.  On the reference page, write the Y and I with red to clearly show the action between the two.  When sounding out the plural form of the word, at the point of substitution, say, "Change! With red write I.  With regular pencil add E-S."  Example:  baby —> bab**i**es (E).   An expansion of this concept is taught in Step 34.

   b. F to V — The only difference between F and V is that /f/ is unvoiced (motor off) and /v/ is voiced (motor on).  We often end words with a /f/ sound.  In some instances when we add an ending, we change to the voiced version *(elf/elves)*.  In other cases, we retain the unvoiced sound and spelling *(beliefs, briefs, chiefs, cliffs, dwarfs, proofs, puffs, roofs)*.

On the reference page when sounding out the plural form, at the point of substitution,  say, "Change! With red write V. Go back to regular pencil and add E-S." Example: *life —> lives*.

   Other examples include:
*wife/ wives (K-6)      loaf/ loaves (K-6)      knife/ knives (K-6)      half/ halves (L-1)*
*leaf/ leaves (L-5)     thief/ thieves (O-1)    self/ selves (Q-2)       calf/ calves (Q-2)*
*shelf/ shelves (R-2)   wharf/ wharves          wolf/ wolves*

5. OR MAY END WITH O:  *vetoes*.  With red write the O.

   Words that end with O are the most unstable.  They **may or may not** take -es.  Foreign words that end with O like  *kimono, kangaroo* take -s. Some words have an acceptable spelling either with -es or -s. Teach that we MAY need -es after O, but not necessarily. We need to memorize when to use which.

O + -es  examples include:

| | |
|---|---|
| *heroes (K-6)* | *dominoes* |
| *zeroes (K-7)* | *embargoes* |
| *echoes (R-2)* | *innuendoes* |
| *tomatoes (R-2)* | *potatoes* |
| *mosquitoes (V-1)* | *tornadoes* |
| *buffaloes* | *torpedoes* |
| *cargoes* | *vetoes* |

**Plural Page**
**Primary Learning Log.**
**Teach at least**
**the first 2 columns**
**before teaching**
**Section J-4.**

**Bold represents**
**work in red.**

| To Make a Word Plural Just . . . | | |
|---|---|---|
| Add an -S | UNLESS the word ending. . . | |
| | *hisses | *changes |
| *bones* | *riches* | *baby → babies* |
| *banks* | *kisses* | → |
| *girls* | *dishes* | → |
| *arms* | *boxes* | *life → lives* |
| | *buzzes* | → |
| | | → |
| | *Just ends with O | |
| | *vetoes* | |
| | Occasional words have . . | |

| No change . . . | an internal change. . . | a foreign spelling |
|---|---|---|
| *dust dust* | *man – men* | *solos* |

6. OCCASIONAL WORDS HAVE NO CHANGE:  dust/ dust (J-3).

This includes no count nouns (dust/dust), words that always look singular (I caught one *fish*. I caught two *fish*.), and words that always look plural *(pants)*. Other examples: *perch (J-3), rain (K-5), clothes (L-1), furniture, (M-7), police, (O-1), sheep (R-2), celery (S-4), salmon, gallows (S-4), scissors (T-3), artillery (V-1), spaghetti (V-1)*.

7. AN INTERNAL CHANGE:  man/ men (D/H-2).

Other examples: *foot/feet (I-1/I-3); goose/geese (K-6); woman/women (N-2); tooth/teeth (R-1/S-6); mouse/mice (R-2/Q-4); louse/lice.* Should we say *house/hice?* Of course not, but I bet I got your attention.

8. A FOREIGN SPELLING: solo/ solos.

Musical terms ending with O are usually Italian and will just add -S *(pianos, altos, sopranos, cellos, trios, banjos, concertos)*. The only music some play is **radios** (R-2), **stereos,** or **videos** (R-2). We can listen while we sit on **patios** or visit **studios**.

Only two of the foreign plural words in the chart below are included in *WISE Guide*: Old English plural *children (M-4)*, and Greek *parenthesis (Y-1)*.

| | singular | change | foreign plural | alternative plural |
|---|---|---|---|---|
| **A D V A N C E D** | antenna<br>vertebra | a —> ae | antennae (insects)<br>vertebrae | antennas (TV)<br>vertebras |
| | cherub | b —> bim | cherubim | cherubs |
| | chateau | eau —> eaux | chateaux | chateaus |
| | ox<br>child<br>brother | + en | oxen<br>children<br>brethren | brothers |
| | analysis<br>crisis<br>parenthesis<br>thesis<br>hypothesis | is —> es | analyses<br>crises<br>parentheses<br>theses<br>hypotheses | |
| | appendix<br>index<br>matrix | ix —> ices | appendices (book)<br>indices (algebra)<br>matrices | appendixes (organ/ book)<br>indexes (books)<br>matrixes |
| | criterion<br>phenomenon<br>agendum<br>curriculum<br>datum<br>memorandum<br>stadium<br>medium | on —> a<br><br>um —> a | criteria<br>phenomena<br>agenda<br>curricula<br>data<br>memoranda<br>stadia<br>media | agendas<br>curriculums<br><br>memos, memorandums<br>stadiums<br>mediums |
| | alumnus (male)<br>crocus<br>focus<br>radius | us —> i | alumni<br>croci<br>foci<br>radii | alums<br>crocuses<br>focuses<br>radiuses |

## Reinforce Plurals.

Spelling Enrichment assignments involving plurals can be found in Sections:  J-6; K-6; N-3; O-6; P-7; Q-2; R-2; S-4; T-3; U-3; V-1; X-2.

## 28. COLLECT CONTRACTIONS. (After J-5)

Objectives:
      To introduce the most commonly used contractions.
      To build a contractions reference page. See Appendix C (B21).

Prepare to Teach:
      Find contraction rule card [R13].

> *don't*
>
> Don't connect the letters under an apostrophe.

### Present the Concept

    Teach the rule: *Contractions replace a letter or letters with an apostrophe to contract or shorten a phrase.* To aid memory, add motions. Hold your arm out to your side parallel to the floor. When you say **contract**, draw your arm up contracting your bicep. Your arm does not look as long.

### Collect Contractions

    The base words used to form contractions have been taught by the sections listed below. The words in bold are in the top one hundred most frequently misspelled words.

| Section | Words | Contractions | Section | Words | Contractions |
|---|---|---|---|---|---|
| A | is not<br>did not | isn't<br>didn't | G | let us | let's* |
| B/J | cannot* | **can't** | H-1<br>H-2 | one is<br>that is | one's*<br>that's |
| C | I am<br>he is<br>she is<br>it is | I'm<br>he's<br>she's<br>it's | I<br>I-2<br>J-2 | it is<br>what is<br>here is | it's*<br>what's<br>here's |
| D | must not<br>are not<br>was not<br>has not<br>have not<br>had not<br>you are<br>we are<br>he, she has<br>it has<br>I have<br>you have<br>we have<br>I had<br>you had<br>he, she had<br>we had | mustn't*<br>aren't<br>wasn't<br>hasn't<br>haven't<br>hadn't<br>you're<br>we're<br>he's, she's<br>it's<br>I've<br>you've<br>we've<br>I'd<br>you'd<br>he'd, she'd<br>we'd | K-3 | I would<br>you would<br>he, she would<br>we would<br>**should** not<br>**would** not<br>**could** not | I'd<br>you'd<br>he'd, she'd<br>we'd<br>shouldn't<br>wouldn't<br>couldn't |
|  |  |  | K-4 | where is | where's |
|  |  |  | K-7 | they are<br>they have<br>they will<br>they would | they're<br>they've<br>they'll<br>they'd |
|  |  |  | L-4 | were not | weren't |
|  |  |  | M-1 | who will<br>who is | who'll<br>who's |
| E | I will<br>you will<br>she will<br>he will<br>it will<br>we will<br>will not | I'll<br>you'll<br>she'll<br>he'll<br>it'll<br>we'll<br>**won't*** | M-5 | **does** not | doesn't |
|  |  |  | N-1 | there is | there's |
|  |  |  | O-6 | do not | **don't** [R19]* |
|  |  |  | P-4 | of the clock | o'clock |

\* These need special attention.
  *Cannot* is a compound word.
  In *mustn't* the first T is silent.

Words *lets, ones, its* differ from *let's, one's* and *it's.*
He *lets* the ball go. She counts by *ones.* The cat licks *its* paw.
*Let's* go home. *One's* getting hungry. *It's* time to go home.

**29.** <u>**DICTATE E'S DROPPING PAGE**</u>. (Before K-3)

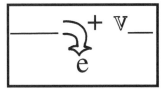

<u>Objectives</u>:

To teach students when "to drop or not to drop" a silent final E.
To build a Discovery Reference Page to teach and review this rule.

<u>Prepare to Teach</u>:

Pull Spelling Rule Cards for Rules: 2, 3, 4, 16, 19, and 7 (all five cards)
Copy and cut suffix cards on page 98 of Wise Guide.

**Introduce the Concept**.

1. RECITE THE RULE. *Silent final E words commonly lose the need for the E when adding a vowel suffix.* The pun on "eavesdropping" gives us a fun name for the rule.

2. DEFINE THE TERMS.

| | |
|---|---|
| **silent final E word**? | A word that ends with an E that is silent. |
| **five reasons for silent E's**? | Review 5 silent final E rule cards. |
| **suffix**? | A word part added to the end of a word to change meaning. |
| **vowel suffix**? | A suffix that begins with a vowel. |
| **consonant suffix**? | A suffix that begins with a consonant. |

3. SORT THE SUFFIX CARDS (optional). Students separate consonant and vowel suffixes.

**Use process of elimination questions to identify an E's dropping word.**

> *Does the word end with a <u>silent E</u>?*
> *Are we adding a vowel suffix?*
> *But, will dropping the E harmonize with other spelling needs?*

Our rule begins, "Silent final E words commonly..." In ***common*** cases a vowel suffix replaces a silent E. Consonants do not. The type of silent final E may influence if the E is still needed when adding a suffix. In uncommon cases other rules may lead us to keep the E before a vowel suffix. When that happens we add an asterisk* to the word. In even more rare cases, we may drop the E before a consonant suffix. These words take two asterisks ** (See further explanation on p.146).

**Introduce the Reference Page**.

Dictate "place" for students to write in the first column. With red add the silent final E markings. (The E in *place* is needed for two reasons. We mentally note both, but mark the first type that works.) Ask process of elimination questions to determine if we drop or keep the silent final E.

| plac͡e | end with silent E? | yes (continue to next question) | | |
|---|---|---|---|---|
| | | | \multicolumn{2}{c}{action to take} | |
| | **vowel suffix?** | **harmonize?** | **drop e** | **keep e** |
| **+ -ing** | yes | yes | *plac ing* | |
| **+ -ment** | no | — | | *place ment* |
| **+ -able** | yes | no | | *place a ble\** |
| \multicolumn{5}{l}{*C says /k/ before A. Keep the E to keep the sound.} | | | | |

**Select several review level words as start-up examples.**

Dictate the base word. Use regular spelling, divide words into syllables and mark them. Use red for all silent final E markings. Identify the suffix to add. Determine how to apply the rule.

| | | questions | | action | |
|---|---|---|---|---|---|
| | | vowel suffix? | harmonize? | **drop e** | **keep e** |
| bone | + -y | yes | yes | bon y | |
| | + -less | no | – | | bone less |
| force | + -ible | yes | yes  (C says /s/ before I. [R2]) | forc i ble | |
| | + -ful | no | – | | force ful |
| dye | + -ed | yes | yes | dyed | |
| | + -ing | yes | no (Mark with *.) | | dye ing* |

* A vowel suffix can replace a silent final E, BUT here we need to keep the E to keep the meaning (dying).

**Watch for places where related rules do not harmonize.**

Reasons we don't drop an E before a vowel suffix. (On the chart, mark examples with an *.)

1. **Keep the E to keep the sound.**
   *C usually says /k/, but C says /s/ before E, I, Y. [R2]*
   bal-ance-a-ble (N-1), trace-a-ble (P-2), no-tice-a-ble (P-2),
   brace-a-ble (Q-5), ser-vice-a-ble (R-5), peace-a-ble (S-6)
   *G usually says /g/, but G may say /j/ before E, I, Y.  [R3]*
   change-a-ble (M-1), ar-range-a-ble (Q-1), cour-age-ous (Q-5)
2. **Keep the E to keep the meaning or pronunciation.**
   mile-age (K-7), shoe-ing (L-3), ca-noe-ing (O-5), singe-ing (Y-2)
   dye-ing, tinge-ing, toe-ing, hoe-ing
3. **Keep the E for vowel requirement.**
   *Every syllable must have a vowel.* [R7, type 4] a-cre-age (V-2), o-gre-ish

**Prepare for advance situations.**

We expect to keep an E before a consonant suffix *(valueless, virtueless, accruement, wholesome, awesome, wisely)*. However, at least seven similar words in English drop an E before adding a consonant suffix *(truly, duly, argument, wholly, ninth, awful, wisdom)*. These are clearly exceptions to the rule, BUT we can see a secondary reason why the E could be dropped even though our rules do not require it to do so.

Reasons exception words drop an E before a consonant suffix.  (On the chart, mark examples with **.)

1. **Another rule may replace the need for the E.**
   *U says /U/ at the end of a syllable.* [R4] tru-ly (O-5), du-ly (R-3) ar-gu-ment (T1)
   *I and O MAY say /I/ and /O/ before two consonants.* [R19] whol-ly (O-2), ninth (P-4)
2. **The original requirement for the E is gone.**
   An odd job E initially added to give main idea word at least three letters.
   awe -- aw-ful (P-7)
   The vowel sound changes in the derivative. The I no longer says /I/.
   wise -- wis-dom (S-6)

© 2012, Wanda Sanseri

**Continue through the Year to Collect E's Dropping Samples.**

Words that stump many educators can be explained using the spelling rules and common sense. When we know the reasons for silent final E's we can see consistency with the E's Dropping principle.

Over the year collect examples for the E's Dropping Page in log. Tailor the word selection by picking words either taught in an earlier spelling section or from the list you are currently teaching. Use the following chart to help locate appropriate examples for your student's level.

In uncommon cases with "BUT" words have students put one asterisk (*) if the silent final E is retained before a vowel suffix and two asterisks (**) if the silent E is dropped before a consonant suffix. Identify the reason on the chart at the bottom of page 146.

| Section | base word | drop e | | keep e | |
|---------|-----------|--------|--|--------|--|
| K-3 | care | cared | car ing | care ful | care less |
|  | state | stat ed | stat ing | state hood | state ment |
| K-7 | mile |  |  | mile age* |  |
| L-3 | shoe | shoed |  | shoe ing* |  |
| L-5 | false | fal si fy |  | false hood |  |
| M-1 | change | chang ing | changed | change a ble* |  |
| M-3 | pro vide | pro vid er | pro vid ed |  |  |
|  | solve | solved | solv a ble |  |  |
| M-4 | noise | nois y |  | noise less |  |
|  | pic ture | pic tured | pic tur esque |  |  |
| M-6 | wire | wir ing | wir y | wire less |  |
| M-7 | charge | charg er | charged | charge a ble* |  |
| N-1 | bal ance | bal anc ing | bal anc er | bal ance a ble* |  |
|  | use | us er | used | use ful |  |
| N-2 | ex cuse | ex cus a ble | ex cus ing |  |  |
|  | mis take | mis tak en | mis tak ing |  |  |
| N-6 | wise | wis dom** |  | wise ly |  |
| O-2 | whole | whol ly** |  | whole some |  |
| O-3 | sur face | sur faced | sur fac er |  |  |
| O-4 | pleas ure | pleas ur a ble |  |  |  |
|  | lo cate | lo cat ing | lo cat ed |  |  |
|  | fi gure | fi gur a tive | fi gur ine |  |  |
| O-5 | ca noe | ca noed |  | ca noe ing* |  |
|  | true | tru er | tru ly** |  |  |
| P-1 | set tle | set tler | set tled | set tle ment |  |
|  | val ue | val u a ble |  | val ue less |  |
|  | for tune | for tun ate |  |  |  |
| P-2 | no tice | no tic ing | no ticed | no tice a ble* |  |
|  | trace | trac er | Trac y | trace less | trace a ble* |
| P-4 | nine | ninth** |  | nine ty |  |
| P-6 | im i tate | im i ta tive | im i ta tor |  |  |
|  | ap prove | ap prov ing | ap proved |  |  |
|  | share | shared | shar ing |  |  |

| Section | base word | drop e | | keep e | |
|---|---|---|---|---|---|
| P-7 | engine | en gin eer | | | |
| | awe | aw ful** | | awe some | |
| Q-1 | meas ure | meas ured | meas ur a ble | mea sure less | |
| | ar range | ar rang ing | ar ranged | ar range ment | ar range a ble* |
| | con tin ue | con tin ued | con tin u ous | | |
| Q-2 | pri vate | pri vat ize | | pri vate ly | |
| Q-4 | re la tive | re la tiv i ty | | re la tive ly | |
| | cul ture | cul tur al | cul tured | | |
| | pre side | pre sid ed | pres i dent | | |
| | en close | en clos ure | en clos ing | | |
| Q-5 | brace | braced | | brace a ble* | |
| | cour age | | | cour age ous* | |
| R-1 | loose | loos er | loos est | loose ly | |
| R-3 | due | du ly** | | | |
| | fierce | fier cer | fier cest | fierce ly | |
| | hum ble | hum bler | hum bly | hum ble ness | |
| | se cure | se cur i ty | se cur ing | se cure ness | |
| R-4 | pur pose | pur posed | pur pos ing | pur pose ful | |
| | vir tue | vir tu ous | | vir tue less | |
| R-5 | ser vice | ser vic ing | ser viced | ser vice a ble* | |
| S-1 | na ture | nat u ral | na tured | | |
| S-5 | pres sure | pres sured | pres sur ize | | |
| S-6 | peace | | | peace ful | peace a ble* |
| T-1 | ar gue | ar gued | ar gu ment** | | |
| T-2 | ac cel er ate | ac cel er a tor | | | |
| | mi nute | mi nut er | mi nut est | mi nute ly | |
| T-3 | fa vor ite | fa vor i tism | | | |
| U-1 | con serve | con ser va tive | | | |
| | re hearse | re hears al | | | |
| U-3 | scene | scen ic | sce na ri o | | |
| V-2 | a cre | | | a cre age* | |
| W-1 | cal cu late | cal cu lat or | cal cu lat ed | | |
| W-2 | sin cere | sin cer i ty | | sin cere ly | |
| | ex treme | ex trem ist | ex trem i ty | ex treme ness | |
| X-1 | fi nance | fi nan cial | fi nanced | | |
| | seize | seized | seiz ure | | |
| | per ceive | per ceived | per ceiv a ble | | |
| | o paque | | | o paque ness | |
| Y-2 | singe | singed | | singe ing* | |

\* Keep E before a vowel suffix.  Why?  See page 146.
\*\* Drop E before a consonant suffix.  Why?  See page 146.

**30.**   **COLLECT HOMOPHONES & HETERONYMS**. (After K-5)

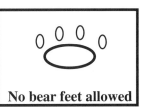

**No bear feet allowed**

Objective:
   To avoid miscommunication caused by using the wrong word.

Prepare to Teach:
   Select review words to use to introduce the concept.
   Note more examples to collect from current spelling list.
   See key to formatted black log at: www.bhibooks.net/multimedia.html

**Define Terms.**

   1. HOMOPHONES sound the same but have different meanings and different spellings (sea, see) [homo- (same) + phone (sound)]. Page 130 of *WISE Guide* has sketches for several homophones. Students may enjoy illustrating others.

   2. HETERONYMS have the same spelling but a different meaning and pronunciation [hetero- (different) + nym (name)]. The context determines how we say each ("bow" -- bend, tied ribbon).

**Collect Homophones from the WISE List.**

   Collect homophones "after" the listed spelling section.  First teach the most common spelling. Later, after teaching related words independently, show them together, compare, and note the differences. Timing instruction this way minimizes the chance of confusion.

| After K-5 | sea | see | son | sun | hour | our |
|---|---|---|---|---|---|---|
| | read (past tense) | red | won | one | sent | cent |
| | wood | would | bear | bare | mail | male |
| | I | eye | | | | |

| After K-6 | week | weak | | |
|---|---|---|---|---|
| After L-2 | by | buy | *bye* | (Words in italics are not in *WISE Guide*.) |
| | for | four | | |
| After L-3 | meat | meet | | |
| After L-4 | no | know | | |
| | road | rode | | |
| | rows | rose | | |
| After L-5 | lead | led | | |
| After M-1 | wheel | we'll | | |
| After M-5 | so | sew | *sow* | |
| After M-7 | stare | stair | | |
| After N-1 | right | write | | |
| | hear | here | | |
| After N-6 | plane | plain | | |
| | pare | pear | pair | |
| After N-8 | fair | fare | | |
| After O-1 | ant | aunt | | |
| | mourn | morn | | |
| After O-2 | waste | waist | | |
| | ate | eight | | |
| | whole | hole | | |
| | threw | through | | |
| After O-3 | new | knew | | |
| After O-4 | holy | wholly | | |
| After P-4 | sale | sail | | |
| After Q-2 | whose | who's | | |
| After Q-6 | theirs | there's | | |

> **Homophones are often confused, sometimes for artistic purpose and sometimes with humorous results.**

| | |
|---|---|
| oops! | In a cafe window: " No **bear** feet allowed." |
| oops! | **Eye** came today. |
| catchy! | Seven days without prayer makes one **weak**. |
| oops! | I will go **buy** you. |
| oops! | I won the Olympic **meat**. |
| oops! | Yes, I **no**. |
| oops! | I **road** on the **rode**. |
| oops! | Please sit in the second or third **rose**. |
| oops! | I have a **led** pencil. |
| catchy! | You can have joy in the **mourning**. |
| catchy! | I'll eat a **whole** donut and give you a **hole**. |

| After R-3 | dew | due | do |
| After R-4 | patients | patience | |
| After R-5 | weigh | way | *whey* |
| After S-6 | to | two | too |
| After S-6 | peace | piece | |
| After T-2 | rain | rein | reign |
| After T-3 | him | hymn | |
| After U-1 | kernel | colonel | |
| After U-3 | air | heir | |
| After U-3 | scene | seen | |
| After U-3 | aisle | I'll | *isle* |
| After V-1 | birth | berth | |
| After V-2 | coarse | course | |
| After V-3 | wait | weight | |
| After V-3 | sense | cents | |
| After Z-2 | stationary | stationery | |

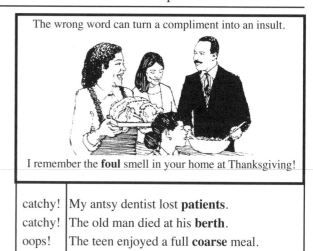

The wrong word can turn a compliment into an insult.

I remember the **foul** smell in your home at Thanksgiving!

| catchy! | My antsy dentist lost **patients**. |
| catchy! | The old man died at his **berth**. |
| oops! | The teen enjoyed a full **coarse** meal. |

## Collect Heteronyms from the WISE List.

| After A | do | **Do** you know how to sing, "**Do**, ray, me, fa, so, la, te, **do**?" |
| After G | live | I **live** in California and saw a **live** bear. |
| After H-1 | house | My **house** will **house** all the guests. |
| After H-2 | row | **Row** the boat quickly to escape the **row** of the mob. |
| After I-2 | putting | He was **putting** his bag down on the **putting** green. |
| After I-4 | bow | He dropped his **bow** and took a **bow**. |
| After J-1 | read | I like to **read**. Yesterday, I **read** a great book. |
| After J-3 | wind | **Wind** up the toy before the **wind** blows again. |
| After K-5 | drawer | The talented **drawer** put away his coloring pencils in his desk **drawer**. |
| After L-4 | close | **Close** the door and sit **close** to the window. |
| After L-5 | lead | The team was in the **lead** but I broke my pencil **lead**. |
| After M-1 | sew(er) | The **sewer** accidentally dropped her thread in the open **sewer**. |
| After M-5 | sow | **Sow** the seed and then feed the **sow** and her piglets. |
| After M-5 | does | **Does** he know where to find the female **does**? |
| After M-5 | learned | The **learned** man **learned** much from his favorite teacher. |
| After M-6 | object | I **object** to letting you sell my favorite **object**. |
| After M-7 | record | The secretary will **record** in the book a **record** of the sale. |
| After N-1 | use | What's the **use** in trying to **use** the broken dish? |
| After N-1 | number | My finger is **number** now than when I wrote my phone **number**. |
| After N-4 | subject | A king can **subject** his **subject** to anything. |
| After O-1 | address | Tomorrow, the president will **address** the crowd at the following **address**. |
| After O-1 | refuse | I **refuse** to let you treat my special treasure as **refuse**. |
| After O-4 | perfect | I will keep trying to **perfect** the drawing until it is **perfect**. |
| After P-2 | produce | I cannot **produce** the **produce** in the field, but I can happily eat it. |
| After P-5 | entrance | She will **entrance** the crowd with that graceful **entrance**. |
| After Q-4 | convict | I saw the jury **convict** the **convict** of another crime. |
| After Q-5 | present | I want to **present** this **present** to you. |
| After S-3 | wound | His **wound** hurt when he **wound** the clock. |
| After S-3 | concert | She had to **concert** a lot of effort to make it to the **concert**. |
| After T-5 | minute | It will only take a **minute** to count that **minute** amount. |
| After U-2 | rebel | It is just like a **rebel** to **rebel**. |
| After V-3 | permit | Dad will **permit** me to get my driver's **permit**. |
| After W-2 | separate | Can you **separate** the white clothes into a **separate** pile? |
| After W-2 | grease | I will **grease** the pan with bacon **grease**. |
| After W-2 | associate | I do not **associate** with my **associate** after work hours. |
| After X-1 | digest | Let me **digest** my food in peace as I read Reader's **Digest**. |
| After X-2 | desert | A cruel person would **desert** the starving group in a barren **desert**. |
| After Y-2 | appropriate | It was not an **appropriate** way to **appropriate** funds. |

# 31. IMPROVE COMPREHENSION WITH McCALL BOOKS. (Before L)

<u>Objectives</u>:
>   To teach comprehension techniques.
>   To improve standardized test scores.
>   To chart individual student progress.

<u>Prepare to Teach</u>:
>   Determine appropriate level.
>   Be ready to do a sample lesson together.

**Train Students for Effective Reading Comprehension.**

McCall-Crabbs

Standard
Test Lessons
in Reading

Five Volumes in One

To *comprehend* means to take hold of the meaning intended by the author. The McCall books reveal how well a student can understand what she reads. They should be used as a diagnostic tool at the beginning of the year. Routine assignments with the books should then be given throughout the year. Progress can then be measured as the year progresses.

While learning to read is one of our goals, we did not start with reading assignments for a reason. According to Jeanne Chall's Stages of Learning discussed in Step 5, comprehension will always be hindered until foundational tools are mastered. Dr. McGuinness concurs. "While traditional comprehension activities, such as "finding the main ideas," answering questions about specific information, and writing summaries, are important and useful activities, they will not have any impact on a child's comprehension unless the child is reading accurately and efficiently." (McGuinness p. 276).

First things need to be first. For over half a century few people have learned the fundamental keys to the English language. As a result, many highly intelligent people struggle with reading, spelling, and writing. Students who learn to see words as phonograms combined into syllables according to set spelling rules can read rapidly without wasting mental energy. They can write more fluidly because they can subconsciously transcribe words correctly. They can concentrate on the ideas they want to communicate rather than stumble over the mechanics of how to spell them. They can read with greater understanding because their minds are free to focus on content.

A student is ready to build higher level analytical skill only after he can automatically recognize words in print without guessing. The McCall books train students in various techniques for effective reading comprehension. Each book has a number of short reading assignments with questions about the text. Questions reveal whether the student knows how to find the main idea, put thoughts into a logical sequence, use the context, draw conclusions, and identify inferences. The discipline of reading with an eye to answering a series of well-designed questions in a limited time helps guide students to gain the most from anything they read or study. These exercises are similar to the type of assignments given by the end-of-the-year state diagnostic tests. As a bonus, working regularly with these books strengthens the student's ability to take standardized tests. High scores often open opportunities for academic honors and college scholarships.

We recommend assigning a lesson in these non-consumable books several times a week. BHI purchased the right to reprint the original *McCall-Crabbs* series, so this excellent resource can continue to be available. We prefer the 1961 text over the more recent, dumbed-down version.

> **A student can build higher level analytical skills only after he can automatically recognize words in print without guessing.**

**Select the Appropriate Level Books**.

   With SWR beginning students can start with "living books" of your choice. Basal readers are not required. Some even begin with the King James Bible. Others start with BHI publications like the *New England Primer* or *Play by the Sea*. Students second grade and above may be ready for the McCall-Crabbs Books.

   1. THE NEW ENGLAND PRIMER. Many use stories in the BHI edition of *The New England Primer of 1777* as a first official "reading assignment." Pages 16-17 have lists of words three columns to a page. These make up 102 of the early words the SWR teacher dictates for a student to write into his Primary Log. First the student reads the words in his own handwriting. Now he can read those words typed in a book in a different order. Once he can read these fluently, he can progress to reading the same words within the context of stories.

**Sample from the
"I Can Read a Book"
section in BHI's historic reprint
of the *New England Primer***

---

### Will he go in the street?

The little child is three.

He cannot go in the street.

His mother will not let him.

The boy is to play in his yard.

Come see. His ball is in the street.

He looks and looks, but he is good.

He will not go for it.

I am big. I will get it for him.

◇◇◇◇◇◇◇◇◇◇◇◇◇◇◇◇◇

### The Good Book

"Children obey your parents in the Lord
for this is right."

Ephesians 6:1

---

   After the child has read a selection, you can check orally for understanding. You might ask: *How old is the boy? Where can he play? Where can he not play? What happened to test him? Did he do the right thing? Does the story have a good ending? How does the Bible verse go with this story?* You can phrase *yes* or *no* questions like: *Does the story ask, "Will he go to school?" Is the child three? Does his mother want him to play in the yard? Does she want him to play in the street?* Such questions encourage a child to think about the meaning of what he reads.

   Students first "learn to read." They see the words and recognize them. After they can fluidly see and recognize words, then they can start developing the ability to "read to learn." BHI publishes worthwhile aids for this like *Lessons from Nature* by John Bunyan. Each selection has questions that test understanding of the text.

2. McCALL-CRABBS. The McCall-Crabbs books plus answer keys to be the best resource available to train the sub-skills of good comprehension up to college level and beyond. BHI publishes the original versions of A-E in one hardcover edition.

*The McCall-Crabbs Standard Test Lessons in Reading* gives a series of short Normed Reference Tests. These are not Criterion Reference Tests where the expectation is 100% mastery. Students do not need to experience test anxiety. Think of them as a training tool for exercising comprehension sub-skills. Students learn from incorrect answers. They go back and reread the selection and apply various sub-skills of comprehension. My adult son recently thanked me for these books. He remembers enjoying them and also appreciated how they trained him to quickly grasp the meaning of text on the first read.

Book A may be first used as early as second semester of first grade for a very strong reader, but usually is not presented until second grade or later. Books B through E are progressively more difficult with some overlap. The skill range in each book is broad and can be used by a number of different grades. Each book contains 78 lessons with multiple choice questions. Some are simple "get the facts" type questions. "Select the best title" trains students to "get the main idea." Others involve inferences. The story may not state the location but mentions cutting apples, measuring, and stirring. Is the setting in the kitchen, den, or bedroom?

Grade level of comprehension can be determined when lessons are timed for three minutes. Young children tend to measure success by the ability to finish an assignment. Instead of making them stop after three minutes, you can have them switch to their red pencils at that time. For an accurate grade level score, count only the correct answers written in regular pencil. This tip from Liz FitzGerald will give students a sense of completion without destroying an accurate assessment of their ability.

Think of the lessons as positive workouts that help train students to be more efficient in reading comprehension. Don't panic if a student's score one day is lower than the day before. It is normal to see ups and downs. Scores can vary for several reasons. Students may do better if they have previous knowledge of or interest in the subject, know the vocabulary used, or just had a good day. Some days we are more alert than others. Each lesson was normed by those taking that particular test. The ages of the participants varied. The highest possible grade-level indicator on different selections depended on the sample group for that particular selection. A student could get all answers right two lessons in a row, but his scores may appear to have dropped even several grade levels in ability.

For a reliable indicator of overall progress, average every ten lessons. By averaging a set of tests, the good days and bad days balance out to give a more accurate profile of achievement. The variations with the test group will even out. Record the average grade-level achieved for each set of ten tests. Use the average scores to trace overall student progress. You can plot them on a graph.

Some people object to two of the selections. Book A, Lesson 11 talks about the much-loved *New England Primer* in a negative manner. Book D in Lesson 57 has a questionable presentation of origins presented as fact. The two selections on the next page not only illustrate the style of the McCall books, but also provide alternative lessons for these two stories. You may photocopy these replacement exercises for student use.

-- Alternative Lesson A-11 --

In the early schools of our country, boys and girls used a book called the New England Primer. This book gave wise instruction, Bible verses, and prayers. The alphabet was the first important part of the reader. After each letter of the alphabet was a cute woodcut picture, and beside it a rhyme. For over a hundred and fifty years this was the main textbook in the country. Our founding fathers learned to read using this book. Children studied their lessons out loud so that the teacher might know how well they were doing. When they had learned their lessons, they stood in a row in front of the teacher, with their toes touching a crack in the floor, and recited.

1. One of the first books used in schools was (a) geography (b) an arithmetic (c) a primer (d) a speller.

2. This book was called the (a) Massachusetts Reader (b) New England Primer (c) New York Primer (d) Children's Reader.

3. The first important part of it was the (a) pictures (b) stories (c) rhymes (d) alphabet.

4. After each letter of the alphabet was a (a) picture (b) story (c) poem (d) lesson.

5. The children studied (a) softly (b) carefully (c) out loud (d) quietly.

6. When the children knew their lessons they recited them to their (a) neighbor (b) brother (c) mother (d) teacher.

7. Reading this book helped make students (a) ugly (b) silly (c) wise (d) sad.

8. This book was used for (a) only a short while (b) 20 years (c) over 150 years (d) 2 months.

9. The children studied out loud (a) to please themselves (b) to annoy their neighbors (c) so the teacher could hear (d) to learn more quickly.

| No. right | 1 | 2 | 3 | 4 | 5 | 6 | 7 | 8 | 9 |
|---|---|---|---|---|---|---|---|---|---|
| G. score | 2.3 | 2.5 | 2.8 | 3.1 | 3.5 | 3.8 | 4.2 | 4.6 | 5.3 |

## -- Alternative Lesson  D-57 --

William Laiton squinted from the glare of the sun as he stared at the miles of vacant ocean.  The captain felt responsible for the seven sailors stranded with him on a lifeboat.  God had preserved them from a sinking ship and a raging storm.  Now the men's water rations dwindled to only a spoonful a day. Without help soon they would die.

On their eighteenth day afloat, a flying fish landed in their skiff.  They used the fish for bait to catch two dolphins.  Meanwhile, the storm had redirected Samuel Scarlet's ship their way.  But Captain Scarlet had his own problem.  His men risked starvation.  They begged him not to take more people on board, but he could not ignore the distressed sailors.

As it turned out, each boat had what the other needed.  Scarlet's ship had water enough to spare, and Laiton's men had plenty of food.  Within days the men arrived safely back home in colonial New England.

1. Captain Laiton was stranded on a lifeboat at sea with (a) four dolphins (b) seven sailors (c) eighteen sailors (d) two other men.

2. Their daily ration of water was a (a) cup (b) bucket (c) spoonful (d) sip.

3. Without help they would (a) sing (b) cry (c) laugh (d) die.

4. Laiton's ship lacked (a) fuel (b) men (c) drink (d) food.

5. Scarlet's ship lacked (a) drink (b) men (c) food (d) fuel.

6. What landed in Laiton's boat? (a) a bird (b) a frog (c) a spoon (d) a fish

7. Scarlet's ship had extra (a) water (b) food (c) music (d) beds.

8. Laiton's men caught (a) crabs (b) two dolphins (c) shrimp (d) snails.

9. These men lived in (a) New England (b) Skiff (c) Florida (d) Spain.

| No. right | 1 | 2 | 3 | 4 | 5 | 6 | 7 | 8 | 9 |
|---|---|---|---|---|---|---|---|---|---|
| G score | 4.2 | 4.7 | 5.0 | 5.3 | 5.5 | 6.0 | 6.9 | 8.1 | 9.4 |

**32.**   **DICTATE 1-1-1 PAGE** (Before Wise List Section L-3)

<u>Objectives</u>:
> To teach spelling rule 14.
> To build a 1-1-1 reference page in the Learning Log.
> To teach logic in application to spelling.

```
__V C    C + V__
        v = vowel
        c = consonant
```

<u>Prepare to Teach</u>:
> Have on hand the Suffix cards prepared in step 24. (Optional)
> Have handy Spelling Rule Cards 14 and 16.
> Preview a sample page in Appendix C. (P9/B11)
> Plan extra time for introducing this concept. Review the page as it applies to later spelling especially in L-3, M-3, N-4, O-5, P-3, Q-3, R-3, S-2, T-5, and V-3.

**Present the Concept**.

1. STIMULATE INTEREST. Draw this problem on the blackboard.

| If | **hope + ing = hop ing** |
|---|---|
| how do you spell | **hop + ing  =    ?** |

2. RECITE THE SPELLING RULE. *With a ONE-syllable word ending in ONE vowel, then ONE consonant, double the last consonant before adding a vowel suffix* [Rule 14]. Students repeat.

3. CLARIFY THE TERMS.

    a. **Syllable**: a rhythmic "chunk" of a word. *Hop* is a one syllable word.

    b. **One vowel**. Hold up the O phonogram card. Ask, "Is this one vowel?" (yes). The single vowels are: a, e, i, o, u, y. Hold up the OA phonogram card. Ask, "Is this one vowel?" (No, it takes two letters to make that vowel sound.)

    c. **One consonant.** Hold up P. Ask, "Is this one consonant? (yes). Hold up the PH. Ask, "Is this one consonant? (No, it takes two consonants to make that sound.)

    d. **Vowel suffix**: A word ending that begins with a vowel. Organize suffixes into vowel suffixes (-ed, -er, -ing, -y) and consonant suffixes (-ly, -ness, -less, -ful).

4. ANSWER QUESTIONS. Is "hop" a <u>one</u> syllable word? (yes); that ends with <u>one</u> vowel? (yes); then <u>one</u> consonant? (yes). Is -ing a vowel suffix (yes). This is a 1-1-1 word and we will need to double the P before adding the suffix ending. Underline the added silent P twice.

**hop ping**

5. CONSIDER ADVANCED CHALLENGES. We need to think of this rule more deeply than simple face value. Consider it as seeing and hearing one vowel then one consonant at the end.

    a. **X** looks like one consonant but it does not sound like one /ks/ (taxing).

    b. **W** is not a consonant in OW, AW, EW just as the U is not a vowel in QU (towing).

    c. **R-controlled vowels** are two-letter phonograms that look and sound like one vowel then one consonant: ar, er, ir, or, ur. The R distorts the vowel sound (stirring).

**Build a Reference Page for the 1-1-1 Rule**.

Students with a Primary Learning Log will find a page already formatted for this rule. Students with black notebooks will build the page by following teacher instructions. *To double or not to double, that is the question*. Doubling the consonant keeps the vowel sound short. With young beginners you may choose at first to teach only the first three words *(get, sin, mad)* and their derivatives.

Dictate the base words for the students to write in the first column. At the top of the board write the suffix we want to add to a word. Use the process-of-elimination questions below to determine whether we need to double the consonant or not before adding the ending. Continue questioning as long as the answer is "yes." If all answers are "yes," then write the derivative in the "yes" column and double the last consonant. **With red** underline the added consonant twice to emphasize that the silent letter was added for a 1-1-1 word. We will think the consonant for spelling but not for normal speech [R. 29]. If you get a "no" answer, write the derivative in the "no" column and just add the ending.

Process-of-Elimination Questions:

    &lt;   **Is it a <u>one</u>-syllable word?**
    &lt;   **Does it end with <u>one</u> vowel, then <u>one</u> consonant (that we can see and hear)?**
    &lt;   **Are we adding a <u>vowel suffix</u>?**

|  | **yes** | **no** | **reason for no** |
|---|---|---|---|
| get | get-ting |  |  |
| sin | sin-ner | sin-ful | *-Ful* is not a vowel suffix. |
| mad | mad-den | mad-ly | *-Ly* is not a vowel suffix. |
| quip | quipped |  |  |
| pick |  | pick-er | CK is not one consonant. |
| ship | ship-ping | ship-ment | *-Ment* is a consonant suffix. |
| big | big-gest | big-ness | *-Ness* is a consonant suffix. |
| fur | fur-ry |  | R distorts the vowel sound, but |
|  |  |  |         UR is a vowel then a consonant. |
| meet |  | meet-ing | EE is not one vowel. |
| box |  | box-er | X looks like one, but sounds like two. |
| row |  | rowed | OW doesn't have a consonant sound. |

**BLACK LOG**

**Introductory exercise of 1-1-1 Page**

**Add elimination questions to bottom of page. See p. 215.**

**Add other 1-1-1 examples in conjunction with new spelling words or as needed.**

**Refer to this page when building derivatives.**

| | 1-1-1 | |
|---|---|---|
| | (yes) | (no) |
| get | get ting | |
| sin | sin ner | sin ful |
| mad | mad den | mad ly |
| quip | quipped | |
| pick | | pick er |
| ship | ship ping | ship ment |
| big | big gest | big ness |
| fur | fur ry | |
| meet | | meet ing |
| box | | box er |
| row | | rowed |

**Consider Additional Examples of 1-1-1 Words.**

The following words from the Wise List could be used for extra practice or as a basis for selecting alternative words for this reference page in subsequent years. The words in bold do not double the consonant, for the reason stated.

1. 1-1-1 WORDS TAUGHT BEFORE L-3 WITH DERIVATIVES.

| red | (5) | red-der | red-dest | **red-ness** | -Ness is a consonant suffix. |
|-----|-----|---------|----------|--------------|------------------------------|
| can | (22) | can-ning | can-nery | | |
| bag | (31) | bag-gage | bagged | | |
| beg | (32) | begged | beg-gar (1239) | | |
| step | (40) | step-ping | stepped | | |
| man | (61) | manned | man-nish | **man-ly** | -Ly is a consonant suffix. |
| hot | (103) | hot-ter | hot-test | **hotly** | -Ly is a consonant suffix. |
| flat | (110) | flat-ten | flat-test | **flatness** | -Ness is a consonant suffix. |
| zip | (247) | zip-per | zipped | | |
| sun | (297) | sun-ny | sun-ning | **sunless** | -Less is a consonant suffix. |
| glad | (350) | glad-der | glad-dest | **gladness** | -Ness is a consonant suffix. |
| stop | (545) | stop-per | stop-pa-ble | | |

2. "NO" WORDS TAUGHT BEFORE L-3.

| school | (66) | **schooled** | **school-ing** | OO is not one vowel. |
|--------|------|--------------|----------------|----------------------|
| jump | (72) | **jumped** | **jump-er** | M-P is not one consonant. |
| toy | (93) | **toy-ing** | **toyed** | OY is not one vowel. |
| soft | (148) | **soft-er** | **soft-est** | F-T is not one consonant. |
| low | (173) | **low-er** | **low-est** | OW has no consonant sound. |
| sick | (186) | **sick-er** | **sick-est** | CK is not one consonant. |
| show | (199) | **showed** | **show-y** | OW has no consonant sound. |
| blow | (215) | **blow-er** | **blow-ing** | OW has no consonant sound. |

3. 1-1-1 WORDS TAUGHT AFTER L-3 AND SOME OF THEIR DERIVATIVES

| war | (568) | war-ring | war-ri-or | | |
|-----|-------|----------|-----------|---|---|
| spot | (677) | spot-ter | spot-ty | spot-ta-ble | |
| shop | (694) | shop-per | shop-ping | shopped | |
| swim | (699) | swim-mer | swim-ming | swim-ma-ble | |
| clap | (821) | clap-per | clapped | clap-ping | |
| drug | (845) | drug-gist | drugged | **drug-less** | -Less is a consonant suffix |
| hem | (848) | hem-ming | hemmed | | |
| slip | | slip-per-y | slip-per | slipped (1642) | |

4. 1-1-1 WORDS NEEDING EXTRA ATTENTION.

gas (124)  gas-ses -- (Uses the 1-1-1 rule.)  *My husband gasses up the car.*
gas-es -- (Uses the plural rule.)  *The gases at the plant are poisonous.*

quit (1102) and quiz (1419). Q always needs a U. U is not a vowel here. [R.1]
quit-ter  quit-ted  quit-ting
quiz-zed  quiz-zing

star (113), spur (339), stir (1058), blur (1104)  R distorted vowel + consonant
star-ry  star-ring  spurred  stir-ring  blur-ry

5. "NO" WORDS TAUGHT AFTER L-3.

| fix (700) | **fixed** | **fix-er** | **fix-a-ble** | X looks like one, but sounds like 2. |
|-----------|-----------|------------|---------------|--------------------------------------|
| tax (791) | **taxed** | **tax-er** | **tax-ing** | X sounds like 2 consonants. |

## 33. REFINE COMPOSITION SKILLS. (After L-4)

Objectives:
    To teach students to organize ideas in writing.
    To reinforce spelling along with teaching composition.

Prepare to Teach:
    Get a sword or knife and a writing pen.
    Write on the board: *The pen is mightier than the sword.*

Would you fight a man with a sword if all you have is a ballpoint pen? Who would win? A sword slices flesh with a razor-sharp edge. Why do we say the pen is mightier? Ideas put in writing can penetrate deeper than any blade. Well-written books, whether good or bad in what they teach, can change the way people think and act and transform history. Writing crystallizes thought. To explain something on paper, you are forced to fine-tune your thinking. Someone who can communicate clearly with the written word can do much to comfort, persuade, and motivate.

Writing starts with a well-crafted sentence. A **sentence** is a complete thought. A **paragraph** consists of several sentences about a single subject. The first sentence often explains the topic of the paragraph (the topic sentence). Indent the first word in a paragraph.

**Priming the Pump for Writing Ideas.**

The blank page stared at the student in cold silence. What could he say? His frozen thoughts immobilized him. How can we unlock the stream of ideas nestled inside? The novice writer usually needs help in learning to activate his flow of words. Pre-writing work helps make ideas flow more naturally when the students write. When we start with spelling words, we have something to give a good jump start.

1. DISCUSS AN IDEA ORALLY FIRST. Early in the program we had students compose oral sentences as a preliminary step to writing sentences. Now we compose oral paragraphs as a preliminary step to writing paragraphs. A paragraph is composed of a series of related sentences.

The teacher may say a simple sentence like, "I like to play in the snow." Next she can ask the student to name things that he likes to do in the snow. She can write the ideas on the board:

throw snow balls
build a snow man
make snow cream
go sledding

My sons and I once had such a discussion. By talking out their ideas before they tried to compose them, they connected speaking and writing. The blank paper was not as threatening. I have kept and treasured the first paragraph my then-six-year-old son wrote.

> *Playing in the Snow*
>
> *I like to play in the snow. We slide down the hill on a box top. I make my own snowman and have snowball fights with my two brothers. We eat my mom's snow cream.*

2. USE A SENTENCE IN *WISE GUIDE* FOR A TOPIC SENTENCE.

    a. In L-4 you could select the sentence, "The ground drank the raindrops like a thirsty man." This sentence gives the setting. Can you connect the other words in this list to that concept?

*Good from Disaster*

*The <u>ground</u> drank the raindrops like a thirsty man.* The <u>flowers</u> no longer <u>held</u> up their heads, but <u>fell</u> drooping <u>close</u> to the <u>ground</u>. The <u>butcher</u> had felt on <u>edge</u> since the <u>climate</u> changed. He didn't <u>know</u> what to do. He <u>rose</u> to leave the <u>kitchen,</u> but he <u>tripped</u> on <u>flour</u> and his <u>body</u> rolled down the <u>stairs</u>. His son <u>flew</u> into the room and <u>drew</u> him into his arms. Together they <u>rode</u> to the doctor. <u>Nothing</u> had ever made him feel so loved. Would you have helped if you <u>were</u> there?

b. In R-2 you could select the sentence, "Common is to gravel as rare is to diamond." One of my students, Jonathan Dahlin, wrote the following.

*Ordinary or Special?*

*Common is to gravel as rare is to diamond. Gravel is so ordinary you can find it anywhere from the rain forests to the ice of the North and South Poles. Diamonds are more expensive and rare. Miners excavate them from select caves in Brazil, Africa, and Australia. The world's biggest diamond was found in South Africa. It was three thousand one hundred six carats. Jewelers cut the huge stone into nine large gems and ninety-six small ones.*

3. BRAINSTORM TO FIND CONNECTIONS BETWEEN WORDS. Look for ways to tie spelling words together. For example, we decided to design a story using the words in Section L-4. What words could give us a setting, characters, a conflict to resolve, and a resolution?

| | |
|---|---|
| **Possible Setting:** | kitchen, stairs, ground |
| **Characters:** | butcher, Rose |
| **Conflict:** | fell, trip, climate, held |
| **Moral:** | Kindness is better than bitterness. Work has benefits. |

The following papers grew out of the brainstorming session. Students went in entirely different directions. They got extra credit for using correctly all twenty words.

*The Fallen Flower*

*A girl with <u>flour</u> on her nose sat on the <u>edge</u> of her seat in the <u>kitchen</u>. She <u>held</u> <u>close</u> the <u>flowers</u> that were given to her by the <u>butcher</u>. <u>Nothing</u> grows as nicely as <u>roses</u> in her <u>climate</u>. Suddenly a boy <u>rode</u> a skateboard down the <u>stairs</u> and <u>tripped</u>. His <u>body</u> knocked her <u>flowers</u> to the <u>ground</u>. Do you <u>know</u> what she did? She ran to where he <u>fell</u> and <u>drew</u> him up. <u>Were</u> you glad she was kind?*

*The Danger of Escaping Work*

*The <u>butcher</u> planned a <u>trip</u> to a warm <u>climate</u> to avoid <u>kitchen</u> duty. He <u>rode</u> to the airport and <u>flew</u> to where he could to do <u>nothing</u>. When he landed, he <u>held</u> the <u>stair</u> rail. A person <u>rose</u> to <u>close</u> the door and <u>tripped</u>. They both <u>fell</u> over the <u>edge</u> to the <u>ground</u>. Did you <u>know</u> that a warm <u>climate</u> is not the best place for a body cast?*

4. TIE WORDS TO A CURRENT EVENT. Concepts come alive when we can make them relevant to our everyday life. The week after the infamous terrorist attacks on the United States, the following was written using spelling words in Sections R-1 and R-2.

*A Common Enemy*

*Everyone from <u>lawyer</u> to <u>prisoner</u> watched the <u>video</u> as quiet as a <u>mouse</u>. The terrorist flew a plane and <u>wrecked</u> the Twin Towers in New York. For <u>eternity</u> we will not forget September 11, 2001. We have heard the <u>idea</u> that all like <u>sheep</u> have gone astray. Now we see how evil someone can be. We will try to be <u>patient</u> with extra security and <u>congratulate</u> our <u>heroes</u>.*

*Help came in a <u>variety</u> of ways. Some sold <u>precious diamonds</u> or gave their <u>salary</u>. Others played the <u>piano</u> for comfort. Some brought food to eat, like <u>tomatoes</u> or grilled <u>moose</u>. Before September 11 we were divided. One minority student on the television said, "Today, we have dropped all <u>prefixes</u>. We are all just Americans." The <u>radio</u> on the <u>shelf</u> <u>echoed</u> through the <u>valley</u> the song, "God Bless America." We are united. We want <u>success</u> in stopping our <u>enemy</u> from hurting others.*

5. LINK WORDS TO A SPECIFIC THEME. The Wise List lends itself to a variety of themes that can be easily tied to the spelling words of that section. The following ideas may or may not be suggested in the reinforcement activities.

| | |
|---|---|
| Happiness (H-1) | Whole Truth (O-6) |
| Seasons (I-2) | Election Time (P-3) |
| Transportation (J-6) | Unity (P-4) |
| Flowers (L-4) | FamilyVacation (P-7) |
| Lying (L-5) | Diamonds (R-2) |
| Colors (M-1) | Biscuit Burglar (T-3) |
| Math (M-2) | Conceit (U-2) |
| Attack (M-3) | An Elaborate Apparatus (U-3) |
| Tax Time (N-1) | Senator's Plan (U-4) |
| Rough Choice (N-6) | A Grievance (V-1) |
| Friendship (O-1) | A Problem (X-1) |
| Adventure (O-4) | Martyrs (Y-2) |
| Trials (O-5) | A Humorous Occurrence (Z-1) |

**Perfecting the Paper**.

1. ENCOURAGE THE PREPARATION OF A ROUGH DRAFT. Good writing usually requires at least two drafts. In the first draft, focus on gathering the content and capturing thoughts. In the final draft clean up the presentation. The format should be neat, the words spelled properly, the grammar correct, and the ideas clearly and interestingly stated.

2. SELECT VIVID WORDS. Rudolf Flesch in *How to Write, Speak and Think More Effectively,* states that the lack of well-used verbs is the main trouble with modern English writing. "Clearly, most of the power, movement, and beauty of the best literary works of all times, The Bible and Shakespeare, come from the succession of active verbs." Verbs power thoughts with momentum, vitality, and flair. In my professional writing classes I learned to go through my paper and circle passive verbs like *is, was, were, are.* Then I would try to rewrite the sentence with a more powerful action verb. This simple exercise caused stunning changes in my work.

Vivid words are encouraged in Sections E, M-4, N-2, O-1, P-6, T-5. Strong writing always uses concrete verbs and nouns, rather than vague, abstract words. As an exercise to demonstrate how some words paint stronger word pictures than others,  start with bland, general words, and search more specific, definite words. For example, find substitutes for the word *move* in the sentence, "I saw an animal move." Good choices might include *attack, bolt, climb, crawl, creep, cruise, dart, dash, dive, drag, drift, float, flutter, fly, gallop, glide, hobble, hop, hover, jump, meander, pace, run, scamper, scoot, slide, slink, slip, slither, sprint, stagger, strike, strut, surge, swim, tramp, zoom.*

Have the students list vivid verbs and nouns to substitute for the bland words in the sentence.

| A *woman* | *went* | *into a room* | *and got* | *a book.* |
|---|---|---|---|---|
| spy | sneaked | bedroom | stole | diary |
| teacher | strolled | library | scanned | atlas |
| widow | hurried | study | grabbed | Bible |
| hostess | slipped | pantry | selected | cookbook |
| grandmother | limped | den | perused | catalog |
| secretary | dashed | office | studied | dictionary |

A game of charades can demonstrate the value of vivid words. For example, write on little slips of paper the vivid words for *person* and *speaks* in Section T-5. A student comes up and acts out word combinations like *electrician argues. Person* could be a baby, a basketball player, a little girl, an old man. The word is too general to give us a clear mental picture. An *electrician* is an adult with a specific skill. We imagine him wearing work clothes and carrying a tool box.

The choice of vivid words can transform a mediocre paper into a professional-sounding paragraph. Consider my son Michael's drafts of a paper he wrote.

*I Want to Be Like Mike* (First Draft)

> *As a little kid, I would watch Michael Jordan do his spectacular moves and then I would go out and "shoot hoop" trying to be like Mike. I have been playing basketball since first grade. I will work hard so I can go to Chapel Hill University.*

I asked my son to list active verbs describing what Michael would "do" in his moves in basketball. He quickly called out *dribble, guard, dunk, score, grin, entertain, dance, handle, fake, spin, shift, slam, glide, pivot, roll, wheel, surge, leap, slide, explode, relocate.* Next I asked for other descriptive basketball words. He named *powerful, fast, agile, quick, explosive, accurate, smooth, deadly aim, intricate moves, happy, calm, focused, brisk.* Then I asked him to use some of these words. Within thirty minutes he had rewritten the paper.

*I Want to Be Like Mike* (Revised Version)

> *As a little kid I watched Michael Jordan spin, fake, slide, and glide to the basket in an explosive leap for a powerful jam. His smooth, agile performance made me want to be like Mike. I have been playing basketball since first grade. When I "shoot hoop," I imitate Mike's spectacular moves. I try to spin fake, pump fake, pivot, surge, and score. If I work diligently and study, maybe someday I can attend the University of Chapel Hill, too.*

3. OMIT NEEDLESS WORDS. Concise writing is vigorous. Padded words slow down the flow of thought like leaves clogging a drain pipe. Clear the debris to further the action and increase the impact. Often these terms drag the power from sentences: *there is, the fact that, the reason I like that is, which was.* Use the word *very* only if it is VERY important.

Bulky:    The fact that there are people who can play musical instruments who do not know how to read any notes amazes me.

Concise:   I am amazed that some people can play piano by ear.

Bulky:    The fact of the matter is that sometimes there is very deep down in me a sort of, shall we say, desire, for one of those cold, creamy drinks that are made up from some ice cream blended with milk and various flavors.

Concise:  Sometimes I crave a milk shake.

Bulky:   "On November 10, 1483, when Hans and Margaret Luther laid glad eyes upon the face of their newborn son, they little thought or even dreamed that they were looking into the face of one who would not only change the destinies of nations, but who would change the aspect of human history for all time to come." — *Martin Luther: The Great Reformer* by J. A. Morrison.

Concise:  On November 10, 1483, when Hans and Margaret Luther laid glad eyes on their newborn son, they never dreamed they were looking into the face of one who would change human history.

4.  GRAB AND HOLD THE READER'S ATTENTION.  Use hooks to arrest the reader's curiosity, especially at the beginning of a paper.  A good lead will start with more than facts or setting. It establishes a hint of a problem or conflict from the beginning.

Study the opening sentences in books.  Find one that stirs your curiosity to read more.  Find another that is flat or uninviting.  Even some older classics can have a boring beginning.

a. *Luther,* by Richard Marius:  "Martin Luther was born on November 10, 1483, in a little town of Eisleben in east-central Germany." — This sentence does not draw one to keep reading like the concise quote in point three which tells us why this birth was significant.

b. *The Hound of the Baskervilles,* by Arthur Conan Doyle:  "Mr. Sherlock Holmes, who was usually very late in the mornings. . . was seated at the breakfast table." — The sentence piques our interest because something has roused the great detective earlier than usual.

c. *Robinson Crusoe*, by Daniel Defoe:  "I was born in the year 1632, in the city of York, of a good family, though not of that country, my father being a foreigner of Bremen, who settled first at Hull." — This classic could have opened with greater flair.

d. *Little Women,* by Louisa May Alcott:  "Christmas won't be Christmas without any presents," grumbled Jo. — Will the circumstances change or Jo's complaining spirit improve?

e. *The Voyage of the Dawn Treader*, by C.S. Lewis:  "There was a boy called Eustace Clarence Scrubb, and he almost deserved it." — Eustace sounds like someone we all know who annoys us.  Maybe this book will give us some help.

5.  ADD FLAIR. Adding variety to sentence patterns can improve a paper.  Instead of always starting the sentence with a noun, sometimes use an adverbial clause or prepositional phrase. Use LY adverbs.  Increase interest by adding sensory words, rhyme, figurative language (similies, metaphors, personification), alliteration, or oxymorons. Avoid misplaced modifiers. These terms are defined in the glossary pp.231-235.  Examples of these techniques occur in the Spelling Enrichments in *Wise Guide*.

| **Ways to add flair** | **Spelling Section where technique is practiced** |
|---|---|
| Adverbial Clauses | G (if), Q-6, R-6 |
| Prepositional Phrases | J-2, N-1 |
| LY Adverbs | N-6, O-5, Q-2, R-3, S-1 |
| Sensory Words | F |
| Rhyming, lyrical words | M-4, O-1, P-3, P-4, Q-2, R-3, T-4, Y-1 |
| Figurative Language | M-4, N-8, R-3 |
| Alliteration | K-6, N-4, O-6, Q-4, T-1, U-1, X-2 |
| Oxymorons | M-7, P-3, T-1 |
| Avoid misplaced modifiers | N-7, R-4, R-5, S-1 |

6. REPLACE REDUNDANT WORDS. English has a rich collection of synonyms. An excellent paper can be strengthened by substituting similar words instead of repeating the same word over again. One student retold a story of sea deliverances from Increase Mather's *Remarkable Providences in Colonial New England*. Consider highlights of her original paper.

*God's Providences* (First submission)

*Disaster struck! A leak sprang forth like a bat out of hell. Fourteen hours the **crew** worked to hold back the sea. They never succeeded and were left with only one option, to abandon the ship and get aboard their **lifeboat**. Quickly, they gathered up some bread, a tub of butter, and the water they had, and they boarded their **lifeboat**. William Laiton's ship was roughly seven hundred fifty miles from New England when this calamity fell. For nineteen dreadful days they lived on the **lifeboat**.*

*. . . Meanwhile, the storm threw Mr. Samuel Scarlet's ship off course, redirecting it towards Laiton's **lifeboat**. Scarlet's **crew** spotted the **boat**. They pleaded with their master not to take the men aboard. Although Scarlet's ship had water to spare, they barely had any food. Samuel did not listen to the selfish suggestion of his **crew.** Instead, he simply said, "It may be that these distressed men are our countrymen, or if not, they are men in misery; therefore, whatever come of it, I am resolved to take them in, and to trust in God who is able to deliver us all." With that they sailed up to the **lifeboat**. Having together two fresh dolphins, some dry bread, and plenty of water, both **crews** were soon refreshed.*

The word *lifeboat* is used five times and *boat* once. For variety and interest she could easily omit the first reference, "and get aboard their lifeboat" and substitue other references with synonyms like *stranded vessel, skiff* and *dinghy*. The word *crew* is used four times. We could omit the phrase "of his crew" and change another *crew* to *sailors*. Notice the difference this simple change can make.

*God's Providences* (Revised Version)

*Disaster struck! A leak sprang forth like a bat out of hell. Fourteen hours the **crew** worked to hold back the sea. They never succeeded and were left with only one option, to abandon the ship. Quickly, they gathered up some bread, a tub of butter, and the water they had, and they boarded their **lifeboat**. William Laiton's ship was roughly seven hundred fifty miles from New England when this calamity fell. For nineteen dreadful days they lived on this **stranded vessel**. The bread was dry; their tub of butter went bad within a day of being in the violent sun, and their supply of water only allowed them one spoonful a day. At times they could feel their skin frying from the scalding sun.*

*After twelve days, things started to take a turn. First, the sun hid and then an angry storm arose. Out of God's providence they survived. A few days later, like a miracle, a flying fish jumped out of the ocean and landed in their boat. Having a hook and some line they decided to use it as bait and caught two dolphins.*

*Meanwhile, the storm threw Mr. Samuel Scarlet's ship off course, redirecting it towards Laiton's **lifeboat**. Scarlet's **sailors** spotted the **skiff**. They pleaded with their master not to take the men aboard. Although Scarlet's ship had water to spare, they barely had any food. Samuel did not listen to the selfish suggestion. Instead, he simply said, "It may be that these distressed men are our countrymen, or if not, they are men in misery; therefore, whatever come of it, I am resolved to take them in, and to trust in God who is able to deliver us all." With that they sailed up to the **dinghy**. Having together two fresh dolphins, some dry bread, and plenty of water, both **crews** were soon refreshed. A few days later they all arrived safely in New England.*

7. SHOW, DON'T TELL. When we show, we engage the reader. Contrast two versions of the same event in the life of a petite missionary to China named Gladys Aylward. The dynamic version comes from a now out-of-print book, *The Small Woman*, by Alan Burgess. I wrote the more boring version to establish a contrast.

| | |
|---|---|
| Telling: | A messenger from the yamen ran into the house. He waved a piece of paper and began talking. It seemed there was a riot. The yamen had sent an order for Gladys to come to the prison. |
| Showing: | A messenger rushed in waving a piece of scarlet paper. He gabbled at such a rate that Gladys found it difficult to understand him.<br>"It's an official summons. A riot has broken out in the men's prison."<br>Gladys was not much concerned, "Oh, has it?"<br>The messenger reiterated loudly, "It's an official order." He hopped from one foot to the other in impatience.<br>Lu Yung-cheng insisted, "When that piece of red paper arrives from the yamen, you must go." There was a nervous tremor in his voice. |
| Telling: | Gladys went with the messenger. As they got closer loud screams could be heard. The governor and six soldiers were waiting. |
| Showing: | "All right," she said mildly. "I'll come, but I certainly don't see what a riot in the prison has to do with me..."<br>They hurried up the road. From the prison they could hear an unholy noise: screams, yells, the most horrible sounds. The governor of the prison, small, pale-faced, his mouth set into a worried line, met her at the entrance. Behind were grouped half a dozen of his staff. |
| Telling: | "The convicts are killing each other and the soldiers are too frightened to go inside," he said. "You must stop the fighting." |
| Showing: | "We're so glad you have come," he said quickly. "The convicts are killing each other."<br>"So I can hear," she said. "But why don't you send in the soldiers to stop it?"<br>"The convicts are murderers, bandits, thieves," said the governor, his voice trembling. "The soldiers are frightened. There are not enough of them. You must go in and stop the fighting."<br>"I must go in! Are you mad?" . . . The governor's eyes fixed on her with hypnotic urgency. Gladys felt a small, cold shiver down her back. When she swallowed, her throat seemed to have a gritty texture. . . She looked up at the governor's pale face, knowing that now hers was the same color. |

8. OBSERVE MODELS OF GOOD WRITING. Study master writers. In addition to sentences in *Wise Guide,* you can write your own sample paragraphs or dictate recommended selections.

See Sections H-2, I-2, J-1, J-4, K-1, K-2, K-5, K-7, L-1, L-2, N-5, O-1, O-2, O-3, O-6, P-2, P-3, P-4, Q-3, Q-4, Q-6, R-1, R-2, R-6, S-4, S-5, S-6, T-1, T- 2, U-1, U- 4, U- 5, V-1, V-3, Y-1, Z-1, Z-2.

9. PRACTICE CREATIVE WRITING. Spelling Enrichments in *Wise Guide* include:
　　composing a story (J-6, K-2, K-5, L-1),
　　designing a card (H-2),
　　composing a diary entry (N-5),
　　drafting a personal note (I-1, J-1, W-2, Z-2), or
　　writing a newspaper article (R-6).

10.  PROVIDE AN AUDIENCE FOR STUDENT WORK.  Instead of dead-end exercises that no one will ever see, have the student enter a writing contest, read his original work to the class, enclose his final draft in a letter to Grandma, or tack his best work on a bulletin board.

When my oldest son, Samuel, was twelve, he entered a contest sponsored by the Plymouth Rock Foundation.  The coveted money prize drove him to give special attention to the task.  His diligence paid off and he won first in the nation.  However, even if he had not placed in the contest, he would still have been a winner.  Hard work brings its own satisfaction and reward.  He learned more about our nation's history, and he developed better writing skills, because of the bonus motivation of the contest.  Notice especially his use of vivid verbs in the first paragraph.

---

### Self-Government with Union

#### by Samuel Sanseri

*King George, wanting to maintain his power as king, taxed excessively, punished unjustly, corrupted, stole and in general stirred up the American colonists.  He broke the laws and violated the rights of the people.*

*This oppression is exactly what the LORD warned the Israelites about in 1 Samuel 8: a king will make the citizens slaves.*

*Gary Amos, in <u>Defending the Declaration</u>, writes, "Tyranny and despotism on the part of the government break the compact (between the government and the people), so that the people are free to alter or abolish the form of government and institute a new one."*

*The Founding Fathers risked their lives to institute a "new government laying its foundation on such principles and organizing its powers in such form, as to them shall seem most likely to effect their safety and happiness."  They implemented self-government with union, a concept which is demonstrated in Exodus 18.*

*Self-government with union is a corporate interest and responsibility.  Or, as William Tyler Page put it, "A government of the people, by the people, for the people."  Civil government was established by God to restrain evil, punish wrongdoing, reward good and to protect against foreign invasion.  The purpose of government is to serve, not to be served.*

*The Declaration of Independence states, "All men are created equal. . . . They are endowed by their Creator with certain unalienable rights, that among these are life, liberty, and the pursuit of happiness. . . To secure these rights, governments are instituted among men, deriving their just powers from the consent of the governed."*

*The Founding Fathers envisioned a country that would protect personal freedom without harming the freedom of others.  Every individual, accountable to God, would be able to pursue his own interest in union with the needs of the nation.*

---

**34.** <u>**DICTATE Y'S EXCHANGING PAGE**</u>. (Before L-6)

<u>Objectives</u>:

To teach how to add a suffix to words ending in Y.
To start building a discovery page in the Learning Log.

<u>Prepare to Teach</u>:

Have handy rule cards: 6, 14, 16, 24.
Have available phonograms: ay, oy, ey, y.
Gather the suffix cards prepared in Step 23. (Optional)
Write on the board or a sentence strip: any suffix except -i__.
Preview Reference Page in Appendix C (P10/ B13). Adapt to the level you are teaching.
Plan to spend at least twenty minutes introducing this concept initially.

**Introduce the Idea**.

1. STIMULATE INTEREST. Move from the known to the unknown. Ask, "What happens if we want to add the suffix -est to the following words?"

| clean | = | clean-est | Write the word and add the ending. |
| grave | = | grav-est | Drop the E and add the ending. [R.16] |
| mad | = | mad-dest | Double the last consonant and add the ending. [R.14] |
| easy | = | eas-i-est | Change the Y back to I. [R. 24] |

When is it smart to trade the Y and I, or shall we say, to make a "wise exchange?"

2. DISCUSS WHAT WE ALREADY KNOW ABOUT THE I.

a. <u>Review Rule 6</u>. "English words do not end in I."

b. <u>Explain words in the dictionary that do end with I</u>.

(1) Foreign spelling. Advertisers use foreign words for flair. These words may come into our vocabulary without adjusting to English spelling norms.

Norwegian: *ski*        Maori (New Zealand): *kiwi*        Spanish: chili
Yiddish: *pastrami*    Japanese: *hibachi, bonsai*
Arabic: *safari*        Italian: *spaghetti, macaroni, broccoli, zucchini*

(2) Slang. For convenience, an English word may be abbreviated. *Taxi* is a shortened form of *taxicab*. *Hi* is a shortened form of *hello*.

c. <u>Ask, "How do we spell English words that end with the sound of I?"</u>
We use a Y to substitute or stand in for the I sound.

3. EXPLAIN THE Y'S EXCHANGING RULE. Sometimes when we add a suffix to a word ending in Y, we change the Y back to the I. When should we do this? That is the object of this lesson. *To change or not to change, that is the question.*

a. <u>Discuss the Meaning of the Rule</u>: *The single vowel Y changes to I when adding ANY ending, unless the ending starts with I.* Let's analyze this rule.

< What is a single vowel Y? [Hold up the phonogram Y.]
< What is not a single vowel Y? [Any vowel plus Y, especially phonograms ay, oy, ey.]
< What type of suffixes work with this rule? Any suffix except one that starts with I.
    [Find the suffix cards that start with I. For this rule we could add the suffix *-ish*.]

b. Contrast with E's Dropping and 1-1-1 Rules. While those rules concern VOWEL suffixes; the Y's Exchanging Rule applies to ANY suffix, UNLESS the ending starts with I. English words avoid two I's in a row.

**Teach the Reference Page.**

Students will work through this discovery process as they build a reference page for their Learning Log. Guide the class through questions to determine the correct spelling of the new derivative.

&lt; *Does it end with a <u>single vowel Y</u>?*
&lt; *Does the suffix begin with <u>ANY</u> letter other than I?*

Dictate the base word to consider for the first column. Then work through the process-of- elimination questions to determine if this is a smart place to make a trade (a wise exchange). If we need to change a Y to I, say "CHANGE" and with a red pencil write the letter I, then go back to regular pencil for the remainder of the word.

**Introductory exercise of the Y's Exchanging Page of the Primary Learning Log.**

**Add other examples in conjunction with new spelling words or as needed.**

| Y's Exchanging Rule | | |
|---|---|---|
| basic word | + any suffix . . . | EXCEPT an I suffix |
| ba by | ba tried | ba by ish |
| fly | fli er | fly ing |

| | | | | yes | no |
|---|---|---|---|---|---|
| ba-by + | **-ed** | Is Y a single vowel Y? | (yes) | | |
| | | A not- I suffix? | (yes) | ba-bied | |
| + | **-ish** | A not- I suffix? | (no) | | ba-by-ish |
| fly + | **-er** | Is Y a single vowel Y? | (yes) | | |
| | | A not- I suffix? | (yes) | fli-er | |
| + | **-ing** | A not- I suffix? | (no) | | fly-ing |
| like-ly + | **-hood** | Is Y a single vowel Y? | (yes) | | |
| | | A not- I suffix? | (yes) | like-li-hood | |
| fun-ny + | **-est** | Is Y a single vowel Y? | (yes) | | |
| | | A not- I suffix? | (yes) | fun-ni-est | |
| play + | **-er** | Is Y a single vowel Y? | (no -- ay) | | play-er |
| hap-py + | **-ness** | Is Y a single vowel Y? | (yes) | | |
| | | A not- I suffix? | (yes) | hap-pi-ness | |

You may add additional words to the Learning Log, space permitting. Reinforcement activities can be done on loose-leaf paper. See L-6, M-4, N-3, O-6, P-5,7, Q-5, R-2, S-1, T-3, V-1, 2, 3.

As follows examples of words ending in Y in *Wise Guide* are listed with possible derivatives. The "no" words are in bold, with parenthetical answers as to why.

| Section | Word | Word # | Derivatives | Reasons for not Changing Y |
|---------|------|--------|-------------|----------------------------|
| **L** | buy | (548) | **buyer, buying** | (U+Y not lone vowel) |
| | body | (585) | bodily, bodies | |
| | early | (629) | earlier, earliest, earliness | |
| | birthday | (631) | **birthdays** | (AY not single vowel) |
| | tiny | (635) | tinier, tiniest | |
| **M** | army | (701) | armies | |
| | ready | (710) | readier, readiest, readiness, **readying** | (I suffix) |
| | monkey | (715) | **monkeys, monkeying** | (EY not single vowel) |
| | bury | (778) | buries, buried, burial, **burying** | (I suffix) |
| | pretty | (779) | prettier, prettiest, prettily, **prettying** | (I suffix) |
| **N** | study | (781) | studies, studied, **studying** | (I suffix) |
| | try | (782) | tried, tries, **trying** | (I suffix) |
| | cry | (788) | cries, crier, cried, **crying** | (I suffix) |
| | sky | (823) | skies | |
| | category | (833) | categories, categorical, categorize | |
| | bury | (834) | buried, buries, burial, **burying** | (I suffix) |
| | energy | (836) | energies | |
| | empty | (839) | emptier, emptiest, emptied, **emptying** | (I suffix) |
| | fancy | (847) | fancier, fanciful, fancied, **fancying** | (I suffix) |
| | dirty | (849) | dirtied, dirtier, dirtiest, dirtiness, **dirtying** | (I suffix) |
| | hurry | (850) | hurried, hurries, **hurrying** | (I suffix) |
| | copy | (856) | copier, copies, **copyist, copying** | (I suffix) |
| | diary | (872) | diaries | |
| | history | (873) | historical, historic, historian | |
| | sorry | (875) | sorrier, sorriest, sorriness, sorrily | |
| | yesterday | (880 | yesterdays | (AY not single vowel) |
| **O** | weary | (970) | wearied, weariness, wearisome, **wearying** | (I suffix) |
| | forty | (985) | forties, **fortyish** | (I suffix) |
| | worry | (999) | worried, worrier, **worrying** | (I suffix) |
| | holy | (1017) | holiness, holier, holiest, holies | |
| | duty | (1044) | duties, dutiful | |
| | liberty | (1045) | liberties | |
| | company | (1048) | companies, companion, accompanied | |
| | penny | (1050) | pennies, penniless | |
| **P** | lengthy | (1141) | lengthiest, lengthiness, lengthily | |
| | naughty | (1143) | naughtier, naughtiest, naughtiness | |
| | hungry | (1144) | hungrier, hungriest, hungriness | |
| | heavy | (1145) | heavier, heaviest, heaviness, heavily | |
| | simply | (1147) | simplify, simplified, **simplifying** | (I suffix) |
| | guilty | (1148) | guiltier, guiltiest, guiltiness | |
| | destroy | (1158) | **destroyed, destroying** | (OY not single vowel) |
| | reply | (1179) | replied, **replying** | (I suffix) |
| | family | (1181) | families | |
| | beauty | (1183) | beauties, beautiful, beautify | |
| | (en)joy | (1194) | **joyful, joyous, joyless** | (OY not single vowel) |
| | carry | (1196) | carried, carriage, carrier, carries, **carrying** | (I suffix) |
| | industry | (1199) | industrial, industrious | |
| **Q** | primary | (1232) | primaries, primarily | |
| | glory | (1259) | glorify, glorious, **glorying** | (I suffix) |

|   |   |   |   |   |
|---|---|---|---|---|
|   | employ | (1286) | **employment, employer, employed** | (OY not single vowel) |
|   | magnify | (1289) | magnifier, magnification, **magnifying** | (I suffix) |
|   | dry | (1317) | drier, dried, **drying** | (I suffix) |
|   |   |   | Exceptions: **dryness, dryly** |   |
| **R** | valley | (1344) | **valleys** | (EY not single vowel) |
|   | salary | (1348) | salaries |   |
|   | vary | (1353) | variety, varieties, **varying** | (I suffix) |
|   | enemy | (1360) | enemies |   |
|   | busy | (1366) | busier, busiest, busily, busied, **busying** | (I suffix) |
|   | angry | (1370) | angrily, angrier, angriest |   |
|   | satisfy | (1389) | satisfied, satisfier, **satisfying** | (I suffix) |
|   | injury | (1398) | injurious, injuries |   |
| **S** | temporary | (1446) | temporarily, temporariness |   |
|   | handy | (1458) | handiest, handicraft, handiwork, handily |   |
|   | century | (1461) | centuries, centurion |   |
|   | marry | (1467) | married, marriage, **marrying** | (I suffix) |
|   | ability | (1476) | abilities |   |
|   | sympathy | (1495) | sympathize, sympathizer, sympathized |   |
|   | majesty | (1498) | majestic, majesties |   |
|   | dictionary | (1513) | dictionaries |   |
|   | community | (1514) | communities |   |
|   | grocery | (1516) | groceries |   |
|   | society | (1530) | societies |   |
|   | supply | (1540) | supplier, supplied, supplies, **supplying** | (I suffix) |
|   | carry | (1558) | carriage, carried, **carrying** | (I suffix) |
| **T** | accompany | (1569) | accompaniment, **accompanying** | (I suffix) |
|   | chimney | (1605) | **chimneys** | (EYnot single vowel) |
|   | lily | (1618) | lilies |   |
|   | discovery | (1619) | discoveries |   |
|   | vary | (1636) | various, **varying** | (I suffix) |
| **U** | ceremony | (1672) | ceremonies, ceremonial, ceremonious |   |
|   | colony | (1674) | colonies, colonial, colonize, colonist |   |
|   | necessary | (1698) | necessarily |   |
|   | city | (1704) | citizen, citified, citied |   |
|   | attorney | (1705) | **attorneys** | (EY not single vowel) |
|   | majority | (1707) | majorities |   |
|   | difficulty | (1718) | difficulties |   |
|   | apply | (1746) | applied, application, **applying** | (I suffix) |
|   | occupy | (1748) | occupied, occupier, **occupying** | (I suffix) |
| **V-Z** | mystery | (1781) | mysterious, mysteriousness, mysteriously |   |
|   | testimony | (1791) | testimonies, testimonial |   |
|   | magnify | (1820) | magnifier, magnificent, **magnifying** | (I suffix) |
|   | vicinity | (1828) | vicinities |   |
|   | confectionery | (1829) | confectioneries |   |
|   | anniversary | (1831) | anniversaries |   |
|   | opportunity | (1832) | opportunities |   |
|   | controversy | (1840) | controversial, controversies |   |
|   | apply | (1866) | application, applied, **applying** | (I suffix) |
|   | extraordinary | (1941) | extraordinarily |   |
|   | cemetery | (1950) | cemeteries |   |
|   | apology | (1953) | apologies, apologize |   |

**35.**  <u>**CONSTRUCT  PLUS ENDINGS PAGE**</u>. (After L-6)

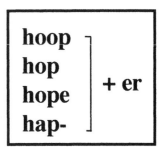

<u>Objectives</u>:

To link together the rules already taught for adding endings.

<u>Prepare to Teach</u>:

Have handy the suffix cards and  rule cards 14, 15, 16, 24.

Preview the sample finished page in Appendix C (P14/ B17).

Realize that the 2-1-1 rule (taught in Step 39) can be applied
     here for upper level students.

**Introduce the Concept.**

Normally we just add a suffix to a base word: teach, teacher; farm, farmer.  But sometimes we have to make a change in the word in order to add an ending.  Can anyone name the three places where we need to make a change?  Let's review how this works.

Write *hoop, hop, hope, happy* on the board.  What do we do if we add the suffix -er to these words?  Most of the time we just add the suffix (hoop-er).  With a 1-1-1 word we have to double the consonant before we add a vowel suffix (hop-per).  With a silent final E word we usually drop the E before we add a vowel suffix (hop-er).  With a word that ends with a single vowel Y we change the Y to I when adding any suffix unless the suffix begins with I (hap-pi-er).

**Build a Reference Page.**

Select some review words.  With red have the students write the base words in the first  column. Divide the words into syllables and mark them with routine spelling markings.  Pick a suffix to be added. Then ask process-of-elimination questions to determine if you should drop an E, add a consonant, or exchange a Y. If any special action is needed, build the derivative in the column designed for that action.  With red, underline the letter added for the 1-1-1 rule or write a red I (changed from a Y) in a Y's Exchanging word.  If no special action is needed,  with regular pencil simply add the ending to the red base word in the first column.

Just add an ending UNLESS you can say "Yes."  Does the word end with...

> a silent E  + a vowel suffix?

> 1 vowel + 1 consonant (accented) + a vowel suffix?

> a single vowel Y  + a suffix that does not begin with  I?

**Introductory
exercise on
Rules for
Adding Endings
in the Primary
Learning Log.**

| Rules for Adding Endings | | | |
|---|---|---|---|
| + ending | E's dropping | 1-1-1 | Y's Exchanging |
| *mad* | | *mad dest* | |
| *eas y* | | | *eas i est* |
| *grave* | *grav est* | | |
| *clean est* | | | |

None of these concepts are new.  This assignment reviews spelling words and links together  rules already taught.  It can be used after L-6 with any spelling section throughout the rest of the program.  Some of the following words can be analyzed as classwork review on the board and some dictated to the Reference Page.  The bold letters that follow indicate where we use red.

| | + ending | E's Dropping | 1-1-1 | Y's Exchanging |
|---|---|---|---|---|
| After L-6 | **mad**<br>**eas** y<br>**grave**<br>**clean** er | grav est | mad **d**est | eas **i** ly |
| After M-1 | **ston** y<br>**white**<br>**red**<br>**green** est | whit est | red **d**est | ston **i** est |
| After M-2 | **spot**<br>**hold** er<br>**might** y<br>**angle** | an gler | spot **t**er | might **i** er |
| After M-3 | **follow** er<br>**swir** ly<br>**pro vide**<br>**swim** | pro vid er | swim **m**er | swir li **i** er |
| After M-4 | **read** y<br>**hat**<br>**climb** er<br>**file** | fil er | hat **t**er | read **i** ness |
| After M-7 | **charge**<br>**bur** y<br>**trust** ed<br>**zip** | charg ing | zip **p**ing | bur **ied** |
| After N-1 | **stud** y<br>**bal ance**<br>**tax** ed<br>**step** | bal anced | ste**pp**ed | stu **di** ous |
| After N-3 | **clap**<br>**mis take**<br>**cat e go ry**<br>**need** ed | mis tak en | cla**pp**ed | cat e gor **i** cal |
| After N-5 | **vote**<br>**plan**<br>**feel** er<br>**sor** ry | vot er | plan **n**er | sor **ri** er |

|  | + ending | E's Dropping | 1-1-1/2-1-1 | Y's Exchanging |
|---|---|---|---|---|
| After O | **ex plain** er<br>**fan cy**<br>**re prove**<br>**hem** | re prov er | hem **m**er | fan cier |
| After O-2 | **wea ry**<br>**waste**<br>**board** ed<br>**stop** | wast ed | stop**p**ed | wea ried |
| After O-3 | **sur face**<br>**quit**<br>**wor ry**<br>**con fir**med | sur fac ing | quit ting | wor ri er |
| After O-4 | **ho ly**<br>**lo cate**<br>**shed**<br>**quiet** er | lo cat er | shed **d**er | ho li er |
| Before P-6 | **trav el** er<br>**red**<br>**pro duce**<br>**guilt y** | pro duc er | red **d**er | guilt i er |
| After R-3 | **an gry**<br>**hum ble**<br>**bright** est | hum blest |  | an gri est |
| Before R-5 | **pur pose**<br>**sat is fy**<br>**in ter est** ed<br>**con trol** | pur posed | con trolled | sat is fied |
| After S-5 | **sup ply**<br>**ac cuse**<br>**lis ten** er | ac cus er |  | sup pli er |
| After T-4 | **va ry**<br>**re al ize**<br>**for feit** ed | re al ized |  | va ried |
| After T-5 | **es ti mate**<br>**slip**<br>**guess** er<br>**ac com pa ny** | es ti ma tor | slip **p**ing | ac com pa nist |
| After U-1 | **sur vive**<br>**drop**<br>**ear ly**<br>**weird** er | sur viv or | drop**p**ed | ear li est |

**INTRODUCE DICTIONARY SKILLS**. (After M)

Objective:

　　To teach students to use the dictionary.

Prepare to Teach:

　　Have a dictionary handy for each student.

**Expose Students to Components of the Dictionary.**

> DIC'TIONARY, *n.* [Fr. *dictionnaire*; It. *dizionario*; Sp. *diccionario*; from L. *dictio*, a word, or a speaking.]
>
> A book containing the words of a language arranged in alphabetical order, with explanations of their meanings; a lexicon.
>
> *Johnson.*
>
> *An American Dictionary of the English Language*
> Noah Webster — 1828

　　The dictionary is a valuable resource. Many don't know how to fully use the information nestled in this valuable reference aid. Each dictionary entry is listed in alphabetical order and gives us certain key information: syllabification, accent, pronunciation, etymology, definition, part of speech, and derivatives. *Wise Guide* addresses many of these skills at various times.

　　1. ALPHABETIZING. To look up words in a dictionary, a student needs to understand alphabetical order. Practice of this skill is suggested in Sections M-1, P-3, P-7, Q-6, S-4, and T-1.

　　2. ACCENT. The accent syllable can be marked in various ways. The traditional way is with a stress mark ('). A stressed syllable can also be either bolded or capitalized. Noah Webster calls **accent** "the more forcible utterance of a particular syllable of a word, by which it is distinguished from the others. The accented syllable of a word serves therefore as a kind of resting place or support of the voice which passes over the unaccented syllable with more rapidity and a less distinct utterance."

　　3. SYLLABIFICATION. Words are divided into syllables. Some dictionaries use a dot or hyphen between syllables and some just give a space. We practice syllabification with every spelling dictation because the rules of English spelling are syllable-dependent. See page 80.

　　4. ETYMOLOGY. The word **etymology** comes from Greek *etymos* (true) + *logos* (word). Webster defines it as "a study of the origin and development of a word; the tracing of a word back as far as possible." To write his 1828 dictionary, he learned twenty languages. The introduction to *Wise Guide* and *Alpha List* describe our format for showing foreign language dervatives. In a nutshell:

> Etymology information is placed in brackets [ ].
> The language of origin is indicated by a < sign and an abbreviation for the language.
> The English meaning of the word parts is placed in parentheses ( ).
> The origin for "etymology" would be written [<Gk *etymos* (true) + *logos* (word)].

　　Other dictionaries use different patterns. How is the etymology coded in the insert to the right? The listing of languages shows a progressive history of "excite" tracing it backwards from a Middle English word that came from an Old French word that originated in a Latin word. **A study of the etymology of words can be an exciting adventure. Plant seeds with your students to start them on this lifetime adventure.** Practice identifying the etymology of words as suggested in Sections S-4, W-3, X-2, Y-1, and Z-2.

　　5. USAGE NOTES. The dictionary will clarify what would be considered standard English. For example the word *good* may carry a warning not to say "He sang good" for "He sang well."

> ex-cite' (eks-), *v.t.*; excited, *pt.*, *pp.*; exciting, *ppr.* [ME. *exciten*; OFr. *exciter*; L. *excitare*, to call out or forth, to stimulate, excite; *ex*, out, and *ciere*, to call, summon.]
>
> 1. To rouse; to call into action; to agitate; to stir up to activity; to cause to act, as that which is dormant, sluggish, or inactive; as, to *excite* the spirits; to *excite* a mutiny or insurrection.
>
> 2. To stimulate, as an organ of the body; as, to *excite* the liver.
>
> 3. In electricity, to induce magnetic properties in.
>
> Syn.—Incite, arouse, stimulate, kindle, agitate, awaken, irritate, stir up, inflame.—When we *excite*, we rouse into action feelings which were less strong; when we *incite*, we urge forward to acts correspondent to the feelings awakened.

> *Webster's New Twentieth Century Dictionary,* 1956,1983
> from copyright by World Publishing 1904-1952

6. DEFINITIONS. Entries are explained in simple, direct terms and listed by number in order of importance.

7. PARTS OF SPEECH. An italicized abbreviation flags the parts of speech. Usually *n.* means "noun," *adj.* means "adjective," etc. *Wise Guide* activities to locate these are in Sections S-6, V-3, and X-2.

---

Notice the Y treated as a short I sound.

**ba by** (bā′bi), *n., pl.* **-bies,** *adj., v.,* **-bied, -by ing.** —*n.* **1.** a very young child. **2.** the youngest of a family or group. **3.** person who acts like a baby; childish person. **4.** *Slang.* term of praise or approval applied to a person or thing. —*adj.* **1.** of or for a baby. **2.** young. **3.** small for its kind; small. **4.** childish. —*v.* treat as a baby; pamper. [ME *babi*] —**ba′by like′,** *adj.*

*Thorndike Barnhart High School Dictionary,* 1957

---

8. PRONUNCIATION KEY. Current dictionaries respell words to try to match pronunciation. I prefer providing students a dictionary that generally avoids giving a conflicting image of the word.

9. DERIVATIVES. New words can be built by simply adding prefixes or suffixes to the foundational word. Most dictionaries include such derivatives within the entry of the base word. The meanings of prefixes and suffixes are separately defined. When the meaning of a word like *mushroom* differs from that which can be deduced from the sum of its parts, it is listed as a separate entry. Practice forming derivatives is given in every lesson of *Wise Guide*. See Step 24 for more details.

10. SYNONYMS. Other words with the same meaning are given, usually with the most commonly used word. For example the word *excite* may list *incite* and *agitate* as synonyms.

**Select a Dictionary**.

Frequently educators ask me to recommend a dictionary. Noah Webster's *First Edition of an American Dictionary of the English Language, 1828* gives profound definitions. Words influence thinking, and Webster's lifetime work for the American people impacted the moral condition of the country. Gradually, his definitions have been watered down, and a conflicting sound key has been added.

CONTRAST THE DEFINITION OF *EDUCATE*.

- <u>Webster's 1828</u> — **ED′ U ᄃATE:**  To bring up, as a child; to instruct; to inform and enlighten the understanding; to instill into the mind principles of the arts, science, morals, religion, and behavior.  To educate children well is one of the most important duties of parents and guardians.

- <u>Webster's New 20th Century</u> — **ed′ū · c̄ate:**  To provide schooling for; to develop the mind and morals especially by instruction.  Education suggests a general course of instruction in a school with stress on mental development.

- <u>21st Century (online)</u> — **ed·u·cate:**  /ej-oo-keyt/  or  /ĕj-ə-kāt′/  or  /ˈe-jə-ˌkāt/: To develop the faculties and powers of (a person) by teaching, instruction or schooling.  Synonyms: school, drill, indoctrinate.  "Parents trust schools to educate their children."

Webster's 1828, excels in definitions and etymology. He avoided respelling words for pronunciation. **Webster linked the code for spelling and the code for speech while giving room for regional variations in speech.**  We extend that approach to our spelling markings. Webster's limited pronunciation markings are on correctly spelled words. (In "educate" a tiny horizontal line on C shows that it says /k/.) The tradition to not respell words for pronunciation continued for at least 155 years. The most recent dictionaries "based on the broad foundation laid down by Noah Webster" were edited by Jean McKechnie under different titles and publishers. Maybe someone today will revive the practice!

Contrast Webster's approach to simplified markings on a correctly spelled word with the confusing pronunciation key found in most current dictionaries. While it is helpful to reference a current dictionary for new vocabulary, I highly recommend searching for a reliable classic dictionary as well.

**37.**   **COLLECT DISMISS L WORDS**. (After M-5)

Dismiss an L

Objectives:
    To demonstrate that while many words are formed by
        simply adding two words joined together, *all* and *full*
        drop (or dismiss) an L when added to another syllable.
    To find Dismiss L derivatives of spelling words.

Prepare to Teach:
    Realize these words are collected over time as they occur.
    Have handy Spelling Rule Cards 17 and 21.
    Preview the Black Learning Log Page in Appendix C (B22).
    Write each of these review words on a separate 3x5 card:
    *hand, bag, cart, hold, stand, writing, full, all, mighty.*

**Present the Idea.**

    1. RECITE THE RULE. *All and full, when added to another syllable, are written with one L.*

    2. DEFINE THE TERMS. A **compound word** combines two or more words together to form a new word. Compound comes from the Latin root com- (together) + ponere (put).

| | | | |
|---|---|---|---|
| Hand + bag | = | a lady's bag held in her hand | **handbag** |
| Hand + cart | = | a cart pushed by hand | **handcart** |
| Hand + hold | = | something to hold by hand for support | **handhold** |
| Hand + stand | = | balancing on hands rather than feet | **handstand** |
| Hand + writing | = | writing done by hand | **handwriting** |
| Hand + full | = | as full as the hands can get | hand**ful** |
| All + mighty | = | mighty over all | **al**mighty |

    In *handbag, handball, handcart, handhold, handstand,* and *handwriting,* we just combined two words, but when we add *hand* and *full* together we make a change. Hold up spelling rule card #21. We call this rule the Dismiss L Rule, a pun on "dismissal." Also, if we add the words *all* and *mighty (M-2, 662)* together, we will eliminate an L *(almighty)*.

    What sound does the second L make in *all* and *full?* (It is silent.) Why did we double it? Hold up Spelling Rule Card 17. Say the rule: **We often double F, L, S after a single vowel at the end of a base word.** All and full become a word part (either a prefix or a suffix) when added to other words. When these are no longer a base word, the added silent L is no longer needed. See Rule 21. **ALL and FULL are written with one L when added to another syllable.**

    3. APPLY THE RULE. Many base words taught before M-5 that can take the suffix -FUL: will (95), thank (200), forget (276), hope (319), rest (353), help (371), fruit (417), care (433), mouth (452), fear (467), watch (573), wish (574), color (641). Dictate some or all of the review words. Have students write a derivative meaning "full." Don't forget to drop the L.

| | | | | | |
|---|---|---|---|---|---|
| full of will | = | will-ful | full of care | = | care-ful |
| full of thanks | = | thank-ful | full in the mouth | = | mouth-ful |
| full of forgetting | = | for-get-ful | full of fear | = | fear-ful |
| full of hope | = | hope-ful | full of watching | = | watch-ful |
| full of rest | = | rest-ful | full of wishes | = | wish-ful |
| full of help | = | help-ful | full of color | = | col-or-ful |
| full of fruit | = | fruit-ful | | | |

**Collect Dismiss L Words Taught after M-5.**

Students should search like detectives for possible Dismiss L words in the Wise List or in outside reading. Students with the Black Learning Log can add these to the Reference Page designed for that purpose, but there is no Reference Page for the Dismiss L Rule in the Primary Learning Log. If you reach this rule while using the Primary Log, just build a Reference Page on loose-leaf paper to be placed in their three-ring binder or on a classroom wall chart.

| Section | Dismiss L Words | | | |
|---|---|---|---|---|
| | **al-** | | **-ful** | |
| M | almost<br>also | (721)<br>(723) | truthful<br>regretful<br>eventful | (729)<br>(734)<br>(757) |
| N | always | (899) | useful<br>thoughtful<br>needful<br>cheerful<br>delightful<br>faithful | (790)<br>(792)<br>(825)<br>(882)<br>(892)<br>(898) |
| O | | | mournful<br>wasteful<br>dutiful | (960)<br>(961)<br>(1044)  [R. 24] |
| P | | | careful<br>wrongful<br>beautiful<br>awful | (1182)<br>(1185)<br>(1193)<br>(1200)  [R.16] |
| Q | although | (1301) | wonderful<br>prideful | (1226)<br>(1250) |
| R | already | (1380) | | |
| S | | | grateful | (1448) |
| T | altogether | (1632) | resourceful | (1590) |
| U | | | respectful | (1752) |

1. EXPLAIN THE WORD "AWFUL." The compound word *awe* + *full* means "full of awe." With trembling and respect, people describe the *awful* power of God. The primary meaning of *awful* in Webster's 1828 Dictionary was, "that which strikes with awe; that fills with profound reverence; as the awful majesty of Jehovah." The meaning has been corrupted to mean "something extremely bad, disagreeable, or terrible." Why do we drop the silent E when -ful is a consonant suffix? See p. 148.

2. SPELL CORRECTLY "ALL RIGHT." People commonly misspell *all right*. These are two separate words, not a compound word. In this case, we need to keep the second L in all. The phrase "all right" is the opposite to "all wrong." If you spell *all right* as a compound word, you are *all wrong*.

**38.**   **TEACH ADVANCED PHONOGRAMS.** (Before N-2)

Objectives:

To show that additional phonogram combinations occur with upper level words.

Prepare to Teach:

With a yellow highlighter, mark in *Wise Guide* all the references to advanced phonograms.

For example, on page 132, in the Preliminaries, highlight *augh*.

On page 133, beside *caught* and *taught*, highlight *augh* = /aw/.

Preview the Extra Phonogram Page.  See Appendix C (P2/ B4).

**Explain the Idea.**

Spelling will never have the consistency of mathematics.  Since the Tower of Babel, mankind no longer speaks only one language.  The rules that govern English do not always accommodate new words that come from foreign tongues.  When I lived in Asia, I learned to eat with chopsticks, the ancient utensil for eating in the Orient.  However, many in Asia use forks and eat hamburgers and fries. At MacDonald's in Seoul, Korea you can read in Korean letters: hamboga (hamburger).  You can ask for a foka (fork).  They adapt our words to accommodate their alphabet and sounds. Likewise,  when we assimilate a word from another language, we retain some of the uniqueness of the spelling from that culture.  English can do this more easily than many other languages.  This may be a reason that English is a key alternative language in places like India, where the native people speak many languages.

The 70 basic phonograms cover the 1000 most frequently used words.  As our vocabulary grows, we will occasionally discover new ways to spell the sounds we have already learned.  Key examples are listed later in this step.  Students do not need to drill these in the same way we did the basic seventy.

**Add Advanced Phonograms to the Log.**

1. PRIMARY LEARNING LOG.  ⟶

Primary Log users start with red adding EU under EW.  With regular pencil bracket the two. Now they can be a "sleuth" looking for additional advanced phonograms.  Add any with red to the final column of the Multi-letter Phonogram Page. GU, the first one, appears in *Wise* in Section N-2. Primary Log students will not reach all the extra phonograms. See end of second grade sample on page 208.

2. BLACK LEARNING LOG.  ⟶

Black Log students should, with red, add EU under EW on page B3.  Also, with red add the two new spellings for /er/.  All other advanced phonograms will be written with red on page B4. Write in alphabetical order on the far left edge of Page 4 the rest of the advanced phonograms. This plugs them into the book in an orderly fashion for discussion later. The teacher can dictate these by letter name.

| Multi-letter Phonograms | | | |
|---|---|---|---|
| sh | ng | igh | ough 6 |
| th 2 | ar | ie 3 | ew 2 |
| oo 3 | wh | dge | eu 2 |
| ee | [aw | ur | gu |

| | | | |
|---|---|---|---|
| sh | | ng | igh |
| th | 2 | ar | ie 3 |
| oo | 3 | wh | dge |
| ee | | [aw | ur |
| [oy | | [au | [ti |
| [oi | | ck | [ci |
| ch | 3 | [oe | [si 2 |
| [ow | 2 | [oa | tch |
| [ou | 4 | ed 3 | [eigh |
| [ay | | [er | ei 3 |
| [ai | | ur | ey 3 |
| ea | 3 | ir | ph |
| or | | wor | [kn |
| ui | | [ear | [gn |
| | | our | ough 6 |
| | | yr | [ew 2 |
| | | | [eu 2 |

### Presentation order of all Advanced Phonograms in Wise Guide.

| 803 | gu | guide | 1673 | et | bouquet |
|---|---|---|---|---|---|
| 851 | qu -- 2 | conquer | 1691 | eu | neutral |
| 1072 | augh | caught | 1719 | ai | aisle |
| 1099 | augh -- 2 | laugh | 1779 | gh | spaghetti |
| 1114 | gu --2 | language | 1824 | eau | bureau |
| 1291 | our | journal | 1860 | rh | rhyme |
| 1293 | gi | region | 1867 | ae | aerospace |
| 1522 | ge | sergeant | 1949 | yr | martyr |
| 1572 | aigh | sraight | 1975 | au -- 2 | chauffeur |
| 1602 | cu | biscuit | 1996 | pn | pneumonia |
| 1620 | sc | scissors | 2000 | ah | hallelujah |

### Words that use Advance Phonograms:  EU, OUR, YR.

**eu** — /OO/-/U/ that we may not use at the end of English words.
An alternate for the native English spelling EW.

| | | | |
|---|---|---|---|
| Old Norse = /OO/ | sleuth | | |
| French and Latin = /OO/ | neutral (1691)<br>chauffeur (1975)<br>lieutenant (1995) | amateur (1908)<br>maneuver (1985)<br>entrepreneur | neuter<br>grandeur<br>leukemia |
| Greek = /OO/ | neutron<br>pneumonia (1996) | neurology<br>pseudo | rheumatism |
| Greek = /U/ | eucalyptus<br>eureka<br>Eutychus | eulogy<br>euro<br>feud | eunuch<br>Europe<br>Eugene |

**our** — French = /er/

| journal (1291)<br>journey (1711) | courage (1295)<br>courtesy (1751) | adjourn (1691) |
|---|---|---|

**yr** — Greek = /er/

| martyr (1949) | myrrh | myrtle |
|---|---|---|

*Syrup* was spelled *sirup* in 1828.  Was this non-Greek word changed to match Greek spelling conventions to get attention in food advertising?

## Add the other advanced phonograms.

A Black Log user adds to the B4 advanced phonogram list a guide word for each new phonogram that he covers in *Wise Guide* or in outside reading.  See sample of a fourth grader's completed page on SWR page 213.  The advanced phonograms do not need to be drilled the way we did the original 70.  There are no new sounds.  We can show that other letters can team together like the basic 70.  We can often trace the reason back to the derivative language.

On SWR pages 180-181, we provide a more extensive list of word examples.  This gives you flexibility if you want to use a different word.  Several phonograms on that page (ay, ps, pt, x--2) do not occur in the Wise List at all.  They are included because they may come up in other subjects.  It is impossible to analyze in an exhaustive manner a living language with 500,000 words and growing. I think you will be amazed that more advanced phonograms, if any, will be rare.

## Additional Advanced Phonograms with Word Examples

| | | | | |
|---|---|---|---|---|
| **ae** | Greek and Latin = /A/ | **ae**rospace (1867)<br>**ae**robics | **ae**rosol (1868)<br>**ae**rial | |
| | Greek and Latin = /E/ | alg**ae**<br>Cae**sar** | archa**e**ology<br>Zacch**ae**us | **Ae**sop<br>**ae**on |
| **ah** | Hebrew = /ah/ | halleluj**ah** (2000)<br>Jon**ah** | hurr**ah**<br>Messi**ah** | Jehov**ah**<br>Sar**ah** |
| | Swedish/ Native American | da**h**lia | Uta**h** | |
| **ai** ₂ | Old French/ Polynesian = /I/ | **ai**sle (1719) | **ai**oli | |
| **aigh** | Old English = /A/ | str**aigh**t (1572) | | |
| **au** ₂ | French = /O/ | cha**u**ffeur (1975) | cha**u**vinism | |
| **augh** | Old English = /aw/ | c**augh**t (1072)<br>n**augh**ty (1143) | t**augh**t (1073)<br>d**augh**ter (1166) | sl**augh**ter |
| | Old English = /af/ | l**augh** (1099) | l**augh**ter (1100) | |
| **ay** ₂ | Native American = /I/ | b**ay**ou | c**ay**enne | k**ay**ak |
| **cu** ₂ | /k/   U added so C = /k/. | bis**cu**it (1602) | cir**cu**it | |
| **cu** | /kw/   U = /w/ as in QU. | **cu**isine | | |
| **eau** | French = /O/ | bur**eau** (1824) | plat**eau** | chat**eau** |
| **et** | French = /A/ | bouqu**et** (1673)<br>buff**et**<br>gourm**et** | ball**et**<br>croch**et**<br>val**et** | ber**et**<br>croqu**et** |
| **ge** | French G = /j/ | ser**ge**ant (1522)<br>sur**ge**on (1770) | pi**ge**on (1701)<br>pa**ge**ant | **Ge**orgia |
| **gh** | Italian G = /g/<br>Old English = /g/ | spa**gh**etti (1779)<br>**gh**ost | **gh**etto<br>**gh**astly | a**gh**ast |
| | GH also shadows Old English sounds in: *igh, ough, aigh, eigh, augh.* | | | |
| **gi** | French G = /j/ | re**gi**on (1293)<br>alle**gi**ance (1998) | reli**gi**on (1303)<br>conta**gi**ous | Geor**gi**a<br>presti**gi**ous |
| **gu** | French = /g/ | **gu**ide (803)<br>**gu**ess (1647)<br>**gu**arantee (1964)<br>dis**gu**ise<br>lea**gue**<br>vo**gue** | **gu**ilty (1148)<br>va**gue** (1886)<br>ro**gue**<br>mor**gue**<br>pla**gue**<br>epilo**gue** | **gu**est (1167)<br>fati**gue** (1959)<br>ton**gue**<br>intri**gue**<br>fati**gue**<br>synago**gue** |
| | **gu**ild<br>**gu**ile<br>**gu**itar<br>**gu**y<br>**gu**erilla | | | |
| **gu** ₂ | /gw/<br>U = /w/ as in QU | lang**u**age (1114)<br>ang**u**ish | distin**gu**ish (1731)<br>peng**u**in | jag**u**ar<br>lang**u**ish |

| pn | Greek = /n/ | **pn**eumonia (1996) | **pn**eumatics | |
| ps | Greek = /s/ | **ps**ychic (No examples in *Wise Guide*. See below.) | | |
| pt | Greek = /t/ | **pt**omaine (No examples in *Wise Guide*. See below.) | | |

| 2<br>qu | Spanish / French = /k/ | con**qu**er (851)<br>bou**qu**et (1673)<br>anti**qu**e (1851)<br>mos**qu**e | li**qu**or (1639)<br>mos**qu**ito (1773)<br>opa**qu**e (1899)<br>techni**qu**e | cli**qu**e<br>criti**qu**e<br>cro**qu**et |

| rh | Greek = /r/ | **rh**yme (1860)<br>**rh**apsody<br>**Rh**ode Island<br>**rh**ubarb<br>**rh**ythm<br>**rh**eumatism | **rh**inoceros (1982)<br>**rh**inestone<br>**rh**izome<br>**rh**ododendron<br>**rh**ebok (African antelope)<br>diar**rh**ea | myr**rh**<br>**Rh**ein<br>**rh**etoric<br>**Rh**odesia |

| sc | Latin = /s/ | **sc**issors (1620)<br>de**sc**end (1679)<br>con**sc**iousness (1803)<br>fluore**sc**ent | **sc**ience (1671)<br>de**sc**ent (1680)<br>con**sc**ience (1870)<br>ob**sc**ene | **sc**ene<br>**sc**ent<br>**sc**epter<br>**sc**ythe |

| 2<br>x | Greek = /z/<br>Used only at the beginning of a word. | **X**erox® | **x**ylophone | **X**erxes |

## Make Observations about Advanced Phonograms.

1. CONNECT ADVANCED PHONOGRAMS WITH RULES WE HAVE LEARNED.
*C and G only say /s/ or /j/ before E, I or Y* [Rules 2, 3]. These rules explain the addition of silent letters in CU, GU, GH, GE, GI.

**cu** — The silent U separates C from E or I so it will say /k/ (circuit). U is not a vowel here.

**gu** — The silent U separates G from E or I so it will say /g/ (guest). U is not a vowel here.

**gh** — The silent H is added to separate a G from an E or I so it will clearly say /g/ (ghetto).

**ge** — The silent E is added to make the G say /j/ (pigeon). E is not a vowel here.

**gi** — The silent I is added to make the G say /j/ (religion). I is not a vowel here.

2. RECOGNIZE THE INFLUENCE OF THE GREAT VOWEL SHIFT. As English developed, the basic vowel sounds changed from those of other European languages. Asian languages use the Spanish sounds when transliterating words. In the Roman alphabet, "A" consistently says /ah/ and "I" consistently says /E/. The island of Japan named *Shi-ko-ku* is pronounced /shE-kO-kOO/. The common name Tanaka is pronounced /Tah-nah-kah/.

3. IDENTIFY THE SILENT P IN GREEK WORDS. The P in PN, PS, and PT represents a forgotten sound in Greek-based words. PS and PT are not illustrated in the Wise List.

| ps | Greek = /s/ | **Ps**alm<br>**ps**ychology | **ps**eudonym<br>**ps**ychopath | **ps**eudo |
| pt | Greek = /t/ | **pt**erodactyl | **Pt**olemy | a**pt**yalism |

## **39.**  **EXPLAIN 2-1-1 ACCENT RULE**. (Before P-3)

Objective:
   To expand the 1-1-1 Rule.

Prepare to Teach:
   Write on the board the words: *get, for-get*.
   Have handy Rule Cards 14, 15.
   Preview a sample 2-1-1 Page for the Black Learning Log.
   See Appendix C. (B12)
   Recognize that this Reference Page is built over time after introducing the concept.

> Don't **forget**
> to double the T in
> **getting** and **forgetting.**

**Stimulate Interest.**

   A common spelling problem is whether to double the consonant in words when we add a vowel suffix. Do we spell the following words:

   acquited or acquitted?      labeling or labelling?      refered or referred?

   Must we memorize the correct form for every individual word, or do we have some principle to guide us? In American English we do and it is similar to a rule we already know. (Unfortunately, British English does not follow this rule.)

**Introduce the Concept.**

   1. REVIEW THE 1-1-1 RULE. With a **one**-syllable word ending in **one** vowel, then **one** consonant, double the last consonant before adding a vowel suffix.

   2. SHOW THE CONNECTION BETWEEN 1-1-1 AND 2-1-1 RULES. The 2-1-1 Rule: "With a **two**-syllable word ending in **one** vowel, then **one** consonant, double the last consonant before adding a vowel suffix **if** the accent is on the last syllable."

   How is this rule different from the 1-1-1 Rule?
      a. more than one syllable.
      b. last syllable accented.

   3. DEFINE ACCENT. To **accent** means to utter a syllable with a particular stress or modulation to the voice. To determine accent, first say the word emphasizing the first syllable. Then say it emphasizing the second syllable (FOR-get/ for-GET).

   > An accented syllable is louder, longer, and higher (for-GET).
   > Prefixes and suffixes are not accented (re-MIT).
   > The base part of a word is usually the accented syllable (FLY-ing).
   > The vowel sound of the accented syllable is more true-to-sound (HU-man, a-BOUT).
   > The second syllable with a fourth type of silent E is never accented (AP-ple).

   Practice accent with the following:

   ac-QUIT      — ac-quit-ting                    CAN-cel      — can-cel-ing
   COV-et       — cov-et-ing                      EN-ter       — en-ter-ing
   e-QUIP       — e-quip-ping, e-quip-ment        LA-bel       — la-bel-ing
   OF-fer       — of-fer-ing                      per-MIT      — per-mit-ting
   OR-der       — or-der-ing                      LIM-it       — lim-it-ing
   VIS-it       — vis-i-tor                       O-pen        — o-pen-ing

**Build a Reference Page for the 2-1-1 Rule**.

The Primary Learning Log does not have a page formatted for this rule. If you reach the first reference for a 2-1-1 word, just write *for-get / for-get-ting* on the board and discuss the concept. Few examples will occur in the whole program, and none in the first half of the list.

Students with a Black Learning Log will build a Reference Page for the 2-1-1 Rule. Although closely related to the 1-1-1 rule, the elimination questions vary slightly.

> < Is it a <u>two-syllable</u> word?
> < Does it end with <u>one</u> vowel then <u>one</u> consonant (that we can see and hear)?
> < Is the <u>accent</u> on the last syllable?
> < Are we adding a <u>vowel suffix</u>?

With red, mark the accent and underline twice the consonant doubled for the 2-1-1-Accent Rule.

**2-1-1 Page after Section T in the Black Learning Log**

**See B-12 in Appendix C to format questions at bottom of page.**

**Review the Concept**.

We retain new concepts through repetition over a period of time. Introduce the 2-1-1 concept with several sample words. Periodically add more words to the Reference Page. See the following list of some 2-1-1 words that come up in the program. More words are given than will fit on any one Reference Page. Select from this wider range of examples for extra reinforcement when needed.

For an added challenge ask, "Why do we double the R in **preferred** and **referring** but not in **preference** or **reference**?" The accent is on the last syllable in pre-fer′ (pre-fer-red), but the accent shifts AND the vowel in the first syllable changes in pre′fer-ence and ref′er-ence. While our head knows that these words all trace back to a 2-1-1 type base word, our ear does not. An accent shift alone does not override the standard rule (ex-cel′, ex-cel′-ling, ex′-cel-lent).

Notice the connection between some of the 2-1-1 sample words and the 1-1-1 words on the same line in the facing page in the Learning Log.

| | | |
|---|---|---|
| for-get′ting | get-ting | |
| be-gin′ner | sin-ner | |
| e-quipped′ | quipped | Q needs a U. U is not a vowel here. |
| wor′ship-ing | ship-ping | Do not double if syllable is unaccented. |
| con-fer′-ring | fur-ry | /er/ = a consonant + a vowel sound |

## Word Examples from *Wise Guide* for Teaching the 2-1-1 Rule

| | | double | | just add ending | reason to not double |
|---|---|---|---|---|---|
| for-get' | J-1 | for-get-ting<br>for-get-ta-ble | U-1 | for-get-ful | Consonant Suffix |
| be-gin' | L-5 | be-gin-ner<br>be-gin-ning | U-1 | | |
| o-mit' | M-2 | o-mit-ting | | | |
| e-quip' | N-5 | e-quipped | | e-quip-ment | Consonant Suffix |
| ad-mit' | P-3 | ad-mit-ted<br>ad-mit-tance | U-5 | | |
| trav' el | P-3 | | | trav-el-er | Accent first syllable |
| com-mit' | P-6 | com-mit-ting<br>com-mit-ta-ble<br>com-mit-tee | X-4 | com-mit-ment | Consonant suffix |
| con-trol' | R-4 | con-trol-ling<br>con-trol-ler<br>con-trol-la-ble | V-3 | | |
| pre-fer' | R-5 | pre-ferred | | pref' er-a-ble<br>pref' er-a-bly<br>pref' er-ence | Accent Shift/Vowel Chg. |
| wor'ship | T-1 | | | wor-shiped<br>wor-ship-ing<br>wor-ship-er | Accent first syllable |
| med' al | T-3 | me-dal'lion | | med' al-ist | Accent first syllable |
| con-fer' | T-5 | con-ferred<br>con-fer-ring | | con' fer-ence   T-5 | Accent Shift/Vowel Chg. |
| re-fer' | T-5 | re-ferred<br>re-fer-ring | | ref' er-ee<br>ref' er-ence      V-2<br>ref' er-a-ble | Accent Shift/Vowel Chg.<br>Accent Shift/Vowel Chg.<br>Accent Shift/Vowel Chg. |
| re-bel' | | re-bel-lious<br>re-bel-ling<br>re-belled | U-2 | | |
| ex-cel' | | ex-cel-lent<br>ex-celled<br>ex-cel-lence | U-4 | | |
| per-mit' | | per-mitted<br>per-mit-ting | V-5 | | |
| prof' it | V-3 | | | prof-it-a-ble<br>prof-it-ing<br>prof-it-ed | Accent first syllable |
| trans-mit' | | trans-mit-ted<br>trans-mit-ting<br>trans-mit-ter | W-3 | | |
| oc-cur' | | oc-cur-rence | Z-1 | | |
| re-lax' | | | | re--lax' a-tion | X sounds like 2 consonants |

## DICTATE THE IE/ EI PAGE. (Before Q-1)

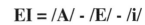

Objectives:
> To spell with confidence words with IE or EI phonograms.
> To collect words for the IE/ EI Reference Page.

Prepare to Teach:
> Pull out the IE and the EI phonogram cards.
> Pull out Spelling Rule Card 9.
> Preview completed IE Page. See Appendix C (P15/ B23).
> Realize that this Reference Page is built over time as words occur in *Wise Guide*.

**Expose the Need**.

Hold up the IE, EI phonogram cards. "Why are these often confused in spelling words?"

< Both phonograms use the same two letters.

< Both make three possible sounds.

< Both commonly say two of the same sounds: /E/ and /i/.

> **EI = /A/ - /E/ - /i/**
>
> **IE = /E/ - /I/ - /i/**

**Explain the Rule**.

1. SAY THE RULE. Fortunately there are clues that can help us remember which phonogram to use in words. *Use I before E except after C, if we say /A/, and in some exceptions.*

2. ANALYZE THE RULE STEP-BY-STEP USING LETTER NAMES.

> a. Use I before E. Of the two phonograms IE and EI, we use IE most often. All the initial words in the Wise List use IE. (Unless someone misspells those words, there is not a need to even bring up this rule until we have an EI word.)

> b. Except after C. After a single letter C (not CI saying /sh/), in the same syllable of a base word spelled with the EI phonogram.

> c. If we say /A/. Only EI says /A/, the same sound as the four-letter A, EIGH.

> d. And in some exceptions. Three silly sentences contain the EI exception words.

3. INTRODUCE THE EXCEPTION SENTENCES.

> a. ***Either weird foreign sovereign forfeited leisure.***

**Sovereign** is another word for king.
To **forfeit** is to give up.
**Leisure** is relaxing activities done for pleasure.

**work-a-holic kings**

What things do you do for leisure? (paint, read, skate, swim, etc.)
Would you agree that **either** of the kings from a foreign country
who would only work, work, work, but never relax, are **weird**?
We call them work-a-holic kings.

b.  *Neither heifer seized counterfeit protein or caffeine.*

**Heifer** is another word for a young female cow.
**Seized** means grabbed or took.
**Counterfeit** is artificial, not genuine.
**Protein** is a key element in food needed for life.
**Caffeine** is a drug-like stimulant.

smart calves

> If **neither** heifer would eat fake protein or drink too much cola and coffee, then these calves are more intelligent than some of us. We drink chemically flavored water that "tastes like the real thing," and gorge on caffeine-laden drinks.

c.  Advanced: *Feisty Mr. Fahrenheit heisted seismic steins and kaleidoscopes.*
These six words use EI to say /I/. None are in the Wise List.

**Feisty** means ill-tempered.
**Fahrenheit** is a temperature scale.
**Heist** means to steal.
**Seismic** is shaking caused by an earthquake.
**Steins** are beer mugs.
**Kaleidoscope** is a small tube for viewing changing
patterns of color.

a shaking thief

We can remember this hot criminal as a shaking thief.

**Build an IE/ EI Reference Page for the Black Learning Log.**

1. REVIEW IE/ EI WORDS. In the first column, under IE, write *chief*. The first word on the Wise List that uses either the IE or EI phonogram is in Section N-2. Find it so we can add it to this reference page. Three more are in Section O and four in Section P. We will add these as well. Which phonogram is used the most often? We started with *chief* because IE is the CHIEF or main phonogram. It is the most common. Our nine review words all used IE.

In Section Q-1 we encounter a word that uses the EI. If a base word meets one of three conditions, we need EI. If not we use IE. With red, we underline each IE or EI. We build this discovery page to reinforce which phonogram to use when.

> **> Is it after a single C?**
> **> Do we say /A/?**
> **> Is it an exception?**

2. ASK PROCESS-OF-ELIMINATION QUESTIONS. As we continue through the program, we will add words to this collection page. To determine placement on the page we will ask three questions. If you answer "yes," put the word under that column. If you say "no" to all three questions, put the word under the IE column.

| ceiling | Is it after C? | Yes, put it under the CEI. | With red, underline /E/, put a 2 over it. |
|---|---|---|---|
| veil | Do we say /A/? | Yes, put it under EI = /A/. | With red, underline /A/. |
| either | Is it an exception? | Yes, put it under exception. | With red underline /E/. |
| fierce | Is it after C?<br>Do we say /A/?<br>Is it an exception? | No.<br>No.<br>No, put it under the IE. | With red, underline /E/. |

**The IE/ EI Page in the Primary Learning Log as taught in Section Q-1.**

*Ceiling* and *veil* can be taught early if need be to give examples of EI words.

| ie or ei ??? | | | |
|---|---|---|---|
| ie | cci | ei says /A/ | Exceptions |
| *chief* | *ceiling* | *veil* | |
| *priest* | | | |
| *thief* | | | |
| *friend* | | | |
| *lie* | | | |

3. CONTINUE BUILDING THE REFERENCE PAGE. Other words are added to the IE/ EI collection page as they occur in the spelling list, reading assignments, or the student's original work. The words in order of introduction on the Wise List are:

| **IE** | | | | | | | |
|---|---|---|---|---|---|---|---|
| priest | N-2 | brief | P-5 | handkerchief | S-6 | grievance | V-1 |
| chief | O-1 | pie | P-5 | piece | S-6 | relieve | V-2 |
| thief | O-1 | field | Q-1 | pierced | T-2 | mischief | Y-1 |
| friend | O-1* | fierce | R-3 | yield | U-2 | mischievous | Y-1 |
| lie | O-6 | believe | S-2 | siege | U-2 | chandelier | Y-1 |
| shield | P-2 | tie | S-3 | achieve | U-2 | menagerie | — |
| grief | P-3 | niece | S-5 | prairie | V-1 | | |

IE is used most often and in more common words. We can wait to bring up this reference page until after we come to EI words. Then we can draw from review words that we learned that used IE. You, of course, can introduce this rule sooner if a student is writing EI when she should use IE.

| **CEI** | | | | | | | |
|---|---|---|---|---|---|---|---|
| ceiling | S-6 | receive | U-2 | conceive | W-3 | receipt | X-2 |
| deceived | T-2 | conceit | U-2 | perceive | X-1 | deceit | — |

| **EI = /A/** | | | | | | | |
|---|---|---|---|---|---|---|---|
| veil | Q1 | reign | T-2 | surveillance | Z-2 | reindeer | — |
| their | Q-6 | vein | U-2 | feign | — | sheik** | — |
| beige | R-6 | heir | U-3 | feint | — | skein | — |
| rein | S-6 | heirloom | Y-1 | heinous | — | inveigle | — |

| **Exceptions** | | | | | | | |
|---|---|---|---|---|---|---|---|
| either | Q-4 | foreign | U-2 | counterfeit | X-1 | caffeine | — |
| neither | S-6 | leisure | V-2 | protein | X-2 | codeine | — |
| weird | T-2 | heifer | W-1 | sovereign | — | sheik** | — |
| forfeit | T-4 | seize | X-1 | sovereignty | Z-2 | | |

Only three exceptions (either, neither, foreign) are in the 1000 most commonly used words.

* An alternate markng can be fri-end.. Treat it as a one syllable word that we think to spell as two.
**In *sheik* the EI can be pronounced /A/ or /E/.

4. RESPOND TO UNFOUNDED CRITICISM. The unknown author of this poem believed that all the bolded words are exceptions to the IE/EI rule. Can you show how he is wrong?

---

"Use I before E, except after C." Really Now?

We **deify** concepts we learned once in school
    We will always **reiterate** our most sacred rule.
**Being** a fact that is simple, concise and **efficient,**
    For all **species** of spelling it's more than **sufficient**.
It gives guidance impartial, **scientific** and fair
    In this language, this tongue to which we are all **heir**.
**Albeit** some in **society** seek to deride,
    To consider **deficient** this most **ancient** guide.
These **atheists** follow a **foreign** agenda,
    A plot hatched in **their** vile **hacienda**.
They **counterfeit** truth and think we are **weird**
    We refuse to **forfeit** the **juciest** law they have smeared.
Resist **glaciers** of ignorance that icily frown,
    **Either** hold to your standards or slide down and drown.
In our work and our **leisure**, our **agencies** and schools,
    Let us follow our **conscience**, **seize** proudly this rule!

---

The rule relates to the phonograms IE and EI in an Anglicized root word.

    a. <u>Consider syllable breaks</u>. The syllable break is vital for properly understanding spelling rules. The following words are clearly not examples of the EI phonogram.

de-i-fy    re-it-erate    be-ing    al-be-it    a-the-ists

We should not look at *be-ing* and connect E and I together any more than we should look at the word *water-melon* and connect it to the word *term*. In *being*, E goes with the base word *be*, and *-ing* is an added suffix.

    b. <u>Clarifying C</u>. "Except after C" words requires EI, but only with a single phonogram C + the two-letter phonogram EI in a base word.

| | | | | |
|---|---|---|---|---|
| CI = /sh/: ef-fi-<u>ci</u>ent | spe-<u>ci</u>es | suf-fi-<u>ci</u>ent | de-fi-<u>ci</u>ent | an-<u>ci</u>ent |
| C-I = ends syllable: | <u>sci</u>-en-ti-fic | so-<u>ci</u>-ety | ha-<u>ci</u>-en-da | |
| | juic-i-est | gla-<u>ci</u>-er | con-<u>sci</u>-ence | |

-CY + suffix    (Y changing to I to add an ending like -es creates IE)
                        a-gen-cy    a-gen-ci + -es  (a-gen-cies)

    c. <u>Apply the whole rule</u>. Some have never learned our full IE/ EI rule.

| | | | | |
|---|---|---|---|---|
| EI says /A/: | heir | their | | |
| Exceptions: | either | weird | foreign | forfeit |
| | leisure | seize | counterfeit | |

This unknown author incorrectly listed twenty-six violations of the IE/ EI rule. Recognizing phonograms and the spirit behind spelling rules resolves most areas of confusion with English words. We are heirs to a truly magnificent language. Unfortunately, most of us don't realize what a treasure we have.

# APPENDIX A:
## Senate Hearing Speech

Literacy Today:  What is Wrong and How Can We Fix it?

Oregon Senate Hearing Presentation, February, 2001
by Wanda Sanseri

I'm holding a set of amazing, wonderworking tools. (I held up a stack of cards.) Before I finish my speech you'll understand why these simple, profound, but little known concepts work like magic.

### An Undervalued Language

Most of us do not appreciate or properly value our language. We've been told English is illogical, irregular, and filled with endless exceptions. We flounder teaching spelling and reading. I have transformational news. English is NOT as perplexingly difficult as we've been led to believe. With the information in my hand, just 98 cards, you can unlock most words in our dictionary. This news is particularly amazing considering the international significance of our language.

English is the most vital language in the world, the first truly global language. Over half of the people who use English do not speak it as their mother tongue. English has the richest vocabulary on the planet. The modern Chinese dictionary has about 12,000 entries. The French vocabulary less than 100,000 words. But the Oxford English Dictionary lists 500,000 words! (McCrum, p.10)

While the world values English as a key means to personal advancement, a growing number of native English speaking people have trouble recognizing words in print. With the most highly funded educational system in the world, we assume everyone can read. We find it hard to believe that 30% of high school graduates cannot read the warning on a can of Drano ®, fill out a job application, interpret a bus schedule, or decipher the menu in a restaurant. The reports of massive illiteracy do not ring true because most of us do not think we personally know anyone with this problem. The chances are that more than one of your friends struggles with the language but tries to pretend otherwise. Non-readers in a culture such as ours do not broadcast their handicap. Victims of this subculture go to great lengths to disguise their secret.

magic in my hands

Consider John Corcoran, author of *The Teacher Who Could Not Read*. This award-winning high school instructor could not read the sign on the bathroom door to know if it said men or women. Jonathan Kozol in *Illiterate America,* describes a well-dressed draftsman who carefully places a fresh edition of *The New York Times* on his desk at work each day just to appear informed. At night he trashes the paper he cannot read. (Kozol, p. 3). Ones you least expect, the student next door, the mechanic who repairs your airplane, or the CEO at your company may be part of this invisible but growing minority.

I would have trouble comprehending the severity of the situation, if I had not witnessed epidemic academic failure in the classroom and with various highly intelligent adults who have over the years come to me secretly for help.

## My Experience:  Witnessing the Problem

I first became aware of the literacy problem as a high school English teacher in the early 1970s. I taught in three distinct settings:  an inner-city all-black school, a small farming community, and a settled middle class suburb.  Low skill levels in all three locations made my job of teaching literature, grammar, and upper-level composition close to impossible.

One year I was assigned a high school remedial class.  The students had high intelligence (an IQ of at least 120 or above)  but had major problems with spelling and reading.  They came from intact, middle-class families and had involved, concerned parents.  My budget for supplies exceeded my needs.  The principal begged me to buy supplies.  If I didn't spend all the money allowed, the school would lose funds the next year.  Our best and brightest struggled with the most foundational academic skills.  I realized that the blame could not be placed on the students, their parents, or the supposed lack of money spent on education.  I began to suspect a problem with the teaching methods themselves.

I did not fault individual teachers.  I belonged to the ranks.  Some of the most caring people I know go into teaching.  People, however, can be sincere and still be wrong.  I started investigating ways to correct the problem.  A friend told me about phonics.  I did not know what that meant. She showed me that letters represented sounds of speech.  The letter A said /a/ in *apple*.  I couldn't believe her.  I had never heard this in my life.  She gave me a recording so I could practice hearing and saying the short vowel sounds.  I would listen to the recording at night  and then teach the sounds to my class the next day.   I understood how handicapped I had been because of whole language instruction.  Nothing can measure the unnecessary stress and limitations I had needlessly endured.  I developed a passion to learn what I had missed so I could give others a better start in life.

> **Sincere teachers can be wrong!**

## My Experience:  Victory over the Problem

That was over thirty years ago.  Since that time I have experienced success teaching all learning types, various ages, and in different settings.  Classroom teachers trained by me have reported amazing progress, as have tutors and home educators.   I have not only witnessed success with average and above average students, but also with ones others termed unteachable.  I guided a dedicated mother of a highly retarded daughter.  The Downs Syndrome girl can now spell at the twelfth grade level!  I tutored an illiterate mother with two juvenile delinquent sons.  In five hours of instruction, she jumped two-and-a-half grade levels.  For the first time she had hope that she could help her troubled sons.

My experience verifies what scientific research confirms.  With the right teaching techniques virtually all students can learn to spell and read English.  I believe three main problems hinder progress in many schools today: whole word instruction, faulty phonics, and the separation of spelling from reading.  The language arts program that you select should guard against these roadblocks to success.

1. PROBLEM NUMBER ONE: WHOLE-WORD INSTRUCTION.  English needs to be taught by component parts rather than by a whole-word approach.  People assume whole word teaching is possible because they think that Chinese is taught that way.  It is not.  A student does not learn distinctly different pictures for each dictionary entry.  Chinese is a combination of a limited number of tonal syllable characters and classifier symbols fused together in various ways.  Whole words have never been used in any language as the sole basis for writing.  "Ordinary people (including children) can only remember about 1,500 to 2,000 abstract visual symbols." (McGuinness, p. 50).

The first step in teaching any language is to isolate the most basic components used to make up that language.  In English we have 500,000 words.  Trying to learn each word one at a time will restrict the student.  Sadly, most elementary teachers, in fact most college professors of education, do not know the basic components of English.  Do you?  How many ways do we have to spell the basic sounds of English? (70)  We call the letter or letters that represent the sounds of English, phonograms.

The next step is to learn the rules that govern the use of these symbols. How many rules do we have in English? (28). With a working knowledge of the 70 phonograms plus 28 spelling rules (our 98 cards), we can phonetically explain 99% of the most commonly used words in the language and at least 87% of all the words in our dictionary. Does it sound unbelievable that the language with the most voluminous vocabulary can be reduced to 98 key components? It seems more incredible that such valuable information has been kept as a secret from people in high places.

2. PROBLEM NUMBER TWO: FAULTY PHONICS INSTRUCTION. Some think that phonics has been tried and didn't work, but phonics works consistently if taught properly. Often it is not. The whole-word method became the rage in the early part of the twentieth century. Periodically, a backlash of complaint would restore phonics for a time. Teachers unschooled in phonics would then combine the unfamiliar material with the whole-word techniques they knew. When this did not produce the promised success, teachers returned again to whole-word instruction. Each time teachers made the switch between whole words and phonics, our understanding of phonics became more frayed. Some of what is now taught as phonics is a weak substitute with worthless rules.

Teachers who fail using phonics usually use an inadequate version. At least three characteristics of weak phonics could be the cause. Evaluate any program by asking if it uses phony phonics, pokey phonics, or fickle phonics.

a. **Phony phonics**. I reviewed a state-approved textbook for beginning reading. Every lesson in the teacher's manual had a section boldly titled, "Phonics." I read every word in the flagged segments. Nothing even remotely related to phonics. In one lesson the text told the teacher to draw an elephant on the board. Under the picture she should write "elephant." She was to point to the picture and have the class repeat, "Elephant." Next she was to point to the word and have the class say, "Elephant." Many teachers like me never learned as children that letters represent sounds. Such a teacher could be deceived by this type of text and might naively tell parents that she uses phonics with every lesson.

elephant

b. **Pokey phonics**. Phonics instruction should be first and fast. Some systems take years to introduce the key components to the language. Unnecessarily delaying this vital instruction will force children to invent their own inadequate and unreliable systems.

Fragmenting key information into bits and pieces which are introduced separately over time makes retrieval hard. Instead of teaching only short vowel sounds or long vowel sounds, it is easier for a student to file together in one place of her mind all the common sounds a phonogram can make. A student who learns only the short vowel sound of O will experience frustration trying to read words like OPEN or DO. A person who knows from the beginning that the letter O has three possible sounds will not be discouraged that the first sound did not work. She has two other choices on the tip of her tongue to try.

The same concept applies to multi-letter phonograms. CH can make three different sounds. Even a retarded or very young child can see CH and say the three sounds it can make. In many programs these sounds are taught separately over a period of years. Students in first grade may have a list of words using CH to say /ch/ as in *child*. In second or third grade they may have a list of words using CH to say /k/ as in *chord*. In fourth grade they might have a long list of words using CH to spell /sh/ as in *chef*. The three distinct sounds are rarely presented together in an uncluttered way.

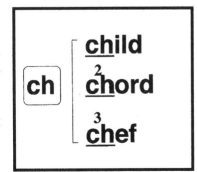

c. **Fickle phonics**.   Phony phonics is not real phonics.  Pokey phonics may include correct information, but it is presented too slowly.  Fickle phonics is unreliable.  Like a fickle girl who flits between more than one lover, it muddles phonics with whole language ideas.  It may involve bogus rules, a cluttered code, a backward focus, or misleading exercises.

(1) <u>Bogus Rules</u>.  Fickle phonics teaches useless ideas like the cute sounding rule, "When two vowels go walking the first one does the talking."  In other words, if we see two vowels together, the first one will say the name of the letter and the second one will be silent. (OA = /O/).  Back in the '70s, I had my students mark page after page of words that illustrated this principle.  The concept worked on screened worksheets, but in real life it failed repeatedly.  I discovered why.  The "two vowels going walking" rule is reliable only 27% of the time!  It only **works consistently** with *aigh, ee, oa, oe*.  It **commonly works** with *ay, ai*.  It **possibly works** with *ea, ae*.  It **usually does not work** with *ei, ey, ie, oo, ou*.  It **never works** with *au, augh, ear, eau, eu, oi, oy, ui*.

The effective way to deal with vowel pairs is to teach each vowel team as a separate phonogram that the student recognizes instantly by sound.  Our goal should be to establish the most instant response between the symbols and the sound, not to waste time with unfruitful mental gymnastics.

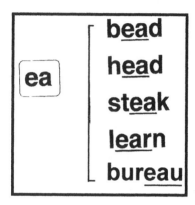

A student can be easily taught all the  sounds that EA regularly makes.   Such a student is prepared for EA to say /E/ in *bead*, /e/ in *head*, /A/ in *steak*,  /er/ in *learn*, and the /O/ in *bureau*.  A student who learned the Two Vowels Go Walking rule might stumble over words like *head, steak, learn*, and *bureau*. People conclude, because of bogus rules like this, that English is so complex and                     is spelled so unpredictably that teaching phonics is useless.  They don't understand that the problem is not the language, it is a faulty presentation of the language.

(2) <u>A Cluttered Code</u>.   The ideal way to teach a complex subject is to identify the most essential core parts.  The phonograms and rules (my magic cards) are the consistent components to a proper understanding of English.  Elevating blends to the level of the phonograms adds needless complexity and creates unnecessary confusion.

A blend is made by running together the sounds of two or more phonograms. For example, if we quickly say the sound of the B plus the sound of the L we have the blend /bl/.  A student who knows the individual sounds can easily combine them for the blend.   Contrast BL with the phonogram PH. Together P and H can represent  /f/, a sound distinctly different from the sounds these letters would make being blended together normally.

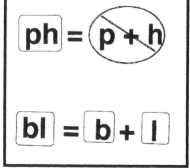

The idea of blending can and should be taught with spelling words, but presenting blends in the same way as phonograms weakens the core foundation.  If we teach blends in isolation, we add 76 or more unnecessary units that water down the essential foundation.

(3) <u>A Backwards Focus</u>.  The eye should be trained to move from left to right in reading English.  Some systems group words by word endings.  Activities include reading a series of words by simply changing the first letter: *day, may, pay, ray, say*. This misleads the student to expect words that look alike will sound alike.

English is built from phonogram units, but cannot be consistently organized by appearance.  Many words that sound alike are spelled differently (rowed, road).  Likewise, numerous phonetically reliable words sound different but look alike (timber, climber/ rose, lose/ home, some/ to, go/ have, cave/ put, but/ pant, want/ are, care/ both, cloth/ hat, what/ etc.).

| Words that end the same may not  sound the same ||
|---|---|
| **day** | **gas** |
| **may** | **has** |
| **pay** | **was** |

Students who expect all look-alike words to sound alike will stumble over words like *gas, has, was*.  The letter S and the letter A can represent more than one sound.  *Has* and *was* are not irregular.  One or more of the phonograms use a predictable alternative sound:  gas = /g-a-s/; has = /h-a-z/; was = /w-ah-z/.

Focusing on the final rhyme confuses eye sequencing from back to front, a problem with dyslexia.  Organizing by rhyme burdens the mind with an unnecessary overload.  English has over 1260 rhymes.  It is better to teach 70 phonograms than to memorize a multitude of unpredictable rhymes.  While *heard* and *beard* appear irregular in so-called "word family" programs, these words are regular in a phonogram based program.  *(Beard* uses four phonograms /b-ea-r-d/.  *Heard* uses three phonograms /h-ear-d/.)

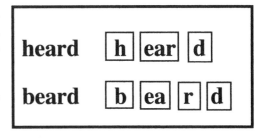

(4)  Misleading Exercises.  Phonics ladders are tools to teach blending.  The plan is to give a consonant or two and then a single vowel.  The  student is taught to use the short vowel sound and form new words by adding different consonants.

This type of exercise is unsound phonemically for two reasons.  First, a vowel at the end of a syllable rarely has the short sound.  Contrast the words *co-ma* and *comma*.  If a student sees CLO as a separate unit, he should  expect  the final vowel sound to be OH (as in clo-sure) not AH (as in clock).

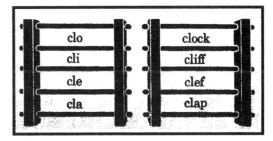

Secondly, if the vowel is not at the end, we need to see the next letter or letters before we can determine the sound it will make.  Several simple patterns commonly change the vowel sound.  Is it  a part of a two-letter phonogram team (OA, OW, OU)?  If so, we might read the words as: *cloak, clown, clout.*  Is the vowel sound influenced by a silent final E *(clove)?*

| The vowel sound cannot be determined without seeing the entire word. ||||
|---|---|---|---|
|  | **long vowel at end** | **2-letter vowel** | **silent letter effect** |
| clo | **clo**-sure, **clo**-ver | **cl**oak, **cl**ois-ter, **cl**oud, **cl**own | **clo**ve, **clo**the |
| cli | **cli**-ent, **cli**-max | -- | **cl**imb, **cl**ime |
| cle | **Cle**-o-pat-ra | **cl**ean, **cl**ear, **cl**eek, **cl**erk | **Cl**eveland, un-**cle** |
| cla | **cla**-vate, **cla**-vier | **cl**aim **cl**ause, **cl**aw, **cl**ay | **Cl**are, de-**clare** |

Leonard Ayres scientifically organized a list of the one thousand most frequently used words in the English language. With phonics ladders, over a third of this core list of words would appear to be exceptions. With a phonogram plus simple rule base, less than one percent of these words are "rule breakers."

Spelling and reading skills should progress to an instantaneous, almost subconscious, response. This happens by building in the student a second nature instinct for the language. Teaching methods should logically build such automatic responses. Avoid methods that do the opposite. Effective phonics deals with the sounds represented by phonograms and gives a complete, uncluttered, reliable presentation of the code as soon as possible.

3. PROBLEM NUMBER THREE: SEPARATING SPELLING AND READING. Dr. Hilde Mosse, an expert in children's reading disorders, proclaimed, "Contrary to the prevailing educational theory, reading and writing belong together; they reinforce each other." (Mosse, p. 14). Typically today, reading is taught first and spelling is delayed as an unrelated afterthought. Children are taught to read /k-a-t/ and spell /See-A-Tee/. While reading utilizes the sounds the letters represent, spelling is taught using alphabet letter names. The two skills seem unrelated.

For all children to understand the magical idea that letters represent speech sounds, the code must be presented as reversible. We should think to spell /k-a-t/ and read /k-a-t/. This is best done by teaching spelling as the foundation to reading, as teachers did in the old days. Students should spell their way into reading. In spelling we analyze the individual parts that make up a word. We teach a child to unglue a word syllable by syllable and sound by sound as he writes it. This is best done by dictation, not by copying. Reading thereby becomes a natural side effect. The student blends back together what he has learned to take apart and analyze.

The author of *The Writing Road to Reading* said, "The failings of most of the phonics methods may be summarized in that they neglect spelling and do not teach the saying and writing of the forty-five basic sounds of the phonograms of the language before trying to read." (Spalding p. 27).

**Findings of Scientific Research**

Eighty percent of students today are taught with whole-word methods. Massive academic failure shows we need change, and scientific evidence shows where. Correctly taught phonics must form the foundation for spelling and reading instruction.

*Illiteracy in America,* a book published by the U.S. Government Printing Office in Washington, D.C., explains, among other things, the achievement decline in our country. The National Council reports, "Since 1911, a total of 124 studies have compared the look-say eclectic approaches with phonics-first programs. Not one found look-say superior." Yet, "since 1955 approximately 85 percent of our 16,000 school districts have been using this eclectic approach. . . Regardless of labels, only about 15 percent of the nation's primary children have received instruction in direct, systematic, and intensive phonics." (National Advisory Council on Adult Education, p. 23)

Susan Hall, the president of the Illinois Branch of the International Dyslexia Association, comments, "Millions of capable children are not learning to read well in America's schools today. The causes and cures are well-known in the research community, but classroom practice has been slow to change. Almost all children can learn to read well if taught with appropriate methods. But not all children in today's classrooms are receiving the type of instruction that will equip them to be good readers." (Hall, p. xvii).

> **With the 98 keys, virtually all students can learn to spell and read English!**

In a publication of the International Reading Association a leading Canadian reading expert, Dr. Keith E. Stanovich, confirms the necessity of phonics. "That direct instruction in alphabetic coding facilitates early reading acquisition is one of the most well-established conclusions in all behavioral science." (Stanovich, pp. 285-6)

Dr. Diane McGuinness, in a newly published book, summarizes the last 25 years of empirical studies on reading instruction. "From research in the classroom and the clinic, we have discovered that when the sequence of reading and spelling instruction is compatible with the logic of the alphabet code and with the child's linguistic and logical development, learning to read and spell proceeds rapidly and smoothly for all children and is equally effective for poor readers of all ages." (McGuinness, p. xiii)

Students need to internalize the symbols that form the code for written English. This information must be considered vital, not just an afterthought. A little dab won't do. For the most effective results, we need to teach early, direct, systematic, intensive phonics.

EARLY--first and fast  (Teach the code as the foundational beginning.)
DIRECT-- straightforward, precise instruction
SYSTEMATIC -- scientifically ordered, not incidental
INTENSIVE -- one or more times a day
PHONICS -- link the sounds of speech to letters that represent the sounds.

Correctly taught phonics replaces the frustration and insecurity of whole-word chaos. Instead of word-by-word memory or random guessing by context, the student has a logical basis for mastering the language. The fog lifts and the student is free to explore independently the wonderful world of print.

## Conclusion

A kind mistress started teaching the young slave child about letters and the sounds they represent in English. This changed his life forever and impacted the lives of many others. He had progressed to spelling three-or four-letter words when the master discovered what was happening. He forbade her to teach the boy any more and explained why when he screamed, "If you teach [him] to read, it would forever unfit him to be a slave!"

Frederick Douglass

*Reading is the pathway to freedom!*

In his autobiography, Frederick Douglass wrote, "From that moment on, I understood the pathway to freedom. Though conscious of the difficulty of learning without a teacher, I set out with high hope and a fixed purpose, at whatever cost of trouble, to learn how to read." (Douglass, p. 48)

Once Douglass had a taste of the alphabetic code and how it worked, he searched for the missing pieces. He would tease the little white boys to tell him more. He might say to them, "I bet I know more words than you do." He would write in the dirt several words he had learned. They would then write some more. Eventually he mastered the language well enough to compose a letter giving him permission to travel, sign it with his master's name, and use the paper to escape. This runaway slave became an internationally famous spokesman for the anti-slavery movement and helped lead his people to freedom.

Slavery has been overturned as an institution in America, and yet 93 million in our nation are in bondage. People who cannot read and write fluidly can never reach their full potential. We can and must help set them free. We have the tools to do so. I hold them in my hands. If we will provide a logical presentation of our language using the most basic component parts, massive illiteracy will become a thing of the past.

| DIAGNOSTIC SPELLING TEST # _____ |
| --- |

*Name* _____ *Age*_____*Grade*_____ *Date* _____

*Total Right* ____ *Grade Equivalent* ____*First Missed* ____ *Tension of Learning Level* ___*Section Placement* ___

1 _____

2 _____

3 _____

4 _____

5 _____

6 _____

7 _____

8 _____

9 _____

10 _____

11 _____

12 _____

13 _____

14 _____

15 _____

16 _____

17 _____

18 _____

19 _____

20 _____

21 _____

22 _____

23 _____

24 _____

25 _____

26 _____

27 _____

28 _____

29 _____

30 _____

31 _____

32 _____

33 _____

34 _____

35 _____

36 _____

37 _____

38 _____

39 _____

40 _____

41 _____

42 _____

43 _____

44 _____

45 _____

46 _____

47 _____

48 _____

49 _____

50 _____

**For teacher use permission is granted to photocopy this form and the graph on SWR page 229.**

# APPENDIX B:  Diagnostic Spelling Scale

These eight interchangeable standardized tests contain 50 words arduously arranged by increasing difficulty by Leonard P. Ayres.  All words are also included in *Wise Guide*.

**Who Should Take this Test?**

STUDENTS WHO CAN READ take the test immediately at the beginning of a new school year.  Use the results to establish a benchmark for measuring improvement throughout the year.  Results are often dramatic.

BEGINNING NON-READERS take this test after covering the first 140 spelling words in *Wise Guide* (about two months into the program).

ALL STUDENTS should be tested periodically throughout the year.  Subsequent tests, administered every month or so, can confirm progress and identify places needing extra attention.

**What is the Purpose of this Test?**

PLACE FIRST-TIME OLDER STUDENT.  Second grade or above can begin the Wise List at their tension of learning level rather than beginning at Section A.  See SWR Steps 4, 11.

MONITOR PROGRESS. We can determine spelling mastery from 1.0 (beginning first grade) to 13.0 (post-college).  This objectively records the pace of development.  Do NOT show student the corrected test.  To do so would invalidate this tool for future use.

EVALUATE ACHIEVEMENT.  Diagnostic tests contain sample words from each level in the Wise List. See which previously covered words are retained. Observe how a student attacks a word not yet taught. If long-term mastery is weak, increase reinforcement activity.

**How Should We Give this Test?**

TEST MULTIPLE LEVELS AT ONCE.  Since the words are progressively difficult you can test many levels together, if need be. Younger students may stop after ten or fifteen words, second graders after twenty-five to thirty-five words, while third graders and above may attempt all fifty words.  Assure students before you begin that they will probably not spell all the words correctly yet. Someday they will be that proficient, if you continue in this program.

ROTATE THE TESTS.  With eight interchangeable tests, you could give a new test each month for a year.  The following year start back over with test one.

ADMINISTER THE TEST.  Read these instructions word for word: *I will dictate each spelling word, read a sentence containing that word, and then say the word again.  You will probably not spell all the words correctly, but do your best.  I cannot give you any hints.  We are testing for what you already know, not teaching you at this time.  Dot your I's and cross your T's.*

Enunciate each word clearly, as in normal speech.  Collect the student's paper as soon as he is finished.  Do NOT show him this paper again.

**How is the test scored?**

Any mistake, including uncrossed T's or incorrectly capitalized words, makes a word incorrect. Write the proper spelling beside words missed. See Step 11, especially page 65 for placement ideas.

DETERMINE GRADE LEVEL. Find the number right on the chart below and follow across to the column titled "Grade Status" to determine grade equivalent. A student with ten correct words is spelling at 2.4 (second grade, fourth month). Record this information on the test form.

IDENTIFY *TENSION-OF-LEARNING* LEVEL. Find the first word missed. Look in the third column for the corresponding Spelling Section. The letter shows the tension-of-learning level or a place where the student can comfortably work and still be challenged. If a student missed any of the first ten words, in most cases you should begin a new year in Section A. If a student misses only one word such as "led" (number 8 in test one) but does not miss again until number 18, you may place him in M. All of the A-I words will be reviewed in Sections M-N.

## EVALUATION TABLE

| WORDS CORRECT | GRADE STATUS* | SPELLING SECTION | WORDS CORRECT | GRADE STATUS* | SPELLING SECTION |
|---|---|---|---|---|---|
| 0 | 1.0 |   | 26 | 4.9 | Q |
| 1 | 1.3 | A | 27 | 5.1 | Q |
| 2 | 1.5 | A | 28 | 5.2 | R |
| 3 | 1.7 | A | 29 | 5.4 | R |
| 4 | 1.8 | A | 30 | 5.6 | R |
| 5 | 1.9 | A | 31 | 5.8 | S |
| 6 | 2.0 | A | 32 | 6.0 | S |
| 7 | 2.1 | H | 33 | 6.2 | T |
| 8 | 2.2 | H | 34 | 6.4 | T |
| 9 | 2.3 | I | 35 | 6.6 | T |
| 10 | 2.4 | I | 36 | 6.8 | U |
| 11 | 2.5 | J | 37 | 7.0 | U |
| 12 | 2.6 | J | 38 | 7.3 | V |
| 13 | 2.7 | K | 39 | 7.5 | V |
| 14 | 2.9 | K | 40 | 7.7 | V |
| 15 | 3.1 | L | 41 | 8.0 | W |
| 16 | 3.3 | L | 42 | 8.4 | W |
| 17 | 3.4 | M | 43 | 8.8 | W |
| 18 | 3.5 | M | 44 | 9.3 | X |
| 19 | 3.7 | N | 45 | 9.8 | X |
| 20 | 3.9 | N | 46 | 10.5 | X |
| 21 | 4.1 | O | 47 | 11.2 | Y |
| 22 | 4.2 | O | 48 | 11.7 | Y |
| 23 | 4.3 | O | 49 | 12.5 | Y |
| 24 | 4.5 | P | 50 | 13.0 | Z |
| 25 | 4.7 | P |   |   |   |

*Grade 1.0 means beginning first grade. Grade 1.3 means first grade, third month.

# Diagnostic Test 1

| 1. | go | I will *go* to the store.................................................................go |
|----|----|------|
| 2. | last | The *last* person in line will shut the door.............................last |
| 3. | will | *Will* you help me, please?...................................................will |
| 4. | all | I want *all* of you to join me in the circle............................all |
| 5. | over | When the concert is *over* we will go home..........................over |
| 6. | hot | The *hot* desert sands burned my feet.....................................hot |
| 7. | his | Tell Mike *his* papers are ready.............................................his |
| 8. | led | He *led* the way to the prayer meeting...................................led |
| 9. | spent | She *spent* all her money foolishly, and now she's sad..........spent |
| 10. | spring | *Spring* blossoms decorate the trees and bushes.................spring |
| 11. | card | Write your memory verses on a 3X5 *card*............................card |
| 12. | blue | The sky is painted a peaceful *blue* color..............................blue |
| 13. | mail | We eagerly wait for each day's *mail* delivery......................mail |
| 14. | stamp | Do you have a *stamp* from Germany in your collection?.........stamp |
| 15. | within | I will finish reading the book *within* the time allotted.............within |
| 16. | body | My *body* ached all over after that exercise session..................body |
| 17. | provide | Parents *provide* for their children.........................................provide |
| 18. | born | I was *born* on Columbus Day................................................born |
| 19. | suffer | We often *suffer* for wrong choices.......................................suffer |
| 20. | rule | I know a spelling *rule* that helps explain that word...............rule |
| 21. | elect | The people did not *elect* a ruler with integrity .....................elect |
| 22. | request | May I please *request* a favor?...............................................request |
| 23. | address | My mailing *address* will be changing next month................address |
| 24. | nearly | I *nearly* dropped the flower vase but caught it just in time.......nearly |
| 25. | carried | I watched as waves *carried* the bottle out to sea...................carried |
| 26. | employ | Dad's boss wanted to *employ* my brother, too......................employ |
| 27. | connection | Is there a *connection* between the season and my allergy?.......connection |
| 28. | entertain | Jan will *entertain* our guest while I finish cooking supper......entertain |
| 29. | publication | I read the Sunday *publication* of the newspaper ..................publication |
| 30. | treasure | Dan tried to dig for Blackbeard's hidden *treasure*.................treasure |
| 31. | piece | He looks ragged with a *piece* torn from his pants...................piece |
| 32. | therefore | Debt creates bondage; *therefore*, I will not be in debt...........therefore |
| 33. | official | The report with the *official* statement arrived today...............official |
| 34. | concern | A compassionate person shows *concern* for others.................concern |
| 35. | various | I enjoy cooking, gardening, and *various* other activities........various |
| 36. | relief | The rain came as a *relief* after the long drought....................relief |
| 37. | foreign | A *foreign* student from Japan visited our family...................foreign |
| 38. | association | A wise man avoids deep *association* with fools....................association |
| 39. | discussion | The *discussion* stimulated my thinking...............................discussion |
| 40. | career | The teaching profession is a satisfying *career*......................career |
| 41. | athletic | *Athletic* training is useful in sports......................................athletic |
| 42. | disease | Louis Pasteur discovered that germs cause *disease*................disease |
| 43. | convenient | The store on the corner is *convenient*...................................convenient |
| 44. | familiar | The girl looked *familiar,* but I could not remember her name.................familiar |
| 45. | accommodate | How many people can this room *accommodate?*.............................accommodate |
| 46. | parliament | *Parliament* was formed to restrain the king.........................parliament |
| 47. | acquaintance | Paul was not a close friend, only an *acquaintance*..........................acquaintance |
| 48. | physician | He went to the *physician* when he was ill............................physician |
| 49. | appropriate | That song was not *appropriate* for the wedding...............................appropriate |
| 50. | occurrence | A comet is an unusual *occurrence*.......................................occurrence |

---

## Diagnostic Test 2

| | | | |
|---|---|---|---|
| 1. | and | You *and* I are friends............................................................................ | and |
| 2. | up | Please get *up* now................................................................................ | up |
| 3. | you | Did *you* read your lesson?...................................................................... | you |
| 4. | this | *This* is the day that the Lord has made..................................................... | this |
| 5. | hat | The boy removed his *hat* when he came inside ....................................... | hat |
| 6. | child | The *child* obeyed his parents.................................................................. | child |
| 7. | lay | Be careful how you *lay* down the vase...................................................... | lay |
| 8. | five | *Five* pennies are worth one nickel............................................................ | five |
| 9. | white | The US flag is red, *white*, and blue.......................................................... | white |
| 10. | block | Walk with me around the *block,* please................................................... | block |
| 11. | cast | The doctor put a *cast* on the boy's broken arm........................................ | cast |
| 12. | inside | Come *inside* the house from the thunderstorm......................................... | inside |
| 13. | light | Turn on the *light,* please........................................................................ | light |
| 14. | cent | A penny is called one *cent*...................................................................... | cent |
| 15. | done | What have I *done* with your shirt?............................................................ | done |
| 16. | buy | Did you *buy* or make a present for Mother's Day?.................................... | buy |
| 17. | file | Can you help me *file* these papers?......................................................... | file |
| 18. | fix | Do you know how to *fix* a broken lamp?................................................... | fix |
| 19. | offer | What did he *offer* in exchange for your baseball card?............................. | offer |
| 20. | front | The *front* door is open, but the back is locked......................................... | front |
| 21. | raise | My friend wants to *raise* chickens........................................................... | raise |
| 22. | personal | That information is *personal*, but I'll tell my friends................................. | personal |
| 23. | getting | Now that winter is here, it is *getting* colder............................................. | getting |
| 24. | rapid | You have made *rapid* improvement in spelling.......................................... | rapid |
| 25. | importance | We must consider the *importance* of an education.................................... | importance |
| 26. | addiction | Avoid *addiction* to drugs or other harmful substances............................. | addiction |
| 27. | select | Be careful how you *select* friends............................................................ | select |
| 28. | popular | It may be *popular*, but it is not wise........................................................ | popular |
| 29. | consider | Will you *consider* tutoring me in algebra?................................................ | consider |
| 30. | interest | What subjects most *interest* you?............................................................ | interest |
| 31. | supply | My *supply* of pencils is almost gone........................................................ | supply |
| 32. | particular | I am *particular* about the foods I eat........................................................ | particular |
| 33. | accident | My brother broke his arm in an *accident*................................................... | accident |
| 34. | impossible | It is not *impossible* to learn to play an instrument.................................... | impossible |
| 35. | automobile | The *automobile* replaced the horse and carriage....................................... | automobile |
| 36. | citizen | I am an American *citizen* by birth............................................................. | citizen |
| 37. | unfortunate | It was *unfortunate* that you missed camp this year................................... | unfortunate |
| 38. | height | My *height* and weight are average for my age.......................................... | height |
| 39. | extremely | He was *extremely* sad when his dog died................................................. | extremely |
| 40. | innocent | I am *innocent* of any crime..................................................................... | innocent |
| 41. | athletic | He received *athletic* training from his father........................................... | athletic |
| 42. | calendar | Where is the *calendar* for next year?....................................................... | calendar |
| 43. | preliminary | He did well in the *preliminary* but not in the final race............................ | preliminary |
| 44. | disappoint | I'm sorry to *disappoint* you, but the picnic is cancelled........................... | disappoint |
| 45. | principle | The Boston Tea Party was conducted as a point of *principle*.................... | principle |
| 46. | restaurant | Tonight we will eat at home, not in a *restaurant*...................................... | restaurant |
| 47. | cemetery | I went to a Memorial Day service at the *cemetery* .................................. | cemetery |
| 48. | mortgage | We worked hard to pay off the debt on our *mortgage* .............................. | mortgage |
| 49. | persistence | Stick with it, because *persistence* often pays........................................... | persistence |
| 50. | guarantee | Our *guarantee* assures the customer we mean well................................... | guarantee |

# Diagnostic Test 3

| | | | |
|---|---|---|---|
| 1. | it | *It* is not my birthday yet. | it |
| 2. | bed | Please make up your *bed* soon. | bed |
| 3. | good | That watermelon tasted so *good* to eat. | good |
| 4. | did | I *did* my best on the test. | did |
| 5. | ice | In the summer I like *ice* in my beverages. | ice |
| 6. | play | I am learning to *play* the piano. | play |
| 7. | soft | A *soft* answer turns away wrath. | soft |
| 8. | tell | I can *tell* when you are angry. | tell |
| 9. | north | Canada is *north* of the United States. | north |
| 10. | blow | It feels colder in the winter when the winds *blow*. | blow |
| 11. | sister | I have a brother, and I wish I had a *sister* too. | sister |
| 12. | room | My favorite *room* is the kitchen. | room |
| 13. | night | The moon shines brightly at *night*. | night |
| 14. | shut | *Shut* the door gently. | shut |
| 15. | track | The train jumped the *track,* but no one was injured. | track |
| 16. | fight | Join the *fight* for justice. | fight |
| 17. | collect | I used to *collect* sea shells. | collect |
| 18. | stood | Everyone *stood* to show respect for the president. | stood |
| 19. | bridge | The suspension *bridge* swayed in the breeze. | bridge |
| 20. | there | I left my book *there* by the sofa. | there |
| 21. | struck | The clock *struck* twelve. | struck |
| 22. | friend | A *friend* loves at all times. | friend |
| 23. | proper | Be careful to use *proper* manners. | proper |
| 24. | travel | I will *travel* cross-country by plane. | travel |
| 25. | entrance | The front *entrance* to the palace is carefully guarded. | entrance |
| 26. | arrange | He will *arrange* another appointment for you. | arrange |
| 27. | connection | There is a *connection* between virtue and happiness. | connection |
| 28. | salary | I requested a raise in *salary*. | salary |
| 29. | machine | The *machine* made funny noises and then stopped. | machine |
| 30. | honor | *Honor* your father and your mother. | honor |
| 31. | century | A *century* means one hundred years. | century |
| 32. | certain | I am *certain* that I mailed that letter yesterday. | certain |
| 33. | national | Tea time is a *national* custom in England. | national |
| 34. | celebration | July 4th is a time of *celebration* in the United States. | celebration |
| 35. | political | When *political* leaders show integrity, the people live at peace. | political |
| 36. | occupy | We should be careful what we let *occupy* our time. | occupy |
| 37. | expense | The phone *expense* was tax deductible. | expense |
| 38. | principal | The *principal* of the local school lives next door to me. | principal |
| 39. | campaign | A veteran soldier has served in more than one *campaign*. | campaign |
| 40. | secretary | The boss will dictate a letter to his *secretary*. | secretary |
| 41. | proceed | We cannot *proceed* until the work is finished on the house. | proceed |
| 42. | separate | *Separate* the light and dark clothes before washing them. | separate |
| 43. | development | The new *development* changes our plan of action. | development |
| 44. | finances | The businessman needs to understand *finances*. | finances |
| 45. | orchestra | The *orchestra* played Beethoven's Fifth Symphony. | orchestra |
| 46. | surgeon | The *surgeon* removed the bullet from the wounded man's leg. | surgeon |
| 47. | allege | The lawyer will *allege* the man committed the crime. | allege |
| 48. | endeavor | We must *endeavor* to live peaceably with one another. | endeavor |
| 49. | discipline | A father will *discipline* the son he loves when he disobeys. | discipline |
| 50. | pneumonia | He died of *pneumonia* last winter. | pneumonia |

## Diagnostic Test 4

| | | | |
|---|---|---|---|
| 1. | see | I cannot *see* because you are in the way | see |
| 2. | man | When does a boy become a *man*? | man |
| 3. | little | The *little* puppy is cute. | little |
| 4. | six | *Six* is half a dozen. | six |
| 5. | say | We will *say* the pledge of allegiance. | say |
| 6. | live | I *live* near my grandmother. | live |
| 7. | low | Reach high and then bend *low* as an exercise. | low |
| 8. | bring | I will *bring* your book back tomorrow. | bring |
| 9. | got | They *got* chicken-pox two weeks after I did. | got |
| 10. | foot | I stubbed my *foot* on the chair. | foot |
| 11. | hope | I *hope* I get to go with you. | hope |
| 12. | same | We have the *same* color of eyes. | same |
| 13. | easy | Reading is *easy* when you can spell well. | easy |
| 14. | could | I *could* finish my math soon if I tried. | could |
| 15. | suit | Dad looks handsome in a *suit* and tie. | suit |
| 16. | fell | John *fell* and broke his leg. | fell |
| 17. | begun | We had not *begun* to fight. | begun |
| 18. | sight | The blind man longed to have his *sight* restored. | sight |
| 19. | tax | The government *tax* is much too high. | tax |
| 20. | number | Give me a *number* between one and one hundred. | number |
| 21. | perfect | Try to write *perfect* letters on your paper. | perfect |
| 22. | objection | His *objection* to the movie was based on too much violence. | objection |
| 23. | population | The *population* of our city is one million people. | population |
| 24. | flight | The *flight* to Chicago was delayed. | flight |
| 25. | trouble | The *trouble* with him is lack of motivation. | trouble |
| 26. | their | *Their* parents are on vacation. | their |
| 27. | written | Laws are *written* to protect us. | written |
| 28. | diamond | She has a diamond ring. | diamond |
| 29. | success | *Success* comes through hard work and right thinking. | success |
| 30. | wreck | Drive carefully so you don't *wreck* your car. | wreck |
| 31. | mention | Do not *mention* what happened again. | mention |
| 32. | assist | I will *assist* you with your math assignment | assist |
| 33. | really | He *really* likes baseball. | really |
| 34. | refer | *Refer* to page ten of your book for the answer to the question. | refer |
| 35. | minute | Philip has one *minute* to finish the test. | minute |
| 36. | probably | He will *probably* go to college. | probably |
| 37. | beginning | Mike is *beginning* to learn Spanish. | beginning |
| 38. | testimony | We listened to every *testimony* before making our decision. | testimony |
| 39. | columns | The newsletter contains two *columns* on each page. | columns |
| 40. | imagine | I can only *imagine* what tomorrow will be like. | imagine |
| 41. | emergency | The *emergency* of the situation caused him to act promptly. | emergency |
| 42. | practical | Dale's desire to quit his job is not *practical*. | practical |
| 43. | immediate | He gave *immediate* attention to the problem. | immediate |
| 44. | intelligent | Thomas Edison was very *intelligent*. | intelligent |
| 45. | recommended | She *recommended* that I take your writing class | recommended |
| 46. | thoroughly | The instructor *thoroughly* taught the principles of economics. | thoroughly |
| 47. | enthusiasm | Dave's *enthusiasm* helped us win the game. | enthusiasm |
| 48. | stationery | May I borrow a piece of *stationery* to write a letter? | stationery |
| 49. | privilege | Driving a car is a *privilege*, not a right. | privilege |
| 50. | lieutenant | The army *lieutenant* desires to become a general. | lieutenant |

# Diagnostic Test 5

1. she — *She* and I are friends...............................................................she
2. now — Please get up *now*..................................................................now
3. old — Her grandfather is very *old*.....................................................old
4. book — Mary read her first *book* today............................................book
5. street — The *street* in front of our house is busy..............................street
6. ring — Father lost his wedding *ring*..................................................ring
7. yes — *Yes*, he approved of our going................................................yes
8. yard — Our neighbor's *yard* is very small..........................................yard
9. sick — John is *sick* with the flu........................................................sick
10. sold — David *sold* his bike for ten dollars........................................sold
11. glad — He was *glad* to give us directions to the park.........................glad
12. with — He came to the game *with* his father......................................with
13. upon — *Upon* our arrival, Jill began preparing dinner.........................upon
14. any — Barefoot Jim doesn't have *any* shoes.......................................any
15. gone — He has *gone* to visit his grandmother....................................gone
16. dash — He loves to run the one-hundred-yard *dash*............................dash
17. happen — Gaining wealth doesn't just *happen*...................................happen
18. wire — The *wire* to the telephone was cut........................................wire
19. change — Bill will have to *change* his clothes....................................change
20. reason — He had no *reason* for his absence......................................reason
21. retire — Dad will *retire* from work..................................................retire
22. royal — The king signed the *royal* decree.........................................royal
23. fourth — Mary's *fourth* child is a girl...............................................fourth
24. beautiful — The *beautiful* speech moved the entire audience................beautiful
25. repair — The washing machine *repair* was costly..............................repair
26. whose — *Whose* shirt is in the laundry?............................................whose
27. perhaps — *Perhaps* he will change his mind......................................perhaps
28. visitor — We have a *visitor* from Japan.............................................visitor
29. tomorrow — *Tomorrow* I will fix it...................................................tomorrow
30. promise — Fulfill every *promise* you make........................................promise
31. total — His *total* bill was $100.00...................................................total
32. examination — The math *examination* will take one hour.....................examination
33. summon — I will *summon* the boys for dinner....................................summon
34. conference — The sales *conference* lasted two days...........................conference
35. absence — His *absence* was noticed by all........................................absence
36. divide — John was asked to *divide* the candy with his brothers...........divide
37. application — An *application* must be completed before hiring.............application
38. apparent — He had no *apparent* reason for going to bed early..............apparent
39. coarse — The wood he used to build the fort was very *coarse*.............coarse
40. individual — Each *individual* is responsible for his own behavior.........individual
41. extreme — His *extreme* political ideas lost him many votes...............extreme
42. cordially — All are *cordially* invited to come to our house...............cordially
43. committee — His *committee* is in charge of hosting the event.............committee
44. receipt — He got a *receipt* when he bought the tires..........................receipt
45. seized — She *seized* the opportunity to make the sale........................seized
46. precipice — They stood at the edge of the *precipice* with great care......precipice
47. syllables — Divide the word into *syllables*........................................syllables
48. extraordinary — Samson's *extraordinary* strength was taken from him...extraordinary
49. vaguely — He *vaguely* remembers where he lived ten years ago............vaguely
50. villain — The *villain* was caught and put in prison.............................villain

# Diagnostic Test 6

| | | | |
|---|---|---|---|
| 1. | is | He *is* happy that he can read..................................................................................is |
| 2. | ten | I can count to *ten*..................................................................................................ten |
| 3. | red | He saw the *red* fire engine.....................................................................................red |
| 4. | time | The *time* is eight o'clock.......................................................................................time |
| 5. | make | He likes to *make* cookies........................................................................................make |
| 6. | hand | He shook the *hand* of the famous man.....................................................................hand |
| 7. | door | He closed his bedroom *door*...................................................................................door |
| 8. | stand | We had to *stand* in line for forty-five minutes.......................................................stand |
| 9. | told | She *told* us a story about George Washington.........................................................told |
| 10. | form | With this clay the potter will *form* a statue..............................................................form |
| 11. | mine | The bicycle is *mine*, not yours ..............................................................................mine |
| 12. | stay | He wanted us to *stay* another day...........................................................................stay |
| 13. | party | Mary is having a birthday *party* on Saturday.........................................................party |
| 14. | would | John said he *would* come to the party.....................................................................would |
| 15. | able | Sally was not *able* to come.....................................................................................able |
| 16. | watch | Grandpa loves to *watch* basketball games.............................................................watch |
| 17. | few | Dad is looking for a *few* good men to help him......................................................few |
| 18. | picture | I took a *picture* of Niagara Falls............................................................................picture |
| 19. | fifth | David is in the *fifth* grade......................................................................................fifth |
| 20. | death | I was sad at the *death* of my cat.............................................................................death |
| 21. | shed | My mother *shed* tears over what I did....................................................................shed |
| 22. | restrain | He could not *restrain* himself from eating the ice cream..........................restrain |
| 23. | navy | I wore *navy* blue shoes with my new dress.............................................................navy |
| 24. | vacation | He took a *vacation* to rest from his work...............................................................vacation |
| 25. | sail | He learned to *sail* in the navy................................................................................sail |
| 26. | surprise | The *surprise* party caught him off guard...............................................................surprise |
| 27. | attempt | Tomorrow he will *attempt* to run one mile..............................................................attempt |
| 28. | search | After a careful *search* we found the lost boy..........................................................search |
| 29. | drown | He saved the little girl so she did not *drown*.........................................................drown |
| 30. | secure | She felt *secure* in her mother's arms.....................................................................secure |
| 31. | arrive | The governor will *arrive* in town at four o'clock.....................................................arrive |
| 32. | difference | He cannot tell the *difference* between blue and green...........................difference |
| 33. | victim | The innocent *victim* filed charges regarding the crime............................victim |
| 34. | invitation | He received an *invitation* to the party....................................................................invitation |
| 35. | business | He owns his own *business*......................................................................................business |
| 36. | majority | In a democracy, the *majority* vote wins.................................................................majority |
| 37. | necessary | It is *necessary* for you to obey your parents..........................................................necessary |
| 38. | ascending | She fell while *ascending* the stairs.........................................................................ascending |
| 39. | desirable | It was *desirable* for her to take piano lessons.......................................................desirable |
| 40. | leisure | *Leisure* time follows work.....................................................................................leisure |
| 41. | sincerely | She *sincerely* believes that you can do better work ...............................................sincerely |
| 42. | organization | Good *organization* is needed for running a business..........................organization |
| 43. | especially | He *especially* enjoys reading history....................................................................especially |
| 44. | annual | The *annual* fee is due at the first of the year........................................................annual |
| 45. | possess | He does not wish to *possess* a gun........................................................................possess |
| 46. | thoroughly | Study the materials *thoroughly* before taking the test............................thoroughly |
| 47. | physician | The *physician* told me to take this medicine..........................................................physician |
| 48. | tortoise | The *tortoise* moves very slowly..............................................................................tortoise |
| 49. | immediately | He came home *immediately* after the game...........................................................immediately |
| 50. | incessant | I tried to avoid her because she is an *incessant* talker..............................incessant |

# Diagnostic Test 7

| 1. | can | You and I *can* go to the park this afternoon.................................................................can |
| 2. | top | Put the book on *top* of the dresser please...............................................................top |
| 3. | my | *My* mother teaches me at home............................................................................my |
| 4. | out | Father is *out* for the evening..............................................................................out |
| 5. | make | He said he would *make* me a banana split.............................................................make |
| 6. | come | She will *come* home at nine o'clock....................................................................come |
| 7. | belong | The guard told me I do not *belong* here...............................................................belong |
| 8. | ran | He *ran* all the way home..................................................................................ran |
| 9. | far | Steve does not live *far* from here.......................................................................far |
| 10. | alike | The twin brothers look *alike*............................................................................alike |
| 11. | deep | The pool is ten feet *deep*................................................................................deep |
| 12. | town | He lives in a small *town*................................................................................town |
| 13. | glass | John broke his favorite drinking *glass*...............................................................glass |
| 14. | they | *They* refused to come to the party....................................................................they |
| 15. | began | He *began* to work at eight this morning.............................................................began |
| 16. | third | That was his *third* hit this season....................................................................third |
| 17. | money | He bought the book with his own *money*.............................................................money |
| 18. | omit | I will *omit* nothing from the report...................................................................omit |
| 19. | center | He moved to the *center* of the room...................................................................center |
| 20. | chain | He could not break the iron *chain*....................................................................chain |
| 21. | jail | *Jail* is a place for lawbreakers.........................................................................jail |
| 22. | district | We live in *district* four.................................................................................district |
| 23. | pleasure | He gets much *pleasure* out of walking................................................................pleasure |
| 24. | cities | New York is one of our major *cities*..................................................................cities |
| 25. | known | She speaks five *known* languages.....................................................................known |
| 26. | property | A person's *property* is what he owns.................................................................property |
| 27. | region | My father supervises *region* one.......................................................................region |
| 28. | wear | She likes to *wear* attractive, modest dresses.......................................................wear |
| 29. | toward | Zeke lives *toward* town.................................................................................toward |
| 30. | adopt | They want to *adopt* a baby..............................................................................adopt |
| 31. | investigate | Sherlock Holmes loves to *investigate* strange crimes.............................investigate |
| 32. | system | Our computer *system* broke down again today......................................................system |
| 33. | folks | His *folks* live in California...............................................................................folks |
| 34. | accept | He is willing to *accept* a compromise.................................................................accept |
| 35. | entitle | This pass will *entitle* you to three free rides......................................................entitle |
| 36. | assure | He will *assure* my safe arrival.........................................................................assure |
| 37. | responsible | She is *responsible* for the broken window...............................................responsible |
| 38. | arrangement | The *arrangement* for our meeting is complete............................................arrangement |
| 39. | evidence | The *evidence* was strong enough to convict him.................................................evidence |
| 40. | experience | They hired someone with *experience*................................................................experience |
| 41. | character | The new worker has good moral *character*..........................................................character |
| 42. | bicycle | Susan received her first *bicycle* for her birthday..............................................bicycle |
| 43. | associates | His *associates* are a good influence.................................................................associates |
| 44. | exquisite | He eats only in *exquisite* restaurants................................................................exquisite |
| 45. | perceived | He *perceived* that I was telling the truth..........................................................perceived |
| 46. | superintendent | John is *superintendent* of the whole store...........................................superintendent |
| 47. | recommend | I *recommend* him for the job.........................................................................recommend |
| 48. | acquaintance | He made my *acquaintance* this morning............................................acquaintance |
| 49. | kerosene | During the power shortage, we needed a *kerosene* lamp...........................kerosene |
| 50. | cantaloupe | *Cantaloupe* is his favorite fruit...................................................................cantaloupe |

## Diagnostic Test 8

| | | | |
|---|---|---|---|
| 1. | run | I will *run* in the track meet | run |
| 2. | the | *The* garden needs to be planted | the |
| 3. | we | *We* enjoy his company | we |
| 4. | your | This is *your* book | your |
| 5. | must | We *must* go now | must |
| 6. | sea | Columbus sailed the *sea* | sea |
| 7. | was | He *was* happy to see me | was |
| 8. | that | *That* car is mine | that |
| 9. | add | He wants me to *add* his name to the list | add |
| 10. | river | The *river* runs through the city | river |
| 11. | fire | He built a fire in the fireplace | fire |
| 12. | post | The *post* holding up the roof is cracked | post |
| 13. | eye | The dog is blind in one *eye* | eye |
| 14. | two | Sue gave me *two* red apples | two |
| 15. | push | He wants to *push* his little brother in the wagon | push |
| 16. | point | The *point* of the knife is very sharp | point |
| 17. | anyway | We asked him to stay home, but he came *anyway* | anyway |
| 18. | goes | Their father *goes* regularly to church | goes |
| 19. | built | Grandfather *built* his own house | built |
| 20. | carry | John wants to help *carry* the groceries | carry |
| 21. | aboard | She climbed *aboard* the train | aboard |
| 22. | refuse | He will *refuse* to cooperate | refuse |
| 23. | truly | She *truly* desires to do what is right | truly |
| 24. | several | One was not enough; he owns *several* cars | several |
| 25. | desire | Why do you *desire* to join the Marines? | desire |
| 26. | period | They walk for a brief *period* each day | period |
| 27. | firm | He held on to me with a *firm* grip | firm |
| 28. | weigh | He wants to *weigh* himself every day | weigh |
| 29. | against | He is standing *against* the wall | against |
| 30. | complete | Tim has the *complete* set of *The Chronicles of Narnia* | complete |
| 31. | pleasant | Jane is a *pleasant*, courteous worker | pleasant |
| 32. | affair | The *affair* at work caused him much grief | affair |
| 33. | estimate | He got an *estimate* for the damage | estimate |
| 34. | accept | He refused to *accept* my phone call | accept |
| 35. | decide | He wants us to *decide* on a color by tomorrow | decide |
| 36. | colonies | The early Puritan *colonies* settled in New England | colonies |
| 37. | elaborate | He wants me to *elaborate* on what I said | elaborate |
| 38. | session | The first *session* lasted for two hours | session |
| 39. | reference | She found the *reference* book at the library | reference |
| 40. | independent | Sam is an *independent*, reliable worker | independent |
| 41. | appreciate | He does not *appreciate* my help | appreciate |
| 42. | bicycle | His ten-speed *bicycle* was stolen | bicycle |
| 43. | artificial | The war veteran has an *artificial* leg | artificial |
| 44. | employees | He has twelve *employees* working for him | employees |
| 45. | decision | She has a hard *decision* to make | decision |
| 46. | immense | The job seemed too *immense* to handle | immense |
| 47. | parallel | The freeway runs *parallel* to the river | parallel |
| 48. | exquisite | The dress from Paris was *exquisite* | exquisite |
| 49. | dispensary | He went to the *dispensary* for the medicine | dispensary |
| 50. | proficiency | He operates the machine with great *proficiency* | proficiency |

# APPENDIX C

# Sample Pages from a Student's *Learning Log*

Information for building the reference pages is given in the text of *Spell to Write and Read*. Cross reference reminders of when to teach them are provided in *Wise Guide*. The Consonant/Vowel, Silent Final E, and the A-E-I-O-U Pages are build as a unified assignment. The Multi-letter Page keeps the same order but will be built gradually with students starting at the spelling Section A. Other reference pages are built in increments over the course of the year. Word examples on these pages will vary according to where the student is in the spelling list. Words are collected over time from the new words taught. Review words and vocabulary from outside sources can be added.

A student builds a new notebook every year. All logs have a section for new spelling words and a section for reference pages. Reference pages train students to analyze spelling rules, develop vocabulary building skills, and highlight grammar concepts. (Reference page work done in red pencil will be bold in the sample pages in this appendix.)

## Primary Learning Log

The Primary Learning Log segments illustrated on the following pages will include a sample spelling section and completed reference pages as they might look at the end of second grade. The student started the year at Section J and completed the year with Section O.

## Black Learning Log

The build-from-scratch Black Learning Log segments illustrated in the following pages include a sample page for new spelling words and completed reference pages as they might look at the end of fourth grade. The student started the year at Spelling Section P and completed the year with Section Z.

The new Formatted Black Log has all of these pages plus more. It shifts the reference pages to the front of the book because of the expanded table of contents. Nine new pages are added. P 26 covers rule 17. Homophones are moved to B38 next to a new page for Heteronyms. See www.bhibooks.net, under Free Downloads, for an answer key for the additions to the new log.

## Front of the book

J-1

| | |
|---|---|
| why | read |
| very | word |
| proud | daddy |
| happy | girl |
| son | never |
| with | forget |
| our | think |
| same | life |
| fine | under |
| name | lord |

Best original sentence for this lesson rewritten neatly and correctly

I am happy to be "Daddy's girl."
I will never forget our fine name

**Section J words -- starting on the opening page of this second grader's log.**

## Back of the book

### Con so nants

b c d f g h j k l m n p qu r s t
v w x (g) y

C says /s/ before E, I, or Y.
G may say /j/ before E, I, or Y.
Q always needs a U. U is not a vowel here.
Z never S says /z/ at the beginning of a base word.

### Vow els

| | most common (short sound) | says name (long sound) | third sound |
|---|---|---|---|
| a | am | a pron | wasp [3] |
| e | elk | me | |
| i | is | i tem | |
| (u) | gym | cry | |
| o | ox | go | to [3] |
| u | up | a mit | put [3] |

© 2001, Wanda Sanseri

**P1 -- Primary Log Reference Page 1**

### Multi-letter Phonograms

| | | | |
|---|---|---|---|
| sh | ng | igh | ough 6 |
| th 2 | ar | ie 3 | ew 2 |
| oo 3 | wh | dge | |
| ee | aw | ur | |
| oy | au | ti | |
| oi | ck | ci | |
| ch 3 | oe | si 2 | |
| ow 2 | oa | tch | |
| ou 4 | ed 3 | eigh | |
| ay | er | ei 3 | |
| ai | ur | ey 3 | |
| ea 3 | ir | ph | |
| or | wor | kn | |
| ui | ear | gn | |

P-2
© 2000, 2002 Wanda Sanseri

**P2 -- Primary Log Reference Page 2**

### SH Spells /sh/

| ...at the beginning of a word | | ...at the end of a syllable | |
|---|---|---|---|
| show | shut | fish | fashi on |
| ship | shoe | wash | fresh |
| shape | shop | fin ish | |
| shore | shine | dash | |
| shall | shed | push | |
| should | shrink | wish | |

| but NOT at the beginning of any syllable after the first one | | |
|---|---|---|
| ti | si | ci |
| so lu tion | ex pres sion | fa cial |
| col lec tion | con fes sion | spa cious |
| de fi ni tion | | |
| sub jec tion | | |
| ex haus tion | si | EXCEPT for the ending -ship |
| in spec tion | con fu sion | son ship |
| sta tion | in clu sion | hard ship |
| pop u la tion | | head ship |
| res ur rec tion | | lead er ship |

© 2002, Wanda Sanseri

**P3 -- Primary Log Reference Page 3**

## Five Spellings of /er/

| er | ur | ir | wor | ear |
|----|----|----|-----|-----|
| Her | church | first | wor ships | ear ly |
| o ver | spurs | girl | word | earth |
| moth er | hurt | bird | work | urn |
| oth er | burn | thirst | worms | heard |
| riv er | turn | sir | world | learn |
| pa per | pur ple | third | wor ry | pearl |
| af ter | re turn | birth day | wor th | |
| sum mer | fur nish | swirl | | |
| win ter | hur dle | dirt | | |
| din ner | curb | con firm | | |
| bit ter | hur ry | skirt | | |
| ev er y | sur face | stir | | |
| nev er | cur tain | | | |
| un der | res ur rec tion | | | |
| cov er | | | | |

| 90% of the time we use this /er/. | Each /er/ is listed in order of frequency. | | OR may say /er/ when W comes before OR. | Ear ( in *hear*) is 2 phonograms (ea-r). The phonogram EAR says /er/ as in *heard*. |

© 2001, Wanda Sanseri

**P4 -- Primary Log Reference Page 4**      **P5 -- Primary Log Reference Page 5**

---

## Silent Final E Words

dime

have

dance

Bi ble

were

true

targe

**There are at least five reasons for a silent final E.**

1. A vowel may say its name before a consonant(s) + a silent final E.
2. English words do not end with V or U.
3. C says /s/ before E, I, or Y.  G may say /j/ before E, I, or Y.
4. Every syllable must have a written vowel.
5. The odd job E covers any miscellaneous reason not listed above.

© 2002, Wanda Sanseri

**P6 -- Primary Log Reference Page 6**

---

## E's Dropping Rule

| | | | | Vowel Suffixes |
|---|---|---|---|---|
| fine | fin est | fine ness | | -able |
| place | plac ing | place ment | | -ed |
| time | tim er | time ly | | -en |
| bone | bon y | bone less | | -er |
| drive | driv en | | | -est |
| care | car ed | care ful | | -ing |
| | | | | -y |
| | | | | **Consonant Suffixes** |
| | | | | -ful |
| | | | | -ly |
| | | | | -less |
| | | | | -ment |

Silent final E words commonly lose the need for the E, when adding a vowel suffix.

© 2001, Wanda Sanseri

**P7 -- Primary Log Reference Page 7**

---

## Ways a Single Vowel Says Its Name (Its Long Sound)

| | | short vowel | long vowel |
|---|---|---|---|
| 1. at the end of a syllable | a | cat | ca ter |
| | e | met | me ter |
| | o | rob | ro bot |
| | u | cub | cu bic |

*A-E-O-U usually say [A-E-O-U] at the end of a syllable.*

| | | | |
|---|---|---|---|
| | i | di tem ma³ | di rt |
| | y | hob by | try |

*I and Y usually say [i] at the end of a syllable, but MAY SAY [I].*

| 2. before a silent final E | a | can | cane |
|---|---|---|---|
| | e | pet | Pete |
| | i | pin | pine |
| | o | rod | rode |
| | u | cut | cute |
| | y | gyp | type |

*A vowel may say its name before a consonant(s) + a silent final E.*

| 3. before 2 consonants | i | mint | mind |
|---|---|---|---|
| | o | pond | poll |

*I and O may say [I] and [O] before 2 consonants.*

**P8 -- Primary Log Reference Page 8**

## 1-1-1 Rule

| mad | mad dest | mad ly |
|---|---|---|
| stir | stir ring | |
| run | run ny | |
| top | topped | |
| cut | cutter | |
| let | let ting | |
| pet | pet ted | |
| dog | dog gy | |
| flat | flat ten | flat ness |
| step | step ping | |
| fun | fun ny | |

With a ONE syllable word
ending with ONE vowel
then ONE consonant
double the last consonant before adding a vowel suffix.

*© 2001, Wanda Sanseri*

**P9 -- Primary Log Reference Page 9**

## Y's Exchanging Rule

| base word | + any suffix | EXCEPT an I suffix |
|---|---|---|
| ba by | ba bied | ba by ish |
| fly | fli er | fly ing |
| like ly | like li hood | |
| fun ny | fun ni est | |
| play | | play er |
| hap py | hap pi ness | |
| eas y | eas i er | |
| read y | read i ness | read y ing |
| cry | cried | cry ing |
| stud y | stud ies | stud y ing |
| cop y | cop i er | cop y ist |
| wor ry | wor ried | wor ry ing |

The single vowel Y changes to I when adding any suffix
except a suffix that starts with I.

*© 2001, Wanda Sanseri*

**P10 -- Primary Log Reference Page 10**

## To Make a Word Plural Just . . .

| Add an -S | UNLESS the word ending. . . | | |
|---|---|---|---|
| | | * hisses | *changes |
| sons | | | |
| banks | riches | baby → babies | |
| girls | kisses | sky → skies | |
| arms | dishes | duty → duties | |
| freedoms | boxes | life → lives | |
| toys | buzzes | wife → wives | |
| gulfs | classes | loaf → loaves | |
| horses | glasses | *just ends with O | |
| stomachs | waltzes | vetoes | heroes |

Occasional words have . .

| No change . . . | an internal change. . . | a foreign spelling |
|---|---|---|
| dust–dust | man–men | solos |
| rain–rain | foot–feet | oxen |
| deer–deer | goose–geese | children |

To make a word plural just add an -s UNLESS the word hisses (ends with ch, s, sh, x,
z), changes (f→ v) (y→ i), or just ends with O. In these cases add -es.
Occasional words have no change, an internal change or a foreign spelling.

*© 2001, Wanda Sanseri*

**P11 -- Primary Log Reference Page 11**

## Primary Log Reference Page 12 & 13

| Numbers | | | | Months of the Year | Days of the Week |
|---|---|---|---|---|---|
| 0 | zero | | | Jan u a ry | Sun day |
| 1 | one | 1st | first | Feb ru a ry | Mon day |
| 2 | two | 2nd | sec ond | March | Tu es day |
| 3 | three | 3rd | third | A pril | Wed nes day |
| 4 | four | 4th | fourth | May | Thurs day |
| 5 | five | 5th | fifth | June | Fri day |
| 6 | six | 6th | sixth | July | Sat ur day |
| 7 | sev en | 7th | sev enth | Au gust | |
| 8 | eight | 8th | eighth | Sep tem ber | **Period of Years** |
| 9 | nine | 9th | ninth | Oc to ber | dec ade |
| 10 | ten | 10th | tenth | No vem ber | |
| 11 | e lev en | 11th | e lev enth | De cem ber | doz en |
| 12 | twelve | 12th | twelfth | | |
| 100 | hun dred | | | | cen tu ry |
| 1,000 | thou sand | | | | mil len ni um |
| 1,000,000 | mil li on | | | | |

## Primary Log Reference Page 14 & 15

| Rules for Adding Endings | | | | ie or ci ??? | | | |
|---|---|---|---|---|---|---|---|
| + ending | E's dropping | 1-1-1 | Y's Exchanging | ie | cei | ei says /A/ | Exceptions |
| eas y | | | eas i ly | chief | ceil ing | veil | |
| read y | | | read i ness | priest | | | |
| climb er | | | | thief | | | |
| file | fil er | | | friend | | | |
| zip | | zip per | | tie | | | |
| stud y | | | stud i ous | | | | |
| tax ed | | | | | | | |
| clap | | clapped | | | | | |
| vote | vot er | | | | | | |
| sur face | sur fac er | | | | | | |
| quit | | quit ter | | | | | |
| ho ly | | | hol i est | | | | |
| quiet er | | | | | | | |
| shed | | shed ding | | | | | |
| **Just add ending UNLESS** | a silent final E word + a vowel suffix ... | a 1-1-1 word + a vowel suffix ... | a single final Y word + any suffix that does not begin with I. | I before E... except after C... if we say /A/ ... and in some exceptions. | | | |

(Either weird foreign sovereign forfeited leisure. Neither heifer seized counterfeit protein.)

The Spelling Section,
starting with the front page
of a fourth grade student's
Black Learning Log.

No red pencil is used
in the spelling list itself. →

The Reference Section
starting with B1
in the back of
the student's Black Log
as it appeared at the end of the
school year.

Places where red pencil
is used are in bold.

↓

P-1

| | |
|---|---|
| im por tant | re pair |
| but ton | caught |
| hu man | taught |
| match | flight |
| set tle | tri al |
| re gard | scale |
| val ue | sup port |
| u su al | fa vor |
| for tune | known |
| count | dou ble |

P-2

| | |
|---|---|
| no tice | trace |
| no tic ing | cough |
| no tice a ble | style |
| ob tain | re treat |
| es cape | pat tern |
| vis it | shield |
| coast | o blige |
| com pli cate | trou ble |
| de sire | laugh |
| pro duce | laugh ter |

---

Con so nants

b c̆ d f ğ h j k l  m n p qu r s̆ t v w x (y) z

c usually says /k/          g usually says /g/

| | |
|---|---|
| cap | gap |
| cot | got |
| cuts | guts |
| clip | grip |
| arc | bag |

but c says /s/ ... and g may say /j/ before e, i, y

| | | | |
|---|---|---|---|
| e | **cent** Kent | **gent** | get (not jet) |
| i | **cit y** kitty | **gin** | be gin |
| y | **cyst** Kyoto | **gyp** | gy ne col o gy |

Vowels²

| | | | |
|---|---|---|---|
| a | Acts | A mos | Ez ra³ |
| e | Ex o dus | Pe ter | |
| i | Le vi ti cus | Ti tus | |
| (y) | Tim o thy | cry | |
| o | Prov erbs³ | Jo el | to³ |
| u | Na hum | Josh u a³ | bush |

**B1 -- Black Log Reference Page 1**

---

A-E-I-O-U

1. at the end of a syllable

| | | | |
|---|---|---|---|
| a | cat | ca ter | |
| e | met | me ter | |
| o | rob | ro bot | |
| u | cub | cu bic | |
| i | di lem ma | di et | |
| y | hob by | by | |

2. before a silent final e

| | | | |
|---|---|---|---|
| a | can | cane | |
| e | pet | Pete | |
| i | pin | pine | |
| o | rod | rode | |
| u | cut | cute | |
| y | gyp | type | |

3. before two consonants

| | | |
|---|---|---|
| i | mint | mind |
| o | pond | poll |

4. no known reason          con trol

**B2 -- Black Log Reference Page 2**

2

## B3 -- Black Log Reference Page 3

| | | | | | |
|---|---|---|---|---|---|
| sh | | ng | | igh | |
| th | 2 | ar | | ie | 3 |
| oo | 3 | wh | | dge | |
| ee | | aw | | wr | |
| oy | | au | | ti | |
| oi | | ck | | ci | |
| ch | 3 | oe | | si | 2 |
| ow | 2 | oa | | tch | |
| ou | 4 | ed | 3 | eigh | |
| ay | | er | | ei | 3 |
| ai | | ur | | ey | 3 |
| ea | 3 | ir | | ph | |
| or | | wor | | kn | |
| ui | | ear | | gn | |
| | | our | | ough | 6 |
| | | yr | | ew | 2 |
| | | | | eu | 2 |

## B4 -- Black Log Reference Page 4

| Phonogram | Sound | Example | Example 2 |
|---|---|---|---|
| ae | /A/-/E/ | ae ro space | Cae sar |
| ah | /ah/ | Sa rah | |
| ai | /I/ | aisle | |
| aigh | /A/ | straight | |
| au | /O/ | chauf feur | |
| augh | /aw/-/af/ | caught | laugh |
| ay | /A/ | bay ou | |
| cu | /k/-/kw/ | bis cuit | cui sine |
| eau | /O/ | bu reau | |
| et | /A/ | bou quet | |
| ge | /j/ | ser geant | |
| gh | /g/ | spa ghet ti | |
| gi | /j/ | re gion | |
| gu | /g/-/gw/ | guide | lan guage |
| pn | /n/ | pneu mo ni a | |
| ps | /s/ | Psalms | |
| pt | /t/ | pto maine | |
| qu | /k/ | con quer | |
| rh | /r/ | rhyme | |
| sc | /s/ | scis sors | |
| x | /z/ | xy lo phone | |

## B5 -- Black Log Reference Pages 5-6

| Her | church | first | wor ships | ear ly | (and) ad journs |
|---|---|---|---|---|---|
| win ter | hurt | bird | worm | yearn | jour nal |
| sup per | spur | girl | work | earth | cour age |
| nev er | burn | thirst | world | earn | jour ney |
| fa ther | curb | dirt | word | heard | cour te sy |
| or der | pur ple | swirl | han di work | pearl | |
| sis ter | burp | thirst y | wor ry | earth ling | |
| con quer | hur dle | sir | worth | learn | |
| pat tern | blur | firm | wor thy | hearse | |
| laugh ter | nurse | cir cus | un wor thy | search | |
| verb | sur prise | vir tue | worse | ear li est | |
| sev er al | mur der | vir tual | worst | re hears al | |
| cat er pil lar | pur pose | cir cu lar | wor ship ful | | |
| news pa per | pur chase | cir cle | | | |
| pas sen ger | fur ther | cir cum fer ence | | | |
| daugh ter | bur glar | cir cum stance | | | |
| clerk | sur vive | | | | yr |
| an swer | sur geon | | | | mar tyr |
| whis per | oc cur rence | | | | syr up |
| term | sur veil lance | | | | myr tle |
| won der ful | | | | | |
| mur der | | | | | |

## B7 -- Black Log Reference Pages 7-8

sh, ti

ci, si, ch

**sh**

at the beginning of a word...

| | |
|---|---|
| ship | shine |
| shape | shed |
| shore | shrink |
| shall | shield |
| should | shadow |
| shut | share |
| shoe | shelf |
| shop | sheep |

at the end of a syllable...

| | |
|---|---|
| fish | fash i on |
| wish | fresh |
| fin ish | red dish |
| dash | pub lish |
| push | dis tin guish |
| wish | ac com plish |

with the ending ship

hard ship
lead er ship
court ship
friend ship
pen man ship

**ti** at the

e lec tion
va ca tion
po si tion
ac tion
sec tion
con nec tion
di rec tion
in for ma tion
ad di tion
pa tient
con ven tion
at ten tion
pub li ca tion
pa tience
ed u ca tion
ob jec tion
cre a tion
im par tial
ex am i na tion
con di tion
mo tion

beginning of any syllable after the first one

| **ci** | **si** | **ti** |
|---|---|---|
| fa cial | pro gres sion | pro vi sion |
| pré cious | ten sion | di vi sion |
| gra cious | pro fes sion | tel e vi sion |
| mu si cian | mis sion a ry | con ver sion |
| cru cial | man sion | vi sion |
| ra cial | com pres sion | oc ca sion |
| e lec tri cian | dis cus sion | de ci sion |
| of fi cial | ses sion | ex plo sion |
| an cient | as cen sion | |
| de li cious | dis sen sion | |
| so cial | Rus sia | |
| ar ti fi cial | | French words |
| ben e fi cial | | **ch** |
| a tro cious | | chef |
| pe di a tri cian | | ma chine |
| es pe cial ly | | chan de lier |
| sus pi cious | | chauf feur |
| mor ti cian | | Mi chi gan |
| phy si cian | | Chi ca go |
| suf fi cient | | |
| pro fi cien cy | | |

7

8

---

## B9 -- Black Log Reference Page 9

**ē**

Silent Final E's

dime

have      true

dance      large

Bi ble

were

1. Does the vowel sound change because of the E?
2. Is the E needed for V or U?
3. Is the E needed for C or G?
4. Is the E needed to give the syllable a vowel?
5. Is the E needed for any other reason?

9

---

## B10 -- Black Log Reference Page 10

**e↓**

E's Dropping

| | (yes) | (no) |
|---|---|---|
| hope | hop ing | hope less |
| love | lov a ble | love ly |
| force | for ci ble | force ful |
| charge | charg er | charge a ble |
| lit tle | lit tlest | |
| olive | olived | |
| a cre | | a cre age |
| dye | | dye ing |
| be | | be ing |
| no tice | no tic ing | no tice a ble |
| trace | Trac y | trace a bility |
| out rage | out raged | out ra geous |
| singe | | singe ing |

* Does it end with a silent E?
* Are we adding a vowel suffix?
* Will dropping the E harmonize with other spelling needs?

10

---

## B11 -- Black Log Reference Page 11

1-1-1

1-1-1

| | (yes) | (no) |
|---|---|---|
| get | get ting | |
| sin | sin ner | sin ful |
| mad | mad den | mad ly |
| quip | quipped | |
| pick | | pick er |
| ship | ship ping | ship ment |
| big | big gest | big ness |
| fur | fur ry | |
| meet | | meet ing |
| box | | box er |
| roar | | roar ed |
| war | war ri or | |
| toy | | toy ing |
| slip | slip per y | |
| quiz | quiz zing | |

* Is it a one-syllable word?
* ... ending in one vowel then one consonant (that we can see and hear)?
* Are we adding a vowel suffix?

## B12 -- Black Log Reference Page 12

2-1-1

2-1-1

| | (yes) | (no) |
|---|---|---|
| for get' | for get' ting | for get' ful |
| be gin' | be gin' ner | |
| o mit' | o mit' ting | |
| e quip' | e quipped' | e quip' ment |
| pre fer' | pre ferred' | pref' er ence |
| wor' ship | | wor' ship er |
| med' al | me dal' fi on | med' al ist |
| con fer' | con fer' ring | con' fer ence |
| re bel' | re bel' fi ous | |
| ex cel' | ex cel' lent | |
| ad mit' | ad mit' tance | |
| con trol' | con trol' la ble | |
| prof' it | | prof' it a ble |
| trans mit' | trans mit' ter | |
| com mit' | com mit' tee | com mit' ment |

* Is it a two-syllable word?
* ... ending in one vowel then one consonant?
* Is the accent on the last syllable?
* Are we adding a vowel suffix?

## B13 -- Black Log Reference Page 13

y's

y's Exchanging

| | (yes) | (no) |
|---|---|---|
| cry | cried | cry ing |
| wea ry | wea ri est | wea ry ing |
| cop y | cop i er | cop y ist |
| beau ty | beau ti ful | |
| glo ry | glo ri ous | glo ry ing |
| em ploy | | em ploy ment |
| va ry | va ri e ty | va ry ing |
| tem po ra ry | tem po ra ri ness | |
| hand y | hand i craft | |
| car ry | car ri age | car ry ing |
| ac com pan y | ac com pan i ment | |
| col o ny | col o nize | |
| ap ply | ap pli ca tion | ap ply ing |
| tes ti mo ny | tes ti mo ni al | |
| mag ni fy | mag ni fi cent | mag ni fy ing |

* Does it end with a single y (not ey, ay, oy)?
* Does the suffix begin with any letter except i?

## B14 -- Black Log Reference Page 14

plurals

s/es

Add an -s unless the word ending...

hisses

| | |
|---|---|
| riches | inches |
| kisses | classes |
| dishes | wishes |
| boxes | taxes |
| buzzes | quizzes |

changes

| (f → v) | | (y → i) | |
|---|---|---|---|
| life → lives | baby | → | babies |
| wife → wives | funny | → | funnies |
| loaf → loaves | summary | → | summaries |
| knife → knives | story | → | stories |
| leaf → leaves | lady | → | ladies |
| thief → thieves | city | → | cities |
| calf → calves | party | → | parties |
| shelf → shelves | country | → | countries |

ends with o

| | |
|---|---|
| heroes | zeroes |
| echoes | tomatoes |

| no change | internal change | foreign |
|---|---|---|
| dust | man → men | solo → solos |
| rain | tooth → teeth | ox → oxen |
| celery | foot → feet | child → children |

# &#35;                                                    mo. / days / yrs.

## Numbers²

| | | | |
|---|---|---|---|
| 0 | zero | | |
| 1 | one | first | 1st |
| 2 | two³ | second | 2nd |
| 3 | three | third | 3rd |
| 4 | four | fourth | 4th |
| 5 | five | fifth | 5th |
| 6 | six | sixth | 6th |
| 7 | seven | seventh | 7th |
| 8 | eight | eighth | 8th |
| 9 | nine | ninth | 9th |
| 10 | ten | tenth | 10th |
| 11 | eleven | eleventh | 11th |
| 12 | twelve | twelfth | 12th |
| 100 | hundred | | 100th |
| 1,000 | thousand | | 1,000th |
| 1,000,000 | million | | 1,000,000th |

## Months,                    Days²

| Months | Days |
|---|---|
| January | Sunday |
| February | Monday |
| March | Tuesday |
| April | Wednesday |
| May | Thursday |
| June | Friday |
| July | Saturday |
| August | |
| September | Period of years² |
| October | decade |
| November | |
| December | dozen |
| | century |
| | millennium |

**B15 -- Black Log Reference Pages 15-16**

15                                                        16

---

+ endings²                                                + endings²

| + | e̱ |
|---|---|
| red | |
| trav'el er | |
| guilt y | |
| pro duce | pro duc er |
| pur pose | pur posed² |
| sat is fy | |
| in ter est ed | |
| con trol | |
| es ti mate | es ti ma tor |
| slip | |
| guess er | |
| ac com pan y | |
| sur vive | sur viv or |
| drop | |
| ear ly | |
| weird est | |

| 1-1-1 or 2-1-1 | y |
|---|---|
| red dest | |
| | guilt i er |
| | sat is fied |
| con trolled² | |
| slip ping | |
| | ac com pan ist |
| dropped² | |
| | ear li est |

Just add an ending
unless the word ends with ...

| a silent e | 1 vowel + 1 consonant | a single y |
|---|---|---|
| + a vowel suffix | + a vowel suffix | + a "not i" suffix |
| + harmonizes | + accent | |

**B17 -- Black Log Reference Pages 17-18**

17                                                        18

---

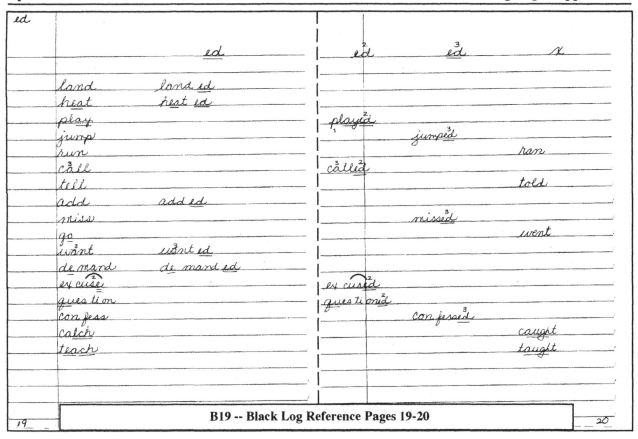

**B19 -- Black Log Reference Pages 19-20**

*19*          *20*

| Contractions | + not | + is | + will |
|---|---|---|---|
| is | = isn't | he = he's | he = he'll |
| do | = don't | she = she's | she = she'll |
| did | = didn't | it = it's | it = it'll |
| can | = can't | one = one's | I = I'll |
| has | = hasn't | that = that's | you = you'll |
| have | = haven't | what = what's | we = we'll |
| had | = hadn't | here = here's | they = they'll |
| must | = mustn't | where = where's | who = who'll |
| are | = aren't | who = who's | |
| was | = wasn't | there = there's | + would |
| will | = won't | | I = I'd |
| should | = shouldn't | + are | you = you'd |
| would | = wouldn't | you = you're | we = we'd |
| could | = couldn't | we = we're | they = they'd |
| does | = doesn't | they = they're | |
| | | | + have |
| let us | = let's | + has | I = I've |
| I am | = I'm | he = he's | you = you've |
| | | she = she's | we = we've |
| of the | | it = it's | they = they've |
| clock | = o'clock | | |

**B21 -- Black Log Reference Page 21**

*21*

Dis miss L

| all | full |
|---|---|
| al most | truth ful |
| al so | re gret ful |
| al ways | e vent ful |
| al though | use ful |
| al read y | thought ful |
| al to gether | need ful |
| | cheer ful |
| | de light ful |
| | faith ful |
| | mourn ful |
| | waste ful |
| | du ti ful |
| | care ful |
| 2 words | wrong ful |
| all right | bea u ti ful |
| all wrong | aw ful |
| | won der ful |
| | pride ful |
| | grate ful |
| | re source ful |

**B22 -- Black Log Reference Page 22**

*22*

ie / ei ?

| ie | cei |
|---|---|
| chief | ceil ing |
| shield | de ceived |
| grief | re ceived |
| brief | con ceit |
| pie | con ceive |
| field | per ceive |
| pierce | re ceipt |
| be lieve | |
| tie | |
| niece | |
| hand ker chief | |
| piece | |
| pierced | |
| yield | |
| siege | |
| a chieve | |
| re lief | |
| prai rie | |
| griev ance | |

Use ie unless
we can say "yea"... ✱ Is it after c?

23

ie / ei ?

| ei says /A/ | X |
|---|---|
| veil | ei ther |
| their | nei ther |
| beige | weird |
| rein | for feit |
| reign | for eign |
| vein | lei sure |
| heir | heif er |
| hei nous | sov er eign |
| heir loom | seize |
| sur veil lance | coun ter feit |
| feign | pro tein |
| feint | sov er eign ty |
| sheik | shek |
| skein | caf feine |
| | feis ty |
| | Fahr en heit |
| | heist |
| | seis mic |
| | stein |
| | ka lei do scope |

✱ Do we say /A/ ?        ✱ Is it an exception we learned?

24

**B23- Black Log Reference Pages 23-24**

---

abbrev.

Ab bre vi a tions

| @ | = | at | acct. | = | account |
|---|---|---|---|---|---|
| St. | = | Street, Saint | mts. | = | mountains |
| yr. | = | year | mo. | = | month |
| yd. | = | yard | no. | = | number |
| ft. | = | foot, feet | mkt. | = | market |
| ea. | = | each | doz. | = | dozen |
| Mr. | = | Mister | qt. | = | quart |
| W | = | West | sec. | = | second |
| w/ | = | with | N. | = | North |
| gal. | = | gallon | S. | = | South |
| in. | = | inch | Mrs. | = | Mistress |
| E. | = | East | amt. | = | amount |
| w/o | = | without | sq. | = | square |
| hr. | = | hour | Ave. | = | Avenue |
| Dr. | = | Drive, Doctor | cm | = | centimeter |
| 1st | = | first | gov't | = | government |
| lb. | = | pound | Is. | = | Island |
| bro. | = | brother | min. | = | minute |
| wk. | = | week | TV | = | television |
| mi. | = | mile | vol. | = | volume |
| pd. | = | paid | assoc. | = | association |
| Rd. | = | Road | misc. | = | miscellaneous |

25

**B25 -- Black Log Reference Page 25**

---

sea / see

Hom o phones

| won | – one | mourn | – morn |
|---|---|---|---|
| hour | – our | waste | – waist |
| cent | – sent – scent | ate | – eight |
| bear | – bare | whole | – hole |
| mail | – male | threw | – through |
| I | – eye | new | – knew |
| weak | – week | sale | – sail |
| by | – buy | dew | – due – do |
| meat | – meet | patients | – patience |
| no | – know | weigh | – way – whey |
| road | – rode | to | – two – too |
| rows | – rose | peace | – piece |
| lead | – led | rain | – rein – reign |
| for | – four – fore | him | – hymn |
| so | – sew – sow | kernel | – colonel |
| stare | – stair | air | – heir |
| right | – write | scene | – seen |
| hear | – here | aisle | – isle – I'll |
| plane | – plain | birth | – berth |
| pare | – pear – pair | coarse | – course |
| fair | – fare | wait | – weight |
| ant | – aunt | sense | – cents |

26

**B26 -- Black Log Reference Page 26**

---

## Parts of Speech | Examples

| Parts of Speech | Examples |
|---|---|
| noun - names a person, place, thing, or idea | boy, school, book, freedom |
| pronoun - takes the place of a noun | I, you, he, she, it, we, they, her, none |
| verb - expresses action or state of being | look, see, love, wave, kill, wash / be (am, is, are, was, were, been) |
| adjective - describes a noun or pronoun | old, little, hot, cold, green, wild / Articles: a, an, the |
| adverb - modifies a verb, adjective or another adverb. It can tell how, when, where, why, to what extent | how? kindly    when? soon / where? here    why? why / to what extent? never |
| preposition - shows the relationship between a noun or pronoun and some other word | over, under, above, below, in, out |
| conjunction - connects words, phrases, clauses | and, but, or, yet, so, nor, since, as |
| interjection - stands alone to express strong feelings | Help! Fire! Oh! Ouch! Hallelujah! |

27 | 28

**B27- Black Log Reference Pages 27-28**

---

## Diagramming Sentences

subject | verb    Children | read

subj. | vb. | direct object    Children | read | books

subj. | vb. | d.o.    Children | read | books
indirect object    me

subj. | vb. | d.o.    children | read | books
adj. adv. adj. adj.    may quickly classical even

subj.    Children
verb    and
subj.    adults    read

subj. | vb. \ predicate nominative    Novels | are \ books.

subj. | vb. \ predicate adjective    Children | are \ happy
prepositional phrase    with books

29 | 

**B29 -- Black Log Reference Page 29**

---

## Prepositions

| | | |
|---|---|---|
| in | under | past |
| by | outside | beyond |
| out | inside | among |
| to | from | except |
| into | along | through |
| up | near | throughout |
| on | between | aboard |
| onto | without | until |
| over | upon | during |
| at | across | regarding |
| of | behind | since |
| like | within | beneath |
| for | above | underneath |
| about | before | toward |
| after | off | against |
| down | below | concerning |
| with | beside | |

**B30 -- Black Log Reference Page 30**

30

**B 31 -- optional -- See Wise Guide, pp. 7, 97**

---

# APPENDIX D: Keys to the Language

## Explanation of Special Spelling Markings

1. Syllabication:
   Words are broken into syllables to illustrate relationships to rules more clearly.

2. Single Underline:
   a. Multi-letter phonograms that represent one unit of sound (**eight**)
   b. Single vowels at the end of a syllable if they say A-E-I-O-U (**me, my**)
   c. U, V, C, or G before a silent E to show why we need the E. (**blue** $_2$, **have** $_2$, **lance** $_3$, **large** $_3$)

3. Double Underline:
   a. Silent letters, like a silent final E, or unexpected letters like the "b" in "**lamb**."
   b. To emphasize 1-1-1 rule (**hop ping**), or the 2-1-1 rule    (**be gin ning**).

   A double underline is unnecessary in words like "**till**" [Rule 17] or "**ap-ple**" [Rule 29]
       In these cases the verbal emphasis is adequate. In dictating the word "till" after the child
       sounds the first /l/ the teacher should interject the rule: "We often double F, L, and S..." In
       dictating words like "apple" the teacher should say, "We think to spell ap-ple, we say "aple.""

4. A Bridge:
   A bridge is drawn from a bold vowel, over the consonant, to the silent E (**time**).

5. Numbers:
   a. Above a phonogram to show which sound other than the first is used ($\overset{3\ 2}{\textbf{was}}$, $\overset{2}{\textbf{slow}}$),
   UNLESS the possibility of a second sound can be readily seen.
       The number 2 is understood and not needed when:
       1. A single consonant follows Rules 2 (**cent**), 3 (**gym**)
       2. A single vowel follows Rules 4 (**me**), 5,6 (**my**), 7 (**dime**), 19 (**old**).
       Note: Occasionally a single vowel will make the second sound and not be covered by any
       of the vowel rules. In such a case, it will need a 2 ($\overset{2}{\textbf{an}}$ **cient**, con $\overset{2}{\textbf{trol}}$).
   b. Beside the double underline for silent final E to show the reason for the E (**ap ple** $_4$, **come** $_5$).
   c. Number 1 is placed above a phonogram to clarify that it is a single phonogram rather
   than a multi-letter one ($\overset{1}{\textbf{ver}}$ **y**) or where the pronounciation is an exception to a general
   rule ($\overset{1}{\textbf{na}}$ **tion al**).

6. An x:
   An X is placed over a phonogram in place of a number when the phonogram makes a
   distinctly different sound from the sound(s) we taught with the phonograms. ($\overset{x}{\textbf{of}}$, **w**$\overset{x}{\textbf{ou}}$**ld**).

7. A Bracket: Shows relationships between words in the Wise List:
   a. Base word/ derivative                     (day/daily)
   b. Same peculiarity in spelling              (any/many)
   c. Contrasts in sounds that might be easily confused   (picture/pitcher)
   d. Different tenses of the same verb         (run/ran)

| phonogram | sound (s) | [For teacher only—Examples of words] | | | |
|---|---|---|---|---|---|
| a | /a/-/A/-/ah/ | am | a-pron | wasp | |
| b | /b/ | bat | | | |
| c | /k/- /s/ | cat | cent | | |
| d | /d/ | dad | | | |
| e | /e/-/E/ | elk | be | | |
| f | /f/ | fat | | | |
| g | /g/-/j/ | big | gym | | |
| h | /h/ | hat | | | |
| i | /i/-/I/ | it | i-vy | | |
| j | /j/ | job | | | |
| k | /k/ | kit | | | |
| l | /l/ | lap | | | |
| m | /m/ | me | | | |
| n | /n/ | nut | | | |
| o | /ah/-/O/-/OO/ | on | go | to | |
| p | /p/ | pan | | | |
| qu | /kw/—Q always needs a U.  U is not a vowel here. | queen | | | |
| r | /r/ | ran | | | |
| s | /s/-/z/ | sent | as | | |
| t | /t/ | tip | | | |
| u | /u/-/U/-/oo/ | up | u-nit | put | |
| v | /v/ | van | | | |
| w | /w/ | wag | | | |
| x | /ks/ | fox | | | |
| y | /y/-/i/-/I/ | yard | gym | by | |
| z | /z/ | zip | | | |
| ai | /A/ -- 2-letter /A/ that we may NOT use at the end of English words` | laid | | | |
| ar | /ar/ | car | | | |
| au | /aw/ that we may  NOT use at the end of English words | sau-cer | | | |
| aw | /aw/ that we may use at the  end of English words | saw | | | |
| ay | /A/ -- 2-letter /A/ that we may use at the end of English words | play | | | |
| ch | /ch/-/k/-/sh/ | child | Christ-mas | chef | |
| ci | /sh/-- short /sh/ | fa-cial | | | |
| ck | /k/ -- 2-letter /k/ | back | | | |
| dge | /j/ -- 3-letter /j/ | edge | | | |
| ea | /E/-/e/-/A/ | eat | bread | steak | |
| ear | /er/ | ear-ly | | | |
| ed | /ed/-/d/-/t/ -- past tense ending | trad-ed | pulled | picked | |
| ee | /E/ -- double /E/ always says /E/ | tree | | | |
| ei | /A/-/E/-/i/ that we may NOT use at the end of English words | heir | cei-ling | for-eign | |
| eigh | /A/ -- 4-letter /A/ | eight | | | |
| er | /er/ | her | | | |
| ew | /OO/-/U/  that we may use at the end of English words | flew | few | | |
| ey | /A/-/E/-/i/ that we may use at the end of English words | they | key | val-ley | |
| gn | /n/-- 2-letter /n/ used both at the beginning and end of a base word | gnat | sign | | |
| ie | /E/-/I/-/i/ | piece | pie | col-lie | |
| igh | /I/-- 3 letter /I/ | night | | | |
| ir | /er/ | first | | | |
| kn | /n/ -- 2-letter /n/ used only at the beginning of a base word | know | | | |
| ng | /ng/ | sing | | | |
| oa | /O/ -- 2-letter /O/ that we may NOT use at the end of English words. | coat | | | |
| oe | /O/ -- 2-letter /O/ that we may use at the end of English words. | toe | | | |
| oi | /oy/ that we may NOT use at the end of English words * | boil | | | |
| oo | /OO/-/oo-/O/ | food | good | floor | |
| or | /or/ | Lord | | | |
| ou | /ow/-/O/-/OO/-/u/ | house | soul | group | coun-try |
| ough | /O/-/OO/-/uff/-/off/-/aw/-/ow/    though   through | rough | trough | thought | bough |
| ow | /ow/-/O/ | plow | snow | | |
| oy | /oy/ that we may use at the end of English words | boy | | | |
| ph | /f/ -- 2-letter /f/ | phone | | | |
| sh | /sh/ | she | dish | | |
| si | /sh/-/zh/ | ses-sion | di-vi-sion | | |
| tch | /ch/ -- 3-letter /ch/ | butch-er | | | |
| th | /th/- /TH/  (motor off/ motor on) | thin | this | | |
| ti | /sh/ -- tall /sh/ | na-tion | | | |
| ui | /OO/ | fruit | | | |
| ur | /er/ | church | | | |
| wh | /hw/ | whis-per | | | |
| wor | /er/ | wor-ships | | | |
| wr | /r/ -- 2-letter /r/ | wreck | | | |

1. **Q** always needs a U.  U is not a vowel here *(quit)*.

2  **C** usually says /k/ *(cat, cot, cut, clip, music)*. **C** says /s/ before E, I, or Y *(cent, city, cycle)*.
3. **G** usually says /g/ *(gap, got, guts, grip, bag)*, *but* **G** MAY say /j/ before E, I, or Y *(germ, giant, gym)*.

4. **A, E, O, U** usually say /A, E, O, U/ at the end of a syllable *(la-zy, me, go, u-nit)*.

5. **I and Y** usually say /i/ at the end of a syllable *(cli-nic, cy-nic)*, but may say /I/ *(li-on, cry)*.

6. English words do not end in **I, U, V, or J**.  At the end of English words Y stands in for I.

7. **SILENT FINAL Es.**  English has at least five reasons for a silent final E.

| | | |
|---|---|---|
| 1st | dime | (The vowel sound changes because of the E.) |
| 2nd | love, true | (English words do not end with V or U). |
| 3rd | dance, large | (The C says /s/ because of the E.  The G says /j/ because of the E). |
| 4th | ap ple | (Every syllable must have a vowel.) |
| 5th | are | (The Odd Job E includes any miscellaneous reason not covered above). |

8. **O-R** usually says /er/ when W comes before O-R *(worship)*.

9. **IE or EI Phonograms?**  Use I before E *(chief)* except after C *(receive)*, if we say /A/ *(vein)*, and in some exceptions: *Either weird foreign sovereign forfeited leisure.  Neither heifer seized counterfeit protein nor caffeine.*

10. **SH: /Sh/ is used** at the beginning of a base word *(she)* at the end of a syllable *(fish)*, but not at the beginning of any syllable after the first one *(na-tion)* except for the ending -ship *(friend-ship)*.
11. **TI, CI, SI:**  **Latin** spellings of /sh/ come at the beginning of any syllable after the first one *(nation, facial, tension)*.

12. **ABBREVIATIONS** use a few letters to represent a larger word (Mr. = Mister, m = meter, CA = California).
13. **CONTRACTIONS** replace a letter (or letters) with an apostrophe to contract (or shorten) a phrase (I am = I'm).

14. **1-1-1 RULE:**  With a <u>one</u>-syllable word ending in <u>one</u> vowel then <u>one</u> consonant, double the last consonant before adding a vowel suffix *(get, getting)*.
15. **2-1-1-ACCENT RULE:**  With a <u>two</u>-syllable word ending in <u>one</u> vowel then <u>one</u> consonant, double the last consonant before adding a vowel suffix IF the <u>accent</u> is on the last syllable *(for get', for get ting)*.

16. **E's DROPPING RULE:  Silent final E words** commonly lose the need for the E when adding a vowel suffix *(hope/hoping/ hopeless)*. In words like *noticeable* or *changeable* rules 2 and 3 override rule 16.

17. **FF, LL, SS:**  We often double **F,L,S** after a single vowel at the end of a base word *(off, all, confess)*. Occasionally other letters are doubled in this way *(ebb, odd, egg, inn, err, watt, jazz)*.

18. **A-Y** usually spells /A/ at the end of a base word *(may, pay)*.  When a word ends with A it says /ah/ *(ma)*.

19. **I and O** may say /I/ and /O/ before two consonants *(bind, gold)*.

20. **X** is never directly before S. *(boxes, excel)*.  There is a /s/ sound in X.

21. **DISMISS L RULE:**  *ALL* and *FULL* are written with one L when added to another syllable  *(almost, fulfill)*. *All right*  is two words just like *all wrong*.  (TILL has been omitted from this rule since it only applies to *until*.)

22. **PLURALS:**  To make a word **plural** just add an -S, UNLESS the word ending hisses (ch, s, sh, x, z), changes *(wife/ wives; fly/flies)*, or may stop with O *(tomato/tomatoes)*.  In these cases add -es.  Occasional words have no change *(sheep/sheep)*, an internal change *(man/men)*, or a foreign spelling *(alumnus/alumni; piano/pianos)*.

23. **DGE: 3-letter /j/** is only used after a single vowel which says /a-e-i-o-u/ *(badge, edge, bridge, lodge, fudge)*.

24. **Y'S EXCHANGING RULE:  A single vowel Y** (not *ay, ey, oy, uy*) changes to I when adding any ending *(try/tried)*, unless the ending starts with I *(trying, babyish, copyist)*.

25. **CK: 2-letter /k/** is used only after a single vowel which says /a-e-i-o-u/ *(back, peck, pick, pocket, truck)*.

26. **CAPITALIZE** individual names or titles of persons *(Jesus)*, places *(Ohio)* or things *(Bible)*.

27. **Z, NEVER S,** spells /z/ at the beginning of a base word *(zoo, zero)*.

28. **ED:**  /Ed-d-t/ past tense ending forms another syllable if the base word ends with /d/ or /t/ *(loaded, acted)*.  If not it sounds like /d/ or /t/ *(killed, picked)*.

29. **DOUBLE CONSONANTS** in multisyllable words should both be sounded for spelling but not in normal speech *(ap-ple)*. [Note: This rule is a guideline for teachers but not necessary for students to learn.]

## COMMON PREFIXES

| Prefix | Meaning | Examples |
|--------|---------|----------|
| anti- | against | antislavery, antisocial |
| auto- | self | autobiography, automatic, automobile |
| bi- | two | bicycle, bifocal, binoculars, biplane |
| by- | near | bypass, bystander, byway |
| cent- | hundred | cent, centigrade, centimeter, century |
| circu- | around | circulate, circus, circumstance |
| counter- | opposite | counteract |
| de- | opposite, down, away | defrost, depress, deport |
| dec- | ten | decade, decimal |
| di- | two | dilemma, dialogue |
| dis- | opposite | disagree, disappear, discontinue, dishonest |
| dys- | difficult, ill | dysfunction, dyspepsia |
| epi- | upon | epicenter, epidermis |
| ex- | out | exceed, excel, exhaust, exit |
| extra- | outside | extracurricular, extraordinary, extravagant |
| hemi- | half | hemisphere |
| homo- | same | homogenize, homophone |
| hyper- | excessive | hyperactive, hypercritical, hypertension |
| il- | not | illegal, illiterate, illogical |
| im- | into | immigrate, implant, import |
| in- | into, not | inhale, infect, inactive, inaccurate |
| inter- | among, between | interact, international |
| ir- | not | irregular, irresponsible |
| kilo- | thousand | kilometer, kilowatt |
| magni- | great | magnify, magnificent |
| mal- | bad | maladjusted, malfunction |
| mega- | large | megaphone |
| meta- | change | metamorphosis, metaphor, metastasis |
| micro- | small | microscope, microfilm |
| mid- | middle | midnight, midway, midyear |
| milli- | thousand | million, milligram |
| mis- | bad | misspell, misbehave, miscarriage |
| mon-, mono- | one | monarch, monologue, monopoly |
| multi- | many | multicolored, multiply |
| non- | not | nonconformist |
| out- | surpassing | outlive, outnumber |
| over- | too much | overdo, overprice |
| post- | after | postpone, postscript (P.S.) |
| pre- | before | preamble, precaution, prefix |
| pro- | before, favor | prophet, prologue, pro-American, pro-life |
| pseudo- | false | pseudonym |
| re- | again | react, reappear, redo, retake, rewrite |
| semi- | half | semiannual, semicircle |
| sub- | under | subway, submarine |
| super- | more than | superman, supernatural, superpower |
| sym- | together | sympathy, symphony, synonym |
| tele- | distant | telegraph, telephone, television |
| trans- | across | transact, transatlantic, translate |
| tri- | three | tricycle, triplet, trinity, trio |
| ultra- | beyond | ultramodern |
| un- | not | unable, unlikely, unhealthy |
| under- | below | undercover, underpass |

## COMMON SUFFIXES

### Vowel Suffixes

| | | | |
|---|---|---|---|
| -able | perish**able** | -ial | commerc**ial** |
| -ably | remark**ably** | -ian | Christ**ian** |
| -ade | block**ade** | -ible | perfect**ible** |
| -age | marri**age** | -ic | histor**ic** |
| -aire | million**aire** | -ical | econom**ical** |
| -al | natur**al** | -ice | serv**ice** |
| -ance | repent**ance** | -ics | econom**ics** |
| -ant | serv**ant** | -ier | cash**ier** |
| -ar | begg**ar** | -ine | hero**ine** |
| -ard | drunk**ard** | -ing | roof**ing** |
| -arium | planet**arium** | -ion | confess**ion** |
| -ary | infirm**ary** | -ior | Sav**ior** |
| -ate | fortun**ate** | -ious | grac**ious** |
| -ation | inspir**ation** | -ish | child**ish** |
| -ative | talk**ative** | -ism | hero**ism** |
| -ed | steam**ed** | -ist | capital**ist** |
| -ee | employ**ee** | -ity | civil**ity** |
| -en | fatt**en** | -ive | act**ive** |
| -ence | correspond**ence** | -o | concert**o** |
| -ency | depend**ency** | -or | act**or** |
| -ent | resid**ent** | -ory | conservat**ory** |
| -er | teach**er** | -osis | tubercul**osis** |
| -ern | east**ern** | -osity | monstr**osity** |
| -ery | brav**ery** | -ous | joy**ous** |
| -ess | princ**ess** | -ure | clos**ure** |
| -ette | kitchen**ette** | -y | rain**y** |
| -est | happi**est** | -yer | law**yer** |

### Consonant Suffixes

| | | |
|---|---|---|
| -cle | little | parti**cle** |
| -cule | little | mole**cule** |
| -cy | a quality or condition | bankrupt**cy** |
| -dom | state or existence of | free**dom** |
| -fold | division into parts | two**fold** |
| -ful | full of | beauti**ful** |
| -fy | to make, to form | glori**fy** |
| -hood | members of a group, condition | neighbor**hood** |
| -less | without | friend**less** |
| -let | small, little | book**let** |
| -like | resembling | child**like** |
| -ly | manner of acting | friend**ly** |
| -ment | state of, act of | govern**ment** |
| -ness | state or quality of | happi**ness** |
| -ship | quality or condition | friend**ship** |
| -some | more, the same as | awe**some** |
| -tude | quality or degree of | magni**tude** |
| -ty | state of, act of | loyal**ty** |
| -ward | in the direction of | back**ward** |
| -wright | a person who constructs | play**wright** |

## A SAMPLE LESSON PLAN FOR PRIMARY BEGINNERS TO THE PROGRAM
Teacher should regularly read aloud to students. Other activities are listed below.
Note: Phonogram presentation order is updated. If necessary, adjust *Wise Guide* preliminaries to match.

| WK | MON | TUES | WED | THURS | FRIDAY |
|---|---|---|---|---|---|
| 1 | 1. Say, write, quiz phonograms: **a, c, d** <br> 2. Guess Word-SWR p.21 | 1. Say, write, quiz **g, o, qu** <br> 2. Quiz all 6 Pho. | 1.Say, write, quiz **e, l, b, f** <br> 2. Quiz all 10 | 1.Say, write, quiz **h, k. i, j** <br> 2. Quiz all 13 | 1. Say, write,quiz **p, r, s** <br> 2. Quiz all 17 |
| 2 | 1. Say, write, quiz **t, u, v** <br> 2. Quiz 20 Phonograms | 1. Say, write, quiz **w, y, n,** <br> 2. Quiz all 23 | 1.Say, write, quiz **m, x, z** <br> 2. Quiz all 26 | 1. Write **0-3** Numbers <br> 2. Quiz all 26 | 1. Teach **Vowel/ Consonant Pg.** <br> 2. Test all 26 |
| 3 | 1. Review **Vowel Consonant Pg**. <br> 2. Quiz all 26 Pho. | 1. Say, write, quiz **sh, th, oo, ee, er** <br> 2. Add to Ref. Pg. all except **er**. | 1. **Sect A words** <br> 2. Quiz all 31 <br> 3. Read *My Bed* ... SWR p.95, 96 | 1. Original Oral Sentences <br> 2. Number Pg | 1. Test A Words <br> 2. Test all 31 Phonograms |
| 4 | 1. Say, write, quiz **oy, oi, ch, ow, ou** <br> 2. Add to Ref. Pg. <br> 3. Dictate A words to 3x5s. | 1. Dictate Section **B** words <br> 2. Read all 36 pho <br> 3. Read words in Learning Log | 1. Dictate B words to 3x5s. <br> 2. Read all 36 <br> 3. Compose Oral Sentences | 1. Time reading A-B words <br> 2. Read all 36 <br> 3. Put cards in sentences. | 1. Antonym activity. (p. 4). <br> 2. Test all 36 & B Words + ones missed in A. |
| 5 | 1. Say, write, quiz **ay, ai, ea, or, ui** <br> 2. Add to Ref. Pg. <br> 3. Vowel Sound Drill- Wise Guide p. 5 | 1. Dictate **Sect C** words <br> 2. Read all 41 <br> 3. Read words in Learning Log | 1. Dictate C words to 3x5s. <br> 2. Read all 41 <br> 3. Compose Oral Sentences | 1. Time reading A-C words <br> 2. Quiz all 41 <br> 3. Preposition game-Wise p.7 | 1. Compound words (p. 6) <br> 2. Test C words +ones missed in A- B. |
| 6 | 1. Say, write, quiz **ng, ar, wh, aw, au** <br> 2. Add to Ref. Pg. <br> 3. **Silent Final E's** | 1. Dictate **Sect D** words <br> 2. Read all 46 <br> 3. Read words | 1. Do spelling enrichment activities. <br> 2. Read all 46 | 1. Do spelling enrichment activities. <br> 2. Quiz all 46 | 1. Read words <br> 2. Test D words +ones missed in A- C. |
| 7 | 1. Say, write, quiz **ck, oe, oa, ed** <br> 2. Add to Ref. Pg. | 1. Dictate **Sec. E** <br> 2. Read all 50 <br> 3. Read words <br> 4. SH words to P3 | 1. Enrichment activities. <br> 2. Read all 50 | 1. Enrichment activities. <br> 2. Quiz all 50 | 1. Read words <br> 2. Test E + words missed in A-D |
| 8 | 1. Say, write, quiz **er, ur, ir, wor, ear** <br> 2. Add to Ref. Pg. <br> 3. **AEIOU** Pg. | 1. Dictate **Sec. F** <br> 2. Read all 55 <br> 3. Read words | 1. Enrichment activities. <br> 2. Read all 55 | 1. Enrichment activities. <br> 2. Quiz all 55 | 1. Read words <br> 2. Test F + words missed in A-E |

In eight weeks you will expose students to 55 phonograms, dictate them to a reference page in their Learning Log, teach 120 of the most frequently used words in the language, and expose students to half of the foundational spelling rules. You will role model the value of language instruction by reading from "living books" and start to train the student to compose original sentences, first orally and then in writing. From here out, the pace of presenting new concepts will begin to slow. In the first eight weeks you will cover three-fourths of the building blocks to the language. Long-term mastery of these tools will come with time as we use them in learning to spell increasingly difficult words. After the first five weeks, the typical phonogram proficiency is 100% accuracy of the basic alphabet and 60 to 70% for the multi-letter phonograms. It will take time to master them all.

## SAMPLE LESSON PLAN FOR PRIMARY BEGINNERS CONTINUED

| WK | MON | TUES | WED | THURS | FRIDAY |
|---|---|---|---|---|---|
| 9 | 1. Intro Rule Cards 7, 8, 17, 18, 19, 25 +. <br> 2. Teach **igh, ie, dge, wr.** Add Phono Pg. | 1. Start intro capitals. <br> 2. Dictate **Sec. G** <br> 3. Add to # Page. | 1. Oral sentences <br> 2. Start writing original sentences | 1. Enrichment activities. <br> 2. Quiz all 59 | 1. Read words. <br> 2. Test G plus selected A-F review words. |
| 10 | 1. Diagnostic Sp. test <br> 2. Quiz phonograms. <br> 3. Teach **ti, ci, si, tch** Add to Phono. Pg. | 1. Read all 55 phonograms <br> 2. Dictate **Sec H-1** <br> 3. Add to # Page | 1. Oral sentences <br> 2. Write original sentences using H-1 words. | 1. Enrichment activities. <br> 2. Quiz all 63 phonograms | 1. Record student reading words from Log. <br> 2. Test H words |
| 11 | 1. Quiz phonograms. <br> 2. Teach **eigh, ei, ey, ph.** Add Phono Pg. | 1. Read phonograms <br> 2. S. Rule Warm-up <br> 3. Dictate **Sec H-2** | 1. Oral sentences <br> 2. Write original w/ H-2 words. | 1. Enrichment activities. <br> 2. Quiz all 67. | 1. Read words. <br> 2. Test H-2 words +. |
| 12 | 1. Teach **kn, gn, ough, ew.** Add Phono Pg. <br> 2. Begin reading easy books! | 1. Read phonograms <br> 2. S. Rule Warm-up <br> 3. Dictate **Sec I-1** | 1. Oral sentences <br> 2. Write original w/ I-1 words. | 1. Enrichment activities. <br> 2. Quiz all 70. | 1. Read. <br> 2. Test I-1 words +. |
| 13 | 1. Read phonograms <br> 2. S. Rule Warm-up <br> 3. Dictate **Sec I-2** | 1. Teach **mid-, -y.** See p. 129 SWR. Make derivatives. <br> 2. Practice quiz **I-2**. | 1. Oral sentences <br> 2. Write original w/ I-2 words. | 1. Enrichment activities. <br> 2. Quiz all 70 phonograms | 1. Read. <br> 2. Test I-2 words +. |
| 14 | 1. Read phonograms <br> 2. S. Rule Warm-up <br> 3. Dictate **Sec I-3** | 1. Explain abbrev. <br> 2. Practice quiz **I-3** | 1. Oral sentences <br> 2. Write original w/ I-3 words. | 1. Enrichment activities. <br> 2. Quiz all 70 | 1. Read. <br> 2. Test I-3 words +. |
| 15 | 1. Read phonograms <br> 2. S. Rule Warm-up <br> 3. Dictate **Sec I-4** | 1. Homophones & homographs <br> 2. Practice quiz **I-4** | 1. Oral sentences <br> 2. Write original w/ I-4 words. | 1. Enrichment activities. <br> 2. Quiz all 70 | 1. Read. <br> 2. Test I-4 words +. |
| 16 | 1. Read phonograms <br> 2. S. Rule Warm-up <br> 3. Intro **ER** Pg. | 1. Dictate **Sec J-1** <br> 2. Teach **J-1** in sign <br> 3. Practice quiz **J-1**. | 1. Oral sentences <br> 2. Write original w/ J-1 words. | 1. Enrichment activities. <br> 2. Quiz all 70 | 1. Read. <br> 2. Test J-1 words +. |
| 17 | 1. Read phonograms <br> 2. S. Rule Warm-up <br> 3. Dictate **Sec J-2** | 1. Read words. <br> 2. Practice quiz **J-2** <br> 3. Enrichment activities. | 1. Oral sentences <br> 2. Write original w/ J-2 words. | 1. Enrichment activities. <br> 2. Quiz select phonograms | 1. Read. <br> 2. Test J-2 words +. |

Continue the year with a pattern similar to week 17. With each spelling section in *Wise Guide,* follow the preliminary suggestions. Warm up with recommended phonograms and spelling rule cards. By week 17 you can be pleased with an 80% mastery of the phonograms. Set a goal of 100% mastery of the phonograms by the end of the year. Teach the spelling words. During the week, reinforce the new spelling words by using these words in original sentences and through the suggested enrichment activities.

Occasionally you will teach a discovery reference page: the **Plural Page** (J-4; K-6), **E's Dropping Page** (K-3, L-1), **1-1-1 Page** (L-3), **Y's Exchanging Page** (L-6) or add to a collection page: **SH Page** (J-2, J-3, K-2, K-3, K-4, L-1, L-2, L-3 , L-5), **ER Page** (J-4, J-6, K-3, K-5, K-7, L-1, L-3, L-5, L-6, **Number Page** (K-1, K-4, K-7, L-2 , L-6).

| | | LESSON PLAN FOR NEW STUDENTS TO THE PROGRAM THIRD GRADE & ABOVE Teacher should regularly read aloud to students. Other activities are listed below. | | | |
|---|---|---|---|---|---|
| **WK** | **MON** | **TUES** | **WED** | **THURS** | **FRIDAY** |
| 1 | 1. Flip through all 70 phonograms to see how many he can say correctly. 2. Give 1st diagnostic spelling test in Appendix B. | 1. Give 2 timed McCall tests (3 min. ea.) 2. Student starts writing a short paper about self-- due Fri. | 1. Record student reading aloud. 2. Determine Placement in Wise List.* 3. Teach A-Z phonograms. | 1. Format Log 2. Teach Consonant / Vowel Pg. 3. Drill multi-phono using ref. pg. order. | 1. Continue drill of Multi-letter Pho. 2. Start adding to Ref. Pg. Mastery not yet required. 3. Finish paper started Tues. |
| | | | **Lesson plan for student who places in the Wise List at Section M** | | |
| 2 | 1. Review phonograms. 2. Quiz review words (top p. 85 in Wise). 3. Teach Silent E Pg. 4. Mark silent E's in review words. | 1. Give dictation of all review words missed. 2. Teach E's Dropping Pg. 3. Phono. quiz | 1. Phono. Drill 2. Dictate M-1 spelling words. 3. Intro. ER Pg. Add ER words from M-1. | 1. Do spelling enrichment activities. 2. Original sentences words | 1. Test new and review words. 2. Quiz all 70 phonograms. (Test for grade; quiz to practice.) |
| 3 | 1. Quiz all 70 phonograms 2. Quiz **M-2** review words (p. 87). Dictate missed ones. | 1. Review phono. & rule cards listed top p. 86. 2. Dictate M-2 words | 1. M-2 spelling enrichment activities. 2. Original sentences | 1. Start SH Pg. & Number Pg. Add M-2 # review words 2. Quiz words | 1. Test new and review words. 2. Quiz all 70 phonograms. |
| 4 | 1. Time reading 70 phonograms. 2. Quiz **M-3** review words; correct. 3. Read orig. sentences. | 1. Teach 1-1-1 using review words as ex. 2. Drill & quiz phonograms | 1. Review spell -ing rule cards. 2. Dictate M-3 words & review words missed. | 1. Do spelling enrichment activities. 2. Original sentences | 1. Test new and review words w/ 1-1-1 endings. 2. Quiz selected phonograms. |
| 5 | 1. Time reading 70 phonograms. 2. Quiz **M-4** review words; correct. 3. Teach metaphors. | 1. Teach Y's Exchanging Pg. 2. Quiz select phonograms 3. *Eagle* p.90. | 1. Read rule cards. 2. Dictate M-4 words & review words missed. 3. Quiz new wds. | 1. Do spelling enrichment activities. 2. Original sentences | 1. Test new and review words. 2. Test selected phonograms 3. Read words in log. |
| 6 | 1. Warm-up drill phonograms/ rules. 2. Dictate **Section M-5** 3. Quiz immediately. | 1. Enrichment activities. 2. Original sentences | 1. Warm-up drill phon/rules 2. Dictate **M-6**. 3. Quiz new wds. | 1. Enrichment activities. 2. Original sentences | 1. Test M-5 & M-6 2. Add any 10 words taught earlier this year. |

\* If a new student misses any of the first ten words, start instruction at Section A. (See Lesson Plans for Primary Students, and, if possible, pick up the pace .)  Otherwise, look on the chart to where the student first misspelled a word and identify the corresponding spelling level.  You can start the student with the spelling section where he first missed.  With a classroom, select a mid range for the group.

# Key Elements in Planning a Lesson

1. PHONOGRAMS.  Introduce or review consistently throughout the program.

    a. Write from dictation some or all phonograms daily until mastered, weekly afterwards.
    b. Read the phonograms daily initially; reduce to once or twice a week afterwards.

2. REFERENCE PAGES.  Construct reference pages of concepts (as needed according to *Wise Guide*).  Reduce the number of new words taught on weeks when you first present one of the more time-consuming reference pages.

3. SPELLING.  Add new spelling words to the Learning Log using teacher dictation.

    a. Teach 10 to 40 new words a week, depending on age/ ability.
    b. Give practice quiz immediately after teaching new words to help build long term mastery.
    c.  Read the words from the Log in unison as a class or with single individuals.
    d. Assign spelling enrichment activities from *Wise Guide*.
    e. Adapt weekly schedule to your needs.  Choose from sample scenarios below.

    Sample Scenario One:
        Monday-- Dictate all the words for the week.  Read words.  Give practice quiz.
        Tuesday -- Assign enrichment activities with the first half of the words.
        Wednesday-- Give practice quiz of the week's words.  Assign more reinforcements.
        Thursday --Assign enrichment activities with the second half of the words.
        Friday-- Test of all words plus five to ten challenge words from earlier in the
                year.  Make student accountable for all words taught that year.

    Sample Scenario Two:
        Monday-- Dictate half of the words for the week.  Read words.  Give practice quiz.
        Tuesday-- Assign enrichment activities.
        Wednesday-- Dictate second half of the words for the week.  Read words.  Quiz.
        Thursday-- Assign enrichment activities.
        Friday-- Test all the words for that week plus five to ten review words.

4. WRITING.  Write daily.
    a. Practice penmanship initially.
    b. Write original sentences (after Step 20).
    c. Construct paragraphs  (after step 33).
    d. Teach correct grammar usage in conjunction with original composition.

5. READING.  Student initially reads his own original sentences, then books written by others.
    a. Read aloud to the students throughout the program (Step 3).
    b. Surround students with worthwhile books.
    c. Watch the students read independently as a natural side-effect of this program.
    d. Improve comprehension. Use the *McCall Test Lessons in Reading* two to three times a
            week (Step 33)

# SWR Diagnostic Spelling Scale Graph

Name _____

Grade _____ Age _____ School Yr _____

| Spelling Section | Grade Status | Word | Test 1 | Test 2 | Test 3 | Test 4 | Test 5 | Test 6 | Test 7 | Test 8 |
|---|---|---|---|---|---|---|---|---|---|---|
| Z | 13.0 | 50 | | | | | | | | |
| Y | 12.5 | 49 | | | | | | | | |
| Y | 11.7 | 48 | | | | | | | | |
| Y | 11.2 | 47 | | | | | | | | |
| X | 10.5 | 46 | | | | | | | | |
| X | 9.8 | 45 | | | | | | | | |
| X | 9.3 | 44 | | | | | | | | |
| W | 8.8 | 43 | | | | | | | | |
| W | 8.4 | 42 | | | | | | | | |
| W | 8.0 | 41 | | | | | | | | |
| V | 7.7 | 40 | | | | | | | | |
| V | 7.5 | 39 | | | | | | | | |
| V | 7.3 | 38 | | | | | | | | |
| U | 7.0 | 37 | | | | | | | | |
| U | 6.8 | 36 | | | | | | | | |
| T | 6.6 | 35 | | | | | | | | |
| T | 6.4 | 34 | | | | | | | | |
| T | 6.2 | 33 | | | | | | | | |
| S | 6.0 | 32 | | | | | | | | |
| S | 5.8 | 31 | | | | | | | | |
| R | 5.6 | 30 | | | | | | | | |
| R | 5.4 | 29 | | | | | | | | |
| R | 5.2 | 28 | | | | | | | | |
| Q | 5.1 | 27 | | | | | | | | |
| Q | 4.9 | 26 | | | | | | | | |
| P | 4.7 | 25 | | | | | | | | |
| P | 4.5 | 24 | | | | | | | | |
| O | 4.3 | 23 | | | | | | | | |
| O | 4.2 | 22 | | | | | | | | |
| O | 4.1 | 21 | | | | | | | | |
| N | 3.9 | 20 | | | | | | | | |
| N | 3.7 | 19 | | | | | | | | |
| M | 3.5 | 18 | | | | | | | | |
| M | 3.4 | 17 | | | | | | | | |
| L | 3.3 | 16 | | | | | | | | |
| L | 3.1 | 15 | | | | | | | | |
| K | 2.9 | 14 | | | | | | | | |
| K | 2.7 | 13 | | | | | | | | |
| J | 2.6 | 12 | | | | | | | | |
| J | 2.5 | 11 | | | | | | | | |
| I | 2.4 | 10 | | | | | | | | |
| I | 2.3 | 9 | | | | | | | | |
| H | 2.2 | 8 | | | | | | | | |
| H | 2.1 | 7 | | | | | | | | |
| A-G | 2.0 | 6 | | | | | | | | |
| A-G | 1.9 | 5 | | | | | | | | |
| A-G | 1.8 | 4 | | | | | | | | |
| A-G | 1.7 | 3 | | | | | | | | |
| A-G | 1.5 | 2 | | | | | | | | |
| A-G | 1.3 | 1 | | | | | | | | |
| | 1.0 | 0 | | | | | | | | |

# First Stroke Penmanship Guide for Cursive

Cursive letters capture a likeness to book face counterparts. Added connectors help tie letters together in words for greater ease in writing fluidly. Cursive avoids numerous unnecessary stops and starts. Before writing a letter, determine if it is short (a, c, o, e. i, m, n, r, s, u, v, w, x), tall (l, h, k, b, t), short with a tall part (d), short with a tail part (g, j, p, qu, y, z), or tall with a tail (f). Identify the beginning stroke.

**Clock Letters** -- Start at the baseline with an upswing. Round up from 10 to 2. Stop. Reverse.

**Loop Letters** -- Start at the baseline with an upswing that doubles back.

**Uphill Letters** -- Start at the baseline with an upswing.

**Bump Letters** -- Start at the baseline with an upswing that ends with a slight curve.

# APPENDIX F:  Final Matter

# Glossary

**Abbreviation** — Abbreviations use a few letters to represent a larger word; a part stands for the whole. Example:  Dr. = Doctor or Drive. [<L ad- (to) + brevis (short)].

**Accent** — The stressed or accented syllable is distinguished from others in the same word by a greater distinctness of sound or force.  An accented syllable is louder, longer, and higher. The stress is stable in Native English derivatives (MAKing, reMAKing). In Latin-based words the stress shifts as the word changes form (poLITical, POLitics). This definition of accent is used in the 2-1-1 rule.  It does not refer to "regional" differences in speech.  [<L ad- (to) + cantus (sing)].

**Adjective** —  A part of speech that qualifies or limits the meaning of a noun or pronoun. Example: The adjective "little" limits the noun "boy" to a small male child  [<L ad- (to) + jacere (throw)].

**Adverb** —  A part of speech that extends or limits the meaning of verbs, other adverbs, or adjectives. Examples: *here, soon, sadly, very*.  [< L ad-(to) + verbum (verb)].

**Alliteration** — The repetition of words with the same initial sounds. Example: *kitty cat*.

**Alphabetic code** — The relationship between sounds of speech and letters that represent those sounds.

**Alphabetize** — To arrange a list of words in alphabetical order.

**Antonym** — An opposite meaning. Example: *like, dislike*. [<Gk anti- (opposite, against) + onyme (name)].

**Appositive** — A word or phrase placed beside another to explain the first.  Example: Mrs. Smith, *my piano teacher*, came to visit my parents.  [< L ad- (to) + ponere (put)].

**Articles** — The three articles in English *(a, an, the)*, are used before nouns to limit their application. These adjectives are also called "noun indicators" because they alert us that a noun is near.

**Auditory blending** — Joining together isolated sounds into a whole. Example: /k-a-t/ = *cat*.

**Auditory discrimination** — The ability to distinguish distinct units of speech.  Example: *cat* (not *tat*).

**Base line** — The line on which a word is written.

**Base words** —  The smallest word that can stand alone.  Prefixes and suffixes can be added to vary the meaning while maintaining a link to the base word. Examples: *joy, enjoy, joyful, rejoicing*.

**Blends** — Blends are two or more phonograms put together that retain their distinctive sounds.  We blend phonograms when we teach spelling, but we find it counterproductive to present blends in isolation. Examples: pr—*pray*, str—*stream*.  We think-to-spell /p-r-ay/ and /s-t-r-ea-m/.

**Classic dictionary** —  One that continues the broad foundations laid down by Noah Webster. Jean McKechnie edited more recent volumes. The pronunciation is simple and mainly coded on the correctly spelled word. Example: ē-mēr'ġen-cy.  Y in *city* sounds like the Y in *myth*.

**Clock letters** — The letters formed using a reference to points on a clock: a, c, d, g, o, qu.  Manuscript letters also use the clock for: f and s.

**Compound words** — Two or more base words joined together to form a new related word. Example: *door + way = doorway.*

**Composition** — When we write a composition, we put together words and sentences in a way that will clearly express our ideas. [<L com- (together) + ponere (put)].

**Comprehension** — To comprehend means to take hold of the meaning, to understand. In language arts we think of comprehension as the ability to seize the meaning intended by an author as we read a book. [<L com- (together) + prehendere (seize)].

**Conjunction** — The part of speech used to connect words, phrases, and clauses. Examples: *but, and, yet, since.* [< L com- (together) + jugare (join)].

**Consonants** — Consonant sounds are blocked in some way by the organs of speech as they are pushed or exploded past throat, teeth, tongue, nose, or lips. [<L con- (together) + sonare (sound)].

**Contraction** — A contraction replaces a letter or letters with an apostrophe to contract (or shorten) a phrase. Example: *do not = don't.* [<L com- (together) + trahere (draw)].

**Decode** — To see print and translate it into speech. To decode means to break the code.

**Degrees of comparison** — Adjectives illustrating progressive levels like *big, bigger, biggest.*

**Derivatives** — A word obtained from a source of origin like water from a well. Example: "Happiness" is a derivative of "happy." [< L de-(from) + revus (stream)].

**Diacritic** — A dictionary marking that indicates pronunciation. These should not be confused with our spelling markings, which emphasize spelling rules over the pronunciation of a word in the flow of speech. [< Gk dia- (apart) + krinein (separate)].

**Diagnostic test** — A diagnostic test helps evaluate overall achievement of a skill as opposed to mastery of certain subject matter taught that week or that term. It is not used for grading purposes but rather as an evaluation tool for the teacher to help determine long-term mastery of a basic skill and the ability to apply concepts taught in a bigger frame of reference.

**Dialect** — Regional variation in language. Examples: In Maine the word *short* may sound like /shot/. In some parts of the South *good tires* may sound like /guitars/.

**Dictation** — Transcribing spelling words orally as opposed to copying. [< L dicere (say, tell)].

**Dismiss L Rule** — *All* and *full* are written with one L when added to another syllable. We can say it's an expected dismissal when we dismiss an L . Examples: *also, joyful.*

**Dyslexia** — Many link this word to the tendency to reverse words or letters. Some use the term more broadly. This Greek term means "poor with words." The good news is that this disorder, once believed to be based in genetics, is now known to be reversible.

**E's Dropping Rule** — Silent final E words commonly lose the need for the E when adding a vowel suffix [R. 16]. The play on "eavesdropping" gives us a fun title for the rule.

**Encode** — The opposite of decode. We encode a word when we hear it and then write down the sounds we hear. When we spell, we encode words. When we read, we decode them.

**Etymology** — A study of the origin of words. [< Gk etymos (true, real) + logos (word)].

**Fickle phonics** — A program that is based on unreliable phonics rules. See pages 192-4.

**Figurative language** — The comparison between two unlike things to make a point. Figurative language can include metaphors, similes, and personification. A *metaphor* lacks any sign of comparison. (The soldiers were lions in combat.) *A simile* uses the words *as* or *like*. (The soldiers fought like lions in combat.) In personification an animal, idea, or object is given the characteristics of a person. (The sun smiled down on us.)

**Greek and Latin roots** — Word parts that do not stand alone in English but are used as the base words for words we use. Example: *ject* (to throw); *deject* (throw down); *object* (throw against).

**Heteronyms** — Words with the same spelling that differ in sound and sense. Example: *tear* (drop of water from the eye), *tear* (rip). [<Gk hetero (different) + onyma (name)].

**Holy Writ** — A term for the Bible.

**Homonyms** — Words with the same pronunciation but a different meaning, origin, and usually spelling. They include both homophones (same sound) and homographs (same spelling). Example: *run* (move fast), *run* (score in baseball. [< Gk homo- (same) + onyma (name)].

**Homophones** — Words with different meanings that sound alike even though they may be spelled differently. Example: *pare, pair, pear*. Knowing these distinctions is important especially in our day. Computer spell checkers may recognize an acceptable spelling but not specify the proper spelling in that context. [<Gk homo- (same) + phone (sound)].

**Homographs** — Words that look the same but have a different origin and meaning. Example: bow (a tied string), bow (an action of bending forward). [<Gk homo- (same) + graph (write)].

**Incidental phonics** — An informal form of phonics instruction that uses the "appropriate moment." Contrasted by a systematic phonics program such as this one.

**Interjection** — An interjection is an exclamation that can stand alone between sentences. Example: *Hurrah!* [< L inter- (between) + jacere (throw)].

**Kinesthetic approach** — Teaching that involves sensations from muscles and joints, including the movement of speech organs and the writing arm.

**Learning Logs** — Notebooks students transform into personally transcribed spelling textbooks.

**Literature** — Edgar Work defines literature as "the kind of writing that frames noble and useful thought in forms that excel."

**Long vowels** — A term to describe the vowel sounds that match the names of the single vowels.

**Misplaced modifier** — A modifier linked to the wrong words. Example: "The man shot the dog with a gun." This sentence makes it look like a two-way shoot-out between a man and a dog. A more accurate rendering would be, "The man with the gun shot a dog."

**Multi-letter phonograms** — Phonograms made from two or more letters. Examples: sh, th.

**Multi-sensory** — Combining in unison the use of more than one of the senses to teach a subject. We use seeing, hearing, saying and shaping (writing) to teach language arts. Taste and smell can be occasionally used. Example: Link the DGE phonogram to the word "fudge." [< L multi- (much, many) + sentire (know or feel)].

**Noun**— A part of speech naming a person, place, thing, or idea. Examples: *man, town, box, love*.

**Oxymoron** — A writing technique where two words with opposite meanings are combined for a special effect. Examples: *small fortune, good grief, tight slacks, jumbo shrimp, small giant, old news, a cruel kindness, random order, original copy, inside out*. [< GK oxys (sharp) + moros (dull)].

**Phonemes** — The smallest units of sound that people can hear in a word.

**Phonemic awareness** — The ability to isolate and remember the order of phonemes in a word.

**Phoney phonics** — Programs that claim to teach phonics but use whole word recall. See page 191.

**Phonics** — Any reading method that teaches the sounds that letters represent.

**Phonogram** — A single letter or fixed combination of letters symbolizing the sounds of speech.

**Plural** — A plural noun represents more than one. Example: *hand, hands*. [< L pluralis < plus (more)].

**Pokey phonics** — Programs that take years to introduce the key components to the language, often starting with only short vowel sounds. See page 191.

**Prefix** — A syllable added (or fixed) to the beginning of a word to change the meaning. Example: *midday*. Mid- is a prefix that can mean "the middle of" and when added to the base word day means "middle of the day." [< L pre- (before) + figere (fix)].

**Preposition** — A part of speech that comes before a word to show a relationship, often in reference to placement. Examples: *in, over, under* [< L prae- (before) + ponere (place)].

**Pronoun** — A part of speech that takes the place of a noun. Examples: *I, you, he, she, it, we, they, who, this*. [< L pro- (in place of) + nomen (noun)].

**R controlled phonograms** — Any single vowel can be distorted when placed before an R. The consonant sound of the R closely resembles a vowel sound. Each of the R influenced vowels can be multi-letter phonograms: *ar, er, ir, yr, or, ur*. When these letters appear together, but are sounded as two or more distinct sounds, we put a one over the vowel.

**Rime** — This alternative spelling of "rhyme," once again in vogue, refers to words with matching final sounds. Used as the title of the famous 19th century poem by Samuel Taylor Coleridge, *The Rime of the Ancient Mariner*.

**Root word** — A synonym for "base word." It often refers to foreign roots like "jactum" which means "throw" in Latin. From it we get the root *ject*. Even though *ject* is not a stand-alone English word, it is the base word to: *eject* (throw out), *reject* (throw back), *subject* (throw under).

**Schwa** — An indeterminate vowel sound marked in some dictionaries as ə. In *Spell to Write and Read* we think-to-spell the actual vowel in proper spelling, then blend it into normal speech.

**Short vowels** — A term describing the most frequently used vowel sounds for single-letter vowels. Examples: *bag, beg, big, bog, bug*.

**Sentence** — A group of words that expresses a complete thought.

**Sight word** — A word read instantly without thinking. Often refers to a word memorized by appearance only. Ultimately, every student needs a basic sight vocabulary, but we believe in building this pool of words by sound and reasoning rather than by unguided rote memorization.

**Silent Final E's** — We teach five reasons for silent E's at the end of a word. See Step 17.

**Silent letter** — A phonogram in a word that is not sounded in speech. Example: the B in *comb*.

**Spelling markings** — Special markings indicate multi-letter phonograms and other spelling concepts. For example, we flag the different types of silent final E's in different ways.

**Suffix** — A word part that can be added (or fixed) to the end of a word to change the meaning. Example: If we add the suffix **-Y** (containing) to the noun **salt**, we will change the noun to **salty**, an adjective meaning "containing salt." [< L sub- (under) + figere (fasten)].

**Syllable** —A syllable is a rhythmic "chunk" of a word. A syllable is pronounced with one impulse of your voice. It has a written vowel. A word has as many syllables as vowel sounds.

> A fun, fourteen-syllable word to dictate at the end of the year:
>
> su-per-cal-i-frag-i-lis-tic-ex-pi-al-i-do-cious.
>
> It means "a job well done."

**Synonyms** — Another name or word with a similar meaning. Example: *small, tiny*. [< Gk syn- (together) + onyme (name)].

**Systematic phonics** — Direct, explicit phonics instructions, as opposed to indirect, incidental phonics. We believe something so vital to strong literacy should be taught carefully.

**Think-to-Spell** — Exaggerate each phonogram sound distinctly for spelling even if we don't hear the sound as clearly in the flow of normal speech. This creates a vocal image of correct spelling.

**Top guide line** — The line that provides a top margin for student penmanship.

**Verb** — The part of speech used to express action *(look, see)* or state of being *(is, am, was)*.

**Vernacular** — Everyday language, informal speech. Vernacular may refer to one's native tongue.

**Vocabulary** — A stock of words used for reading and writing. More clear communication can take place when the student's word bank is enlarged.

**Vowel** — Vowel sounds pass through the mouth and throat with little obstruction from teeth, tongue, or lips. Only vowels say their letter names in words.

**Whole language** — A system that combines literature with whole word memorization in an attempt to improve on the boring look-say technique taught with Dick and Jane readers. Patrick Groff, a professor of education at San Diego State University says, "The *whole language* method of reading instruction is a highly popular, yet experimentally discredited teaching innovation.... The scientifically invalid nature of WL reading instruction has been known since its inception. None of its unique principles or novel practices is corroborated by relevant experimental research findings" (Groff, Ideas of Liberty, pp. 40, 43).

**Word family** — A group of words built from the same root or base. Rhyming words that look alike *(fall, tall, hall)* should not be called word families. Words in the "fall" family would include: *falling, fallen, unfallen, waterfall, downfall, fallout, rainfall, pitfall*.

**Y's Exchanging Rule** — The single vowel Y changes to I when adding any ending, unless the ending starts with an I [R. 24]. We say the Y makes a smart trade, a wise exchange.

# INDEX

# Bibliography

Andersen, Richard C., et al. *Becoming a Nation of Readers: The Report of the Commission on Reading*. Champaign, IL: Center for the Study of Reading, 1984.

Aukerman, Robert C. *Approaches to Beginning Reading*. New York: Wiley, 1984.

Ayres, Leonard Porter. *A Measuring Scale for Ability in Spelling*. Michigan: Mott Media, 1986.

Bishop, Margaret M. *The ABC's and All Their Tricks*. Michigan: Mott Media, 1986.

Blumenfeld, Samuel. *How to Tutor*. Boise, Idaho: The Paradigm Company, 1977.

Bowen, James A. *English Words as Spoken and Written*. 1900.

Bryson, Bill. *The Mother Tongue*. New York: Harper Collins, 1990.

Chall, J.S. *Stages of Reading Development*. New York: McGraw-Hill, 1983.

-------- *Learning to Read: The Great Debate*. New York: McGraw-Hill, 1983.

Coffin, Charles. *The Story of Liberty*. Gainesville, FL: Maranatha Publications, 1987.

Copperman, Paul. *The Literacy Hoax*. New York: Morrow Quill, 1980.

Corcoran, John, with Carole Carlson. *The Teacher Who Couldn't Read*. Colorado Springs, CO: Focus on the Family, 1994.

Crystal, David. *The Cambridge Encyclopedia of The English Language*. New York, NY: Cambridge University Press, 1996.

Douglass, Frederick. *Narratives of the Life of Frederick Douglass, an American Slave*. New York: Penguin Books, 1986.

Ebner, Louisa. *Learning English with the Bible* series. Chattanooga, TN: AMG Publishers, 2002.

Farnham-Diggory, S. foreword to *Writing Road to Reading*. NY: William Morrow, 1990.

Felix, Antonia. *Laura: America's First Lady, First Mother*. Avon, MA: Adams Media, 2002.

Fischer, David Hackett. *Albion's Seed: Four British Folkways in America*. New York: Oxford University Press, 1989.

FitzGerald, Elizabeth. *Cursive First*. Hayward, CA: LITHBTH Educational Services. 2001.

Fry, Edward Bernard with Jacqueline Kress and Dona Lee Fountoukidis. *The Reading Teacher's Book of Lists*. Paramus, NJ: Prentice Hall, 1993.

Furness, Edna. *Spelling for the Millions*. New York: Thomas Nelson, 1977.

Groff, Patrick. *Preventing Reading Failure: An Examination of the Myths of Reading Instruction*. Portland, OR: National Book Company, 1987.

-------- "Whole Language: Emancipatory Pedagogy or Socialist Nonsense?" *Ideas of Liberty*. Irvington-on-Hudson, NY. July 2000: Vol. 50. No. 7.

Hall, Susan. *Straight Talk about Reading*. Chicago, IL: Contemporary Books, 1999.

Heller, Ruth. *World of Language Series*. New York: Penguin Putnam, 1991.

Irish, Frank. *Fundamentals of the English Language*. Lock Haven, PA: State Normal School, 1888.

Kozol, Jonathan. *Illiterate America*. New York: Plume, 1985.

Ludwig, Charles. *Michael Faraday: Father of Electronics*. Waterloo, Ontario: Herald Press, 1978.

McCrum, Robert with William Cran and Robert MacNeil. *The Story of English*. New York: Penguin Books, 2002.

McGuinness, Diane. *Why Our Children Can't Read and What We Can Do About It*. New York: Simon & Schuster, 1997.

Mosse, Hilde. *You Can Prevent or Correct Learning Disorders*. Beaverton, OR: Riggs Institute, 1982.

National Advisory Council on Adult Education. *Illiteracy in America: Extent, Causes, and Suggested Solutions*. Washington, DC: U.S. Government Printing Office. No date.

Orton, Samuel. *Reading, Writing, and Speech Problems in Children and Selected Papers*. Austin, TX: PRO-ED, Inc., 1989.

Patterson, Calvin. *The American Word Book*. New York: American Book Company, 1897.

Rubin, Bonnie Miller. "Reading Wars: Endless Squabbles Keep Kids from Getting the Help They Need." *Chicago Tribune* (March 2, 1997).

Spalding, Romalda. *Writing Road to Reading*. New York: William Morrow, 1990.

Stanovich, Keith E. "Romance and Reality." *The Reading Teacher* 47, no. 4 (December 1993/ January 1994).

Thorndike, E. L. and Clarence Barnhart. *Thorndike-Barnhart High School Dictionary*. Chicago, IL: Scott Foresman, 1957.

Watts, Isaac. *The Improvement of the Mind: A Discourse on the Education of Children and Youth*. Morgan, PA: Soli Deo Gloria Publication, 1998.

Webster, Noah. *An American Dictionary of the English Language*. Newhaven, NY: Converse, 1828.

--------*A Grammatical Institute of the English Language, Part 1*. Hartford: Hudson & Goodwin, 1783.

--------*Webster's New Twentieth Century Dictionary*, Standard Reference Works: New York, 1956 and edited by Jean McKechnie. Prentice Hall: New York, 1983.

Wiener, Harvey. *Any Child Can Write*. New York: Bantam Books, 1990.

Wilson, Edith. *Books Children Love: A Guide to the Best Children's Literature*. Westchester, IL: Crossway Books, 1987.

Work, Edward Whitaker. *The Bible in English Literature*. London: Fleming H. Revell, 1917.